Third Edition

BEDFORD BASICS
A WORKBOOK FOR WRITERS

Diana Hacker   Wanda Van Goor

Prince George's Community College

BEDFORD/ST. MARTIN'S   Boston ◆ New York

For Bedford/St. Martin's

Developmental Editor: Michelle McSweeney
Production Editor: Stasia Zomkowski
Marketing Manager: Charles Cavaliere
Editorial Assistant: Katherine Gilbert
Production Assistant: Melissa Cook
Copyeditor: Barbara G. Flanagan
Text Design: Claire Seng-Niemoeller
Cover Design: Hannus Design Associates
Composition: Ruttle, Shaw & Wetherill, Inc.
Printing and Binding: Quebecor Printing Kingsport

President: Charles H. Christensen
Editorial Director: Joan E. Feinberg
Director of Editing, Design, and Production: Marcia Cohen
Managing Editor: Elizabeth M. Schaaf

Library of Congress Catalog Card Number: 97–74960

6   5
m   l   k   j

For information, write: Bedford/St. Martin's, 75 Arlington Street, Boston, MA 02116 (617–399–4000)

ISBN: 0–312–15457–7

ACKNOWLEDGMENTS

The American Heritage Dictionary of the English Language, Third Edition, from the entry "regard." Copyright © 1996 by Houghton Mifflin Company. Reprinted by permission from *The American Heritage Dictionary of the English Language,* Third Edition.

Eugene Boe, from "Pioneers to Eternity: Norwegians on the Prairie," from *The Immigrant Experience,* edited by Thomas C. Wheeler. Copyright © 1971 by Thomas C. Wheeler. Reprinted by permission of Doubleday, a division of Bantam Doubleday Dell Publishing Group, Inc.

Jane Brody, excerpts from *Jane Brody's Nutrition Book* by Jane Brody. Copyright 1981 by Jane E. Brody. Reprinted by permission of W. W. Norton & Company, Inc. and Wendy Weil Agency, Inc.

Roger Caras, from "What's a Koala?" Copyright 1983 by Roger Caras. First appeared in *Geo* Magazine, May 1983. Reprinted by permission of Curtis Brown, Ltd.

Bruce Catton, from "Grant and Lee: A Study in Contrasts," from *The American Story,* edited by Earl Schenck Miers. Copyright 1956 U.S. Capitol Historical Society, all rights reserved.

Earl Conrad, excerpt from *Harriet Tubman* by Earl Conrad. Copyright 1943, 1969 by Earl Conrad. Published by Paul S. Erikson. Reprinted by permission of the publisher.

James Underwood Crockett, et al. From *Time-Life Encyclopedia of Gardening: Wildflower Gardening.* By James Underwood Crockett, Oliver Allen, and the Editors of Time-Life Books. © 1977 Time-Life Books, Inc.

Excerpt from *The Dorling Kindersley Encyclopedia of Fishing.* Copyright 1994 Dorling Kindersley. Reprinted with permission.

Stephen Jay Gould, from "Were Dinosaurs Dumb?" Copyright © 1978 by Stephen Jay Gould, from *The Panda's Thumb: More Re-flection in Natural History* by Stephen Jay Gould. Reprinted by permission of W. W. Norton & Company, Inc.

Dan Gutman, from *The Way Baseball Works.* Reprinted with permission of Simon & Schuster. Copyright 1996 by Byron Preiss/Richard Ballantine, Inc.

Hillary Hauser, from "Exploring a Sunken Realm in Australia," National Geographic, January 1984. HILLARY HAUSER/National Geographic Image Collection. Reprinted by permission.

Portland Community College home page and Netscape browser frame. Copyright 1997 by Portland Community College. Reprinted with permission of Russell Banks, Division of Publications, Portland Community College. Copyright 1996 Netscape Communications Corp. All rights reserved. This electronic file or page may not be reprinted or copied without the express written permission of Netscape.

Chet Raymo, excerpt from "Curious Stuff, Water and Ice." *The Boston Globe,* January 27, 1986.

Lewis Thomas, from "On Societies as Organisms." Copyright © 1971 by The Massachusetts Medical Society, from *The Lives of a Cell* by Lewis Thomas. Used by permission of Viking Penguin, a division of Penguin Books USA Inc.

James Thurber, paragraph from "University Days." Copyright 1933, 1961 by James Thurber. From *My Life and Hard Times* by James Thurber, published by Harper & Row. Reprinted by permission.

Olivia Vlahos, from *Human Beginnings.* Published by Viking Penguin, Inc. Reprinted by permission of the author.

Alice Walker, from "In Search of Our Mothers' Gardens," from *In Search of Our Mothers' Gardens.* Copyright 1967 by Alice Walker. Reprinted by permission of Harcourt Brace & Company and David Higham Associates Ltd.

Preface for Instructors

Bedford Basics is both a quick reference guide and a workbook. The text, adapted from *The Bedford Handbook*, Fifth Edition, and the exercises are designed specifically for developmental students. Here are the principle features of the exercises and the text.

The exercises

RESPECTFUL OF THE STUDENT'S COLLEGE STATUS. Although the exercises vary in level of difficulty, all of them respect the age and experience of college students; none insults their intelligence. Most exercises ask students to edit paragraphs and essays, not to fill in blanks or recopy whole sentences when only a word or two may need changing. Where possible, exercises encourage students to think about the impact of errors on readers and to choose revision strategies that are effective, not just "correct."

WRITTEN IN CONNECTED DISCOURSE. Because nearly every exercise in *Bedford Basics* is a paragraph, an essay, or a set of numbered sentences that are connected in meaning, students learn to identify and revise problem sentences in realistic contexts. These connected discourse exercises mimic the process of revision as it occurs in real life. In addition, they provide a rhetorical context to guide students as they choose one revision strategy over another. All of the exercises in a section are thematically linked, usually focusing on the achievements of a famous person or group—such as Harriet Beecher Stowe, Frederick Douglas, Aesop, Sigmund Freud, and Steven Spielberg—so that students are reading real prose on interesting topics rather than unrelated drill sentences.

"GUIDED PRACTICE" EXERCISES. Sections 8–45 all open with a guided practice exercise that gives students special help. Section numbers in the margins of these paragraph-style exercises identify problem sentences and tell students where in the text to look for explanations and revision strategies. Answers to these exercises and the preview exercises in sections 46–50 appear in the back of the book.

VARIED FORMATS. Seldom will the student be asked to do exactly the same thing in two adjacent exercises. Varied ways of working on a topic keep the task interesting. Sometimes students need only to circle the letter of the correct or clearer sentence in a pair of sentences; sometimes they choose between two words or phrases; frequently they edit, crossing out incorrect or confusing forms and adding handwritten revisions; occasionally, they edit the same sentence in two different ways.

EMPHASIS ON READING. As they learn to edit the paragraphs and essays in *Bedford Basics*, students do a considerable amount of reading, and many exercises ask them to respond as readers. In an exercise on mixed constructions, for example, students are asked to discriminate between the easy-to-read and the hard-to-read sentences. Where possible, students are encouraged to think about meaning. For example, an exercise on adjectives and adverbs asks students to consider the difference in meaning between the sentences "Most slaves did not find escape routes easy" and "Most slaves did not find escape routes easily."

CROSS-CURRICULAR CONTENT. Most exercises profile a person or group that students are likely to encounter in college courses across the curriculum: Mary Wollstonecraft, Albert Einstein, Martin Luther King, Jr., Louis Braille, Mother Jones, and so on. Because many of these persons overcame great obstacles to achieve their goals, their stories are often inspirational as well as informative.

ADAPTABLE TO A VARIETY OF TEACHING STYLES. You can use the exercises in a variety of ways.

We have used them successfully for homework or quizzes for nongraded individual study, for class discussions, and for collaborative learning in small groups.

The text

QUICK ACCESS THROUGH MENUS. Designed for student use, a new brief menu inside the front cover displays icons representing the workbook's nine parts and lists only the numbered sections. By consulting this menu, students can quickly locate the icon and section number for the information they need. Then they can follow up the page reference or flip pages in search of the appropriate tabs. The tabs on the left-hand pages display the icons, and those on the right-hand pages give the section numbers.

The traditional, more detailed menu, which is useful for instructors but too daunting for many students, now appears on the back end-papers.

TUTORIALS. Four tutorials in "How to Use This Workbook" show students how to use the brief and detailed menus, the index, and the Glossary of Usage. We like to use two or three of the tutorials as a small-group classroom activity early in the semester; our students teach one another, and they get to know one another at the same time.

HAND-EDITED SENTENCES. Most examples in *Bedford Basics* appear with handwritten revisions over faulty typeset sentences. Unlike paired incorrect and correct examples, hand-edited sentences highlight the revision, allowing students to grasp both the error and its correction at a glance. Further, hand-edited sentences model the process of revision that students should use when working on hard copies of their own drafts.

QUICK REFERENCE CHARTS. Many of the workbook's charts take students back to their own writing, helping them review their drafts for common problems such as fragments and subject-verb agreement. Other charts summarize important material: a checklist for global revision, strategies for avoiding sexist English, the usual order of cumulative adjectives, and so on.

FIFTY GRAMMAR CHECKER BOXES. New to this edition are boxes that show students just what current grammar checkers and spell checkers can do—and what they can't do. As you may have discovered in your own classes, some students produce strange errors because they have taken the advice of a grammar checker without first thinking. And many students believe that once they have run a grammar or spell checker, their problems are over.

To discover the capabilities and limits of current grammar checkers, we have run hundreds of exercise sentences (many containing errors), along with some student drafts, through two grammar checker programs that are commonly used on college campuses. The results, summarized in screened boxes with computer icons throughout the book, show that grammar checkers help with some but by no means all of the typical problems in a draft.

HELP FOR ESL STUDENTS. Part VI focuses exclusively on common problems facing speakers of English as a second language. Section 29 discusses ESL problems with verbs; section 30 explains when to use the articles *a, an,* and *the;* and section 31 alerts students to a variety of other potential trouble spots. ESL boxes throughout the book provide other tips for students who speak English as a second language.

SPECIAL ATTENTION TO DIALECT DIFFERENCES. Section 27, Standard English verb forms, is devoted to written errors caused by the speech patterns of nonstandard English. Students who need help with such matters as omitted verbs and verb endings will find a fuller-than-usual description of important differences between standard and nonstandard English.

A NEW SECTION ON DOCUMENT DESIGN. Both in the business world and in the academic world, writers are becoming increasingly interested in document design—the use of visual cues to help readers. A new section on document design appears in Part I, The Writing Process. It includes the principles of document design, a model MLA paper without secondary sources, sample business formats, and advice on creating effective e-mail and Web pages.

A USER-FRIENDLY INDEX. The index of *Bedford Basics* helps students find what they are looking for even if they don't know grammatical terminology. When facing a choice between *I* and *me*, for example, students may not know to look up "Case" or even "Pronoun, case of." They are more likely to look up "*I*" or "*me*," so *Bedford Basics* includes index entries for "*I* versus *me*" and "*me* versus *I*." Similar user-friendly entries appear throughout the index of the third edition.

Acknowledgments

We would like to thank the following reviewers for setting a high standard and encouraging us to reach it; this workbook has been much improved because of their perceptive comments.

Gwen Benson, Northwestern Oklahoma State University

Anne Eggebroten, Mount St. Mary's College

Margaret Emm, Oxnard College

Rene Braun Hellmann, Western Connecticut State University

Barbara Henry, West Virginia State College

Katherine Hill-Miller, Long Island University

Gladys H. Hines, Texas A&M University

Helen Killoran, Ohio University

Richard A. Peacock, Birmingham-Southern College

David Willard, Bakersfield College

We are also grateful to several people at Bedford Books who were actively involved in the book's development and production. Publishers Charles Christensen and Joan Feinberg helped us plan the book: its trim size, its two-color design, its spiral binding, and its varied styles of exercises. Editorial Assistant Katherine Gillbert, with guidance from Developmental Editor Michelle McSweeney, responded to the manuscript in detail, offering us many intelligent suggestions and much upbeat encouragement along the way. Production editor Stasia Zomkowski and her assistant Melissa Cook guided our complex manuscript expertly through production, with unflappable good humor.

Thanks also go to Claire Seng-Niemoeller for designing clean, uncluttered pages that highlight the workbook's hand-edited sentences and to copyeditor Barbara Flanagan for bringing consistency and grace to the final manuscript.

Finally, for their support and encouragement, we would like to thank our families, our colleagues at Prince George's Community College, and the many students over the years who have taught us that errors, a natural by-product of the writing process, are simply problems waiting to be solved.

Diana Hacker and Wanda Van Goor

Prince George's Community College

How to Use This Workbook

To learn any skill—whether it be basketball, tennis, chess, CPR, computer programming, or the electric guitar—takes practice. English composition is no exception: In a composition class, you will learn to write by writing, and you will learn to revise by revising.

Working the exercises

Bedford Basics sharpens your revision skills by giving you a great deal of controlled, yet realistic, practice. Let's say, for example, that you want to learn to identify and correct sentence fragments. Your first step is to read section 19 and to study the flowchart on page 168. Next you should try the first exercise, called a "guided practice." This exercise gives a number-letter code in the margin next to each fragment. In addition to telling you where to look for fragments, the codes refer to specific rules in the text, so if you have trouble identifying or fixing a particular fragment, you can turn to the book for help. When you have finished the exercise, you should check your answers. Answers to the first exercise in each section appear in the back of the book, beginning on page 419.

Once you have tried the guided practice exercise, attempt the other exercises, consulting the rules in the text whenever you run into trouble. You'll find that the rest of the exercises in a set vary in style and level of difficulty. In the set on fragments, for example, one exercise asks you to identify the correct sentence in each of a series of paired word groups; another, presented in paragraph form, asks you to identify fragments and to think about possible revision strategies; and the final three exercises give you practice in both identifying and revising fragments. Throughout the entire set, the subject you'll be reading about is the Beatles.

Other exercise sets resemble the one on fragments. In these sets you will encounter a number of famous persons you are likely to meet in other college classes: men and women such as Karl Marx, Harriet Beecher Stowe, Frederick Douglass, Albert Einstein, and Althea Gibson.

Finding information with an instructor's help

When you are revising a paragraph or essay that has been marked by your instructor, tracking down information is simple. If your instructor marks a problem with a number such as *19* or a number and letter such as *21b,* you can turn directly to the appropriate section of the workbook. Just flip through the colored tabs on the upper corners of the pages until you find the number in question. The number *19,* for example, leads you to the rule "Repair sentence fragments," and *21b* takes you to the subrule "Make the verb agree with its subject, not with a word that comes between." If your instructor uses an abbreviation such as *frag* or *agr,* consult the list of abbreviations and symbols on page 437, where you will find the name of the problem (*sentence fragment; faulty agreement*) and the number of the section to consult.

Finding information on your own

With a little practice, you will be able to find information in this book without an instructor's help — usually by tracking the icons that appear in the brief menu inside the front cover. At times, you may want to consult the detailed menu inside the back cover, the index, or the Glossary of Usage

THE FRONT ENDPAPERS. Usually the brief menu on the inside front cover is the fastest way into the book. Let's say you are having problems with run-on sentences. Your first step is to find the appropriate section—in this case "Grammatical Sentences," which is represented by a check mark icon. Next, find the appropriate numbered rule: "20 Revise run-on sentences." You can flip directly to the page number given (p. 175), or you can use the icon tabs on the left-hand pages and section number tabs on right-hand pages to help you find section 20.

THE BACK ENDPAPERS.   When the numbered section you're looking for is broken up into quite a few lettered subsections, try consulting the detailed menu on the inside back cover.

THE INDEX.   If you aren't sure which topic to choose from one of the menus, consult the index at the back of the book. For example, you may not realize that the issue of *is* versus *are* is a matter of subject-verb agreement (section 21). In that case, simply look up "*is* versus *are*" in the index and you will be directed to the exact pages you need.

THE GLOSSARY OF USAGE.   When in doubt about the correct use of a particular word (such as *affect* and *effect, among* and *between,* or *hopefully*), consult the Glossary of Usage at the back of the book. This glossary explains the difference between commonly confused words; it also lists colloquialisms and jargon that are inappropriate in formal written English.

Diana Hacker and Wanda Van Goor

Tutorials

The following tutorials will give you practice using the book's menus, index, and Glossary of Usage. Answers to the tutorials begin on page 419.

TUTORIAL 1 Using the menus

Each of the following "rules" violates the principle it expresses. Using the brief menu inside the front cover or the detailed menu inside the back cover, find the section in *Bedford Basics* that explains the principle. Then fix the problem. Examples:

Tutors in
~~In~~ the writing center/~~they~~ say that vague
pronoun reference is unacceptable.   *23*

come
Be alert for irregular verbs that have ~~came~~ to
you in the wrong form.   *27a*

1. A verb have to agree with its subject.
2. Each pronoun should agree with their antecedent.
3. About sentence fragments. You should avoid them.
4. Don't write a run-on sentence you must connect the clauses with a comma and a coordinating conjunction or with a semicolon.
5. Discriminate careful between adjectives and adverbs.
6. Proofread to see if you any words out.
7. Check for *-ed* verb endings that have been drop.
8. In most contexts, passive-voice verbs should be avoided.
9. In choosing proper pronoun case, follow the example of we teachers, whom are the experts.
10. Don't use no double negatives.
11. When dangling, watch your modifiers.
12. Its important to use apostrophe's correctly.
13. A writer must be careful not to shift your point of view.
14. If your sentence begins with a long introductory word group use a comma to separate the word group from the rest of the sentence.
15. Last but not least, avoid clichés like the plague.

TUTORIAL 2 Using the index

Assume that you have written the following sentences and want to know the answers to the questions in brackets. Use the index at the back of the workbook to locate the information you need, and edit the sentences if necessary.

1. Anybody taking the school bus to the volleyball game must bring in a permission slip signed by their parents. [Does the pronoun *Anybody* agree with *their*? If not, what is the best way to fix the problem?]
2. We had intended to go surfing but spent most of our vacation lying on the beach. [Should I use *lying* or *laying*?]
3. We only looked at two houses before buying the house of our dreams. [Is *only* in the right place?]
4. In Saudi Arabia it is considered ill-mannered for you to accept a gift. [Is it okay to use *you* to mean "anyone in general"?]
5. In Canada, Joanne picked up several bottles of maple syrup for her sister and me. [Should I write *for her sister and I*?]

TUTORIAL 3 Using the menus or the index

Imagine that you are in the following situations. Using either the menus or the index, find the information you need.

1. You are Ray Farley, a community college student who has been out of high school for ten years. You recall learning to punctuate items in a series by putting a comma between all items except the last two. In your college readings, however, you have noticed that most writers use a comma between all items. You're curious about the current rule. Which section of *Bedford Basics* will you consult?

2. You are Maria Sanchez, an honors student working in your university's writing center. Mike Lee, who speaks English as a second language, has come to you for help. He is working on a rough draft that contains a number of problems involving the use of articles (*a, an,* and *the*). You know how to use articles, but you aren't able to explain the rather complicated rules on their correct use. Which section of *Bedford Basics* will you and Mike Lee consult?

3. You are John Pell, engaged to marry Jane Dalton. In a note to Jane's parents, you have written *Thank you for giving Jane and myself such a generous contribution toward our honeymoon trip to Hawaii.* You wonder if you should write *Jane and I* or *Jane and me* instead. Upon consulting *Bedford Basics,* what do you learn?

4. You are Selena Young, a supervisor of interns at a housing agency. Two of your interns, Jake Gilliam and Susan Green, have writing problems involving *-s* endings on verbs. Gilliam tends to drop *-s* endings; Green tends to add them where they don't belong. You suspect that both problems stem from nonstandard dialects spoken at home.

    Susan and Jake are in danger of losing their jobs because your boss thinks that anyone who writes *the tenant refuse* or *the landlords agrees* is beyond hope. You disagree. Susan and Jake are more intelligent than your boss supposes, and they have asked for your help. Where in *Bedford Basics* can they find the rules they need?

5. You are Joe Thompson, a first-year college student. Your friend Samantha, who has completed two years of college, seems to enjoy correcting your English. Just yesterday she corrected your sentence *I felt badly about her death* to *I felt bad about her death.* You're sure you've heard many educated persons, including professors, say *I felt badly.* Upon consulting *Bedford Basics,* what do you discover?

TUTORIAL 4 Using the Glossary of Usage

Consult the Glossary of Usage to see if the italicized words are used correctly. Then edit any sentences containing incorrect usage. Example:

an

The pediatrician gave my daughter ~~a~~

injection for her allergy.

1. The *amount* of horses a Comanche warrior had in his possession indicated the wealth of his family.
2. This afternoon I plan to *lie* out in the sun and begin working on a tan.
3. That is the most *unique* floral arrangement I have ever seen.
4. Changing attitudes *toward* alcohol have *effected* the beer industry.
5. Jenny *should of* known better than to attempt that dive.
6. Everyone in our office is *enthused* about this project.
7. George and Pat are selling *there* house because now that *their* children are grown, *their* planning to move to Arizona.
8. Most sleds are pulled by no *fewer* than two dogs and no more than ten.
9. It is *man's* nature to think wisely and act foolishly.
10. Dr. Newman and *myself* have agreed to arrange the retirement party.

Contents

The Writing Process

1 **Generate ideas and sketch a plan.**

2 **Rough out an initial draft.**

3 **Make global revisions; then revise sentences.**

4 **Choose an appropriate document design.**

Since it's not possible to think about everything all at once, most experienced writers handle a piece of writing in stages. Roughly speaking, those stages are planning, drafting, and revising.

1 Generate ideas and sketch a plan.

Before attempting a first draft, spend some time coming up with ideas. Think about your subject while listening to music or driving to work, jot down inspirations on scratch paper, and explore your ideas with anyone willing to listen. At this stage you should be collecting information and experimenting with ways of focusing and organizing it to best reach your readers.

1a Assess the writing situation.

Begin by taking a look at the writing situation in which you find yourself. The checklist on page 2 will help you get started.

1b Experiment with ways to explore your subject.

Instead of just plunging into a first draft, experiment with one or more techniques for exploring your subject, perhaps one of these:

listing
clustering
asking questions
freewriting
annotating texts and
  taking notes

keeping a journal
talking and listening
the Internet
invention software

You can use most of these techniques whether you are working with pencil and paper or entering ideas into a computer.

Checklist for assessing the writing situation

At the beginning of the writing process, you may not be able to answer all of the questions on this checklist. That's fine. Just be prepared to think about them later.

NOTE: It is not necessary to think about the elements of a writing situation in the exact order listed in this chart.

SUBJECT

— Has a subject (or a range of possible subjects) been given to you, or are you free to choose your own?

— Is your subject worth writing about? Can you think of any readers who might be interested in reading about it?

— How broadly can you cover the subject? Do you need to narrow it to a more specific topic (because of length restrictions, for instance)?

— How detailed should your coverage be?

SOURCES OF INFORMATION

— Where will your information come from: Personal experience? Direct observation? Interviews? Questionnaires? Reading? The Internet?

— If your information comes from reading or the Internet, what sort of documentation is required?

PURPOSE

— Why are you writing: To inform readers? To persuade them? To entertain them? To call them to action? Some combination of these?

AUDIENCE

— How well informed are your readers about the subject? What do you want them to learn about the subject?

— How interested and attentive are they likely to be? Will they resist any of your ideas?

— What is your relationship to them: Employee to supervisor? Citizen to citizen? Expert to novice? Scholar to scholar?

— How much time are they willing to spend reading?

— How sophisticated are they as readers? Do they have large vocabularies? Can they follow long and complex sentences?

LENGTH AND DOCUMENT DESIGN

— Are you working within any length specifications? If not, what length seems appropriate, given your subject, your purpose, and your audience?

— Must you use a particular design or format for your document? If so, do you have guidelines or examples that you can consult?

REVIEWERS AND DEADLINES

— Who will be reviewing your draft in progress: Your instructor? A writing center tutor? Your classmates? A friend? Someone in your family?

— What is your deadline? How much time will you need to allow for the various stages of writing, including typing and proofreading the final draft?

Whatever technique you turn to, the goal is the same: to generate a wealth of ideas. At this early stage of the writing process, you should aim for quantity, not necessarily quality, of ideas. If an idea proves to be off the point, trivial, or too far-fetched, you can always throw it out later.

Listing

You might begin by simply listing ideas, putting them down in the order in which they occur to you—a technique sometimes known as "brainstorming." Here, for example, is a list one student writer jotted down:

Lifeguarding—an ideal summer job?

    my love of swimming and lying in the sun

    hired by Powdermill Village, an apartment complex

first, though, there was a test

two weeks of training—grueling physical punishment plus book work

I passed. The work was over—or so I thought.

greeted by manager; handed a broom, hose, bottle of disinfectant

scrubbing bathrooms, cleaning the pool, clearing the deck of dirt and leaves

little kids breaking every pool rule in the book—running on deck, hanging on buoyed ropes, trying to drown each other

spent most of my time blowing the whistle

working the evening shift no better—adults smuggling in gin and tonics, sexual advances from married men by end of day, a headache and broom-handled hands

The ideas appear here in the order in which they first occurred to the writer. Later she felt free to rearrange them, to cluster them under general categories, to delete some, and to add others. In other words, she treated her initial list as a source of ideas and a springboard to new ideas, not as an outline.

Clustering

Unlike listing, the technique of clustering highlights relationships among ideas. To cluster ideas, write your topic in the center of a sheet of paper, draw a circle around it, and surround that with related ideas connected to it with lines. If some of the satellite ideas lead to more specific clusters, write them down as well. The writer of the following diagram was exploring ideas for an essay on home uses for computers.

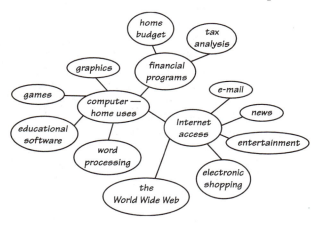

Asking questions

By asking relevant questions, you can generate many ideas—and you can make sure that you have adequately surveyed your subject. When gathering material for a story, journalists routinely ask themselves Who? What? When? Where? Why? and How? In addition to helping journalists get started, these questions ensure that they will not overlook an important fact: the date of a prospective summit meeting, for example, or the exact location of a neighborhood burglary.

Whenever you are writing about events, whether current or historical, the journalist's questions are one way to get started. One student, whose subject was the negative reaction

in 1915 to D. W. Griffith's silent film *The Birth of a Nation,* began exploring her topic with this set of questions:

> *Who* objected to the film?
> *What* were the objections?
> *When* were protests first voiced?
> *Where* were protests most strongly expressed?
> *Why* did protesters object to the film?
> *How* did protesters make their views known?

Freewriting

In its purest form, freewriting is simply nonstop writing. You set aside ten minutes or so and write whatever comes to you, without pausing to think about word choice, spelling, or even meaning. If you get stuck, you can write about being stuck, but you should keep your pencil moving. The point is to loosen up, relax, and see what happens. Even if nothing much happens, you have lost only ten minutes. It's more likely, though, that something interesting will emerge on paper—perhaps an eloquent sentence, an honest expression of feeling, or a line of thought worth exploring.

To explore ideas on a particular topic, consider using a technique known as *focused freewriting.* Again, you write quickly and freely—without regard for word choice, spelling, punctuation, or even paragraphing—but this time you focus on a subject and pay some attention to meaning. The following passage was written freely by a student who was recalling childhood visits to his grandparents' farm.

> Memories. Memories of Canton, Mississippi. We called it The Farm, like it was the only farm in the world. There was lots to keep us busy, 90 acres of untamed pastures. One of the first things that comes to mind is playing in the haybarn, climbing through the hay stacked high to the rafters. We would burrough a path between the bails tunnelling our way to the top. This was alot of fun until someone disturbed one of the many wasp nests making everyone scatter. Cruising the pastures, we enjoyed testing sound travel. We would spread out from each other and still talk at a normal tone audibly. I remember once getting over 100 yards away from my brother—although we would have to talk slowly and clearly, we could

understand each other. An-other game for the pasture was to lie on the ground, be very quiet, slow our breathing, and wait for the buzzards. We could never figure out how they knew we weren't dead.

—David Queen, student

Despite the awkward beginning, the misspellings, and some problems with punctuation, this freewriting has potential. Its writer later polished some of the sentences and included them in an essay.

Annotating texts and taking notes

When you write about reading, one of the best ways to explore ideas is to mark up the text—on the pages themselves if you own the work, on photocopies if you don't.

The following example is a paragraph from William J. Bennett's "Drug Policy and the Intellectuals," with a few comments penciled in the margins:

The issue I want to address is our national drug policy and the intellectuals. Unfortunately, the issue is a little one-sided. There is a very great deal to say about our national drug policy, but much less to say about the intellectuals—except that by and large, they're against it. Why they should be against it is an interesting question, perhaps more a social-psychological question than a properly intellectual one. But whatever the reasons, I'm sorry to say that on properly intellectual grounds the arguments mustered against our current drug policy by America's intellectuals make for very thin gruel indeed.

Who does he mean exactly?

His tone seems sort of arrogant.

Thesis?

Why this metaphor?

In addition to annotating texts, you will often want to take notes on your reading.

Keeping a journal

A journal is a collection of personal, exploratory writings. An entry in a journal can be any length—from a single sentence to several pages—and it is likely to be informal and experimental.

In a journal, meant for your eyes only, you can take risks. In one entry, for example, you might do some freewriting or focused freewriting. In another, you might pose a series of interesting questions, whether or not you have

the answers. In still another, you might play around with language for the sheer fun of it: writing "purple prose," for instance, or parodying the style of a favorite author or songwriter.

Talking and listening

The early stages of the writing process do not have to be lonely. Many writers begin a writing project by brainstorming ideas in a group, debating a point with friends, or engaging in conversation with a professor. Others turn to themselves for company—by talking nonstop into a tape recorder.

If your computer is equipped with a modem, you can "virtually converse" by exchanging ideas through e-mail, by joining an Internet chat group, or by following a listserv discussion. If you are part of a networked classroom, you may be encouraged to exchange ideas with your classmates and instructor in an electronic workshop.

Talking can be a good way to get to know your audience. If you're planning to write a narrative, for instance, you can test its dramatic effect on a group of friends. Or if you hope to advance a certain argument, you can try it out on listeners who hold a different view.

As you have no doubt discovered, conversation can deepen and refine your ideas before you even begin to set them down on paper. Our first thoughts are not necessarily our wisest thoughts; by talking and listening to others we can all stretch our potential as thinkers and as writers.

The Internet

The Internet is a rich source of information that is fast and convenient to use, although its sheer magnitude can be overwhelming. A good way to begin exploring your subject on the Internet is through a search engine such as Yahoo! or Excite. A student looking for trends in teenage smoking, for example, might start by entering *teenage and smoking* in Excite's search box. Even a fairly focused subject such as this can unleash thousands of sites, however, so always be prepared to narrow your search to make it more manageable. In the smoking example, the student might modify the search to read *teenage and smoking and advertising*, which would cut the number of sites listed in half.

Invention software

You may have access to invention software in a networked classroom, in your school's writing center, or even on your own computer. Invention software prompts you to think about your subject by raising a series of exploratory questions and sometimes by generating group discussion. To make the most of invention software, be sure to keep an open mind and allow yourself to explore the subject freely. For invention programs tailored to specific disciplines, check with your instructors.

1c   Settle on a tentative focus.

As you explore your subject, you will begin to see possible ways to focus your material. At this point, try to settle on a tentative central idea.

For many types of writing, your central idea can be asserted in one sentence, a generalization preparing readers for the supporting details that will follow. Such a sentence, which will ordinarily appear in the opening paragraph of your finished essay, is called a *thesis*. A successful thesis—like the following, all taken from articles in *Smithsonian*—points both the writer and the reader in a definite direction.

> Much maligned and the subject of unwarranted fears, most bats are harmless and highly beneficial.

> Geometric forms known as fractals may have a profound effect on how we view the world, not only in art and film but in many branches of science and technology, from astronomy to economics to predicting the weather.

> Aside from his more famous identities as colonel of the Rough Riders and president of the United States, Theodore Roosevelt was a lifelong professional man of letters.

The thesis sentence usually contains a key word or controlling idea that limits its focus. The preceding sentences, for example, prepare for essays that focus on the *beneficial* aspects of bats, the *effect* of fractals on how we view the world, and Roosevelt's identity as a writer, or *man of letters.*

It's a good idea to formulate a thesis early in the writing process, perhaps by jotting it on scratch paper, by putting it at the head of a rough outline, or by attempting to write an introductory paragraph that includes the thesis.

Your tentative thesis will probably be less graceful than the thesis you include in the final version of your essay. Here, for example, is one student's early effort:

> Although they both play percussion instruments, drummers and percussionists are very different.

The thesis that appeared in the final draft of the student's paper was more polished:

> Two types of musicians play percussion instruments—drummers and percussionists—and they are as different as Soundgarden and the New York Philharmonic.

Don't worry too soon about the exact wording of your thesis, however, because your main point may change as your drafts evolve. (See 2a and 3b.)

1d   Sketch a tentative plan.

Once you have generated some ideas and formulated a tentative thesis, you may want to sketch an informal outline. Informal outlines can take many forms. Perhaps the most common is simply the thesis followed by a list of major supporting ideas.

> Hawaii is losing its cultural identity.
> —pure-blooded Hawaiians increasingly rare
> —native language diluted
> —natives forced off ancestral lands
> —little emphasis on native culture in schools
> —customs exaggerated and distorted by tourism

Clustering diagrams, often used to generate ideas, can also serve as rough outlines (see p. 3). And if you began by jotting down a list of ideas (see p. 2), you may be able to turn the list into a rough outline by crossing out some ideas, adding others, and numbering the ideas to create a logical order.

Planning with headings

When writing a relatively long college paper or business document, consider using headings to guide readers. In addition to helping readers follow the organization of your final draft, headings can be a powerful planning tool, especially if you are working on a computer. You can type in your tentative thesis and then experiment with possible headings; once you have settled on the headings that work best, you can begin typing in chunks of text beneath each heading. Here, for example, is what one student typed into his laptop computer when planning a long history paper. The headings, written in the form of questions, are centered.

> Although we will never know whether Nathan Bedford Forrest directly ordered the massacre of Union troops at Fort Pillow, evidence strongly suggests that he was responsible for it.
>
> What happened at Fort Pillow?
>
> Why do the killings qualify as a massacre?
>
> Did Forrest order the massacre?
>
> Did the men have reason to think Forrest wanted a massacre?

For more detailed advice about using headings, see pages 44–45.

When to use a formal outline

Early in the writing process, rough outlines have certain advantages over more formal outlines: They can be produced more quickly, they are more obviously tentative, and they can be revised more easily should the need arise. However, a formal outline may be useful later in the writing process, after you have written a rough draft, especially if your subject matter is complex.

The following formal outline helped its writer improve and clarify the structure of his rough draft. Notice that the student's thesis is an important part of the outline. Everything else in the outline supports the thesis, either directly or indirectly.

Thesis: Although various methods for disposing of nuclear wastes have been proposed, each has serious drawbacks.

I. Antarctic ice sheet disposal is problematic for scientific and legal reasons.
   A. Our understanding of the behavior of ice sheets is too limited.
   B. An international treaty prohibits disposal in Antarctica.

II. Space disposal is unthinkable.
   A. The risk of an accident and resulting worldwide disaster is great.
   B. The cost is prohibitive.

   C. The method would be unpopular at home and abroad.

III. Seabed disposal is unwise because we do not know enough about the procedure or its impact.
   A. Scientists have not yet solved technical difficulties.
   B. We do not fully understand the impact of such disposal on the ocean's ecology.

IV. Deep underground disposal endangers public safety and creates political problems.
   A. Geologists disagree about the safest disposal sites, and no sites are completely safe.
   B. There is much political pressure against the plan from citizens who do not want their states to become nuclear dumps.

In constructing a formal outline, keep the following guidelines in mind.

1. Put the thesis at the top.
2. Make items at the same level of generality as parallel as possible (see 9).
3. Use sentences unless phrases are clear.
4. Use the conventional system of numbers and letters for the levels of generality.

   I.
      A.
      B.
         1.
         2.
            a.
            b.
               (1)
               (2)
                  (a)
                  (b)
   II.

5. Always use at least two subdivisions for a category, since nothing can be divided into fewer than two parts.
6. Limit the number of major sections in the outline; if the list of roman numerals begins to look like a laundry list, find some way of clustering the items into a few major categories with more subcategories.
7. Be flexible; in other words, be prepared to change your outline as your drafts evolve.

EXERCISE 1–1 Freewriting

On a separate sheet of paper or on a computer, begin with one of the following openings and write nonstop for ten minutes. Try to write in sentences, but don't worry about grammar, punctuation, and spelling. Just write and see what happens.

1. For years I have wanted to . . .

2. Who would have thought that . . .

3. What I remember most about . . .

4. I have always loved [or hated] . . .

5. If I had known then what I know now, I would never have . . .

6. In ten years, I imagine computers will be able to . . .

7. When I was a child, my favorite activity was . . .

8. The most frightening moment of my life happened when . . .

9. I wish my family [or my mother or brother or boyfriend or best friend] would . . .

10. Whenever I hear the word "math" [or the name of some other subject], I . . .

11. If I find one more thing I'm allergic to, I'll . . .

12. When my family watches TV together, we . . .

13. My dad doesn't mind asking other people to . . .

14. The first job most people have . . .

15. Buying a car is often . . .

EXERCISE 1–2 Exploring a subject

Choose a subject from one of the following lists and use the technique of listing or clustering to generate ideas that you might later include in an essay or paragraph.

Education: computers in the classroom, an inspiring teacher, sex education in junior high school, magnet schools, a learning disability such as dyslexia, programmed instruction, parochial schools, teacher certification, a local program to combat adult illiteracy, creative means of funding a college education

Careers and the workplace: working in an emergency room, the image versus the reality of a job such as lifeguarding, a police officer's workday, advantages of flextime for workers and employers, company-sponsored day care, mandatory drug testing by employers, gender or racial discrimination on the job, the psychological effects of unemployment, the rewards of a part-time job such as camp counseling, e-mail privacy issues, sexual harassment in the workplace

Families: an experience with adoption, a portrait of a family member who has aged well, the challenges facing single parents, living with an alcoholic, a portrait of an ideal parent, growing up in a large family, the problems of split custody, an experience with child abuse, the depiction of parent-child relationships in a popular TV series, expectations versus the reality of marriage, overcoming sibling rivalry, the advantages or disadvantages of being a twin, overseeing a child's access to the World Wide Web

Health: a vegetarian diet, weight loss through hypnotism, a fitness program for the elderly, reasons not to smoke, the rights of smokers or nonsmokers, overcoming an addiction, Prozac as a treatment for depression, the side effects of a particular treatment for cancer, life as a diabetic, the benefits of an aerobic exercise such as swimming, caring for a person with AIDS

Sports and hobbies: an unusual sport such as free-fall parachuting or bungee jumping, surviving a wilderness program, bodybuilding, a sport from another culture, the philosophy of karate, the language of sports announcers, pros and cons of banning boxing, coaching a Little League team, cutting the costs of an expensive sport such as skiing, a portrait of a favorite sports figure, sports for the handicapped, the discipline required for a sport such as gymnastics, the rewards of a hobby such as woodworking, salary caps for professional athletes

The arts: working behind the scenes at a theater, censorship of rock and roll lyrics, photography as an art form, the Japanese tea ceremony, the influence of African art on Picasso, the appeal of a local art museum, a portrait of a favorite musician or artist, performing as a musician, a high school for the arts, the colorization of black-and-white films, science fiction as a serious form of literature, a humorous description of romance novels or hard-boiled detective thrillers, the role of animation in film

Social justice: an experience with racism or sexism, affirmative action, reverse discrimination, making public transportation accessible for the physically handicapped, an experience as a juror, a local program to aid the homeless, discrimination against homosexuals, pros and cons of a national drinking age of twenty-one

Death and dying: working on a suicide hotline, the death of a loved one, a brush with death, caring for terminally ill patients, physician-assisted suicide, the Buddhist view of death, explaining death to a child, passive euthanasia, death with dignity, an out-of-body experience

Violence and crime: an experience with a gun, a wartime experience, violence on television news programs, visiting a friend in prison, alternative sentencing for first offenders, victims' rights, a successful program to eliminate violence in a public high school, Internet fraud, capital punishment, preventing terrorist attacks, domestic violence and the courts, violence in TV shows and video games marketed to children

Nature and ecology: safety of nuclear power plants, solar energy, wind energy, air pollution in the national parks, forest fires on the California coast, grizzly bears in Yellowstone, communication among dolphins, organic gardening, backpacking in the Rockies, marine ecology, cleaning up Boston Harbor, the preservation of beaches in Delaware

Science and technology: pros and cons of writing on a computer, genetic engineering, an experimental farming technique, a medical breakthrough, free speech and the Internet

EXERCISE 1–3 Planning an essay

In the space below, sketch an informal outline for an essay on one of the subjects listed in Exercise 1–2. Begin with a thesis (a sentence expressing your main point) and then list three or four ideas that support the thesis (see page 5 for an example). Once you have sketched the outline, ask your instructor whether it looks promising. If it needs more work, try again.

Once you have a good informal outline, consult it as you fill out the form that appears on the following pages. Here is how to fill out the form. First put your thesis statement at the end of the box for the introductory paragraph. Then turn each of the items in your outline into a sentence and place your sentences at the beginnings of the body paragraphs, where they will serve as topic sentences. Finally, list as many specific ideas as possible beneath each topic sentence; later you can consult these lists as you draft the essay. (*Note:* Although a box on the form represents the essay's concluding paragraph, leave the space blank for now.)

When you are finished, you should be ready to begin drafting your essay. Notice that some of your most important sentences have already been drafted.

INTRODUCTORY PARAGRAPH

FIRST BODY PARAGRAPH

SECOND BODY PARAGRAPH

THIRD BODY PARAGRAPH

FOURTH BODY PARAGRAPH (*OPTIONAL*)

CONCLUDING PARAGRAPH (*LEAVE BLANK FOR NOW*)

2 Rough out an initial draft.

As long as you treat an initial draft as a rough draft, you can focus your attention on ideas and organization, knowing that problems with sentence structure and word choice can always be dealt with later.

Overcoming writer's block

Before beginning a first draft, gather together your prewriting materials—lists, diagrams, outlines, freewriting, and so on. In addition to helping you get started, such notes and blueprints will encourage you to keep moving. With your earlier thoughts close by, you won't need to pause so frequently, staring at a blank page in search of ideas. Writing tends to flow better when it is drafted relatively quickly, without many stops and starts. The trick, of course, is to relax — to overcome the fear that grips many of us as we face that blank page.

At one time or another, we all experience writer's block. But if writer's block is a chronic problem for you, consider whether you're being too hard on yourself. Do you demand that your sentences all be stylish and perfectly grammatical right from the start? Do you expect your ideas to emerge full-blown, like Athena from the head of Zeus?

Professional writers are not so tough on themselves. Jacques Barzun, for example, lets his rough-draft sentences be "as stupid" as they wish. Joan Didion acknowledges that she discovers ideas *as she writes;* for her, writing is a way of learning, not just a means of revealing already known truths. As Didion puts it, "I write entirely to find out what I'm thinking, what I'm looking at, what I see and what it means."

2a For most types of writing, draft an introduction that includes a thesis.

The introduction announces the main point; the body develops it, usually in several paragraphs; the conclusion drives it home. You can begin drafting, however, at any point. If you find it difficult to introduce a paper that you have not yet written, you can write the body first and save the introduction for later.

For most writing tasks, your introduction will be a paragraph of 50 to 150 words. Perhaps the most common strategy is to open the paragraph with a few sentences that engage the reader and to conclude it with a statement of the essay's main point. The sentence stating the main point is called a *thesis.* (See 1c.) In the following examples, the thesis has been italicized.

> To the Australian aborigines, the Dreamtime was the time of creation. It was then that the creatures of the earth, including man, came into being. There are many legends about that mystical period, but unfortunately, the koala does not fare too well in any of them. *Slow-witted though it is in life, the koala is generally depicted in myth and folklore as a trickster and a thief.*
> —Roger Caras, "What's a Koala?"

> When I was sixteen, I married and moved to a small town to live. My new husband nervously showed me the house he had rented. It was after dark when we arrived there, and I remember wondering why he seemed so apprehensive about my reaction to the house. I thought the place seemed shabby but potentially cozy and quite livable inside. The morning sun revealed the reason for his anxiety by exposing the squalor outdoors. Up to that point, my contact with any reality but that of my own middle-class childhood had come from books. *The next four years in a small Iowa town taught me that reading about poverty is a lot different from living with it.*
> —Julie Reardon, student

Ideally, the sentences leading to the thesis should hook the reader, perhaps with one of the following:

a startling statistic or unusual fact

a vivid example

a description

a paradoxical statement

a quotation or bit of dialogue

a question

an analogy

a joke or an anecdote

Such hooks are particularly important when you cannot assume your reader's interest in the subject. Hooks are less necessary in scholarly essays and other writing aimed at readers with a professional interest in the subject.

Although the thesis frequently appears at the end of the introduction, it can just as easily appear at the beginning. Much work-related writing, in which a straightforward approach is most effective, commonly begins with the thesis.

> *Flextime scheduling, which has proved its effectiveness at the Library of Congress, should be introduced on a trial basis at the main branch of the Montgomery County Public Library.* By offering flexible work hours, the library can boost employee morale, cut down on absenteeism, and expand its hours of operation.   — David Warren, student

For some types of writing, it may be difficult or impossible to express the central idea in a thesis sentence; or it may be unwise or unnecessary to put a thesis sentence in the essay itself. A personal narrative, for example, may have a focus too subtle to be distilled in a single sentence, and such a sentence might ruin the story. Strictly informative writing, like that found in many business memos, may be difficult to summarize in a thesis. In such instances, do not try to force the central idea into a thesis sentence. Instead, think in terms of an overriding purpose, which may or may not be stated directly.

Characteristics of an effective thesis

An effective thesis should be a generalization, not a fact; it should be limited, not too broad; and it should be sharply focused, not too vague.

Because a thesis must prepare readers for facts and details, it cannot itself be a fact. It must always be a generalization demanding proof or further development.

TOO FACTUAL
The first polygraph was developed by Dr. John A. Larson in 1921.

REVISED
Because the polygraph has not been proved reliable, even under the most controlled conditions, its use by private employers should be banned.

Although a thesis must be a generalization, it must not be *too* general. You will need to narrow the focus of any thesis that you cannot adequately develop in the space allowed. Unless you were writing a book or a very long research paper, the following thesis would be too broad.

TOO BROAD
Many drugs are now being used successfully to treat mental illnesses.

You would need to restrict the thesis, perhaps like this:

REVISED
Despite its risks and side effects, Prozac is an effective treatment for depression.

Finally, a thesis should be sharply focused, not too vague. Beware of any thesis containing a fuzzy, hard-to-define word such as *interesting*, *good*, or *disgusting*.

TOO VAGUE
Many of the songs played on station WXQP are disgusting.

The word *disgusting* is needlessly vague. To sharpen the focus of this thesis, the writer should be more specific.

REVISED
Of the songs played on station WXQP, all too many depict sex crudely, sanction the beating or rape of women, or foster gang violence.

In the process of making a too-vague thesis more precise, you may find yourself outlining the major sections of your paper, as in the previous example. This technique, known as *blueprinting*, helps readers know exactly what to expect as they read on. It also helps you, the writer, control the shape of your essay.

2b Fill out the body.

Before drafting the body of an essay, take a careful look at your introduction, focusing especially on your thesis sentence. What does the thesis promise readers? Try to keep this focus in mind.

It's a good idea to have a plan in mind as well. If your thesis sentence outlines a plan (see 2a) or if you have sketched a preliminary outline, try to block out your paragraphs accordingly. If you do not have a plan, you would be wise to pause for a moment and sketch one (see 1d). Of course it is also possible to begin without a plan—assuming you are prepared to treat your first attempt as a "discovery draft" that will almost certainly be tossed (or radically rewritten) once you discover what you really want to say.

For more detailed advice about paragraphs in the body of an essay, see sections 5–7.

2c Attempt a conclusion.

The conclusion should echo the main idea, without dully repeating it. Often the concluding paragraph can be relatively short. By the end of the essay, readers should already understand your main point; your conclusion simply drives it home and perhaps suggests its significance.

In addition to echoing your main idea, a conclusion might summarize the essay's key points, pose a question for future study, offer advice, or propose a course of action. To end an essay detailing the social skills required of a bartender, one writer concludes with some advice:

> If someone were to approach me one day looking for the secret to running a good bar, I suppose I would offer the following advice: Get your customers to pour out their ideas at a greater rate than you pour out the liquor. You will both win in the end.
> —Kathleen Lewis, student

To make the conclusion memorable, consider including a detail, example, or image from the introduction to bring readers full circle; a quotation or bit of dialogue; an anecdote; or a humorous, witty, or ironic comment. To end a narrative describing a cash register holdup, one student uses an anecdote that includes some dialogue:

> It took me a long time to get over that incident. Countless times I found myself gasping as someone "pointed" a dollar bill at me. On one such occasion, a jovial little man buying a toy gun for his son came up to me and said in a Humphrey Bogart impression, "Give me all your money, Sweetheart." I didn't laugh. Instead, my heart skipped a beat, for I had heard those words before.
> —Diana Crawford, student

Whatever concluding strategy you choose, avoid introducing wholly new ideas at the end of an essay. Also avoid apologies and other limp, indeterminate endings. The essay should end crisply, preferably on a positive note.

Do not become discouraged if the perfect conclusion eludes you at the rough-draft stage of the writing process. Because the conclusion is so closely tied to the rest of the essay in both content and tone, you may well decide to rework it (or even replace it) as your drafts evolve.

EXERCISE 2–1 Introductory paragraphs

A. On a separate sheet of paper or on a computer, write a clearly focused thesis statement for two of these subjects. Use blueprinting in one of them.

1. The college cafeteria

2. Commuting to work or school

3. Ways to meet interesting men and women

4. A cause you believe in

5. The advantages (or disadvantages) of writing on a computer

6. The reasons you admire your favorite athlete

7. The dangers of backpacking in remote areas of Alaska (or the dangers of mountain climbing, scuba diving, or some other outdoor activity)

8. Ways to improve the registration process at your college

9. Juggling the demands of work, school, and family

10. Why a certain candidate should be elected president of the student government

B. Choose one of the thesis statements you wrote for A and draft an introductory paragraph that ends with the thesis. You may decide to change the wording of your original thesis to make it fit smoothly with the other sentences in the paragraph. If possible, begin your introduction with one of the hooks suggested on page 13.

EXERCISE 2–2 Introductory paragraphs

As a rule, the opening sentence of an introductory paragraph should hook readers, and the concluding sentence should state the thesis. Which sentence in each of the following sets would work best to hook readers? Circle the letter of that sentence and be prepared to explain the reasons for your choice. Example:

    a. It seems to me that I have an unusual talent for making enemies.

    b. I make enemies easily.

    (c.) "I'll never speak to you again!" yelled my former best friend.

1a. There are four kinds of preachers.

  b. I've gone to church all my life, and I can tell you that preachers come in four varieties.

  c. Preachers can be fit into four different categories.

2a. Statistics indicate that a quarter of the U.S. population will develop cancer.

  b. Cancer threatens many people in America.

  c. Next time you're in a crowd, look around you. Of every four people you see, one is likely to develop cancer.

3a. The New York Yankees have done it again!

  b. New York's baseball team, the Yankees, has set another record.

  c. There is a new record in baseball history.

4a. Prostitution, one of the world's oldest professions, is the act or practice of engaging in sexual intercourse for a fee.

  b. Should the world's oldest profession, prostitution, become legal in the United States?

  c. Many people believe that prostitution should be legalized, but I disagree.

5a. People who are color-blind don't see the same way other people do.

  b. "Roses are red, violets are blue"—but only if you're not color-blind.

  c. Color blindness affects many people in today's society.

EXERCISE 2–3 Introductory paragraphs

An introductory paragraph usually ends with a thesis sentence that asserts the main point of the whole essay. Which sentence in each of the following pairs would work better as a thesis for an essay approximately 500 words long? Circle the letter of that sentence and be prepared to explain your choice. Example:

    a. **Our trip to Disney World was very interesting.**

    (b.) **At Disney World, our family enjoyed the cartoon characters, the food, and most of all the many thrilling rides.**

1a. Elizabeth Blackwell, who came from Europe to study in Boston, was the first female doctor in the United States.

  b. Elizabeth Blackwell, who came from Europe to study in Boston, had to work very hard to become the first female doctor in the United States.

2a. People have different roles in different cultures, and these differences make understanding each other difficult.

  b. Because of their different cultural beliefs, leaders of Iran and the United States have had difficulty understanding one another.

3a. The House of Ruth is a shelter for abused women.

  b. The House of Ruth offers a number of important services to abused women.

4a. Although our two local elementary schools receive equal funding and serve a similar population of students, Lincoln is academically superior to Highland.

  b. Our two local elementary schools receive equal funding and serve a similar population of students, but Lincoln is better than Highland.

5a. Over the past twenty years, medical researchers have made significant advances in the treatment of cancer.

  b. Over the past twenty years, medical researchers have made significant advances in the treatment of breast cancer.

EXERCISE 2–4 Developing the body

_____

Using the thesis you wrote in Exercise 2–1, make a list of at least twenty-five details you might use to develop the thesis. Then group those details into three or more sets. Identify each set with a key word or phrase, and note the numbers of the details you would place in each group. (You do not have to use all twenty-five details, but think of at least that many.)

Thesis: _____

_____

Details:

1. _____   14. _____

2. _____   15. _____

3. _____   16. _____

4. _____   17. _____

5. _____   18. _____

6. _____   19. _____

7. _____   20. _____

8. _____   21. _____

9. _____   22. _____

10. _____   23. _____

11. _____   24. _____

12. _____   25. _____

13. _____

Key words or phrases and numbered details that go with them:

1. _____

_____

2. _____

_____

3. _____

_____

3   Make global revisions; then revise sentences.

For experienced writers, revising is rarely a one-step process. The larger elements of writing generally receive attention first—the focus, organization, content, and overall strategy. Improvements in sentence structure, word choice, grammar, punctuation, and mechanics come later.

NOTE: When working on a computer, print out a hard copy so that you can read the draft as a whole rather than screen by screen. A computer screen focuses your attention on small chunks of text rather than the whole; a printout allows you to look at the entire paper when thinking about what global revisions to make.

Once you have decided what global revisions may be needed, the computer, of course, is an excellent tool. In fact, because the computer saves time, it encourages you to experiment with global revisions. Should you combine two paragraphs? Would your conclusion make a good introduction? Might several paragraphs be rearranged for greater impact? Will the addition of boldface headings improve readability? With little risk, you can explore the possibilities. When a revision misfires, it is easy to restore your original draft.

3a   Get some distance, perhaps with the help of reviewers.

Many of us resist global revisions because we find it difficult to distance ourselves from a draft. We tend to review our work from our own, not from our audience's, perspective.

To distance yourself from a draft, begin by putting it aside for a while, preferably overnight or even longer. When you return to it, try to play the role of your audience as you read. Mark any places where your readers are likely to be confused, misled, or annoyed; look too for sentences and paragraphs that are not likely to persuade.

If at all possible, enlist the help of reviewers—persons willing to play the role of audience for you. Possible reviewers include peers, such as family members, friends, and other students; and professionals, such as professors, trained writing center tutors, and practicing writers. Ask your reviewers to focus on the larger issues of writing, not on the fine points. If they are at first captivated by fine points such as grammar and spelling—and many peer reviewers often are—remind them that you are not yet ready to think about such matters. For the moment, you are interested in their response to the essay as a whole.

Many professors set aside class time for peer review sessions in which students respond to one another's drafts in written comments, discussions, or both. In some classrooms, students use e-mail or other forms of electronic communication to send and receive comments on one another's rough drafts.

Checklists for global revision appear on pages 24 and 25.

3b   Approach global revision in cycles.

The process of global revision can be complex, so it is best to approach it in cycles, with each cycle encompassing a particular purpose for revising. Five common cycles of global revision are discussed in this section:

— Sharpening the focus
— Improving the organization
— Strengthening the content
— Clarifying the point of view
— Engaging the audience

You can handle these cycles in nearly any order, and you may be able to combine some of them. A chart summarizing these cycles appears on page 24.

If you have asked someone to review your draft, you have already begun to see which of these cycles most need your attention. And by giving some thought to your overall purpose and audience, you'll see even more clearly where your essay does—and does not—need major reworking.

Sharpening the focus

A draft is clearly focused when it fixes readers' attention on one central idea and does not stray from that idea. You can sharpen the focus of a draft by clarifying the introduction (especially the thesis) and by deleting any text that is off the point.

EXAMPLE OF GLOBAL REVISIONS

Sports on TV--A Win or a Loss?

Team sports are as much a part of Americain life as Mom and apple pie, and they have a good tendency to bring people together. They encourage team members to cooperate with one another, they also create shared enthusiasm among fans. Thanks to television, this togetherness now seems available to nearly all of us at the flick of a switch. ~~We do not have to buy tickets, and travel to a stadium, to see the World Series or the Super Bowl, these games are on television. We can enjoy the game in the comfort of our own living room.~~

~~After Thanksgiving or Christmas dinner, the whole family may gather around the TV set to watch football together.~~ It would appear that television has done us a great service. But is this really the case?

Although television does make sports more accessible, it also creates a distance between the sport and the fans and between athletes and the teams they play for.

The advantage of television is that it provides sports fans with greater convenience. [insert] ←

We can see more games than if we had to attend each one in person, and we can follow greater varieties of sports.

EXAMPLE OF SENTENCE-LEVEL REVISIONS

Televised
Sports ~~on TV~~--A Win or a Loss?

Team sports, ~~are~~ as much a part of Americain life as Mom and apple pie, ~~and they have~~ *tend* *us* ~~a good tendency~~ to bring ~~people~~ together. They encourage team members to cooperate *and* with one another, they ~~also~~ create shared *Because of* enthusiasm among fans. ~~Thanks to~~ television, this togetherness now seems available ~~to~~ ~~nearly all of us~~ at the flick of a switch. ~~It would appear that television has done us a great service.~~ But is this really the case? Although television *makes* ~~does make~~ sports more accessible, it also creates a distance between the sport and the fans and between *their* athletes and ~~the~~ teams~~, they play for.~~

The advantage of television is that it provides sports fans with greater convenience. We do not have to buy tickets / and travel to a stadium / to see the World Series *but* or the Super Bowl / ~~these games are on~~ *any* ~~television.~~ We can enjoy ~~the~~ game in the *rooms.* comfort of our own living ~~room.~~ We can see more games than if we had to attend each *a* one in person, and we can follow greater *variety* ~~varieties~~ of sports.

Guidelines for peer reviewers

READING THE DRAFT

As you read, you may want to pencil a few marks in the margin: perhaps an asterisk (*) for sentences or passages that seem especially effective, a question mark (?) for spots that confuse you, a plus mark (+) for places where you'd like to hear more details. Don't get carried away, however. Remember that you are not "grading" a finished essay; you are helping a fellow writer get distance from a rough draft. Above all, do not mark errors in grammar, punctuation, and spelling. The writer can deal with such matters later.

WRITING COMMENTS

Although some professors may ask you to write comments on the draft of an essay, most prefer that you respond on a separate sheet of paper or in a separate computer file. In a networked classroom, you may be asked to respond online. Here are some ideas for framing written responses:

1. In a sentence, describe the writer's apparent purpose and audience.

2. In a sentence, explain what the introduction promises readers; in other words, explain what you, as a reader, expect to hear in the rest of the essay.

3. List the two or three passages that best fulfill the promise of the introduction.

4. List a few things that you would like to hear more about.

5. Try to sketch a very simple outline of the draft—just the key ideas in support of the main point. (If this is difficult, the writer may need to work on organization.)

6. Write down two or three sentences from the draft that you found particularly interesting or well written.

TALKING TO THE WRITER

If you have the opportunity to discuss your ideas with the writer—either in person or online—here are some guidelines to keep in mind:

1. Try to open your conversation with descriptive, rather than evaluative, comments. For example, if the writer's subject is physical disabilities, you might begin by saying, "I think your point is that many adults are insensitive when they encounter persons with physical disabilities."

2. When you turn to evaluative comments, make the first ones positive. For example, you might mention that you found the writer's second paragraph a powerful example of insensitivity toward people with physical disabilities.

3. An effective peer review session is a dialogue, not a monologue. Try to get the writer talking by asking questions—about the draft in progress and about the subject. As writers talk about their subject with an interested listener, they often recall useful details and vivid examples that might be included in the essay.

4. If you have suggestions for improvement, try to tie them to the writer's goals. For instance, you might advise the writer to put the most dramatic example of insensitivity toward physically disabled people last, where it will have maximum impact on readers. Or you might suggest that a passage would gain power if abstractions were replaced with concrete details.

5. Throughout the review session, look on yourself as a coach, not a judge, as a proposer of possibilities, not a dictator of revisions. It is the writer, after all, who will have to grapple with the task of improving the essay.

6. At the end of the review session, you might want to express interest in reading the writer's next revision or final draft. Such interest—if it is sincere—can be a powerful motivator for a writer.

CLARIFYING THE INTRODUCTION First you will want to make sure that your introduction looks and reads like an introduction. Can readers tell where the introduction stops and the body of the essay begins? Have you perhaps included material in the introduction that really belongs in the body of the essay? Is your introduction long-winded?

Next check to see whether the introduction focuses clearly on the main point of the essay. Does it let readers know what to expect as they read on? Does it make the significance of the subject clear so that readers will want to read on?

The most important sentence in the introduction is the thesis. (See 2a.) If your essay lacks a thesis, make sure that you have a good reason for not including one. If your thesis is poorly focused or if it doesn't accurately state the real point of the essay, you'll need to revise it.

Checklist for global revision (for writers)

STRENGTHENING THE CONTENT

Look for opportunities

— to add specific facts, details, and examples
— to emphasize major ideas
— to rethink your argument or central insight

SHARPENING THE FOCUS

Look for opportunities

— to clarify the introduction (especially the thesis)
— to delete text that is off the point

IMPROVING THE ORGANIZATION

Look for opportunities

— to add or sharpen topic sentences
— to move blocks of text
— to reparagraph and perhaps add headings

CLARIFYING THE POINT OF VIEW

Look for opportunities

— to make the point of view more consistent
— to use a more appropriate point of view

ENGAGING THE AUDIENCE

Look for opportunities

— to let readers know why they are reading
— to motivate readers to read on
— to use a more appropriate tone

DELETING TEXT THAT IS OFF THE POINT   Compare the essay's introduction, particularly its thesis statement, with the body of the essay. Does the body of the essay fulfill the promise of the introduction? If not, one or the other must be adjusted. Either rebuild the introduction to fit the body of the paper or keep the introduction and delete any sentences or paragraphs that stray from its point.

Improving the organization

A draft is well organized when its major divisions are logical and easy for readers to follow. To improve the organization of your draft, consider taking one or more of the following actions: adding or sharpening topic sentences, moving blocks of text, reparagraphing, and inserting headings.

ADDING OR SHARPENING TOPIC SENTENCES   Topic sentences, as you probably know, state the main ideas of the paragraphs in the body of an essay. (See 5a.) Topic sentences act as signposts for readers, announcing ideas to come.

You can review the organization of a draft by reading only the topic sentences. Do they clearly support the essay's main idea? Do they make a reasonable sentence outline of the paper? If your draft lacks topic sentences, make sure you have a good reason for omitting these important signposts.

MOVING BLOCKS OF TEXT   Improving the organization of a draft can be as simple as moving a few sentences from one paragraph to another or switching the order of paragraphs. Often, however, the process is more complex. As you move blocks of text, you may need to supply transitions to make them fit smoothly in their new positions; you may also need to rework topic sentences to make your new organization clear.

Before moving text, consider sketching a revised outline. Divisions in the outline might become topic sentences in the restructured essay. (See 1d.)

REPARAGRAPHING AND INSERTING HEADINGS   Occasionally you can clarify the organization of a draft simply by combining choppy paragraphs or by dividing those that are too long for easy reading. (See 6d.)

In long documents, such as research papers or business reports, consider using headings to help readers follow your organization. Possible headings include phrases, declarative

Checklist for global revision (for reviewers)

FOCUS

— Does the introduction focus on the main point?

— Is the thesis clear enough? (If there is no thesis, is there a good reason for omitting one?)

— Are any ideas off the point?

ORGANIZATION

— Does the writer give readers enough organizational cues (such as topic sentences or headings)?

— Should any text be moved?

— Are any paragraphs too long or short for easy reading?

CONTENT

— Are there enough facts, examples, and details to support major ideas?

— Are the parts proportioned sensibly? Do major ideas receive enough attention?

— How might the argument be strengthened?

POINT OF VIEW

— Is the draft free of distracting shifts in point of view?

— Is the point of view appropriate?

AUDIENCE APPEAL

— Does the draft accomplish its purpose—to inform us, to persuade us, to entertain us, to call us to action (or some combination of these)?

— Does the opening paragraph make us want to read on? Do we know why we are reading?

— Is the tone appropriate?

---

or imperative sentences, and questions. To draw attention to headings, consider centering them, putting them in boldface, underlining them, using all capital letters, or some combination of these. (See also pp. 44–45.)

Strengthening the content

In reviewing the content of a draft, consider whether any text (sentences, paragraphs, or longer passages) should be added or deleted, keeping in mind your readers' needs. Then, if your purpose is to argue a point, consider how persuasively you have proved your point to an intelligent, discerning audience. When necessary, rethink your argument.

ADDING TEXT If any paragraphs or sections of the essay are developed too skimpily to be clear and convincing (a common flaw in rough drafts), you will need to add specific facts, details, and examples. This necessity will take you back to the beginning of the writing process: listing specifics, brainstorming ideas with friends or classmates, perhaps doing more research.

DELETING TEXT Look for sentences and paragraphs that can be cut without serious loss of meaning. Perhaps you have repeated yourself or strayed from your point. Maybe you

have given undue emphasis to minor ideas. Cuts may also be necessitated by word limits, such as those imposed by a college assignment or by the realities of the business world, where readers are often pressed for time.

RETHINKING YOUR ARGUMENT A first draft presents you with an opportunity for rethinking your argument. You can often deepen your ideas on a subject by asking yourself some hard questions. Is your claim more sweeping than the evidence allows? Have you left out an important step in the argument? Have you dealt with the arguments of the opposition? The more challenging your subject, the more likely you will find yourself adjusting your early thoughts.

Clarifying the point of view

If the point of view of a draft shifts confusingly or if it seems not quite appropriate for your purpose, audience, and subject, consider adjusting it.

There are three basic points of view to choose from: the first person (*I* or *we*), the second person (*you*), and the third person (*he, she, it, one,* or *they*). Each point of view is appropriate in at least some contexts, and you may need to experiment before discovering which one best suits your needs.

THE THIRD-PERSON POINT OF VIEW Much academic and professional writing is best presented from the third-person point of view (*he, she, it, one,* or *they*), which puts the subject in the foreground. The *I* point of view is usually inappropriate in such contexts because, by focusing attention on the writer, it pushes the subject into the background. Consider, for example, one student's first-draft description of the behavior of a species of frog that he had observed in the field.

> Each frog that *I* was able to locate in trees remained in its given tree during the entirety of *my* observation period. However, *I* noticed that there was considerable movement within the home tree.

Here the *I* point of view is distracting, as the student himself noticed when he began to revise his report. His revision focuses more on the frogs, less on himself.

> Each frog located in a tree remained in that tree throughout the observation period. The frogs moved about considerably, however, within their home trees.

Just as the first-person pronoun *I* can draw too much attention to the writer, the second-person pronoun *you* can focus unnecessarily on the reader. In the following sentence from a memo, for example, a supervisor writing to a sales manager needlessly draws attention to the reader:

> When *you* look at the numbers, *you* can clearly see that travel expenses must be cut back.

This sentence would be clearer and more direct if presented without the distraction of the *you* point of view:

> The numbers clearly show that travel expenses must be cut back.

Although the third-person point of view is often a better choice than the *I* or *you* point of view, it is by no means trouble-free. Writers who choose it can run into problems when they want to use singular pronouns in an indefinite sense. For example, when Miss Piggy says that a reason for jogging is "to improve *one's* emotional health and make *one* feel better about *oneself,*" one wishes she wouldn't use quite so many *one's*, doesn't one? The trouble is that American English, unlike British English, does not allow this pronoun to echo throughout a sentence. The repetitions sound stuffy in American English.

Some years ago Americans would have said "to improve a person's emotional health and to make *him* feel better about *himself,*" with the understanding that *him* really meant *him or her.* Today, however, this use of *him* is offensive to many readers and is best avoided. On the other hand, "to make *him or her* feel better about *himself or herself*" is distinctly awkward. So what is poor Miss Piggy to say?

Her only hope, it turns out, is a flexible and inventive mind. She might switch to the plural: *Joggers run to improve their emotional health and to make them feel better about themselves.* Or she could restructure the sentence altogether: *Jogging improves a person's emotional health and self-image.* (See 17f and 22a.)

THE SECOND-PERSON POINT OF VIEW The *you* point of view, which puts the reader in the foreground, is appropriate if the writer is advising readers directly, as in giving tips on raising children or instructions on flower arranging. All imperative sentences, such as the advice for writers in this book, are written from the *you* point of view, although the word itself is frequently omitted and understood. "Sketch a plan" means "*You* should sketch a plan"; everyone knows this, so the *you* is not expressed.

In the course of giving advice or instructions, the actual word *you* may be appropriate and even desired. In advising gardeners about walkways, for example, newspaper columnist Henry Mitchell feels free to use the words *you* and *your* as the need arises:

> If *your* main walk is less than four feet wide, and if it is white concrete, then widen it, no matter what has to be sacrificed . . . and resurface it with brick, stone, or something less glaring and dull. Three flowers against a good-looking pavement will do more for *you* than thirty flowers against white concrete. [Italics added.]

Mitchell might have written this passage from the third-person point of view instead ("If *the gardener's* walk is less than four feet wide . . ."), but the effect would have seemed oddly indirect. Even at the risk of sounding a bit bossy, Mitchell has wisely selected the imperative (*you*) approach instead.

Notice that Mitchell's *you* means "you, the reader." It does not mean "you, anyone in general." Indefinite uses of *you,* such as the following example, are inappropriate in formal writing (see 23d).

> Young Japanese women wired together electronic products on a piece-rate system: The more *you* wired, the more *you* were paid.

Here the writer should have stayed with the third-person point of view instead.

> The more *they* wired, the more *they* were paid.

THE FIRST-PERSON POINT OF VIEW   If much of a writer's material comes from personal experience, the *I* point of view will prove most natural. It is difficult to imagine, for example, how James Thurber could have avoided the word *I* in describing his early university days:

> *I* passed all the other courses that *I* took at my university, but *I* could never pass botany. This was because all botany students had to spend several hours a week in a laboratory looking through a microscope at plant cells, and *I* could never see through a microscope. *I* never once saw a cell through a microscope. This used to enrage my instructor. [Italics added.]   —"University Days"

Thurber's *I* point of view puts the writer in the foreground, and since the writer is in fact the subject, this makes sense.

Writers who are aware that the first-person point of view is sometimes viewed as inappropriate in academic writing often overgeneralize the rule. Concluding that the word *I* is never appropriate, they go to extreme lengths to avoid it.

> Mama read with such color and detail that *one* could fancy *oneself* as the hero of the story.

Since the paper in which this sentence appeared was a personal reminiscence, the entire paper sounded more natural once the writer allowed himself to use the word *I*:

> Mama read with such color and detail that *I* could fancy *myself* as the hero of the story.

Engaging the audience

Considerations of audience often lead to global revision. Many rough drafts need a major overhaul because they are directed at no audience at all for no apparent purpose—written in a vacuum, so to speak. Readers are put off by such writing because when they don't know *why* they are reading, they suspect that a writer may be wasting their time. A good question to ask yourself about your own rough drafts, therefore, is the toughest question that a reader might ask: "So what?" If your draft can't pass the "So what?" test, you will need to rethink your entire approach; in fact, you may even decide to scrap the draft and start over.

Once you have made sure that your draft is directed at an audience—readers who stand to benefit in some way by reading it—you may still need to refine your tone. The tone of a piece of writing expresses the writer's feelings toward the audience, so it is important to get it right. If the tone seems too self-centered—or too flippant, stuffy, bossy, patronizing, opinionated, or hostile—obviously it should be modified.

Any piece of writing drafted in anger or frustration will almost certainly need to be toned down. The following rough draft, for example, was written by a secretary in response to criticisms of a newsletter sent out by the organization for which she worked.

> Dear Mr. Martin:
>
> I know our newsletter is crudely laid out, the reason being that I type it from rough drafts under a tight enough deadline that only major errors of judgment get retyped. Perhaps we'd do better if we had more funding.
>
> I think you were wrong to dismiss the offending story as bragging about *Nuclear War: What's in It for You?* The book was nominated for the prize, a fact worthy of mention despite the fact that it did not win.
>
> In any case, I am glad to hear that you liked the open letter to the president. Would that the *Philadelphia Inquirer* had liked it as well.
>
> Sincerely,
>
> Robbie Nichols

As she reached the last paragraph of the rough draft, the writer saw the need to be more diplomatic. Later, in a calmer mood, she revised the letter like this:

Dear Mr. Martin:

We are glad to hear that you liked Roger Molander's "An Open Letter to the President." Would that the *Philadelphia Inquirer* had liked it as well.

I do think you were wrong to dismiss the sentence about *Nuclear War: What's in It for You?* as "bragging." It is a fairly direct sentence, and there may well be those among the faithful who wouldn't otherwise have known about its nomination for the prize.

Your comments about the physical layout of the story were, in fact, echoed by the staff here. The layout could not be changed, however, because it was typed under a tight deadline that allowed retyping only in cases of major errors of judgment.

Thank you for writing. Even though our newsletter has a limited circulation, we hope that Roger's open letter will elicit serious thought about the president's March 23 address on weapons in space.

Sincerely,

Robbie Nichols

EXERCISE 3 –1 Global revision

Pretend that Alex, the writer of the following rough draft, has come to you for advice about global revision of his essay (see the guidelines on p. 23 and the checklist on p. 25). What will you tell him? Try to resist commenting on grammar, punctuation, and spelling — matters that Alex plans to deal with after he has made global revisions. Whether you write comments directly on Alex's essay, on a separate sheet of paper, or in a computer file is up to you.

If you are concerned enough about the earths environment to make six easy steps a part of your regular routine, your individual actions can help save the planet for this generation and the generations to come.

First of all, people who want to help the planet can recycle. Recycling includes more then cans, bottles, and newspapers. Adopt your grandparents' attitude about reusing things. Don't throw out that lamp, but pass it on to someone else. Pass down clothing from one child to the next. A person concerned about the environment looks at everything real careful, before he puts it in the trash can, and ask himself, whether someone could use that item for anything at all? If the answer is yes, don't throw it away.

Another thing you can do is conserve energy. No, you fool, that doesn't mean loafing in the hammock all day. It means turning off lights and radios and tv's when your not using them. It means planning your errands so that you make one trip instead of three or four. It means carpooling not only for the kids' swimming lessons but for your job. Another way to help is to replace as much of the plastic you use as you can. Does your office or church use styrofoam cups for coffee? Paper may cost more, but its easier on the planet. You might even go all the way and use a ceramic cup that you can reuse endlessly. The only chore that would add to your day would be washing a cup. Is the planet worth that much of your time?

Finally, you can replace some of what you've used. Plant a tree. Cultivate a garden. Grind up the leaves in your yard and compost them to replace the soil. If everyone did these few things, life on our planet would be much safer for all its inhabitants.

EXERCISE 3–2 Choosing a point of view

For each of the following topics, which point of view—first person, second person, or third person—would probably work best? If more than one point of view seems possible, which one would you choose? Why?

1. How to pass a driver's test on the first try _____

    _____

2. A comparison of the prices at two different auto parts stores _____

    _____

3. A humorous experience on your first day as a lifeguard _____

    _____

4. The way fashions seem to go in cycles _____

    _____

5. A review of a restaurant _____

    _____

6. The origins of the civil rights movement in the United States _____

    _____

7. How to dissect a worm in biology lab _____

    _____

8. Your close call with death _____

    _____

9. What it was like to grow up in a large family _____

    _____

10. Science fiction as a serious form of literature _____

    _____

EXERCISE 3–3 Revising for tone

Revise (or rewrite) the following memo to give it a positive tone in spite of its negative content.

Date: July 29, 1997

To: Philip Marks, Assistant Sales Manager

From: Jan Donovan, Division Chief

Subject: Employee orientation meeting

You've got a lot to learn about motivating employees. If yesterday's meeting is any example of your skill, we'll not meet any of our quotas this quarter.

The only good things you did were to start the meeting on time and to introduce everyone. The rest of the meeting was a disaster: Your agenda wasn't organized, you didn't have all the facts on the newest models, and you threatened the new people with loss of their jobs. Maybe I should copy your style and tell you to shape up or ship out.

You've obviously got brains—use them. I'll be watching next week to see if you've learned anything from this experience.

SENTENCE-LEVEL REVISIONS

3c Revise and edit sentences.

When you revise sentences, you focus on effectiveness; when you edit, you check for correctness. As with global revision, sentence-level revision may be approached in cycles, with each cycle focusing on a different purpose for making changes. The main purposes for revising sentences—to strengthen, clarify, vary, and refine them—are detailed in the chart on page 34. A checklist on editing for grammar, punctuation, and mechanics appears on page 35.

Some writers handle most sentence-level revisions directly at the computer, experimenting on screen with a variety of possible improvements. Other writers prefer to print out a hard copy of the draft, mark it up, and then return to the computer. Here, for example, is a rough-draft paragraph as one student edited it for a variety of sentence-level problems:

> *deciding*
> Finally we decided that perhaps our
> dream needed ~~some~~ prompting, ~~and~~ we visited
> a fertility doctor and began the expensive,
> timeconsuming round of procedures that
> *some* *our dream's fulfillment.*
> held out ~~the~~ promise of ~~fulfilling our~~
> *Our efforts, however, were* *As*
> ~~dream. All this was~~ to no avail/~~and as~~ we
> approached the sixth year of our marriage,
> *could no longer*
> we ~~had reached the point where we couldn't~~
> even discuss our childlessness without
> becoming very depressed. We questioned why
> this had happened to us/. Why had we been
> *such a*
> singled out for ~~this~~ major disappointment?

The original paragraph was flawed by wordiness and overuse of *and* as a way of linking ideas. Such problems can be addressed through any number of acceptable revisions. The first sentence, for example, could have been changed like this:

> Finally we decided that perhaps our
> *After visiting*
> dream needed ~~some~~ prompting/~~and we~~

> *we*
> ~~visited~~ a fertility doctor, ~~and~~ began
> the expensive, timeconsuming round of
> *promised hope*
> procedures that ~~held out the promise~~ of
> fulfilling our dream.

Though some writers might argue about the effectiveness of these improvements compared with the previous revision, most would agree that both versions are better than the original.

Some of the paragraph's improvements involve less choice and are not so open to debate. The hyphen in *time-consuming* is necessary; a noun must be substituted for the pronoun *this* in the second sentence, which was being used more loosely than grammar allows; and the question mark in the next to last sentence must be changed to a period.

Software tools

Software can provide help with sentence-level revisions. Most word processors have spell checkers that will catch many but not all spelling errors, and some have thesauruses to help with word choice.

Some word processing programs are equipped with grammar checkers (sometimes called "style checkers" or "text analyzers"). When using a grammar checker, you need to be aware of what this tool can—and cannot—do. Grammar checkers are fairly good at flagging wordy sentences, jargon, slang, clichés, and passive verbs. But such problems represent only a small fraction of the sentence-level problems in a typical draft. Because so many problems—such as faulty parallelism, mixed constructions, and misplaced modifiers—lack mathematical precision, they slip right past the grammar checker. You should not assume, therefore, that once you have run your draft through a grammar checker, your grammar problems are over.

Throughout this book, you will find grammar checker advice linked to specific problems. For example, in section 14 you will learn that grammar checkers can flag most but not all passive verbs and that they flag passive constructions whether or not they are appropriate. In section 20 you will learn that grammar checkers flag some run-ons, miss others, and tell you that some sentences may be run-ons when in fact they are not.

Cycles of sentence-level revision

The numbers in this chart refer to sections in this workbook.

STRENGTHENING SENTENCES

Look for opportunities

— to use more active verbs (14a)
— to prune excess words (16)

CLARIFYING SENTENCES

Look for opportunities

— to balance parallel ideas (9)
— to supply missing words (10)
— to untangle mixed constructions (11)

— to repair misplaced or dangling modifiers (12)
— to eliminate distracting shifts (13)

INTRODUCING VARIETY

Look for opportunities

— to combine choppy sentences (8a)
— to break up long sentences (8d)
— to vary sentence openings (15a)

REFINING THE STYLE

Look for opportunities

— to choose language more appropriate for the subject and audience (17)
— to choose more exact words (18)

The grammar checker advice is based on a large sample of correct and incorrect sentences that were run through two widely used grammar checker programs. For more details, see page iv of the Preface.

Proofreading

After revising and editing, you are ready to prepare the final manuscript. (See 4b for guidelines.) At this point, make sure to allow yourself enough time for proofreading—the final and most important step in manuscript preparation.

Proofreading is a special kind of reading: a slow and methodical search for misspellings, typographical mistakes, and omitted words or word endings. Such errors can be difficult to spot in your own work because you may read what you intended to write, not what is actually on the page. To fight this tendency, try proofreading out loud, articulating each word as it is actually written. You might also try proofreading your essay backward, a strategy that takes your attention away from the meanings you intended and forces you to think about small surface features instead.

Although proofreading may be dull, it is crucial. Errors strewn throughout an essay are distracting and annoying. If the writer doesn't care about this piece of writing, thinks the reader, why should I? A carefully proofread essay, however, sends a positive message: It shows that you value your writing and respect your readers.

EXPOSITORY STUDENT ESSAY: EXPLAINING AN INSIGHT

Lauren Pent, who wrote "E-mail — Return to Sender?" (pp. 39–40), was responding to the following assignment.

ASSIGNMENT: EXPLAINING AN INSIGHT

When you explain an insight on a topic, you offer readers a fresh or interesting way of looking at it. In other words, you give them a way of understanding something that they may have understood differently before.

You might challenge a conventional view that has not been validated by your own experience: the view, for example, that growing up in a small town is idyllic or that work as a flight attendant is glamorous. You might explain an insight about a group with which you are familiar: Harley-Davidson bikers, farmers, the physically challenged, or people from another culture. You might give readers a new way of looking at some aspect of the media: maybe by ridiculing the language of sports announcers, revealing stereotypes in a television series, explaining why *Star Trek* has had such lasting appeal, or showing that the history of rap music is more complex than

An editing checklist

At first this checklist may seem overwhelming, but as your instructor responds to your writing and as you become familiar with the rules in this workbook, you'll begin to see which problems, if any, tend to cause you trouble. You can then devise a personal checklist of errors to look for as you edit. (The numbers in the chart refer to sections in this workbook.)

GRAMMAR

Sentence fragments (19)
Run-on sentences (20)
Subject-verb agreement (21)
Pronoun-antecedent agreement (22)
Pronoun reference (23)
Case of nouns and pronouns (24)
Case of *who* and *whom* (25)
Adjectives and adverbs (26)
Standard English verb forms (27)

Verb tense, mood, and voice (28)
ESL problems (29, 30, 31)

PUNCTUATION

The comma and unnecessary commas (32, 33)
The semicolon (34)
The colon (35)
The apostrophe (36)
Quotation marks (37)
End punctuation (38)
Other punctuation marks (39)

MECHANICS

Abbreviations and numbers (40, 41)
Italics (underlining) (42)
Spelling and the hyphen (43, 44)
Capital letters (45)

---

most people think. Or you might give readers an insight into one of your special interests, such as photography, mountain climbing, or one of the martial arts.

Your insight should appear in a thesis sentence early in the essay, most likely at the end of the introductory paragraph (see pp. 13–14 of this workbook). For this assignment, your information should come from personal knowledge, interviews, or direct observation. Aim for an essay from 500 to 1,000 words long—from two to four typed pages, double-spaced.

Pent's planning materials

When she received her assignment, Lauren Pent considered several possibilities before settling on the topic of e-mail. Having just gone online herself, Pent understood the advantages of e-mail that her family and friends had been raving about. She wondered, though, whether e-mail wasn't perhaps being oversold.

To get started on her paper, Pent typed the following list of ideas into her computer:

```
e-mail--faster than "snail mail"
```

```
easy to use--no licking envelopes etc. (es-
pecially when you're sending lots of copies
of the same message)
```

```
lots of people have free access at school
or work but most people in the world don't
have computers or modems, so e-mail is no
use to them
```

```
I wonder why there isn't more junk e-mail.
Will Ed McMahon ever make it to cyberspace?
```

```
cost of e-mail? fees for online services,
but you can send multiple copies for the
same price as one
```

```
e-mail is sort of impersonal. I'd rather
get a love letter or a birthday card
through regular mail
```

```
what about privacy? especially in the work-
place
```

Later Pent reread her list and concluded that her focus should be the advantages and disadvantages of e-mail, with an emphasis on the disadvantages that some people probably haven't thought about. With this focus in mind, she formulated a tentative thesis and sketched a rough outline.

```
E-mail has many advantages over regular
mail, but there are several disadvantages
that might not be so readily apparent.
```

```
  --Advantages
    --speed
    --low cost
    --easy to use
  --Disadvantages
    --no access for some people
    --lacks a personal touch
    --lack of privacy, especially in
      the workplace
```

NOTE: Pent later revised this rough outline after listening to what her peer reviewers had to say about her first draft.

Working from her list and rough outline, Pent wrote a first draft. She wrote it quickly, focusing more on ideas than on grammar, style, and mechanics. As you read her rough draft, consider what global changes you would recommend. Think about large issues such as focus, organization, content, and audience appeal.

PENT'S ROUGH DRAFT

```
        E-mail--Return to Sender?
     For many people, turning on the
computer and checking for e-mail messages
has become as much a part of their daily
routine as a trip to the mailbox. The
growing popularity of e-mail makes us won-
der how could we have survived without it?
E-mail has many advantages, including
speed, never having to pay for postage and
that we can send messages with ease. At
the same time, however, there are several
disadvantages that might not be so readily
apparent.
     There is no denying that e-mail has
many advantages over regular mail through
the U.S. Postal Service. The most obvious
advantage is speed. We can send e-mail
around the world in a matter of minutes
with no more effort than it takes to press
a few key on the computer. It is this ter-
rific speed that has lead to our calling
regular mail "snail mail." E-mail also has
the advantage of being less expensive. Many
people have access to e-mail for free
through there work or school. And while
```

```
some people may pay for e-mail through an
online service, there is no increase in
cost relative to the number of messages
sent. It is the same price to send one
message to one person as it is to send
messages back and forth all day or to a
hundred people.
     In addition, e-mail allows us to send
the same message to many people at the
same time with little more effort than it
takes to send a message to one person.
There is never the trouble of photocopying
the letter or printing out another copy or
addressing and posting another envelope.
Considering the ease, it is surprising
there is not more junk e-mail then there
is. Someday the direct marketing people
will surely catch up with the electronic
revolution, at least Ed McMahon hasn't made
it to cyberspace yet.
     Despite the convenience that e-mail
provides, it has several disadvantages. For
one thing, each person who uses e-mail must
have their own e-mail address, so e-mail
excludes anyone who doesn't have access to
a computer. Even having a computer still
does not mean that one has e-mail. One
must pay a monthly fee to an online
service to have access to e-mail. It is
only less expensive in the sense that there
is not a per-use charge as there is with
regular mail.
     Assuming one does have access to
e-mail without much effort or expense,
there are still several advantages to regu-
lar mail. With e-mail all messages look
very much alike and this removes some of
the wonder of getting a message in the
first place. We have no handwriting to
scrutinize, no perfumed envelope to smell,
no colors or designs to enjoy. E-mail is
also limited by what one can send. Attached
files might let us send a copy of a photo,
but we wouldn't want to put it in a frame.
One will never get an e-mail care package
from home or an e-mail pop-up birthday
card. For these more personal things we
must always resort to regular mail.
```

```
    In addition, there is the issue of
privacy. Especially in the business world.
For example, its probably not a great idea
to complain about your boss on the company
e-mail, or write anything that you would
not truly mind sharing with others.
    While e-mail gives us the ability to
send messages with convenience, speed, and
little expense, it lacks the personality
of regular mail. There is no reason,
however, to always choose one over the
other. Instead we should take advantage
of both, using each to its best advantage.
E-mail for quick notes, multiple mailings,
and business correspondence. Regular mail
for messages that deserve a more personal
touch. Regular mail will always take
longer, but, as the old saying goes,
good things come to those who wait.
```

Peer review of Pent's draft

Before beginning to revise the draft, Pent brought it to class for a peer review session. Three of her classmates read the draft and responded to it, using the checklist on page 25. Here are some of their most useful comments and suggestions:

I'd like to hear more about why e-mail is convenient.

Your remark about junk mail and Ed McMahon was funny, but wasn't it off the point?

I like your details about personal letters. You made me feel nostalgic.

You talk about the cost of e-mail in two places. Shouldn't this all be together? Also, is e-mail cheaper or not?

Dr. King is going to want you to sharpen your thesis (at the end of the first paragraph).

In places, your use of the word *one* seemed sort of stiff. I like it better when you use *we,* because it sounds friendlier.

I thought your point about privacy was a good one. Once my little sister called up an e-mail sent by my boyfriend, and she hasn't stopped teasing me since.

One of the things I like about e-mail is that people don't seem to care as much if you make mistakes.

You made me see the advantages of e-mail, but maybe you could beef up the part about disadvantages. Isn't the danger of "flaming" a disadvantage? I know some people who have gotten themselves in trouble in the business world.

Your second paragraph seems pretty long. Why not break it up so that you talk about the low cost of e-mail in one paragraph and its convenience in another?

I wasn't sure about your purpose and audience. The concluding paragraph gives advice to readers, but some parts of the paper make more of a social commentary.

Notice that Pent's classmates were focusing on global matters, not on sentence-level revisions. Because the draft needed a fair amount of work, it made little sense to tinker with its sentences, some of which would be thrown out anyway.

Pent's global revisions

With the help of her peer reviewers, Pent saw the need for a number of global revisions. Here, for example, is how she revised her opening paragraph to improve the focus of her paper:

```
    For many people, turning on the
computer and checking for e-mail messages
has become as much a part of their daily
routine as a trip to the mailbox. The
growing popularity of e-mail makes us won-
der how could we have survived without it?
E-mail has many advantages, including
speed, never having to pay for postage and
that we can send messages with ease. At
the same time, however, there are several
disadvantages that might not be so readily
apparent.
```

In our enthusiasm for e-mail, however, it would be unwise of us to abandon the post office altogether. For some purposes, e-mail is a poor sub-

stitute for "snail mail," both in our personal lives and in the business world.

For Pent's sentence-level revisions of this same paragraph, see this page.

In the following paragraph, Pent made three global revisions. She added a topic sentence at the beginning of the paragraph, she deleted text that was off the point, and she added new text describing another way in which e-mail is convenient.

There is no question that e-mail is convenient. It ~~In addition, e-mail~~ allows us to send the same message to many people at the same time with little more effort than it takes to send a message to one person. There is never the trouble of photocopying the letter or printing out another copy or addressing and posting another envelope. ~~Considering the ease, it is surprising there is not more junk e-mail then there is. Someday the direct marketing people will surely catch up with the electronic revolution, at least Ed McMahon hasn't made it to cyberspace yet.~~ *E-mail is also convenient because it lends itself to an informal style that makes composing a message relatively easy; in addition, readers of e-mail tolerate more mistakes than readers of conventional mail, and their tolerance saves us time.*

If you compare Pent's final draft (pp. 39–40) with her earlier draft (pp. 36–37), you will notice other global revisions: breaking a long paragraph into two paragraphs, deleting and adding more chunks of text, sharpening topic sentences, making the point of view more consistent by using *we* instead of *people* or *one*, and so on.

Pent's sentence-level revisions

Once Pent had written a second draft, she felt ready to devote her full attention to matters of style and correctness. Here, for example, are the first two paragraphs as Pent edited them. Notice that even though Pent had run all of her drafts through a spell checker, the second paragraph still contained both a typographical error and a misspelling. The spell checker didn't flag *key* and *lead* because they are real words.

For many ~~people,~~ *of us,* turning on the computer and checking for e-mail messages has become as much a part of ~~their~~ *our* daily routine as a trip to the mailbox. The growing popularity of e-mail makes us wonder how ~~could we have~~ *we ever* survived without it~~.~~*:* E-mail has many advantages */over regular mail,* including speed, ~~never having to pay for postage and that we can send messages with ease~~ *low cost, and convenience.* In our enthusiasm for e-mail, however, ~~it~~ *we* would be unwise ~~of us~~ to abandon the post office altogether. For some purposes, e-mail is a poor substitute for "snail mail," both in our personal lives and in the business world.

There is no denying that e-mail has many advantages over regular mail~~,~~*:* ~~through the U.S. Postal Service.~~ The most obvious advantage is speed. We can send e-mail around the world in a matter of minutes with no more effort than it takes to press a few key*s* on the computer. It is this ~~terrific~~ speed that has ~~lead~~ *led* to our calling regular mail "snail mail."

When Pent finished making all of her revisions, she carefully proofread and corrected her paper before turning in the final draft shown here.

PENT'S FINAL DRAFT

E-mail--Return to Sender?

For many of us, turning on the computer and checking for e-mail messages has become as much a part of our daily routine as a trip to the mailbox. The growing popularity of e-mail makes us wonder how we ever survived without it. E-mail has many advantages over regular mail, including speed, low cost, and convenience. In our enthusiasm for e-mail, however, we would be unwise to abandon the post office altogether. For some purposes, e-mail is a poor substitute for "snail mail," both in our personal lives and in the business world.

There is no denying that e-mail has many advantages over regular mail. The most obvious advantage is speed. We can send e-mail around the world in a matter of minutes with no more effort than it takes to press a few keys on the computer. It is this speed that has led to our calling regular mail "snail mail."

E-mail also has the advantage of being less expensive, for most people, than regular mail. Many people have access to e-mail for free through their work or school. And while some people may pay for e-mail through an online service, there is no increase in cost relative to the number of messages sent. It is the same price to send one message to one person as it is to send messages back and forth all day or to a hundred people. Finally, if we consider the costs saved in long-distance phone bills in addition to the costs saved in postage, most e-mail users surely come out ahead.

There is no question that e-mail is convenient. It allows us to send the same message to many people at the same time with little more effort than it takes to send a message to one person. When sending multiple copies of a message, we avoid the trouble of photocopying the letter, printing out additional copies, addressing envelopes, and posting the mail. E-mail is also convenient because it lends itself to an informal style that makes composing a message relatively easy; in addition, readers of e-mail tolerate more mistakes than readers of conventional mail, and their tolerance saves us time.

Despite the many benefits that e-mail provides, it is not always appropriate. Before dashing off another piece of e-mail-- in our private lives or in the business world--we need to pause and consider whether the post office or a carrier such as Federal Express or UPS might be more fitting.

It would be sad to think that letters from friends might become obsolete. With e-mail, unfortunately, all messages look very much alike, and this sameness removes some of the wonder of getting a message in the first place. We have no handwriting to scrutinize, no perfumed envelope to smell, no colors or textures to enjoy. E-mail is also limited by what we can send. Attached files might let us send a copy of a photo, but we wouldn't want to put it in a frame. We will never receive an e-mail care package from home or an e-mail pop-up birthday card. For these more personal things we must still rely on regular mail. Besides, opening old computer files is never as much fun as pulling a musty shoebox out of the closet to browse through old letters and photos.

In the business world, as in our personal lives, e-mail is not always an appropriate medium. First, there is the issue of privacy. Because of its electronic transmission in networked systems, e-mail may be accessible to co-workers and supervisors. It's probably not a good idea to complain about the boss on the company e-mail or to write anything that shouldn't be shared with strangers or potential ene-

mies. A second problem with e-mail is its
informality. For much company business, a
certain level of courtesy and formality is
desirable; e-mail can seem inappropriate
because of its relatively slapdash quality.
And finally, because of its speed, e-mail
encourages "flaming," sending off rapid-
fire emotional messages that can get a
businessperson in serious trouble.

    While e-mail gives us the ability to
send messages with convenience, speed, and
little expense, it lacks the personality
and authority of regular mail. Luckily,
however, we needn't always choose one over
the other. Instead we should take advantage
of both, using each to its best advantage:
e-mail for quick notes, multiple mailings,
and routine business correspondence; regular
mail for personal messages and for formal
or private business correspondence. Regular
mail will always take a bit longer, but at
times good things are worth waiting for.

EXERCISE 3–4 Revising and editing

In the following essay, revise and edit sentences. Rule numbers in the margin refer to sections in this workbook. The first revision has been made for you.

seven
When people find out our family has moved 7̸ times since my husband and   **41a**

I were married, they say, "Oh, you poor thing!" and roll there eyes. I just smile.   **43b**

Moving has its drawbacks, but I've found that it has some advantages as well.

    Because we have moved so often, I have learn to acquire and to save fewer   **27d**

things. Our house is not crowded with furniture, it's not stuffed with unnecessary   **20**

objects. If a friend offers me cuttings from her gorgeous houseplants I only have to   **32b**

envision packing day to refuse them graciously. When I think about having to

pack all my childrens kindergarten art masterpieces, I can move the old ones from   **36a**

the refrigerator door to the trash can instead of to a bottom drawer. Where they   **19**

would just sit until the next move. One friend offered my husband and I a   **24b**

complete set of novels by Charles Dickens. I told him that even if the set included

a first edition of *A Tale of Two Cities*, I couldn't take it.

    We have also been taught by our frequent moves to become active in our   **14a**

church. Meeting people in the new neighborhood may be hard but we can always   **32a**

count on finding friends at the church. Frequently, someone in the new church

will know someone in the church we just left—or in the one before that—so

getting acquainted is even easier. Because we are willing to help, we easily find

small groups that make learning names and faces easier. My husband has a

strong tenor voice, so the choir is always an option for him. Liking to work with

children, teaching church school gives me a chance to know whole families. Our   **12e**

teenagers use several techniques to meet people at church; joining youth groups,   **34d**

babysitting in the nursery, and they offer to help with any social activity.   **9a**

    Even more important, because we've moved so often, we've developed real   **26a**

close family ties. My husband and I are often the only playmates available for the

younger children when we move to a new town. For several weeks we go with them to playgrounds, play hide-and-seek in the new house and yard, and spend many after-dinner hours with the checker board or the Monopoly game. Even our teenagers depends on us for company and conversation at first. Besides being there for them to complain to or joke with, we take real interest in their worries about making new friends at a new school. We've also evolved lots of family stories and jokes from all these moves. For example, I routinely burn cakes and cookies as I learn to use a new stove, so I get teased a lot. A plate of non-burned cookies will call forth a formal ceremony to celebrate our having settled in.

27c

Although moving so often does result in some major inconveniences, but for our family it has had some significant good results as well.

11a

4 Choose an appropriate document design.

The term *document* is broad enough to describe anything you might write in an English class, in other classes across the curriculum, in the business world, and in everyday life. How you design a document (format it on the page) can affect how it is received.

Instructors have certain expectations about how a college paper should look (see 4b). Employers, too, expect documents such as business letters and memos to be formatted in standard ways (see 4c). Even peers who read your e-mail and World Wide Web pages will appreciate an effective document design (see 4d and 4e).

4a Become familiar with the principles of document design.

Well-designed documents—such as memos, résumés, manuals, and reports—have always been important in the business world, where writers must compete for the attention of readers. By using lists, headings, and a variety of visual cues, business and technical writers make documents accessible to all segments of an audience: readers who want a quick overview, those who are scanning for specific information, those who need in-depth coverage of a topic, and so on.

Document design is becoming increasingly important in the academic world as well. The information explosion has placed unprecedented demands on instructors' and students' time, so professional articles and student essays must be as accessible as possible. Fortunately, today's computers and printers provide academic writers with design tools that were once prohibitively expensive. With access to software, a student can enhance an essay with boldface headings, formally displayed lists, and even graphs, charts, and other visuals.

Good document design promotes readability, but what this means depends on your purpose and audience and perhaps on other elements of your writing situation, such as your subject and any length restrictions. (See the checklist on p. 2.) All of your design choices —word processing options, use of headings, displayed lists, and other visuals—should be made in light of your specific writing situation.

Format options

Most typewriters and word processing programs present you with several format options. Before you begin typing, you should make sure that your margins, line spacing, and justification are set appropriately. If a number of fonts (typeface styles and sizes) are available, you should also determine which is most appropriate for your purposes.

MARGINS, LINE SPACING, AND JUSTIFICATION For documents written on 8½" × 11" paper, you should leave a margin of between one and one and a half inches on all sides of the page. These margins prevent the text from looking too crowded, and they allow room for annotations, such as an instructor's comments or an editor's suggestions.

Most manuscripts in progress are double-spaced to allow room for editing. Final copy is often double-spaced as well, since single-spacing is less inviting to read. But at times the advantages of double-spacing are offset by other considerations. In a business memo, for example, you may single-space to fit the memo on one easily scanned page. And in a technical report, you might single-space to save paper, for both ecological and financial reasons.

Word processing programs usually give you a choice between a justified and an unjustified (ragged) right margin. When the text is justified, all of the words line up against the right margin, as they do on a typeset page like the one you are now reading. Unfortunately, text that has been justified on a computer can be hard to read. The problem is that extra space is added between words in some lines, creating "rivers" of white that can be quite distracting. In addition, right-justified margins may create a need for excessive hyphenation at the ends of lines. Unless you have the technology to create the real look of a typeset page, you should turn off the justification feature.

FONTS   If you have a choice of fonts, you should select a normal size (10 to 12 points) and a style that is not too offbeat. Although unusual styles of type, such as those that look handwritten, may seem attractive, they slow readers down. We all read more efficiently when a text meets our usual expectations.

CAUTION: Never write or type a college essay or any other document in all capital letters. Research shows that readers experience much frustration when they are forced to read more than a few words in a row printed in all capital letters.

Headings

There is little need for headings in short essays, especially if the writer uses paragraphing and clear topic sentences to guide readers. In more complex documents, however, such as research papers, grant proposals, business reports, and even Web-based documents, headings can be a useful visual cue for readers.

Headings help readers see at a glance the organization of a document. If more than one level of heading is used, the headings also indicate the hierarchy of ideas—as they do throughout this book.

Headings serve a number of functions, depending on the needs of different readers. When readers are simply looking up information, headings will help them find it quickly. When readers are scanning, hoping to pick up the gist of things, headings will guide them. Even when readers are committed enough to read every word, headings can help. Efficient readers preview a document before they begin reading; when previewing and while reading, they are guided by any visual cues the writer provides.

CAUTION: Avoid using more headings (or more levels of headings) than you really need. Excessive use of headings can make a text choppy.

PHRASING HEADINGS   Headings should be as brief and as informative as possible. Certain styles of headings—the most common being *-ing* phrases, noun phrases, questions, and imperative sentences—work better for some purposes, audiences, and subjects than others.

Whatever style you choose, use it consistently for headings on the same level. In other words, headings on the same level of organization should be written in parallel structure (see 9), as in the following examples. The first set of headings appeared in a report written for an environmental think tank, the second in a history textbook, the third in a mutual fund brochure, and the fourth in a garden designer's newsletter.

-ING HEADINGS
Safeguarding the earth's atmosphere
Charting the path to sustainable energy
Conserving global forests
Triggering the technological revolution
Strengthening international institutions

NOUN PHRASE HEADINGS
The economics of slavery
The sociology of slavery
Psychological effects of slavery

QUESTIONS AS HEADINGS
How do I buy shares?
How do I redeem shares?
What is the history of the fund's performance?
What are the tax consequences of investing in the fund?

IMPERATIVE SENTENCES AS HEADINGS
Fertilize roses in the fall.
Feed them again in the spring.
Prune roses when dormant and after flowering.
Spray roses during their growing season.

PLACING AND HIGHLIGHTING HEADINGS   Headings on the same level of organization should be positioned and highlighted in a consistent way. For example, you might center your first-level headings and print them in boldface; then you might place the second-level headings flush left (against the left margin) and underline them, like this:

First-level heading

Second-level heading

Headings are usually centered or placed flush left, but at times you might decide to indent them a half inch or five spaces from the left margin, like a paragraph indent. Or in a business document, you might place headings in a column to the left of the text.

To highlight headings, consider using boldface, italics or underlining, all capital letters, color, larger or smaller typeface than the text, a different font, or some combination of these:

boldface   color

italics   larger typeface

underlining   smaller typeface

ALL CAPITAL LETTERS   different font

On the whole, it is best to use restraint. Excessive highlighting results in a page that looks too busy, and it defeats its own purpose, since readers have trouble sorting out which headings are more important than others.

Important headings can be highlighted by using a fair amount of white space around them. Less important headings can be downplayed by using less white space or even by running them into the text (as with the small all-capitals heading in the next column).

Displayed lists

Lists are easy to read or scan when they are displayed rather than run into your text. You might reasonably choose to display the following kinds of lists:

— steps in a process
— materials needed for a project
— parts of an object
— advice or recommendations
— items to be discussed
— criteria for evaluation (as in checklists)

Displayed lists should usually be introduced with an independent clause followed by a colon (see 35a and the preceding list). Periods are not used after items in a list unless the items are sentences.

Lists are most readable when they are presented in parallel grammatical form (see 9). In the sample list, for instance, the items are all noun phrases. As with headings, some kinds of lists might be more appropriately presented as *-ing* phrases, as imperative sentences, or as questions.

To draw the reader's eye to a list, consider using bullets (circles or squares) or dashes if there is no need to number the items. If there is some reason to number the items, use an arabic number followed by a period for each item.

Although displayed lists can be a useful visual cue, they should not be overdone. Too many of them will give a document a choppy, cluttered look. And lists that are very long (sometimes called "laundry lists") should be avoided as well. Readers can hold only so many ideas in their short-term memory, so if a list grows too long, you should find some way of making it more concise or clustering similar items.

Visuals

Visuals such as charts, graphs, tables, diagrams, maps, and photographs convey information concisely and vividly. In a student essay not intended for publication, you can use another person's visuals as long as you credit the borrowing. And with access to computer graphics, you can create your own visuals to enhance an essay, a report, or an electronic document.

This section suggests when charts, graphs, tables, and diagrams might be appropriate for your purposes. It also discusses where you might place such visuals.

USING CHARTS, GRAPHS, TABLES, AND DIAGRAMS In documents that help readers follow a process or make a decision, flow charts can be useful; for an example, see page 111 of this workbook. Pie charts are appropriate for indicating ratios or apportionment, as in the following example.

PIE CHART

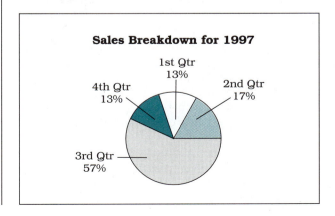

Sales Breakdown for 1997

1st Qtr 13%
2nd Qtr 17%
4th Qtr 13%
3rd Qtr 57%

LINE GRAPH

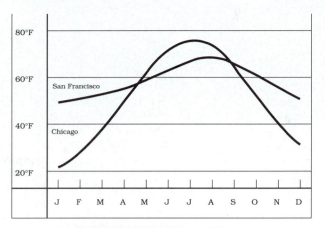

**MONTHLY MEAN TEMPERATURE IN
SAN FRANCISCO AND CHICAGO**

BAR GRAPH

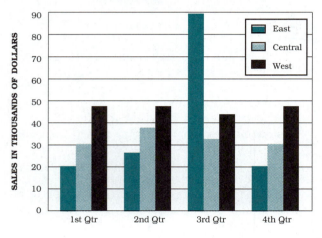

Line graphs and bar graphs illustrate disparities in numerical data. Line graphs are appropriate when you want to illuminate trends over a period of time, such as trends in sales, in unemployment, or in population growth. Bar graphs can be used for the same purpose. In addition, bar graphs are useful for highlighting comparisons, such as vote totals for rival political candidates or the number of refugees entering the United States during different time periods.

Tables are not as visually interesting as line graphs or charts, but they allow for inclusion of specific numerical data, such as exact percentages. The following table presents the responses of students and faculty to one question on a campus-wide questionnaire.

TABLE

Is American education based too much on European history and values?

| | **PERCENT** | | |
	NO	**UNDECIDED**	**YES**
Nonwhite students	21	25	54
White students	55	29	16
Nonwhite faculty	15	20	65
White faculty	57	27	16

Diagrams are useful—and sometimes indispensable—in scientific and technical writing. It is more concise, for example, to use the following diagram than to explain the chemical formula in words.

DIAGRAM

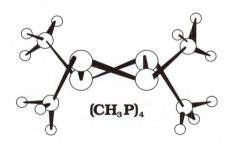

$(CH_3P)_4$

PLACING VISUALS   A visual may be placed in the text of a document, near a discussion to which it relates, or it can be put in an appendix, labeled, and referred to in the text.

Placing visuals in the text of a document can be tricky. Usually you will want the visual to appear close to the sentences that relate to it, but page breaks won't always allow this placement. At times you may need to insert the visual at a later point and tell readers where it can be found or, with the help of software, you may be able to make the text flow around the visual.

In newsletters and in business and technical documents, page layout is both an art and a science. The best way to learn how to lay out pages is to work with colleagues who have had experience solving the many problems that can arise.

4b For academic essays, use standard manuscript formats.

If your instructor provides formal guidelines for formatting an essay—or a more specialized document such as a lab report, a case study, or a research paper—you should of course follow them. Otherwise, use the manuscript format that is standard for the discipline in which you are writing.

In most English and humanities classes, you will be asked to use the MLA (Modern Language Association) format. The following guidelines are consistent with advice in the *MLA Handbook for Writers of Research Papers*, 4th ed. (New York: MLA, 1995).

MATERIALS   Use good-quality 8½" × 11" white paper. If the paper emerges from the printer in a continuous sheet, separate the pages, remove the feeder strips from the sides of the paper, and assemble the pages in order. Secure the pages with a paper clip. Unless your instructor suggests otherwise, do not staple the pages together or use any sort of binder.

TITLE AND IDENTIFICATION   Essays written for English and humanities classes do not require a title page unless your instructor requests one. If you are not using a title page, begin the first page against the left margin about one inch from the top of the page. Type your name, the instructor's name, the course name and number, and the date on separate lines; double-space between lines. Double-space again and center the title of the paper in the width of the page. Capitalize the first and last words of the title and all other words except articles, prepositions, and coordinating conjunctions (see 45c). Double-space after the title and begin typing the text of the paper.

MARGINS, SPACING, AND INDENTATION   Leave margins of at least one inch but no more than an inch and a half on all sides of the page.

Double-space lines and indent the first line of each paragraph one-half inch (or five spaces) from the left margin.

For a quotation longer than four typed lines of prose or three lines of verse, indent each line one inch (or ten spaces) from the left margin. Double-space between the body of the paper and the quotation, and double-space between the lines of the quotation. Quotation marks are not needed when a quotation is set off from the text by indenting. See 37b for an example.

PAGINATION   Put your last name followed by the page number in the upper right corner of each page, one-half inch below the top edge. (If you have a separate title page, the title page is uncounted and unnumbered.) Use arabic numerals (1, 2, 3, and so on). Do not put a period after the number and do not enclose the number in parentheses.

PUNCTUATION AND TYPING   In typing the paper, leave one space after words, commas, semicolons, and colons and between dots in ellipsis marks. MLA allows either one or two spaces after periods, question marks, and exclamation points. To form a dash, type two hyphens with no space between them; do not put a space on either side of the dash.

HEADINGS   MLA neither encourages nor discourages use of headings and currently provides no guidelines for their use. If you would like to use headings in a long essay or research paper, check first with your instructor. Although headings are not used as frequently in English and the humanities as in other disciplines, the trend seems to be changing. (See p. 44 for examples of types of headings.)

VISUALS   MLA classifies visuals as tables and figures (figures include graphs, charts, maps, photographs, and drawings). Label each table with an arabic numeral (Table 1, Table 2, and so on) and provide a clear caption that identifies the subject; the label and caption should appear on separate lines above the table. For each figure, a label and a caption are usually placed below the figure, and they need not appear on separate lines. The word "Figure" may be abbreviated to "Fig."

Visuals should be placed in the text, as close as possible to the sentences that relate to them, unless your instructor prefers them in an appendix.

MLA ESSAY FORMAT

½"

↑ 1"

Weitzel 1

Double-
spacing
throughout

Tom Weitzel
Dr. Fry
English 101
16 April 1997

Title,
centered

Who Goes to the Races?

½"
Indent

A favorite pastime of mine is observing people, and my favorite place to observe is at the horse races. After many encounters with the racing crowd, I have discovered that there are four distinct groups at the track: the once-a-year bunch, the professionals, the clubhouse set, and the unemployed.

The largest group at the track consists of those who show up once a year. They know little about horses or betting and rely strictly on racetrack gimmick sheets and newspaper predictions for selecting possible winners. If that strategy doesn't work, they use intuition, lucky numbers, favorite colors, or appealing names. They bet larger amounts as the day goes along, gambling on every race, including long-shot bets on exactas and daily doubles. The vast majority go home broke and frustrated.

More subtle and quiet are the professionals. They follow the horses from track to track and live in campers and motor homes. Many are married couples, some are retired, and all are easily spotted with their lunch sacks, water jugs, and binoculars. Since most know one another, they section themselves off in a particular area of the stadium. All rely on the racing form and on personal knowledge of each horse, jockey, and track in making the proper bet. They bet only on the smart races, rarely on the favorites. Never do they bet on exactas or daily doubles. More often than not they either break even or go home winners.

Isolated from the others is the clubhouse set. Found either at the cocktail lounge or in the restaurant, usually involved in business transactions, these racing fans rarely see a race in person and do their betting via the waiter. It's difficult to tell whether they go home sad, happy, or in between. They keep their emotions to themselves.

The most interesting members of the racetrack population are the unemployed. They will be found not in the clubhouse, but right down at the rail next to the finish line. Here one can discover the real emotion of the racetrack--the screaming, the cursing, and the pushing. The unemployed are not in it for the sport. Betting is not a game for them, but a battle for survival. If they lose, they must borrow enough money to carry them until the next check comes in, and then, of course, they head right back to the track. This particular group arrives at the track beaten and leaves beaten.

I have probably lost more money than I have won at the track, but observing these four interesting groups of people makes it all worthwhile.

1"

1"

↑ 1"

4c For business documents, use standard business formats.

This section provides guidelines for preparing business letters, résumés, and memos. For a more detailed discussion of these and other business documents—proposals, reports, executive summaries, and so on—consult a business writing textbook or take a look at examples currently being written at the organization for which you are writing.

Business letters

In writing a business letter, be direct, clear, and courteous, but do not hesitate to be firm if necessary. State your purpose or request at the beginning of the letter and include only pertinent information in the body. By being as direct and concise as possible, you show that you value your reader's time.

A sample business letter appears at the bottom of this page. This letter is typed in what is known as "block" style. The return address at the top and the close and signature at the bottom are lined up just to the right of the center of the width of the page. The inside address, the salutation, and the body of the letter are flush left (against the left margin). The paragraphs are not indented.

If you choose to indent your paragraphs, you are using "semiblock" style, which is con-

BUSINESS LETTER IN BLOCK FORM

Return address →

121 Knox Road, #6
College Park, MD 20740
March 4, 1997

Linda Hennessee, Managing Editor
World Discovery
1650 K Street, NW
Washington, DC 20036

← Inside address

Dear Ms. Hennessee: ← Salutation

Please accept my application for the summer editorial internship listed with the Career Development Center at the University of Maryland. Currently I am a junior at the University of Maryland, with a double major in English and Latin American studies.

Over the past three years I have gained considerable experience in newspaper and magazine journalism, as you will see on my enclosed résumé. I am familiar with the basic procedures of editing and photographic development, but my primary interests lie in feature writing and landscape photography. My professional goal is to work as a photojournalist with an international focus, preferably for a major magazine. I cannot imagine a better introduction to that career than a summer at *World Discovery*.

← Body

I am available for an interview almost any time and can be reached at 301-555-2651. My e-mail address is jrichard@umdcp.edu.

I look forward to hearing from you.

Close → Sincerely,

Signature → *Jeffrey Richardson*

Jeffrey Richardson

Enc.

RÉSUMÉ

Jeffrey Richardson
121 Knox Road, #6
College Park, MD 20740
301-555-2651

OBJECTIVE	To obtain an editorial internship with a magazine
EDUCATION Fall 1994– present	University of Maryland • B.A. expected in June 1998 • Double major: English and Latin American studies • GPA: 3.7 (on a 4-point scale)
EXPERIENCE Fall 1995– present	Photo editor, *The Diamondback*, college paper • Shoot and print photographs • Select and lay out photographs and other visuals
Summer 1996	Intern, *The Globe*, Fairfax, Virginia • Wrote stories about local issues and personalities • Interviewed political candidates • Edited and proofread copy • Contributed photographs • Coedited "The Landscapes of Northern Virginia: A Photoessay"
Summers 1994 1995	Tutor, Fairfax County ESL Program • Tutored Latino students in English as a Second Language • Trained new tutors
ACTIVITIES	Photographers' Workshop, Spanish Club
REFERENCES	Available upon request

---

sidered less formal. If you choose to move all elements of the letter flush left, you are using the most formal style, "full block." This style is usually preferred when the letter is typed on letterhead stationery that gives the return address of the writer or the writer's company.

When writing to a woman, use the abbreviation *Ms.* in the salutation unless you know that the woman prefers another form of address. If you are not writing to a particular person, you can use the salutation *Dear Sir or Madam* or you can address the company itself—*Dear Solar Technology.*

Below the signature, flush left, you may include the abbreviation *Enc.* to indicate that something is enclosed with the letter or the abbreviation *cc* followed by a colon and the name of someone who is receiving a copy of the letter.

Résumés

An effective résumé gives relevant information in a clear and concise form. The trick is to present yourself in the best possible light without going on at length and wasting your reader's time.

A sample résumé appears at the top of this page. Notice that the writer has used bullets to make his résumé easy to scan. Notice too that he presents his work experience in reverse chronological order—to highlight his most recent accomplishments.

When you send out your résumé, you should include a letter that tells what position you seek and where you learned about it (see p. 49). The letter should also summarize your education and past experience, relating them to the job you are applying for. End the letter with

BUSINESS MEMO

Commonwealth Press

MEMORANDUM

February 28, 1997

To: Production, promotion, and editorial assistants

cc: Stephen Chapman

From: Helen Brown

Subject: New computers for staff

We will receive the new personal computers next week for the assistants in production, promotion, and editorial. In preparation, I would like you to take part in a training program and to rearrange your work areas to accommodate the new equipment.

Training Program

A computer consultant will teach in-house workshops on how to use our spreadsheet program. If you have already tried the program, be prepared to discuss any problems you have encountered.

Workshops for our three departments will be held in the training room at the following times:

- Production: Monday, March 10, 10:00 a.m. to 2:00 p.m.
- Promotion: Wednesday, March 12, 10:00 a.m. to 2:00 p.m.
- Editorial: Friday, March 14, 10:00 a.m. to 2:00 p.m.

Lunch will be provided in the cafeteria. If you cannot attend, please let me know by March 3.

Allocation and Setup

To give everyone access to a computer, we will set up the new computers as follows: two in the assistants' workspace in production; two in the area outside the conference room for the promotion assistants; and two in the library for the editorial assistants.

Assistants in all three departments should see me before the end of the week to discuss preparation of the spaces for the new equipment.

---

a suggestion for a meeting, and tell your prospective employer when you will be available.

Memos

Business memos (short for *memorandums*) are a form of communication used within a company or organization. Usually brief and to the point, a memo reports information, makes a request, or recommends an action. The format of a memo, which varies from company to company, is designed for easy distribution, quick reading, and efficient filing.

Most memos display the date, the name of the recipient, the name of the sender, and the subject on separate lines at the top of the page. Many companies have preprinted forms for memos, and some word processing programs allow you to call up a memo template that prints standard memo lines—"To," "cc" (for others receiving a copy of the memo), "From," and "Subject"—at the top of the page.

Because readers of the memos are busy people, you cannot assume that they will read your memo word for word. Therefore the subject line should describe the subject as clearly and concisely as possible, and the introductory paragraph should get right to the point. In addition, the body of the memo should be well organized and easy to scan. To promote scanning, use headings where possible and display any items that deserve special attention by setting them off from the text. A sample memo with headings and a displayed list appears at the top of this page.

4d Follow the conventions of e-mail.

Communicating by electronic mail (or e-mail) has many benefits. Unlike conventional "snail" mail messages, e-mail messages are sent and received immediately after they are written—to and from anywhere in the world at any time. And although e-mail can be as quick as a telephone call, it provides a bit more time than conversation allows for framing ideas and thoughtful responses. As with all writing, you should keep your audience and purpose clearly in mind as you draft e-mail. But you should also be aware of the special conventions of this fast-paced form of communication.

Keeping messages brief and direct

Because the purpose of e-mail is to relay and receive information quickly, it is a courtesy to keep each message as brief as possible and to state your point early. Your message may be just one of many that your reader has to wade through. Always fill in the subject line with a clear, concise description of what your message is about (*Dec. 4 meeting agenda* is clearer than *Miscellaneous notes*). If you are making a request or a recommendation, state it right away, if possible in the first few sentences (*Can you get your report to me by Monday?* or *I think we need two committees to study the impact of the proposed building*). For long, detailed messages that may fill more than two computer screens, consider providing a summary at the beginning, such as the following:

> The study on improving the work environment at DeVincent Company includes three key recommendations: (1) acquire additional space for the growing customer service division, (2) improve lighting and reduce background noise in cubicle areas, and (3) add another break room for the third and fourth floors.

Maintaining an appropriate tone

It is appropriate for e-mail to be more informal than other types of writing; you may even alienate your reader if you are too formal. In general, maintain a tone that is friendly and conversational, yet respectful. The first-person (*I*) and second-person (*you*) points of view are standard in e-mail, and contractions are usually acceptable.

Though you should always try to keep messages as brief as possible, you can avoid a blunt tone by including an appropriate greeting and closing. You may also want to open with a brief personal note or include a bit of humor when communicating with friends and colleagues.

TOO FORMAL AND BLUNT
Now that the regional conference has concluded, it is my responsibility to assemble the agenda for the 1997 planning meeting. In order to do so in a timely fashion, I need your ideas about issues to cover in the meeting by October 25.

Expressions like *it is my responsibility* and *in order to do so in a timely fashion* make this message sound formal and stilted, and the lack of a greeting and closing give it a cold, blunt tone.

REVISED

Dear Carolyn,

I enjoyed seeing you and the other members of the steering committee at the regional conference. Now that I'm back in the office, I need to start putting together the agenda for our 1997 planning meeting. If you have any preliminary thoughts about issues to cover, could you please e-mail them to me by October 25? Thanks, Carolyn. I look forward to hearing from you.

Best,
Ada

As with all forms of writing, your tone in e-mail should suit your subject and audience. In business and academic contexts or in writing to someone you don't know well, you will probably want to use a more formal tone than you would when, say, making social plans with friends. Regardless of your subject and audience, you should always avoid harsh or flippant language in e-mail.

NOTE: Some e-mailers use emoticons (combinations of symbols that look like faces turned sideways) and acronyms (such as *TIA* for "thanks in advance"). Though you may be tempted to use these shortcuts, it is usually better to convey your tone and meaning through words, especially in business and academic contexts. Readers who are unfamiliar with emoticons and e-mail abbreviations may be confused by them, and even readers who understand these shortcuts may be annoyed by them.

Designing e-mail

Consider using the following elements to design e-mail messages that are easy to scan and easy to digest. See the sample e-mail message on page 54 for an example of good design.

SHORT PARAGRAPHS   In academic writing, short paragraphs often indicate inadequate development. In e-mail messages, however, short paragraphs make it easier for readers to see divisions among key ideas within the limits of a computer screen. As in other forms of writing, each paragraph in an e-mail message should be built around a main point. Indicate a new paragraph with a hard return and a tab indent or with a line of space.

HEADINGS   In brief e-mail messages of a paragraph or two, headings probably aren't necessary. But in longer messages containing categories of information, headings can break up blocks of text and help readers scan for items of special interest.

Because many e-mail programs cannot produce boldface, underlining, or italics, set off each heading on a line by itself with a line of space above it. Word all the headings in parallel form (see "Phrasing Headings," p. 44).

DISPLAYED LISTS   For an e-mail message that includes a list or steps in a procedure, consider displaying the information with asterisks, dashes, or numbers. (See the sample e-mail message on p. 54.)

SIMPLE FORMATTING   Word processing software allows writers to use an endless variety of fonts and type styles in documents. The type options in e-mail programs, however, are usually more limited. You can't be sure that your recipient's e-mail system will be able to reproduce special formatting even if you can include it. It is best, therefore, to keep formatting simple, relying on white space, indentations, and simple lists to design your messages.

CAUTION: Avoid the temptation to use all capital letters to highlight whole sentences or paragraphs. All-capital text is so difficult to read, especially in long stretches, that among e-mailers it is known as "shouting."

Following e-mail etiquette

E-mail, like other forms of communication, has its own etiquette, which varies slightly depending on your purpose and audience. Essentially, when writing and responding to others, you should take care to be prompt, clear, and courteous. Here are some principles to keep in mind:

—Check your e-mail frequently and respond to messages promptly.

—Fill in subject lines to help readers sort through their messages and set priorities.

—Include a brief greeting (such as *Hi, Gloria* or *Dear Professor Hartley*) and a brief closing (such as *Bye for now* or *Sincerely*).

—Avoid writing in all capital letters or all lowercase letters.

—Resist "flaming" — spouting off angry or insulting messages.

—Forward messages from others only when you are certain the original sender would approve.

—Restrict your use of copyrighted materials to short passages, and always name the author, title, and publication source.

Revising e-mail

Although standards for revision are not as high for fast-paced e-mail as for other forms of written communication, resist the temptation to send off a message without reading it first. Check to make sure that your tone is tactful, that your main point is clear and concise, and that your message is free of errors in grammar, punctuation, spelling, and mechanics.

4e   Creating effective Web sites.

At some point you may be asked to create a World Wide Web site as part of a school or work

E-MAIL MESSAGE

Return-Path: <dportes@umass-boston.edu>
Date: Fri, 22 Nov 1996 22:31:45-0500
To: rdayson@newhoriz.org
From: Danielle Portes <dportes@umass-boston.edu>
Subject: Telephone interview on Dec. 4
cc: Helen Tran <htran@umass-boston.edu>

Dear Ms. Dayson:

Thank you for taking the time to speak with me last week about my research project. As we agreed, I am sending some questions for you to consider before our phone interview on December 4 at 2 p.m.

QUESTIONS ABOUT GUESTS

--What symptoms of stress do guests--both women and their children--show when they first arrive at the shelter?

--What problems, in addition to the abuse itself, must guests deal with (for example, lack of support from family or friends, financial concerns, problems in dealing with police and courts)?

--Can you think of any past or current guests who might agree to an interview?

QUESTIONS ABOUT STAFFERS

--What are the main stresses that staffers face? How do they cope with these stresses?

--What do staffers see as the rewards as well as the drawbacks of the job?

--On average, how many guests does each staffer work with every day? every week?

--Can you think of any past or current staffers who might agree to an interview?

I appreciate your considering these questions and look forward to our interview.

Sincerely,
Danielle Portes
Phone: 617-555-7777

assignment, or you may decide to build one for your personal use. Although this book can't begin to explain all the technical aspects of creating a Web site, included here are design and organizational hints to help you make the most of this new medium. For more detailed information on creating a Web site, see *Style Guide for Online Hypertext* (http://www.w3.org/pub/WWW/Provider/Style), written by Web founder Tim Berners-Lee.

Organizing information

If you have browsed the World Wide Web, you may have noticed that the most effective sites are the simplest ones—those that give you quick and easy access to what you're looking for. The overall organization of a Web site can be found on its home page, which welcomes visitors, introduces them to the site, and gives them an overview of its contents (see the sample on p. 55).

From the home page, visitors navigate via "links," words or visual images that, at the click of the mouse, send them to other pages within the site or to other locations on the Web. In a typical Web site, the home page contains the most general information, and internal pages are more specific.

Before creating a Web site, make an outline of the hierarchy of the information you will present: a home page linked to internal pages, which can in turn be linked to other pages in your site or on the Web. As is true in print documents, important items, such as a company name, should receive more prominence than items of lesser importance, such as a copyright date. To help you weigh the relative importance of material, think about what your readers will most likely be looking for. Why are they visiting your site in the first place? What are they expecting to find?

Breaking up text

Because the Internet is so vast, online surfers move quickly from page to page. Visitors to your page won't have the patience to scroll through long passages of text. To keep your readers' attention, present your material as concisely as possible, and break up text with headings and displayed lists (see pp. 44–45). And, where appropriate, highlight information with visuals such as clip art, photos, or even animation.

Linking to other sites

One of the most useful features of World Wide Web documents is the ability to create links to other Internet locations. You will probably decide to add some links to other sites from your Web page, but use care when doing so. Especially when creating academic or professional Web sites, keep in mind that any links you include should be relevant to your subject.

A link to another site is an implicit endorsement of that site, so you should evaluate potential sites before linking to them. As a courtesy to readers, periodically visit the sites you have links to; remove any links to sites that are outdated or nonfunctioning, and reroute links to sites that have moved.

Testing your site

When you create a Web site, you are publishing a document that represents you or your organization. Therefore, before you upload your new site to the Web, you should be certain that all your links are working and that all your text has been properly coded.

As you would in a print document, you should use a clear and grammatical writing style, carefully proofread your text, and give proper credit to any material you may have borrowed from other sources.

SAMPLE WEB PAGE

Constructing Paragraphs

5 Focus on a main point.

6 Develop the main point.

7 Improve coherence.

Except for special-purpose paragraphs, such as introductions and conclusions (see 2a and 2c), paragraphs are clusters of information supporting an essay's main point (or advancing a story's action). Aim for paragraphs that are clearly focused, well developed, organized, coherent, and neither too long nor too short for easy reading.

5 Focus on a main point.

A paragraph should be unified around a main point. The point should be clear to readers, and all sentences in the paragraph must relate to it.

5a State the main point in a topic sentence.

As readers move into a paragraph, they need to know where they are—in relation to the whole essay—and what to expect in the sentences to come. A good topic sentence, a one-sentence summary of the paragraph's main point, acts as a signpost pointing in two directions: backward toward the thesis of the essay and forward toward the body of the paragraph.

A topic sentence is more general than the material supporting it. Usually the topic sentence is the first sentence in the paragraph.

Nearly all living creatures manage some form of communication. The dance patterns of bees in their hive help to point the way to distant flower fields or announce successful foraging. Male stickleback fish regularly swim upside-down to indicate outrage in a courtship contest. Male deer and lemurs mark territorial ownership by rubbing their own body secretions on boundary stones or trees. Everyone has seen a frightened dog put his tail between his legs and run in panic. We, too, use gestures, expressions, postures, and movement to give our words point. [Italics added.]   —Olivia Vlahos, *Human Beginnings*

Sometimes the topic sentence is introduced by a transitional sentence linking it to earlier material. In the following paragraph, the topic sentence (italicized) has been delayed to allow for a transition.

But flowers are not the only source of spectacle in the wilderness. *An opportunity for late color is provided by the berries of wildflowers, shrubs, and trees.* Baneberry presents its tiny white flowers in spring but in late summer bursts forth with clusters of red berries. Bunchberry, a ground-cover plant, puts out red berries in the fall, and the red berries of wintergreen last from autumn well into winter. In California, the bright red, fist-sized clusters of Christmas berries can be seen growing beside highways for up to six months of the year. [Italics added.]

—James Crockett et al.,
Wildflower Gardening

Occasionally the topic sentence may be withheld until the end of the paragraph—but only if the earlier sentences hang together so well that the reader perceives their direction, if not their exact point. The opening sentences of the following paragraph state facts, making them supporting material rather than topic sentences, but they strongly suggest a central idea. The topic sentence at the end is hardly a surprise.

Tobacco chewing starts as soon as people begin stirring. Those who have fresh supplies soak the new leaves in water and add ashes from the hearth to the wad. Men, women, and children chew tobacco and all are addicted to it. Once there was a shortage of tobacco in Kaobawa's village and I was plagued for a week by early morning visitors who requested permission to collect my cigarette butts in order to make a wad of chewing tobacco. Normally, if anyone is short of tobacco, he can request a share of someone else's already chewed wad, or simply borrow the entire wad when its owner puts it down somewhere. *Tobacco is so important to them that their word for "poverty" translates as "being without tobacco."* [Italics added.]

—Napoleon A. Chagnon,
Yanomamo: The Fierce People

Although it is generally wise to use topic sentences, at times they are unnecessary. A topic sentence may not be needed if a paragraph continues developing an idea clearly introduced in a previous paragraph, if the details of the paragraph unmistakably suggest its main point, or if the paragraph appears in a narrative of events where generalizations might interrupt the flow of the story.

5b Do not stray from the point.

Sentences that do not support the topic sentence destroy the unity of a paragraph. If the paragraph is otherwise well focused, such offending sentences can simply be deleted or perhaps moved elsewhere. In the following paragraph describing the inadequate facilities in a high school, the information about the word processing instructor (in italics) is clearly off the point.

As the result of tax cuts, the educational facilities of Lincoln High School have reached an all-time low. Some of the books date back to 1985 and have long since shed their covers. The lack of lab equipment makes it necessary for four to five students to work at one table, with most watching rather than performing experiments. The few computers in working order must share one dot matrix printer. *Also, the word processing instructor left to have a baby at the beginning of the semester, and most of the students don't like the substitute.* As for the furniture, many of the upright chairs have become recliners, and the desk legs are so unbalanced that they play seesaw on the floor.

Sometimes the cure for a disunified paragraph is not as simple as deleting or moving material. Writers often wander into uncharted territory because they cannot think of enough evidence to support a topic sentence. Feeling that it is too soon to break into a new paragraph, they move on to new ideas for which they have not prepared the reader. When this happens, writers are faced with a choice: Either find more evidence to support the topic sentence or adjust the topic sentence to mesh with the evidence that is available.

EXERCISE 5–1 Topic sentences

Like a thesis statement, a topic sentence should not be too factual, too broad, or too vague. (See 3b.) Instead it should be a general assertion that tells readers exactly what to expect in the paragraph. It must, of course, be a sentence. Which of the following sentences about Sigmund Freud might work well as topic sentences? What is wrong with the others?

1.   Sigmund Freud distinguished between the "manifest" and the "latent" content of dreams.

2.   Freud was born in 1856 in Freiburg, Moravia (Czechoslovakia).

3.   What "identification" means in psychology.

4.   In Freudian psychology, "identification" means identifying with the characteristics of another as a means of gaining emotional support.

5.   According to Freud, the unconscious mind has three major divisions: the id, the ego, and the superego.

6.   Sigmund Freud was an interesting person.

7.   Freud argued that one's personality is established by the age of six or seven.

8.   Much of Freud's work dealt with the role of sexual fantasies in human behavior.

9.   Freud founded the Vienna Psycho-Analytic Society in 1902.

10. To help his patients discover their unconscious desires, Freud used the technique of dream analysis.

EXERCISE 5–2 Revising for focus

Some of the sentences in the following paragraph stray from the focus established in the topic sentence. Improve the paragraph's focus by crossing out any sentences that do not belong.

Sigmund Freud is best known for his theories about the role sex plays in the unconscious mind. He did have theories about other subjects too, however. The whole subject of sex had been taboo for so long that scientific discussion of it had been almost impossible until Freud dared to publish his theories. Then, too, the theories themselves seemed outrageous to most people. His belief that sexual functioning begins at birth was too strange to accept. He also theorized that from childhood to adulthood, children go through specific stages of sexual development. This had certainly not been taught at the University of Vienna, where Freud received his doctor's degree. He almost did not get to go to the university. His family was poor, and they had to make great sacrifices to send him. After he graduated, he started working on these theories. Later Freud developed another theory: that if the normal pattern of sexual development was interrupted in some way, the person would become "fixated" emotionally at that stage. The person would grow physically and mentally, but emotionally that person would stop growing. The result would be emotional problems as an adult. Freud's pioneering work on sex has made him famous throughout the world.

6   Develop the main point.

Topic sentences are generalizations in need of support, so once you have written a topic sentence, ask yourself, "How do I know that this is true?" Your answer will suggest how to develop the paragraph.

6a   Flesh out skimpy paragraphs.

Though an occasional short paragraph is fine, particularly if it functions as a transition or emphasizes a point, a series of brief paragraphs suggests inadequate development. How much development is enough? That varies, depending on the writer's purpose and audience.

For example, when she wrote a paragraph attempting to convince readers that it is impossible to lose fat quickly, health columnist Jane Brody knew that she would have to present a great deal of evidence because many dieters want to believe the opposite. She did *not* write:

> When you think about it, it's impossible to lose—as many diets suggest—10 pounds of *fat* in ten days, even on a total fast. Even a moderately active person cannot lose so much weight so fast. A less active person hasn't a prayer.

This three-sentence paragraph is too skimpy to be convincing. But the paragraph that Brody wrote contains enough evidence to convince even skeptical readers:

> When you think about it, it's impossible to lose—as many diets suggest—10 pounds of *fat* in ten days, even on a total fast. A pound of body fat represents 3,500 calories. To lose 1 pound of fat, you must expend 3,500 more calories than you consume. Let's say you weigh 170 pounds and, as a moderately active person, you burn 2,500 calories a day. If your diet contains only 1,500 calories, you'd have an energy deficit of 1,000 calories a day. In a week's time that would add up to a 7,000-calorie deficit, or 2 pounds of real fat. In ten days, the accumulated deficit would represent nearly 3 pounds of lost body fat. Even if you ate nothing at all for ten days and maintained your usual level of activity, your caloric deficit would add up to 25,000 calories. . . . At 3,500 calories per pound of fat, that's still only 7 pounds of lost fat.
> — Jane Brody, *Jane Brody's Nutrition Book*

6b   Choose a suitable pattern of organization.

Although paragraphs may be patterned in an almost infinite number of ways, certain patterns of organization occur frequently, either alone or in combination: examples and illustrations, narration, description, process, comparison and contrast, analogy, cause and effect, classification and division, and definition. There is nothing magical about these patterns (sometimes called *methods of development*). They simply reflect some of the ways in which we think.

Examples and illustrations

Examples, perhaps the most common pattern of development, are appropriate whenever the reader might be tempted to ask, "For example?" Though examples are just selected instances, not a complete catalog, they are enough to suggest the truth of many topic sentences, as in the following paragraph.

> Normally my parents abided scrupulously by "The Budget," but several times a year Dad would dip into his battered, black strongbox and splurge on some irrational, totally satisfying luxury. Once he bought over a hundred comic books at a flea market, doled out to us thereafter at the tantalizing rate of two a week. He always got a whole flat of pansies, Mom's favorite flower, for us to give her on Mother's Day. One day a boy stopped at our house selling fifty-cent raffle tickets on a sailboat and Dad bought every ticket the boy had left—three books' worth.   —Connie Hailey, student

Illustrations are extended examples, frequently presented in story form. Because they require several sentences apiece, they are used more sparingly than examples. When well selected, however, they can be a vivid and effective means of developing a point. The writer of the following paragraph uses illustrations to demonstrate that Harriet Tubman, famous conductor on the Underground Railroad for escaping slaves, was a genius at knowing how and when to retreat.

> Part of Harriet Tubman's strategy of conducting was, as in all battle-field operations, the knowledge of how and when to retreat. Numerous allusions have been made to her moves when she suspected that she was in danger. When she feared the party was closely pursued, she would take it for a time on a train southward bound. No one seeing Negroes going in this direction would for an instant suppose them to be fugitives. Once on her return she was at a railway station. She saw some men reading a poster and she heard one of them reading it aloud. It was a description of her, offering a reward for her capture. She took a southbound train to avert suspicion. At another time when Harriet heard men talking about her, she pretended to read a book which she carried. One man remarked, "This cannot be the woman. The one we want can't read or write." Harriet devoutly hoped the book was right side up.
> —Earl Conrad, *Harriet Tubman*

Narration

A paragraph of narration tells a story or part of a story. Narrative paragraphs are usually arranged in chronological order, but they may also contain flashbacks, interruptions that take the story back to an earlier time. The following paragraph, from Jane Goodall's *In the Shadow of Man,* recounts one of the author's experiences in the African wild.

> One evening when I was wading in the shallows of the lake to pass a rocky outcrop, I suddenly stopped dead as I saw the sinuous black body of a snake in the water. It was all of six feet long, and from the slight hood and the dark stripes at the back of the neck I knew it to be a Storm's water cobra—a deadly reptile for the bite of which there was, at that time, no serum. As I stared at it an incoming wave gently deposited part of its body on one of my feet. I remained motionless, not even breathing, until the wave rolled back into the lake, drawing the snake with it. Then I leaped out of the water as fast as I could, my heart hammering.
> — Jane Goodall, *In the Shadow of Man*

Description

A descriptive paragraph sketches a portrait of a person, place, or thing by using concrete and specific details that appeal to one or more of our senses—sight, sound, smell, taste, and touch. Consider, for example, the following description of the grasshopper invasions that devastated the midwestern landscape in the late 1860s.

> They came like dive bombers out of the west. They came by the millions with the rustle of their wings roaring overhead. They came in waves, like the rolls of the sea, descending with a terrifying speed, breaking now and again like a mighty surf. They came with the force of a williwaw and they formed a huge, ominous, dark brown cloud that eclipsed the sun. They dipped and touched earth, hitting objects and people like hailstones. But they were not hail. These were live demons. They popped, snapped, crackled, and roared. They were dark brown, an inch or longer in length, plump in the middle and tapered at the ends. They had transparent wings, slender legs, and two black eyes that flashed with a fierce intelligence.
> —Eugene Boe, "Pioneers to Eternity"

Process

A process paragraph is patterned in time order, usually chronologically. A writer may choose this pattern either to describe a process or to show readers how to perform a process. The following paragraph describes what happens when water freezes.

> In school we learned that with few exceptions the solid phase of matter is more dense than the liquid phase. Water, alone among common substances, violates this rule. As water begins to cool, it contracts and becomes more dense, in a perfectly typical way. But about four degrees above the freezing point, something remarkable happens. It ceases to contract and begins expanding, becoming less dense. At the freezing point the expansion is abrupt and drastic. As water turns to ice, it adds about one-eleventh to its liquid volume.
> —Chet Raymo, "Curious Stuff, Water and Ice"

Here is a paragraph explaining how to perform a "roll cast," a popular fly fishing technique:

Begin by taking up a suitable stance, with one foot slightly in front of the other and the rod pointing down the line. Then begin a smooth, steady draw, raising your rod hand to just above shoulder height and lifting the rod to the 10:30 or 11:00 position. This steady draw allows a loop of line to form between the rod top and the water. While the line is still moving, raise the rod slightly, then punch it rapidly forward and down. The rod is now flexed and under maximum compression, and the line follows its path, bellying out slightly behind you and coming off the water close to your feet. As you power the rod down through the 3:00 position, the belly of the line will roll forward. Follow through smoothly so that the line unfolds and straightens above the water.

—*The Dorling Kindersley Encyclopedia of Fishing*

Comparison and contrast

To compare two subjects is to draw attention to their similarities, although the word *compare* also has a broader meaning that includes a consideration of differences. To contrast is to focus only on differences.

Whether a comparison-and-contrast paragraph stresses similarities or differences, it may be patterned in one of two ways. The two subjects may be presented one at a time, block style, as in the following paragraph of contrast.

So Grant and Lee were in complete contrast, representing two diametrically opposed elements in American life. Grant was the modern man emerging; beyond him, ready to come on the stage, was the great age of steel and machinery, of crowded cities and a restless burgeoning vitality. Lee might have ridden down from the old age of chivalry, lance in hand, silken banner fluttering over his head. Each man was the perfect champion of his cause, drawing both his strengths and weaknesses from the people he led.

—Bruce Catton, "Grant and Lee: A Study in Contrasts"

Or a paragraph may proceed point by point, treating the two subjects together, one aspect at a time. The following paragraph uses the point-by-point method to contrast the writer's academic experiences in an American high school and an Irish convent:

Strangely enough, instead of being academically inferior to my American high school, the Irish convent was superior. In my class at home, *Love Story* was considered pretty heavy reading, so imagine my surprise at finding Irish students who could recite passages from *War and Peace.* In high school we complained about having to study *Romeo and Juliet* in one semester, whereas in Ireland we simultaneously studied *Macbeth* and Dickens's *Hard Times,* in addition to writing a composition a day in English class. In high school, I didn't even begin algebra until the ninth grade, while at the convent seventh graders (or their Irish equivalent) were doing calculus and trigonometry.

—Margaret Stack, student

Analogy

Analogies draw comparisons between items that appear to have little in common. Writers turn to analogies for a variety of reasons: to make the unfamiliar seem familiar, to provide a concrete understanding of an abstract topic, or to provoke fresh thoughts or changed feelings about a subject. In the following paragraph, physician Lewis Thomas draws an analogy between the behavior of ants and that of humans. Thomas's analogy helps us to understand the social behavior of ants and forces us to question the superiority of our own human societies.

Ants are so much like human beings as to be an embarrassment. They farm fungi, raise aphids as livestock, launch armies into wars, use chemical sprays to alarm and confuse enemies, capture slaves. The families of weaver ants engage in child labor, holding their larvae like shuttles to spin out the thread that sews the leaves together for their fungus gardens. They exchange information ceaselessly. They do everything but watch television.

—Lewis Thomas, "On Societies as Organisms"

Although analogies can be a powerful tool for illuminating a subject, they should be used with caution in arguments. Just because two things may be alike in one respect, we cannot conclude that they are alike in all respects.

Cause and effect

When causes and effects are a matter of argument, they are too complex to be reduced to a simple pattern. However, if a writer wishes merely to describe a cause-and-effect relationship that is generally accepted, then the effect may be stated in the topic sentence, with the causes listed in the body of the paragraph.

> The fantastic water clarity of the Mount Gambier sinkholes results from several factors. The holes are fed from aquifers holding rainwater that fell decades—even centuries—ago, and that has been filtered through miles of limestone. The high level of calcium that limestone adds causes the silty detritus from dead plants and animals to cling together and settle quickly to the bottom. Abundant bottom vegetation in the shallow sinkholes also helps bind the silt. And the rapid turnover of water prohibits stagnation.
> —Hillary Hauser, "Exploring a Sunken Realm in Australia"

Or the paragraph may move from cause to effects, as in this paragraph from a student paper on the effects of the industrial revolution on American farms.

> The rise of rail transport in the nineteenth century forever changed American farming—for better and for worse. Farmers who once raised crops and livestock to sustain just their own families could now make a profit by selling their goods in towns and cities miles away. These new markets improved the living standard of struggling farm families and encouraged them to seek out innovations that would increase their profits. On the downside, the competition fostered by the new markets sometimes created hostility among neighboring farm families where there had once been a spirit of cooperation. Those farmers who couldn't compete with their neighbors left farming forever, facing poverty worse than they had ever known.
> —Chris Mileski, student

Classification and division

Classification is the grouping of items into categories according to some consistent principle. Philosopher Francis Bacon was using classification when he wrote that "some books are to be tasted, others to be swallowed, and some few to be chewed and digested." Bacon's principle for classifying books is the degree to which they are worthy of our attention, but books of course can be classified according to other principles. For example, an elementary school teacher might classify children's books according to the level of difficulty, or a librarian might group them by subject matter. The principle of classification that a writer chooses ultimately depends on the purpose of the classification.

The following paragraph classifies species of electric fish.

> Scientists sort electric fishes into three categories. The first comprises the strongly electric species like the marine electric rays or the freshwater African electric catfish and South American electric eel. Known since the dawn of history, these deliver a punch strong enough to stun a human. In recent years, biologists have focused on a second category: weakly electric fish in the South American and African rivers that use tiny voltages for communication and navigation. The third group contains sharks, nonelectric rays, and catfish, which do not emit a field but possess sensors that enable them to detect the minute amounts of electricity that leak out of other organisms.
> —Anne Rudloe and Jack Rudloe, "Electric Warfare: The Fish That Kill with Thunderbolts"

Division takes one item and divides it into parts. As with classification, division should be made according to some consistent principle. To divide a tree into roots, trunk, branches, and leaves makes sense; to list its components as branches, wood, water, and sap does not, for the categories overlap.

The following passage describes the components that make up a baseball:

> Like the game itself, a baseball is composed of many layers. One of the delicious joys of childhood is to take apart a baseball and examine the wonders within. You begin by removing the red cotton thread and peeling off the leather cover—which comes from the hide of a Holstein cow and has been tanned, cut, printed, and punched with holes. Beneath the cover is a thin layer of cotton string, followed by several hundred yards of woolen yarn, which make up the bulk of the ball. Slice into the rubber and you'll find the ball's heart—a cork core. The cork is from Portugal, the rubber from southeast Asia, the covers are American, and the balls are assembled in Costa Rica.
> —Dan Gutman, *The Way Baseball Works*

Definition

A definition puts a word or concept into a general class and then provides enough details to distinguish it from others in the same class. For example, in one of its senses the term *grit* names the class of things that birds eat, but it is restricted to those items—such as small pebbles, eggshell, and ashes—that help the bird grind food.

Many definitions may be presented in a sentence or two, but abstract or difficult concepts may require a paragraph or even a full essay of definition. In the following paragraph, the writer defines envy as a special kind of desire.

> Envy is so integral and so painful a part of what animates human behavior in market societies that many people have forgotten the full meaning of the word, simplifying it into one of the synonyms of desire. It is that, which may be why it flourishes in market societies: democracies of desire, they might be called, with money for ballots, stuffing permitted. But envy is more or less than desire. It begins with the almost frantic sense of emptiness inside oneself, as if the pump of one's heart were sucking on air. One has to be blind to perceive the emptiness, of course, but that's just what envy is, a selective blindness. *Invidia,* Latin for envy, translates as "nonsight," and Dante had the envious plodding along under cloaks of lead, their eyes sewn shut with leaden wire. What they are blind to is what they have, God-given and humanly nurtured, in themselves.
> —Nelson W. Aldrich, Jr., *Old Money*

Extended definitions frequently make use of other patterns of development, such as examples, illustrations, or comparison and contrast. Here, for example, is a paragraph that uses a number of illustrations to define the typical teenage victim in a "slasher" film.

> Since teenagers are the target audience for slasher films, the victims in the films are almost always independent, fun-loving, just-out-of-high-school partygoers. The girls all love to take late-night strolls alone through the woods or to skinny-dip at midnight in a murky lake. The boys, eager to impress the girls, prove their manhood by descending alone into musty cellars to restart broken generators or by chasing psychotic killers into haylofts and attics. Entering dark and gloomy houses, young men and women alike decide suddenly that now's a good time to save a few bucks on the family's electric bill—so they leave the lights off. After hearing a noise within the house, they always foolishly decide to investigate, thinking it's one of their many missing friends or pets. Disregarding the "safety in numbers" theory, they branch off in separate directions, never to see each other again. Or the teenagers fall into the common slasher-movie habit of walking backward, which naturally leads them right into you-know-who. Confronted by the ax-wielding maniac, the senseless youths lose their will to survive, close their eyes, and scream.
> —Matthew J. Holicek, student

6c   Consider possible ways of arranging information.

In addition to choosing a pattern of development (or a combination of patterns), you may need to make decisions about arrangement. If you are developing a paragraph with examples, for instance, you'll need to decide how to order the examples. Or if you are contrasting two items point by point, you'll need to decide which points to discuss first, second, and so on. Often considerations of purpose and audience will help you make these choices.

Three of the most common ways of arranging information are treated in this section: time order, spatial order, and order of climax. Other possible arrangements include order of complexity (from simple to complex), order of familiarity (from most familiar to least familiar), and order of audience appeal (from "safe" ideas to those that may challenge the audience's views).

Order of time

Time order, usually chronological, is appropriate for a variety of purposes such as narrating a personal experience, telling an anecdote, describing an experiment, or explaining a process. The following paragraph, arranged in chronological order, appears in *Blue Highways,* an account of the author's travels on the back roads of America.

> Onion Saddle Road, after I was committed to it, narrowed to a single rutted lane affording no place to turn around; if I met somebody, one of us would have to back down. The higher I went, the more that idea unnerved me—the road was bad enough driving forward. The com-

pass swung from point to point, and within five minutes it had touched each of the three hundred sixty degrees. The clutch started pushing back, and ruts and craters and rocks threw the steering wheel into nasty jerks that wrenched to the spine. I understood why, the day before, I'd thought there could be no road over the Chiricahuas; there wasn't. No wonder desperadoes hid in this inaccessibility.
—William Least Heat-Moon

Time order need not be chronological. For example, you might decide to arrange events in the order in which they were revealed to you, not in the order in which they happened. Or you might choose to begin with a dramatic moment and then flash back to the events that led up to it.

Order of space

For descriptions of a location or a scene, a spatial arrangement will seem natural. Imagine yourself holding a video camera and you'll begin to see the possibilities. Might you pan the scene from afar and then zoom to a close-up? Would you rather sweep the camera from side to side—or from top to bottom? Or should you try for a more impressionistic effect, focusing the camera on first one and then another significant feature of the scene?

The writer of the following paragraph describes the contents of a long, narrow pool hall by taking us from the front to the back.

> The pool tables were in a line side by side from the front to the back of the long, narrow building. The first one was the biggest, and the best snooker players used it. Beyond it were the other tables used by lesser players, except for the last one. This was the bank's pool table, used only by the best players in the county.   —William G. Hill, student

Order of climax

When ideas are presented in the order of climax, they build toward a conclusion. Consider the following paragraph describing the effects on workers of long-term blue-collar employment. All of the examples have an emotional impact, but the final one—even though it might at first seem trivial—is the most powerful. It shows us just how degrading blue-collar work can become.

> I met people who taught me about human behavior. I saw people take amphetamines to keep up with ever-rising production rates. I saw good friends, and even relatives, physically attack each other over job assignments that would mean a few cents' difference. I observed women cheating on their husbands and men cheating on their wives. I watched women hand over their entire paycheck to a bookie. I saw pregnant women, their feet too swollen for shoes, come to work in slippers. I saw women with colds stuff pieces of tissue up their nostrils so they wouldn't have to keep stopping to blow their nose.   —Linda Lavelle, student

Because the order of climax saves the most dramatic examples for the end, it is appropriate only when readers are likely to persist until the end. In much business writing, for example, you cannot assume that readers will read more than the first couple of sentences of a paragraph. In such cases, you will be wise to open with your most powerful examples, even at the risk of allowing the paragraph to fizzle at the end.

6d   If necessary, adjust paragraph length.

Most readers feel comfortable reading paragraphs that range between 100 and 200 words. Shorter paragraphs force too much starting and stopping, and longer ones strain the reader's attention span. There are exceptions to this guideline, however. Paragraphs longer than 200 words frequently appear in scholarly writing, where they suggest seriousness and depth. Paragraphs shorter than 100 words occur in newspapers because of narrow columns; in informal essays to quicken the pace; and in business letters, where readers routinely skim for main ideas.

In an essay, the first and last paragraphs will ordinarily be the introduction and conclusion. These special-purpose paragraphs are likely to be shorter than the paragraphs in the body of the essay. Typically, the body paragraphs will mimic the essay's organization: one paragraph per point in short essays, a group of paragraphs per point in longer ones. Some ideas require more development than others, however, so it is best to be flexible. If an idea stretches to a length unreasonable for a paragraph, you should divide it, even if you have presented comparable points in the essay in single paragraphs.

Paragraph breaks are not always made for strictly logical reasons. Writers use them as well to create emphasis, to mark a shift in time or place, to indicate a contrast, to signal a change in speakers (in dialogue), to provide readers a needed pause, or simply to improve the look of a page. Here is a summary of reasons for beginning a new paragraph.

REASONS FOR BEGINNING A NEW PARAGRAPH

— to mark off the introduction and the conclusion
— to signal a shift to a new idea
— to indicate an important shift in time or place
— to emphasize a point (by placing it at the beginning or the end, not in the middle, of a paragraph)
— to highlight a contrast
— to signal a change of speakers (in dialogue)
— to provide readers a needed pause
— to break up text that looks too dense

Beware of using too many short, choppy paragraphs, however. Readers want to see how your ideas connect, and they become irritated when you break their momentum by forcing them to pause every few sentences. Here are some reasons you might have for combining some of the paragraphs in a rough draft.

REASONS FOR COMBINING PARAGRAPHS

— to clarify the essay's organization
— to connect closely related ideas
— to maintain momentum
— to bind together text that looks too choppy

EXERCISE 6–1 Choosing a method of development

What method of paragraph development would you choose for each of the following topics? Be prepared to discuss your reasons.

_____ 1. Showing that your grandmother is an active woman

_____ 2. Explaining how a major event (something like marriage, a new job, death of a loved one, birth of a baby) has affected your life

_____ 3. Reporting on Michelangelo's sculpture of David

_____ 4. Explaining the differences between your family's customs and those of your best friend's family

_____ 5. Giving instructions on how to operate a cash register

_____ 6. Telling about an experience from which you learned something

_____ 7. Analyzing the main parts of a computer

_____ 8. Explaining the meaning of "culture" on an anthropology exam

_____ 9. Grouping all of the items on one floor of your college library into three or four easily remembered sets

_____ 10. Showing how a hamburger and an essay are alike

EXERCISE 6–2 Writing paragraphs

If your instructor assigns paragraphs modeled on the patterns discussed in this section, here are some possible subjects—most of which you would need to restrict.

Examples or illustrations: sexism in a comic strip, ways to include protein in a vegetarian diet, the benefits of a particular summer job, community services provided by your college, violence on the six o'clock news, educational software for children

Narration: the active lifestyle of a grandparent, life with an alcoholic, working in an emergency room, the benefits (or problems) of intercultural dating, growing up in a large family, the rewards of working in a nursing home, an experience that taught you a lesson, a turning point in your life

Description: your childhood home, an ethnic neighborhood, a rock concert, a favorite painting in an art gallery, a garden, a classic car, a hideous building or monument, a style of dress, a family heirloom (such as a crazy quilt or a collection of Christmas tree ornaments), a favorite park or retreat

Process: how to repair something, how to develop a successful job interview style, how to ask someone out on a date, how to practice safe scuba diving, how to build a set for a play, how to survive in the wilderness, how to train a dog, how to quit smoking, how to make bread

Comparison and contrast: two neighborhoods, teachers, political candidates, colleges, products; country living versus city living; the stereotype of a job versus the reality; a change in attitude toward your family's religion or ethnic background

Analogy: between a family reunion and a circus, between training for a rigorous sport and boot camp, between settling an argument and being a courtroom judge, between a dogfight and a boxing match, between raising a child and tending a garden

Cause and effect: the effects of water pollution on a particular area, the effects of divorce on a child, the effects of an illegal drug, why a particular film or television show is popular, why an area of the country has high unemployment, why early training is essential for success as a ballet dancer, violinist, or athlete

Classification: types of clothing worn on your college campus, types of people who join online chat groups, types of dieters, types of television weather reports, types of rock bands, types of teachers

Definition: an Internet addict, an ideal parent or teacher, an authoritarian personality, an intellectual, a sexist, a typical heroine in a Harlequin romance, a typical blind date, anorexia nervosa, concrete poetry, rapping, metacognition, impressionism

EXERCISE 6–3 Paragraphing

Here is a teacher's first draft of an introduction of herself. It is written as one paragraph. Turn it into a five-paragraph essay by putting a paragraph marker [¶] in front of each word that should start a new paragraph.

I've been a fire-tower lookout, a salesperson, a waitress, a singer for commercial radio, a professional writer, and a check girl in a bingo parlor—but none of these jobs held my interest very long. The job I have enjoyed most in my life is teaching. Whether I was pretending, volunteering, or earning my living, I've done some kind of teaching for most of my life. As a child, I did a lot of make-believe teaching. I used to line up my dolls and stuffed animals on the side porch and "teach" them whatever I was currently learning, like the ABC's or numbers. I would "read" stories to them too, trying to sound just like the teacher who read to us at school. When the neighborhood kids played school, I always wanted to be either the bad kid or the teacher. My friend Billy would play school only if he could be the bad kid, so I usually ended up being "teacher." I've done a lot of volunteer teaching, too. I started teaching church school when I was about thirteen—not babysitting in the nursery, but teaching a class of eight-year-old girls. By the time I finished college, I had taught unruly ten-year-old boys, lovesick adolescent girls, and even an adult class or two. When G.I.'s started coming back to my college after World War II, I tutored some who had trouble with freshman English. Later, when displaced persons from World War II immigrated to the United States, I organized, recruited teachers for, and taught night school classes in English. The most unusual volunteer teaching I ever did was at the University of Hawaii dolphin tanks, where two beautiful sleek dolphins were learning grammar. I've taught as a professional for many years. My first salaried teaching job was at the University of Pennsylvania. For four years I taught freshman composition while I worked on my graduate degrees. In the late 1960s, I came to Prince George's Community College, where I've taught English for more than twenty-five years. What job comes next? I don't know, but I'd be willing to bet on one thing: Whatever it is, I'll find some way to turn it into teaching.

—Wanda Van Goor

7 Improve coherence.

When sentences and paragraphs flow from one to another without discernible bumps, gaps, or shifts, they are said to be coherent. Coherence can be improved by strengthening the various ties between old information and new. A number of techniques for strengthening those ties are detailed in this section.

7a Link ideas clearly.

In the first draft of a paragraph or an essay, writers do not always link their ideas as clearly as possible. To check a draft for clear connections among ideas, try to look at it from the point of view of a reader. Think in terms of the reader's expectations.

Linking ideas in paragraphs

As you know, readers usually expect to learn a paragraph's main point in a topic sentence early in the paragraph. Then, as they move into the body of the paragraph, they expect to encounter specific details, facts, or examples that support the topic sentence—either directly or indirectly. Consider the following example, in which all of the sentences following the topic sentence directly support it.

> A passenger list of the early years of the Orient Express would read like a *Who's Who of the World,* from art to politics. Sarah Bernhardt and her Italian counterpart Eleonora Duse used the train to thrill the stages of Europe. For musicians there were Toscanini and Mahler. Dancers Nijinsky and Pavlova were there, while lesser performers like Harry Houdini and the girls of the Ziegfeld Follies also rode the rails. Violinists were allowed to practice on the train, and occasionally one might see trapeze artists hanging like bats from the baggage racks.
> —Barnaby Conrad III, "Train of Kings"

If a sentence does not directly support the topic sentence, readers expect it to support another sentence in the paragraph and therefore to support the topic sentence indirectly. Composition scholar Francis Christensen has invented a useful system for numbering the sentences in a paragraph to depict the hierarchic connections among sentences that readers look for. The topic sentence, being most general, receives the number 1, and any sentences that directly support it receive the number 2. Sentences that support level 2 sentences receive the number 3, and so on. Here, for example, is Christensen's numbering system as applied to a paragraph by columnist Ellen Goodman.

1. In the years since Kitty Genovese's murder, social scientists have learned a great deal about bystander behavior.
   2. They've learned that the willingness to intervene depends on a number of subtle factors beyond fear.
      3. It turns out that people are less likely to help if they are in a crowd of bystanders than if they are the only one.
         4. Their sense of responsibility is diffused.
         4. If the others aren't helping, they begin to reinterpret what they are seeing.
      3. People are also more passive in urban neighborhoods or crowded city spots where they suffer from "excessive overload" or simply turn off.
      3. They rarely get involved if they believe that the victim knows the assailant.
         4. This is especially true if the crime being witnessed is . . . a rape or attempted rape.

Because the sentences in this paragraph are arranged in a clear hierarchy, readers can easily follow the writer's train of thought.

To check one of your own paragraphs for clear connections among ideas, look to see if the hierarchic chain has been broken at any point. The topic sentence should announce the main idea, and the rest of the sentences should support it either directly or indirectly. When a sentence supports the topic sentence indirectly, it must support an earlier sentence that is clearly linked (directly or indirectly) to the topic sentence. If you can't find such a sentence, you'll need to add one or rethink the entire chain of ideas.

Linking ideas in essays

WHAT READERS LOOK FOR IN AN ESSAY Like the sentences within paragraphs, the paragraphs within an essay should be arranged in a clear hierarchy. Readers expect to learn the essay's main point in the first paragraph, often in a thesis statement (see 2a). And by scanning the topic sentence of each paragraph in the body of the essay, readers hope to understand how each paragraph connects with what has come before. As a rule, a topic sentence should tell readers whether the information they are about to read supports the thesis statement directly or supports a key idea in the essay, which in turn supports the thesis.

Consider the following thesis statement and topic sentences, taken from an essay by student Thu Hong Nguyen. Each of Nguyen's topic sentences supports the thesis statement directly.

THESIS STATEMENT IN OPENING PARAGRAPH
From the moment she is mature enough to understand commands, to the day she is married off, to the time when she bears her own children, a Vietnamese woman tries to establish a good name as a diligent daughter, a submissive wife, and an altruistic mother.

TOPIC SENTENCE IN FIRST BODY PARAGRAPH
In order to be approved of by everyone, a Vietnamese daughter must work diligently to help her parents.

TOPIC SENTENCE IN SECOND BODY PARAGRAPH
Once she enters an arranged marriage, a good Vietnamese woman must submit to her husband.

TOPIC SENTENCE IN THIRD BODY PARAGRAPH
Finally, to be recognized favorably, a Vietnamese woman must sacrifice herself for the benefit of the children it is her duty to bear.

Topic sentences do not always have to interlock with the thesis quite so tightly as in Nguyen's essay. Nevertheless, by scanning the opening sentence or two of each paragraph, readers should have at least a rough sense of the connections among ideas within the whole essay.

7b   Repeat key words.

Repetition of key words is an important technique for gaining coherence, because if too much information seems new, a paragraph will be hard to read. To prevent repetitions from becoming dull, you can use variations of a key word (*hike, hiker, hiking*), pronouns referring to the word (*hikers . . . they*), or synonyms (*walk, trek, wander, tramp, climb*).

In the following paragraph describing plots among indentured servants in seventeenth-century America, historian Richard Hofstadter binds sentences together by repeating the key word *plots* and echoing it with variations (all in italics).

> *Plots* hatched by several servants to run away together occurred mostly in the plantation colonies, and the few recorded servant *uprisings* were entirely limited to those colonies. Virginia had been forced from its very earliest years to take stringent steps against *mutinous plots*, and severe punishments for *such behavior* were recorded. Most servant *plots* occurred in the seventeenth century: a contemplated *uprising* was nipped in the bud in York County in 1661; apparently led by some left-wing offshoots of the *Great Rebellion*, servants *plotted* an *insurrection* in Gloucester County in 1663, and four leaders were condemned and executed; some discontented servants apparently joined *Bacon's Rebellion* in the 1670's. In the 1680's the planters became newly apprehensive of discontent among the servants "owing to their great necessities and want of clothes," and it was feared that they would *rise up* and *plunder* the storehouses and ships; in 1682 there were plant-cutting *riots* in which servants and laborers, as well as some planters, took part. [Italics added.]
> —Richard Hofstadter,
> *America at 1750*

7c   Use parallel structures for parallel ideas.

Parallel grammatical structures are frequently used within sentences to underscore the similarity of ideas (see 9). They may also be used to bind together a series of sentences expressing similar information. In the following passage describing folk beliefs, anthropologist Margaret Mead presents similar information in parallel grammatical form.

Actually, almost every day, even in the most sophisticated home, something is likely to happen that evokes the memory of some old folk belief. The salt spills. A knife falls to the floor. Your nose tickles. Then perhaps, with a slightly embarrassed smile, the person who spilled the salt tosses a pinch over his left shoulder. Or someone recites the old rhyme, "Knife falls, gentleman calls." Or as you rub your nose you think, That means a letter. I wonder who's writing?

—Margaret Mead,
"New Superstitions for Old"

A less skilled writer might have varied the structure, perhaps like this: *The salt gets spilled. Mother drops a knife on the floor. Your nose begins to tickle.* But these sentences are less effective; Mead's parallel structures help tie the paragraph together.

7d Maintain consistency.

Coherence suffers whenever a draft shifts confusingly from one point of view to another or from one verb tense to another. (See 13.) In addition, coherence suffers when the subjects of sentences keep introducing new information. As a rule, a sentence's subject should echo a subject or object in the previous sentence.

The following rough-draft paragraph is needlessly hard to read because so few of the sentences' subjects are tied to earlier subjects or objects. The subjects appear in italics.

One goes about trapping in this manner. At the very outset *one* acquires a "trapping" state of mind. A *library* of books must be read, and preferably *someone* with experience should educate the novice. *Preparing* for the first expedition takes several steps. The *purchase* of traps is first. A *pair* of rubber gloves, waterproof *boots*, and the grubbiest *clothes* capable of withstanding human use come next to outfit the trapper for his adventure. Finally, the *decision* has to be made on just what kind of animals to seek, what sort of bait to use, and where to place the traps.

Although the writer repeats a number of key words, such as *trapping*, the paragraph seems disconnected because new information keeps appearing as subjects.

To improve the paragraph, the writer used the first-person pronoun as the subject of every sentence. The revision is much easier to read.

I went about trapping in this manner. To acquire a "trapping" state of mind, *I* read a library of books and talked at length with an experienced trapper, my father. Then *I* purchased the traps and outfitted myself by collecting a pair of rubber gloves, waterproof boots, and the grubbiest clothes capable of withstanding human use. Finally, *I* decided just what kinds of animals to seek, what sort of bait to use, and where to place my traps.

—John Clyde Thatcher, student

Notice that Thatcher combined some of his original sentences. By doing so, he was able to avoid excessive repetitions of the pronoun *I*. Notice, too, that he varied his sentence openings (most sentences do not begin with *I*) so that readers are not likely to find the repetitions tiresome.

7e Provide transitions.

Transitions are bridges between what has been read and what is about to be read. Transitions help readers move from sentence to sentence; they also alert readers to more global connections of ideas—those between paragraphs or even larger blocks of text.

SENTENCE-LEVEL TRANSITIONS Certain words and phrases signal connections between (or within) sentences. Frequently used transitions are included in the following list.

TO SHOW ADDITION
and, also, besides, further, furthermore, in addition, moreover, next, too, first, second

TO GIVE EXAMPLES
for example, for instance, to illustrate, in fact, specifically

TO COMPARE
also, in the same manner, similarly, likewise

TO CONTRAST
but, however, on the other hand, in contrast, nevertheless, still, even though, on the contrary, yet, although

TO SUMMARIZE OR CONCLUDE
in other words, in short, in summary, in conclusion, to sum up, that is, therefore

TO SHOW TIME
after, as, before, next, during, later, finally, meanwhile, then, when, while, immediately

TO SHOW PLACE OR DIRECTION
above, below, beyond, farther on, nearby, opposite, close, to the left

TO INDICATE LOGICAL RELATIONSHIP
if, so, therefore, consequently, thus, as a result, for this reason, since

Skilled writers use transitional expressions with care, making sure, for example, not to use *consequently* when an *also* would be more precise. They are also careful to select transitions with an appropriate tone, perhaps preferring *so* to *thus* in an informal piece, *in summary* to *in short* for a scholarly essay.

In the following paragraph, taken from an argument that dinosaurs had the " 'right-sized' brains for reptiles of their body size," biologist Stephen Jay Gould uses transitions (italicized) with skill.

> I don't wish to deny that the flattened, minuscule head of the large bodied "Stegosaurus" houses little brain from our subjective, top-heavy perspective, *but* I do wish to assert that we should not expect more of the beast. *First of all,* large animals have relatively smaller brains than related, small animals. The correlation of brain size with body size among kindred animals (all reptiles, all mammals, *for example*) is remarkably regular. *As* we move from small to large animals, from mice to elephants *or* small lizards to Komodo dragons, brain size increases, *but* not so fast as body size. *In other words,* bodies grow faster than brains, *and* large animals have low ratios of brain weight to body weight. *In fact,* brains grow only about two-thirds as fast as bodies. *Since* we have no reason to believe that large animals are consistently stupider than their smaller relatives, we must conclude that large animals require relatively less brain to do as well as smaller animals. *If* we do not recognize this relationship, we are likely to underestimate the mental power of very large animals, dinosaurs in particular. [Italics added.]
> —Stephen Jay Gould, "Were Dinosaurs Dumb?"

CAUTION: Do not be too self-conscious about plugging in transition words while you are drafting sentences; overuse of these signals can seem heavy-handed. Usually, you will use transitions quite naturally, just where readers need them. If you (or your reviewers) discover places where readers cannot easily move from sentence to sentence in your rough draft, you can always add transition words as you revise.

PARAGRAPH-LEVEL TRANSITIONS   Paragraph-level transitions usually link the *first* sentence of a new paragraph with the *first* sentence of the previous paragraph. In other words, the topic sentences signal global connections.

Look for opportunities to allude to the subject of a previous paragraph (as summed up in its topic sentence) in the topic sentence of the next one. In his essay "Little Green Lies," Jonathan H. Alder uses this strategy in the following topic sentences, which appear in a passage describing the benefits of plastic packaging.

> Consider septic packaging, the synthetic packaging for the "juice boxes" so many children bring to school with their lunch. [*Rest of paragraph omitted.*]

> What is true for juice boxes is also true for other forms of synthetic packaging. [*Rest of paragraph omitted.*]

TRANSITIONS BETWEEN BLOCKS OF TEXT   In long essays, you will need to alert readers to connections between blocks of text more than one paragraph long. You can do this by inserting transitional sentences or short paragraphs at key points in the essay. Here, for example, is a transitional paragraph from a student research paper by Karen Shaw. It announces that the first part of her paper has come to a close and the second part is about to begin.

> Although the great apes have demonstrated significant language skills, one central question remains: Can they be taught to use that uniquely human language tool we call grammar, to learn the difference, for instance, between "ape bite human" and "human bite ape"? In other words, can an ape create a sentence?

Another strategy to help readers move from one block of text to another is to insert headings in your essay. Headings, which usually sit above blocks of text, allow you to announce a new topic boldly, without the need for subtle transitions.

THE STAND-ALONE PARAGRAPH

Most paragraphs appear with other paragraphs in an essay, a report, a letter, a memo, or some other kind of document. The exception is the stand-alone paragraph, which is meant to be read by itself. Stand-alone paragraphs are assigned in many English classes; you will also use them for essay exams and other short writing assignments in the academic world. In the business world, you will use them for brief reports, evaluations, proposals, and so on.

A stand-alone paragraph is a miniature essay. Like an essay, it has a clear beginning, a middle, and an end. But because it is so much shorter than an essay, it must get to the point faster. Usually a stand-alone paragraph begins with a topic sentence that expresses its main point, as in the following one-paragraph profile of a person. The topic sentence is italicized.

> *Paul Norman has loved airplanes all his life.* Even when he was a little boy, he wanted to be a pilot. He used to draw airplanes on all his schoolwork. He also folded paper airplanes and designed new folding techniques so the planes would fly in certain ways. In high school and college, he studied subjects that would help him become a pilot. He took every geography and math course his high school offered, and in college he took physics and aerodynamics as well as advanced math. Unfortunately, Paul's vision was not acute enough for him to qualify as a professional or a military pilot, so he tried another way of working with planes. He went back to school and earned a master's degree in business administration; now he is the manager of a major airport in Houston. From child to adult, Paul has not changed his major interest—airplanes.

Occasionally a stand-alone paragraph opens with an introductory sentence that attracts readers' attention and prepares them for the main point. In such cases, the topic sentence will be the second sentence of the paragraph. For example, the paragraph about Paul Norman might have started like this:

> Paul Norman smiled broadly as he watched eight planes in a row take off with clocklike precision from the newly opened runways. *Paul has loved airplanes all his life.* Even when he was a little boy. . . .

Because the stand-alone paragraph appears by itself, it needs a conclusion. Usually the concluding sentence sums up the paragraph's main point, as the one about Paul Norman does.

EXERCISE 7–1 Linking ideas clearly

Read the following two paragraphs. Then decide which one was easier for you to follow and try to explain why.

A. Sigmund Freud influenced far more than his own field, psychology. His conclusions about the effects of childhood experiences affected other social sciences too. Most sociologists, for example, accept Freud's idea that a young child's family relationships set the pattern for his or her adult relationships. Many criminologists believe that criminals act out unconscious drives, and courts often refer criminals for psychiatric evaluation or therapy. In addition to the social sciences, the humanities have also used many of Freud's insights. In art, for instance, the surrealist movement tried to paint the unconscious mind. And novelists and playwrights have used Freud's concepts to develop their plots and their characters. Because Freud's work has influenced so many fields, it has changed the way many of us view human beings.

B. No one has figured out how to test many of Freud's theories. Many feel he overemphasized the importance of sex in personality development. What test would show whether President Truman disliked military officers because they reminded him of his father or because big boys bullied him when he was little, or for any number of other reasons? Other causes than guilt or fear about sex might influence a person even more. Guilt and fear about sexual matters may influence a person, but the extent of that influence can't be proved. Freud's theories have received criticism for several reasons.

EXERCISE 7–2 Linking ideas clearly

Use the Christensen system (see p. 73) for numbering the levels of generality in paragraph A in Exercise 7–1.

Next, try another technique for displaying the hierarchic structure of paragraph A. Fill in the following form, using sentences for the main point and conclusion and key words or phrases for the direct and indirect supports.

Main idea: _____

_____

Direct support: _____

Indirect support: _____

Indirect support: _____

Direct support: _____

Indirect support: _____

Indirect support: _____

Conclusion: _____

_____

EXERCISE 7–3 Using transitions

The following paragraph would be easier to read if it had a few transitions. Revise the paragraph by inserting appropriate transition words or phrases where they are needed. Feel free to combine or restructure sentences. The first revision has been made for you.

At first, their

Freud's Psycho-Analytic Society often met to discuss psychoanalytic theories. ~~Their~~

disagreements were not serious. Later, arguments became so serious that several members left the group. One was Carl Jung, who disagreed with Freud's emphasis on the sex instinct and on abnormal personalities. Alfred Adler disputed Freud's emphasis on sex. He refused to accept Freud's pessimistic view of people. Karen Horney rejected Freud's belief in the biological inferiority of women. She quarreled with Freud about instincts. All three of these talented psychiatrists left the Psycho-Analytic Society because of their disagreements with Freud's controversial theories.

EXERCISE 7–4 Recognizing coherence techniques

Discuss the ways in which the writer of the following paragraphs has achieved coherence. You should find examples of these techniques: linking ideas clearly, repeating key words, using parallelism, and providing transitions.

Sigmund Freud claimed that people are born with two drives—the drive for survival and the drive for destruction. He gave both drives (or instincts) Greek names. For the drive for survival, he chose *Eros*, the Greek god of love. For the drive for destruction, he used the Greek word for death, *Thanatos*. After naming the two drives, Freud divided each drive into specific components. Eros includes the need for at least three things: food and drink, warmth, and sex. In contrast, Thanatos contains both the desire to destroy others and the desire to destroy oneself.

Freud tried to show that people's various behaviors come from either Eros or Thanatos. Eros is more than simply love or lust. For example, as the instinct for survival, it makes people work hard, build shelters, and produce children. Likewise, Thanatos is not simply an inclination to homicide or suicide. According to Freud, Thanatos is responsible for several kinds of destructive behavior, such as drinking too much, driving dangerously, or smoking cigarettes. Freud's thinking has been so accepted by Western culture that dictionaries sometimes define *Eros* and *Thanatos* as "life instinct" and "death instinct."

Clear Sentences

8 **Coordinate equal ideas; subordinate minor ideas.**

9 **Balance parallel ideas.**

10 **Add needed words.**

11 **Untangle mixed constructions.**

12 **Repair misplaced and dangling modifiers.**

13 **Eliminate distracting shifts.**

14 **Emphasize your point.**

15 **Provide some variety.**

---

8 Coordinate equal ideas; subordinate minor ideas.

When combining two or more ideas in one sentence, you have two choices: coordination or subordination. Choose coordination to indicate that the ideas are equal or nearly equal in importance. Choose subordination to indicate that one idea is less important than another.

GRAMMAR CHECKERS do not catch the problems with coordination and subordination discussed in this section. Not surprisingly, computer programs have no way of sensing the relative importance of ideas.

Coordination

Coordination draws attention equally to two or more ideas. To coordinate single words or phrases, join them with a coordinating conjunction or with a pair of correlative conjunctions (see 47g). To coordinate independent clauses—word groups that could stand alone as a sentence—join them with a comma and a coordinating conjunction or with a semicolon:

| , and | , but | , or | , nor |
| , for | , so | , yet | ; |

The semicolon is often accompanied by a conjunctive adverb such as *moreover, furthermore, therefore,* or *however* or by a transitional phrase such as *for example, in other words,* or *as a matter of fact.* (See the chart on p. 85 for a more complete list.)

Assume, for example, that your intention is to draw equal attention to the following two ideas.

> Grandmother lost her sight. Her hearing sharpened.

To coordinate these ideas, you can join them with a comma and the coordinating conjunction *but* or with a semicolon and the conjunctive adverb *however.*

> Grandmother lost her sight, but her hearing sharpened.

> Grandmother lost her sight; however, her hearing sharpened.

It is important to choose a coordinating conjunction or conjunctive adverb appropriate to your meaning. In the preceding example, the two ideas contrast with one another, calling for *but* or *however.*

Subordination

To give unequal emphasis to two or more ideas, express the major idea in an independent clause and place any minor ideas in subordinate clauses or phrases. (For specific subordination strategies, see the chart on p. 85.)

Deciding which idea to emphasize is not a matter of right and wrong but is determined by the meaning you intend. Consider the two ideas about Grandmother's sight and hearing.

> Grandmother lost her sight. Her hearing sharpened.

If your purpose is to stress your grandmother's acute hearing rather than her blindness, subordinate the idea about her blindness.

> *As she lost her sight,* Grandmother's hearing sharpened.

To focus on your grandmother's growing blindness, subordinate the idea about her hearing.

> *Though her hearing sharpened,* Grandmother gradually lost her sight.

8a   Combine choppy sentences.

Short sentences demand attention, so you should use them primarily for emphasis. Too many short sentences, one after the other, make for a choppy style.

If an idea is not important enough to deserve its own sentence, try combining it with a sentence close by. Put any minor ideas in subordinate structures such as phrases or subordinate clauses.

► We keep our use of insecticides, herbicides, and
  because we
  fungicides to a minimum/ We are concerned

  about the environment.

A minor idea is now expressed in a subordinate clause beginning with *because.*

► The Chesapeake and Ohio Canal, is a 184-mile

  waterway constructed in the 1800s/, It was a

  major source of transportation for goods during

  the Civil War.

A minor idea is now expressed in an appositive phrase (*a 184-mile waterway constructed in the 1800s*).

                                        E
► Sister Consilio was enveloped in a black robe
                                Sister Consilio
  with only her face and hands visible/, She was

  an imposing figure.

A minor idea is now expressed in a participial phrase beginning with *Enveloped.*

Although subordination is ordinarily the most effective technique for combining short, choppy sentences, coordination is appropriate when the ideas are equal in importance.

► The hospital decides when patients will sleep

  and wake/, It dictates what and when they will
  and
  eat/, It tells them when they may be with family

  and friends.

Using coordination to combine sentences of equal importance

1. Consider using a comma and a coordinating conjunction. (See 32a.)

    , and   , but   , or   , nor
    , for   , so   , yet

    ▶ In Orthodox Jewish funeral ceremonies, the
    and the
    shroud is a simple linen vestment/. ~~The~~ coffin
    is plain wood with no adornment.

2. Consider using a semicolon and a conjunctive adverb or transitional phrase. (See 34b.)

also	for example
as a result	for instance
besides	furthermore
consequently	however
finally	in addition
in fact	of course
in other words	on the other hand
in the first place	otherwise
meanwhile	still
moreover	then
nevertheless	therefore
next	thus
now	

    ▶ Tom Baxter has been irritating me lately/;
    therefore,
    I avoid him whenever possible.

3. Consider using a semicolon alone. (See 34a.)

    ▶ Nicklaus is like fine wine/;
    he
    ~~He~~ gets better with time.

Using subordination to combine sentences of unequal importance

1. Consider putting the less important idea in a subordinate clause beginning with one of the following words. (See 49b.)

after	that
although	unless
as	until
as if	when
because	where
before	which
even though	while
if	who
since	whom
so that	whose

    When my
    ▶ ~~My~~ son asked his great-grandmother if she had
    she
    been a slave/. ~~She~~ became very angry.

    ▶ My sister owes much of her recovery to a body-
    that she
    building program/. ~~She~~ began ~~the program~~ three
    years ago.

2. Consider putting the less important idea in a phrase. (See 49a, 49c, 49d, and 49e.)

    ▶ Karate, ~~is~~ a discipline based on the philosophy
    of nonviolence/. ~~It~~ teaches the art of self-defense.

    E
    ▶ ~~Alvin was~~ encouraged by his professor to apply
    Alvin
    for the job/. ~~He~~ filed an application on Monday
    morning.

    my eyes
    ▶ I reached for the knife out of habit/. ~~My eyes~~
    scanning
    ~~scanned~~ the long shiny blade for a price
    sticker. In a low, steady voice, my customer said,
    "This is a holdup."

8b Avoid ineffective or excessive coordination.

Coordinate structures are appropriate only when you intend to draw the reader's attention equally to two or more ideas: *Professor Naake praises loudly, and she criticizes softly.* If one idea is more important than another—or if a coordinating conjunction does not clearly signal the relation between the ideas—you should subordinate the less important idea.

ESL When combining sentences, do not repeat the subject of the sentence; also do not repeat an object or adverb in an adjective clause. See 31b and 31c.

▶ The apartment that we moved into ~~it~~

  needed many repairs.

▶ Tanya climbed into the tree house that

  the boys were playing in, ~~it.~~

INEFFECTIVE
Closets were taxed as rooms, and most colonists stored their clothes in chests or clothes presses.

IMPROVED
Because closets were taxed as rooms, most colonists stored their clothes in chests or clothes presses.

The revision subordinates the less important idea by putting it in a subordinate clause. Notice that the subordinating conjunction *Because* signals the relation between the ideas more clearly than the coordinating conjunction *and.*

Because it is so easy to string ideas together with *and*, writers often rely too heavily on coordination in their rough drafts. The cure for excessive coordination is simple: Look for opportunities to tuck minor ideas into subordinate clauses or phrases.

  When
▶ Jason walked over to his new Miata, ~~and~~ he saw

  that its windshield had been smashed.

The minor idea has become a subordinate clause beginning with *When.*

  noticing
▶ My uncle, ~~noticed~~ my frightened look, ~~and~~ told

  me that Grandma had to feel my face because

  she was blind.

The less important idea has become a participial phrase modifying the noun *uncle.*

  After four hours,
▶ ~~Four hours went by, and~~ a rescue truck finally

  arrived, but by that time we had been evacuated

  in a helicopter.

Three independent clauses were excessive. The least important idea has become a prepositional phrase.

8c   Do not subordinate major ideas.

If a sentence buries its major idea in a subordinate construction, readers may not give the idea enough attention. Express the major idea in an independent clause and subordinate any minor ideas.

  had polio as a child,
▶ Lanie, who now walks with the help of braces,

  ~~had polio as a child.~~

The writer wanted to focus on Lanie's ability to walk, but the original sentence buried this information in an adjective clause. The revision puts the major idea in an independent clause and tucks the less important idea into an adjective clause (*who had polio as a child*).

  As
▶ I was driving home from my new job, heading

  down Ranchitos Road, ~~when~~ my car suddenly

  overheated.

The writer wanted to emphasize that the car was overheating, not the fact of driving home. The revision expresses the major idea in an independent clause, the less important idea in an adverb clause (*As I was driving home from my new job*).

8d   Do not subordinate excessively.

In attempting to avoid short, choppy sentences, writers sometimes go to the opposite extreme, putting more subordinate ideas into a sentence than its structure can bear. If a sentence collapses of its own weight, occasionally it can be restructured. More often, however, such sentences must be divided.

▶ Our job is to stay between the stacker and the

  tie machine watching to see if the newspapers
  If they do,
  jam, ~~in which case~~ we pull the bundles off and

  stack them on a skid, because otherwise they

  would back up in the stacker.

EXERCISE 8–1 Coordination and subordination: Guided practice

Edit the following paragraph to put major ideas in independent clauses and minor ideas in subordinate clauses or phrases. Rule numbers in the margin refer to appropriate rules in section 8. The first revision has been made for you, and a suggested revision of this exercise appears in the back of the book.

No one who knew Albert Einstein as a young child would ever have believed that he might one day be called the smartest man in the world. None of his teachers could have predicted success for him. ~~Albert was a~~ *A shy,* slow learner~~,~~/ ~~He was shy. He~~ *Albert*   *8a*

always got in trouble in class. He consistently failed some subjects. They were the   *8a*

subjects he did not like. His family could not have predicted his success either. Albert could not even get to meals on time. Night after night his parents had to postpone dinner until servants, after searching the house and grounds, found the boy,   *8d*

at which time he would be full of apologies but have no explanation to offer for his lateness except that he was "thinking." Once his angry father dangled his big gold watch at Albert. He told Albert to figure out how late he was. Albert, who was fasci-   *8a*

nated by the tiny magnetic compass hanging from the watch chain, could not tell   *8c*

time. The boy asked so many questions about the compass that he did not eat much dinner anyway. Albert begged his father to lend him the compass to sleep with, and   *8b*

his father let him borrow it. Years later Einstein wondered whether that little compass had been the beginning of his interest in science.

EXERCISE 8–2 Coordination and subordination

Combine or restructure the following sentences so that the independent clause expresses the idea in brackets and everything else is subordinated. Example:

who ran an electrochemical factory,

Albert Einstein's father, Hermann Einstein, had some interest in science. ~~He owned an electrochemical factory.~~ [Emphasize his father's interest in science.]

1. Hermann Einstein moved his electrochemical business to Munich; the move made it possible for his son to have the best schooling available. [Emphasize the fact that Hermann moved his business.]

2. Albert Einstein's Uncle Jake explained math to the boy and made algebra problems into games. [Emphasize Uncle Jake's making games out of the problems.]

3. Albert's mother was impressed by her son's persistent questions and secretly hoped that Albert would one day be a professor. [Emphasize the mother's hope.]

4. One of Albert's friends was a medical student at the University of Munich. This friend supplied Albert with well-written modern books on natural science. [Emphasize that the friend supplied Einstein with books.]

5. Hermann Einstein kept his business in Munich for several years, and afterward he decided to go to Italy and work with relatives. [Emphasize the decision to go to Italy and work with relatives.]

EXERCISE 8–3 Coordination and subordination

Combine or restructure the following sentences so that the independent clause expresses the idea in brackets and, if necessary, other ideas are subordinated. Example:

When

Hermann Einstein moved his family to Italy, ~~but~~ he left Albert in Munich to finish school.

[Emphasize his leaving Albert in Munich to finish school.]

1. Albert was miserably lonely without his family, and he had always depended on them for his social life. [Emphasize Albert's loneliness without his family.]

2   He did not get along with the other students. He did not get along with his teachers either. [Emphasize both ideas equally.]

3. He had never gotten along well with other students, and they envied his superior work in math and physics. [Emphasize his not getting along with other students.]

4. In mathematics he was smarter than his teachers, so his teachers resented him too. [Emphasize his teachers' resentment of him.]

5. He was desperate to be with his family in sunny Italy, so he faked a nervous breakdown. [Emphasize his faking a nervous breakdown.]

6. Albert convinced a medical doctor to sign a formal request for a six-month vacation and then he found out that the school had expelled him. [Emphasize his discovery that the school had expelled him.]

7. His months in Italy were a welcome change, and they gave him time to enjoy life again and to plan for his future. [Emphasize that the months in Italy were welcome.]

8. Albert spent months thinking about his future while he enjoyed Italy's scenery, art, and music, and then he finally decided that he wanted to be a theoretical physicist. [Emphasize his decision to become a theoretical physicist.]

9. He knew his father's business was not doing well, but he asked his father for enough money to take the entrance exams at the Swiss Federal Polytechnic School. [Emphasize his request to his father.]

10. His father wanted him to succeed, so he found the money somehow. [Emphasize his father's finding the money.]

EXERCISE 8-4 Coordination and subordination: Guided review

Edit the following paragraph to put major ideas in independent clauses and minor ideas in subordinate clauses or phrases. Rule numbers in the margin refer to appropriate rules in section 8. The first revision has been done for you.

Teachers are not always right about their pupils. Certainly Albert Einstein's

teachers, ~~misjudged~~ *misjudging* his ability in math, ~~and they~~ failed to spot the most bril- 8b

liant student they had ever had. Giuseppe Verdi's teachers made similar errors in

judging their pupil's musical ability. Verdi was Italian. He lived in the nineteenth 8a

century. He wanted to be a composer. He applied to the Conservatory of Music in

Milan, and he was rejected because he "showed no aptitude for music." Today his 8b

works are performed more than those of any other opera composer. Scientists have

also been underestimated. Everyone has heard of Charles Darwin, the British sci-

entist. This man, who also had trouble in school, first proposed the theory of evo- 8c

lution. He did so poorly at his school, which was the University of Edinburgh, that 8d

his teachers considered him hopeless, as a result of which they dismissed him. The

first American physicist to win the Nobel Prize for physics was also misjudged by his

teachers. Albert Abraham Michelson was a student at Annapolis. He was in the naval 8a

academy there. One of his teachers told him to pay less attention to science and

concentrate on naval gunnery. Luckily, Einstein, Verdi, Darwin, and Michelson re-

fused to accept their teachers' evaluations of them.

9 Balance parallel ideas.

If two or more ideas are parallel, they are easier to grasp when expressed in parallel grammatical form. Single words should be balanced with single words, phrases with phrases, clauses with clauses.

A kiss can be a comma, a question mark, or an exclamation point. —Mistinguett

This novel is not to be tossed lightly aside, but to be hurled with great force. —Dorothy Parker

In matters of principle, stand like a rock; in matters of taste, swim with the current. —Thomas Jefferson

Writers often use parallelism to create emphasis. (See 14c.)

 GRAMMAR CHECKERS do not flag faulty parallelism. Because computer programs have no way of assessing whether two or more ideas are parallel in meaning, they fail to catch the faulty parallelism in sentences such as this: *In my high school, boys were either jocks, preppies, or studied constantly.*

9a Balance parallel ideas in a series.

Readers expect items in a series to appear in parallel grammatical form. When one or more of the items violates readers' expectations, a sentence will be needlessly awkward.

▶ Abused children commonly exhibit one or more of the following symptoms: withdrawal,
depression.
rebelliousness, restlessness, and ~~they are depressed.~~

The revision presents all of the items as nouns.

▶ Hooked on romance novels, I learned that there is nothing more important than being rich, look-
having
ing good, and ~~to have~~ a good time.

The revision uses *-ing* forms for all items in the series.

▶ After assuring us that he was sober, Sam drove down the middle of the road, ran one red light,
went through
and two stop signs.

The revision adds a verb to make the three items parallel: *drove . . . , ran . . . , went through . . . .*

NOTE: In headings and lists, aim for as much parallelism as the content allows. (See 4a.)

9b Balance parallel ideas presented as pairs.

When pairing ideas, underscore their connection by expressing them in similar grammatical form. Paired ideas are usually connected in one of these ways:

— with a coordinating conjunction such as *and, but,* or *or*
— with a pair of correlative conjunctions such as *either . . . or* or *not only . . . but also*
— with a word introducing a comparison, usually *than* or *as*

Parallel ideas linked with coordinating conjunctions

Coordinating conjunctions (*and, but, or, nor, for, so,* and *yet*) link ideas of equal importance. When those ideas are closely parallel in content, they should be expressed in parallel grammatical form.

▶ At Lincoln High School, vandalism can result in
expulsion
suspension or even ~~being expelled~~ from school.

The revision balances the nouns *suspension* and *expulsion.*

▶ Many states are reducing property taxes for home-
extending
owners and ~~extend~~ financial aid in the form of tax credits to renters.

The revision balances the verb *reducing* with the verb *extending.*

Parallel ideas linked with correlative conjunctions

Correlative conjunctions come in pairs: *either . . . or, neither . . . nor, not only . . . but also, both . . . and, whether . . . or.* Make sure that the grammatical structure following the second part is the same as that following the first part.

▶ The shutters were not only too long but also ~~were~~ too wide.

> The words *too long* follow *not only*, so *too wide* should follow *but also.* Repeating *were* creates an unbalanced effect.

▶ I was advised either to change my flight or *to* ^ take the train.

> *To change my flight*, which follows *either*, should be balanced with *to take the train*, which follows *or.*

Comparisons linked with than or as

In comparisons linked with *than* or *as*, the elements being compared should be expressed in parallel grammatical structure.

▶ It is easier to speak in abstractions than *to ground* ~~ground-~~ ^ ing one's thoughts in reality.

▶ Mother could not persuade me that giving is as *receiving.* much a joy as ~~to receive.~~ ^

> *To speak in abstractions* is balanced with *to ground one's thoughts in reality. Giving* is balanced with *receiving.*

NOTE: Comparisons should also be logical and complete. (See 10c.)

9c Repeat function words to clarify parallels.

Function words such as prepositions (*by, to*) and subordinating conjunctions (*that, because*) signal the grammatical nature of the word groups to follow. Although they can sometimes be omitted, include them whenever they signal parallel structures that might otherwise be missed by readers.

▶ Many smokers try switching to a brand they find *to* distasteful or a low tar and nicotine cigarette. ^

> In the original sentence the prepositional phrase was too complex for easy reading. The repetition of the preposition *to* prevents readers from losing their way.

▶ The ophthalmologist told me that Julie was *that* extremely farsighted but corrective lenses would ^ help considerably.

> A second subordinating conjunction helps readers sort out the two parallel ideas: *that* Julie was extremely farsighted and *that* corrective lenses would help.

NOTE: If it is possible to streamline the sentence, repetition of the function word may not be necessary.

▶ The board reported that its investments had done well in the first quarter but ~~that they~~ had since dropped in value.

> Instead of linking two subordinate clauses beginning with *that*, the revision balances the two parts of a compound predicate — *had done well in the first quarter* and *had since dropped in value.*

EXERCISE 9–1 Parallelism: Guided practice

Edit the following paragraphs to correct faulty parallelism. Rule numbers in the margin refer to appropriate rules in section 9. The first revision has been done for you, and a suggested revision of this exercise appears in the back of the book.

In his own time, this sixteenth century man was known only by his given name, "Leonardo." Today he is still known by that one name. But then and now, that name suggests many different roles for its owner: theatrical producer, biologist, botanist, inventor, engineer, strategist, researcher, and artist.

Sixteenth-century Venetian soldiers knew Leonardo as a military strategist. When the Turkish fleet was invading their country, Leonardo suggested conducting surprise underwater attacks and ~~to flood~~ ^{flooding} the land that the Turkish army had to cross. Engineers knew him as the man who laid out new canals for the city of Milan. Scientists admired him for not only his precise anatomical drawings but also for his discovery that hardening of the arteries could cause death. To Milan's royal court, Leonardo was the artist who was painting impressive portraits, sculpting a bronze horse memorial to the house of Sforza, and at the same time worked on a mural of the Last Supper. *9b* *9b* *9a*

Leonardo understood things others did not. He saw a three-dimensional *s*-curve in all of nature — the flow of water, the movements of animals, and how birds flew. He called this curve "life-force." We recognize the same *s*-curve today in the spiraling form of DNA. Leonardo invented the wave theory. He saw that grain bending as the wind blew over it and water rippling from a stone cast into it were the same scientific event. It was as easy for him to see this wave in sound and light as observing it in fields and streams. The math of his day could not explain all his theories; it was the twentieth century before science showed the world that Leonardo knew what he was talking about. *9a* *9b*

Leonardo was not blind to the negative aspects of his world. He saw very clearly that the powers of nature could be infinitely destructive and human beings could be savage. At the same time, he felt a unity that held all life's varied parts together, a unity he could express in his art. *9c*

"Leonardo" — it's quite a name!

EXERCISE 9–2 Parallelism

All of the following sentences make an attempt to use parallel structure. Half of them succeed. The other five need revision. Put "OK" by the correct ones and edit the other five to correct faulty parallelism. Example:

> Leonardo spent the first years of his life playing in the fields, drawing animals and plants,
> *building*
> and ~~he built~~ miniature bridges and towers along the river.

1. When Leonardo moved to Florence to live with his father, he exchanged a slow-moving rural life for a fast-paced urban one.

2. Because his birth parents had not been married, many job opportunities were not available to Leonardo. He could not become a merchant, a banker, or a skilled craftsman.

3. It was no easier for Leonardo to attend the local university than learning a craft.

4. The obvious choices were to become a soldier or he could join the priesthood.

5. Leonardo did not want his future to be in either the church or the army.

6. Deciding that Leonardo could draw better than he could march or pray, his father placed him with a major artist, Andrea del Verrocchio.

7. Verrocchio's shop did work for all kinds of customers, including trade unions, churches, and they would do work for individuals also.

8. Living in Verrocchio's home and working in his shop, Leonardo heard talk of new theories about geography and science while he learned painting, sculpting, modeling, and how to cast bronze, silver, and gold figures.

9. Perhaps even more important was the variety of instruments Leonardo learned to make, among them musical, navigational, and ones for surgeons to use.

10. Working with Verrocchio was like going to three schools: an art school, a technology institute, and a liberal arts college.

EXERCISE 9–3 Parallelism

Circle the letter of the word or word group that best completes the parallel structure in each sentence. Example:

   Leonardo was handsome, generous, clever, and _____ .

   a. ambidextrous

   b. able to use either hand for most activities

   c. he could use either hand for most activities

1. Leonardo's life had three distinct periods: his childhood in Vinci, his apprenticeship in Florence, and _____ .

   a. when he was an adult

   b. his being an adult and earning his own way

   c. his adulthood in various Italian cities

2. In childhood, Leonardo had not only a loving family and relatives but also _____ .

   a. safe and unspoiled acres to explore

   b. he had the whole gentle slope of a mountain to explore

   c. including fields and vineyards to explore

3. However, two natural events haunted his memory for years: a hurricane destroyed much of the valley below his village, and _____ .

   a. a flood washed away much of the city of Florence

   b. a flood that washed away much of the city of Florence

   c. the boiling, muddy, surging waters of a flood

4. Wind and water became major topics for Leonardo's study. He decided that wind and water did many useful things but _____ .

   a. bad things too

   b. bad things too resulted from them

   c. that bad things too resulted from them

5. Viewers can find in many of Leonardo's works small round pebbles washed by a stream, riverbanks covered with moss and flowers, and _____ .

   a. little freshwater crabs partly hidden beneath rocks

   b. viewers can find small freshwater crabs under rocks

   c. little freshwater crabs sometimes hide beneath rocks

EXERCISE 9–4 Parallelism: Guided review

Edit the following paragraphs to correct faulty parallelism. Rule numbers in the margin refer to appropriate rules in section 9. The first revision has been done for you.

Leonardo's vision of life as one borderless unity affected both his personal   9b

life and ~~it affected~~ his artistic work.

Leonardo did not simply look at the world; he studied it carefully. Watching

the wind ripple the water in a pond, he was observant, intent, and in a serious mood.   9a

Leonardo saw no boundaries in nature; to him, people and animals were parts of

one creation. He ate no meat because he did not want to bring death to a fellow crea-

ture; he bought caged songbirds so that he could set them free. Having no family of

his own, he adopted a boy from another family to be both his son and he would be   9b

his heir. Even right- and left-handedness were the same to him. He filled his note-

books with mirror writing, but he wrote letters, reports, and proposals in the usual

way. When his right hand became crippled, he used his left.

Leonardo's view of all of life as one creation led him to artistic innovations. Be-

fore Leonardo, artists had always used outlines to separate a painting's subject from

its background. Because Leonardo saw everything in nature as interrelated, he decided

that using shadow and gradation of light and color was better than to use an outline.   9b

He wanted one thing to flow into another the way smoke flows into air. This painting

technique is called *sfumato*, Italian for "in the manner of smoke." Looking at Mona Lisa's

hand, for instance, viewers can find no line where one finger ends and the next one be-

gins; the separation is done totally with shadows. This unified vision of the world af-

fected the content of his paintings as well as the technique. Background and subject

often echo each other in a picture: the drapery and folds of the subject's clothing may

reflect background scenes of curving vines or rocky hills or water that flows.   9a

Leonardo recognized the great diversity surrounding him, but he believed

that an even greater unity supported the diversity and his own work was an ex-   9c

pression of that unity.

10 Add needed words.

Do not omit words necessary for grammatical or logical completeness. Readers need to see at a glance how the parts of a sentence are connected.

> **ESL** Languages sometimes differ in the need for certain words. In particular, be alert for missing verbs, articles, subjects, or expletives. See 29e, 30, and 31a.

> **GRAMMAR CHECKERS** do not flag the vast majority of missing words. They can, however, catch some missing verbs (see 27e). Although they can flag some missing articles (*a, an,* and *the*), they often suggest that an article is missing when in fact it is not. (See also 30.)

10a Add words needed to complete compound structures.

In compound structures, words are often omitted for economy: *Tom is a man who means what he says and [who] says what he means.* Such omissions are perfectly acceptable as long as the omitted words are common to both parts of the compound structure.

If the shorter version defies grammar or idiom because an omitted word is not common to both parts of the compound structure, the word must be put back in.

▶ Some of the regulars are acquaintances whom
    who
we see at work or ‸live in our community.

The word *who* must be included because *whom . . . live in our community* is not grammatically correct.

      accepted
▶ I never have ‸and never will accept a bribe.

Have . . . accept is not grammatically correct.

                                in
▶ Many of these tribes still believe ‸and live by

ancient laws.

Believe . . . by is not idiomatic in English.

NOTE: Even when the omitted word is common to both parts of the compound structure, occasionally it must be inserted to avoid ambiguity. The sentence *My favorite English professor and mentor influenced my choice of a career* suggests that the professor and mentor are the same person. If they are not, *my* must be repeated: *My favorite English professor and my mentor influenced my choice of a career.*

10b Add the word *that* if there is any danger of misreading without it.

If there is no danger of misreading, the word *that* may be omitted when it introduces a subordinate clause: *The value of a principle is the number of things [that] it will explain.* Occasionally, however, a sentence might be misread without *that.*

▶ Looking out the family room window, Sarah saw
    that
‸her favorite tree, which she had climbed so often

as a child, was gone.

Sarah didn't see the tree; she saw that the tree was gone.

                            that
▶ Many civilians believe ‸the air force has a

vigorous exercise program.

The word *that* tells readers to expect a clause, not just *the air force,* as the direct object of *believe.*

10c Add words needed to make comparisons logical and complete.

Comparisons should be made between items that are alike. To compare unlike items is illogical and distracting.

▶ Henry preferred the hotels in Pittsburgh to
    those in
‸Philadelphia.

Hotels must be compared with hotels.

▶ Some say that Ella Fitzgerald's renditions of Cole
                                  singer's.
Porter's songs are better than any other ~~singer.~~
                                          ‸

Ella Fitzgerald's renditions cannot be logically compared to a singer. The revision uses the possessive form *singer's*, with the word *renditions* being implied.

Sometimes the word *other* must be inserted to make a comparison logical.

>   *other*
> ▶ Chicago is larger than any city in Illinois.

Since Chicago is not larger than itself, the original comparison was not logical.

Sometimes the word *as* must be inserted to make a comparison grammatically complete.

>   *as,*
> ▶ Ben is as talented/ if not more talented than, the
>
> other actors.

The construction *as talented* is not complete without a second *as*: *as talented as . . . the other actors.*

Finally, comparisons should be complete enough to ensure clarity. The reader should understand what is being compared.

> **INCOMPLETE**
> Brand X is less salty.

> **COMPLETE**
> Brand X is less salty than Brand Y.

Also, there should be no ambiguity. In the following sentence, two interpretations are possible.

> **AMBIGUOUS**
> Ken helped me more than my roommate.

> **CLEAR**
> Ken helped me more than *he helped* my roommate.

> **CLEAR**
> Ken helped me more than my roommate *did*.

10d Add the articles *a, an,* and *the* where necessary for grammatical completeness.

Articles are sometimes omitted in recipes and other instructions that are meant to be followed while they are being read. Such omissions are inappropriate, however, in nearly all other forms of writing, whether formal or informal.

>   *a*   *an*
> ▶ Blood can be drawn only by doctor or by au-
>
> thorized person who has been trained
>   *the*
> in procedure.

It is not always necessary to repeat articles with paired items: *We bought a computer and printer.* However, if one of the items requires *a* and the other requires *an*, both articles must be included.

>   *an*
> ▶ We bought a computer and ink-jet printer.

ESL Articles can cause special problems for speakers of English as a second language. See 30.

EXERCISE 10–1 Needed words: Guided practice

Add any words needed for grammatical or logical completeness in the following paragraphs. Rule numbers in the margin refer to appropriate rules in section 10. The first revision has been done for you, and a suggested revision of this exercise appears in the back of the book.

Mary Wollstonecraft, an eighteenth-century writer, may have been England's first feminist. Her entire life reflected her belief in equal rights for women in all areas of their lives: personal, intellectual, and professional.

From childhood, she never had *accepted* and never would accept the idea that men were superior to women. As a young girl, she knew that her drinking and gambling father deserved less respect than her long-suffering mother. As an adult, she demanded that society give her the same freedom it gave to men. *10a*

Wollstonecraft also demanded men pay attention to her ideas. She did not argue about an idea. Instead, she gave an example of what she objected to and invited her readers to think about it from various points of view. Working this way, she made few enemies among intellectuals. Indeed, she was attracted and respected by some of the leading intellectuals of her day. Among them she was as well known on one side of the Atlantic as on the other. Tom Paine, the American orator and writer, probably knew her better than Samuel Johnson, the English writer. *10b* *10a* *10c*

Professionally, she was a governess, teacher, and writer. When her father's drinking destroyed the family, she and her sisters had to support themselves. After a stint as governess, Mary joined her two sisters in starting a girls' school. Eventually, financial problems forced the school to close, but not before Mary had acquired enough firsthand experience to write *Thoughts on the Education of Daughters* (1786). As competent or more competent than other writers of the day, she was a more persuasive advocate for women than most of them. *10c*

Modern feminists may find it ironic that current encyclopedia entries for "Wollstonecraft" refer researchers to "Godwin," her married name—where they will find an entry for her longer than her famous husband, William Godwin. *10c*

EXERCISE 10–2 Needed words

Circle the letter of the clearer sentence in each pair. Example:

a. Mary Wollstonecraft felt a woman did not have to marry a man in order to live with him.

(b.) Mary Wollstonecraft felt that a woman did not have to marry a man in order to live with him.

1a. She never married, or wanted to, her first liaison.

b. She never married, or wanted to marry, her first liaison.

2a. With Gilbert Imlay, she discovered that travel could teach her much about the business world.

b. With Gilbert Imlay, she discovered travel could teach her much about the business world.

3a. She had a more intellectual relationship with William Godwin than Gilbert Imlay.

b. She had a more intellectual relationship with William Godwin than with Gilbert Imlay.

4a. In one way she may have been as conservative as, if not more conservative than, other women of her day.

b. In one way she may have been as conservative, if not more conservative, than other women of her day.

5a. Marrying Godwin when she became pregnant may have shown that she believed in and acted by society's rules for pregnant women.

b. Marrying Godwin when she became pregnant may have shown that she believed and acted by society's rules for pregnant women.

EXERCISE 10–3 Needed words

Missing words make some of the following sentences ambiguous. Add the needed words so that only one meaning is possible. If a sentence is clear as written, mark it "OK." Example:

did.

Mary Wollstonecraft approved of the French Revolution more than Edmund Burke/
            ^

1. Mary Wollstonecraft blamed women's problems on the structure of society more than the men of her time.

2. Her ideas about women frightened other people less than her husband.

3. Her daughter, Mary Shelley, who wrote *Frankenstein*, became as famous as Wollstonecraft herself.

4. The readers Mary Shelley attracted were different from those who enjoyed her mother's work.

5. Modern readers know Mary Shelley better than Mary Wollstonecraft.

EXERCISE 10–4 Needed words: Guided review

Add any words needed for grammatical or logical completeness in the following paragraphs. Rule numbers in the margin refer to appropriate rules in section 10. The first revision has been done for you.

  Most people in her era found *that* Mary Wollstonecraft used very persuasive tech-   *10b*
niques. She did not argue and never had by directly attacking those who disagreed   *10a*
with her.

  More astute than other women of her day, she used anecdotal "observations."
She knew disarming stories and anecdotes would make her point best. Since she   *10b*
did not argue, her listeners never felt they had to defend their own positions and
were able to listen to her stories with reasonably open minds. The stories, which
often made clever use of allegory and metaphor, came from her own experience and
observation. Preferring examples from dressmaking to other occupations, she chose   *10c*
stories that illustrated her points and let the anecdotes speak for themselves. Her
technique was as convincing, or more convincing than, outright argument.   *10c*

  Mary Wollstonecraft's sense of timing was also good. In 1790, she wrote a
pamphlet entitled *A Vindication of the Rights of Men.* Part of her reason for writing
it was to respond to the excitement caused by the French Revolution (1789–99).
People liked her pamphlet very much. While enthusiasm was still high, she produced
A Vindication of the Rights of Woman in 1792. It, too, was well received.

  No doubt part of Mary Wollstonecraft's unusually effective writing came from
the fact that she not only believed in but also lived the ideas she wrote about.   *10a*

11   Untangle mixed constructions.

A mixed construction contains parts that do not sensibly fit together. The mismatch may be a matter of grammar or of logic.

> **GRAMMAR CHECKERS** can flag *is when, is where,* and *reason . . . is because* constructions (11c), but they fail to identify nearly all other mixed constructions, including sentences as tangled as this one: *Depending on the number and strength of drinks, the amount of time that has passed, and one's body weight determines the concentration of alcohol in the blood.*

11a   Untangle the grammatical structure.

Once you head into a sentence, your choices are limited by the range of grammatical patterns in English. (See 48 and 49.) You cannot begin with one grammatical plan and switch without warning to another.

> **MIXED**
> For most drivers who have a blood alcohol content of .05 percent double their risk of causing an accident.

> **REVISED**
> For most drivers who have a blood alcohol content of .05 percent, the risk of causing an accident is doubled.

> **REVISED**
> Most drivers who have a blood alcohol content of .05 percent double their risk of causing an accident.

The writer began with a long prepositional phrase that was destined to be a modifier but then tried to press it into service as the subject of the sentence. This cannot be done. If the sentence is to begin with the prepositional phrase, the writer must finish the sentence with a subject and verb (*risk . . . is doubled*). The writer who wishes to stay with the original verb (*double*) must head into the sentence another way: *Most drivers . . . .*

>   *Being*
> ▶ ~~When an employee is~~ promoted without warning
>   ^
>
>   can be alarming.

The adverb clause *When an employee is promoted without warning* cannot serve as the subject of the sentence. The revision replaces the adverb clause with a gerund phrase, a word group that can function as the subject. (See 49c.)

> ▶ Although many pre-Columbian peoples achieved a
>
>   high level of civilization, ~~but~~ they were unfamiliar
>
>   with the wheel.

The *Although* clause is subordinate, so it cannot be linked to an independent clause with the coordinating conjunction *but.*

Occasionally a mixed construction is so tangled that it defies grammatical analysis. When this happens, back away from the sentence, rethink what you want to say, and then say it again as clearly as you can.

> **MIXED**
> In the whole-word method children learn to recognize entire words rather than by the phonics method in which they learn to sound out letters and groups of letters.

> **REVISED**
> The whole-word method teaches children to recognize entire words; the phonics method teaches them to sound out letters and groups of letters.

> **ESL**
> English does not allow double subjects; nor does it allow an object or an adverb to be repeated in an adjective clause. See 31b and 31c.
>
> ▶ The squirrel that came down our chimney
>
>   ~~it~~ did much damage.
>
> ▶ Hearing screams, Serena ran over to the
>
>   pool that her daughter was swimming
>
>   in~~, it~~.
>   ^

11b Straighten out the logical connections.

The subject and the predicate should make sense together; when they don't, the error is known as *faulty predication.*

> ► We decided that ~~Tiffany's welfare~~ would not be
>
> safe living with her mother.
>
> *Tiffany*

Tiffany, not her welfare, may not be safe.

> ► Under the revised plan, the elderly/~~who now~~
>
> ~~receive a double personal exemption~~, will be
>
> abolished.
>
> *the double personal exemption for*

The exemption, not the elderly, will be abolished.

An appositive and the noun to which it refers should be logically equivalent. When they are not, the error is known as *faulty apposition.*

> ► ~~The tax accountant,~~ a very lucrative field,
>
> requires intelligence, patience, and attention to
>
> detail.
>
> *Tax accounting,*

The tax accountant is a person, not a field.

11c Avoid *is when, is where,* and *reason . . . is because* constructions.

In formal English many readers object to *is when, is where,* and *reason . . . is because* constructions on either grammatical or logical grounds. Grammatically, the verb *is* (as well as *are, was,* and *were*) should be followed by a noun that renames the subject or by an adjective that describes it, not by an adverb clause beginning with *when, where,* or *because.* (See 48b and 49b.) Logically, the words *when, where,* and *because* suggest relations of time, place, and cause — relations that do not always make sense with *is, was,* or *were.*

> ► Anorexia nervosa is ~~where people,~~ believing they
>
> are too fat, diet to the point of starvation.
>
> *a disorder suffered by people who,*

Anorexia nervosa is a disorder, not a place.

> ► ~~The reason~~ I missed the exam ~~is~~ because my
>
> motorcycle broke down.

The writer might have changed *because* to *that* (*The reason I missed the exam is that my motorcycle broke down*), but the revision above is more concise.

EXERCISE 11–1 Mixed constructions: Guided practice

Edit the following paragraphs to eliminate problems with mixed constructions. Rule numbers in the margin refer to appropriate rules in section 11. The first revision has been done for you, and a suggested revision of this exercise appears in the back of the book.

Sometimes it's hard to separate fact from fiction, to know what is history and what is folklore. For example, was there really a Casey Jones? Or are the stories about him simply legends? Casey Jones, John Henry, Johnny Appleseed, Uncle Sam, Santa Claus—which of these ~~names~~ were real men? Although we've been told **11b** stories about them all of our lives, but are those stories true? **11a**

There really was a railroad engineer people called "Casey" Jones; the reason he got that nickname was because of his birthplace, Cayce, Kentucky. There really **11c** was a "Cannonball" too; it was the Illinois-Central's fast mail train. And there really was a train wreck: Engine Number 382 rammed into some freight cars. The accident was not Casey's fault, and he died trying to save his passengers. When workers found his body in the wreckage, Casey's hand was still on the air brake lever. (The use of air brakes had recently been installed on trains to increase their braking power.) **11b**

John Henry was an African American railroad worker of great strength. In legend and song, he died after a timed contest against a steam drill. By using a hammer in each hand made him win the contest. John Henry drilled two holes seven **11a** feet deep; the steam drill bored only one nine-foot hole. The real John Henry died on the job too, crushed by rocks that fell from the ceiling of a railroad tunnel.

John Chapman, better known as Johnny Appleseed, was a wealthy and well-liked nurseryman who kept moving his place of business west as the frontier moved west. His boyhood friend Sam Wilson supplied meat to the United States troops during the War of 1812. A worker told a government inspector that the "U.S." stamped on the meat stood for "Uncle Sam." Although it was a joke, but it caught on, and **11a** Congress made the "Uncle Sam" identification official in the 1960s.

That leaves Santa Claus. As far as historians know now, Santa was not real. But legends say that there was once a man who . . .

EXERCISE 11-2 Mixed constructions

Use the technique suggested in brackets to correct the mixed constructions in the following sentences. Example:

> **What European first set eyes on America? If you say Amerigo Vespucci, from whom the name "America" is said to derive, ~~so~~ you'll be only half right. [Delete one word.]**

1. Although Vespucci claimed to have found a new continent, but there is no evidence that he ever got to any land in the Western Hemisphere. [Delete one word.]

2. Columbus may have seen parts of the Americas first, but when a German mapmaker believed Vespucci's claim and put Vespucci's name on the map explains why the lands became known as America. [Delete two words and add a comma.]

3. If Vespucci wasn't the first European to find land across the Atlantic, so who was? [Delete one word.]

4. For most British historians who have worked on the question say John Cabot got there first. [Delete one word and capitalize another.]

5. Early mariners, a very dangerous occupation, often sailed under several names. [Insert *who worked at* where it best fits.]

6. "John Cabot" was the name for Italian mariner Giovanni Caboto used when he worked for the English. [Delete one word.]

7. Some people say that Leif Eriksson saw the coast of North America first; their reason is because he established a small community on Newfoundland about A.D. 1000. [Change one word to *that*.]

8. Even though Eriksson's community was established five hundred years before the time of Vespucci, Columbus, and Cabot, but the Norse sagas claim that Bjarni Herjulfsson sighted North America before Eriksson did. [Delete one word.]

9. The growth in the number of theories increases as new evidence is found. [Delete three words.]

10. So who was the first European on American shores? As these bits of history indicate that no one can really answer that question. [*Either* delete one word and capitalize another *or* delete one word and add a comma.]

EXERCISE 11–3 Mixed constructions

Read through each sentence just once. If it sounds correct to you, put "OK" after it. If it sounds like a mixed construction, put "MC" after it. Then go back and check; only four of the sentences should have "OK" after them. Fix the others. Example:

Do you believe that ~~because of~~ Paul Revere's late-night horseback ride alerted minutemen from Boston to Lexington to Concord that the British were coming? _MC_

1. In college, most American students discover that their knowledge of history is a mixture of fact and fiction. _____

2. For example, most students believe that Paul Revere rode alone, alerting citizens from Boston to Concord that the British were coming. In fact, Revere did not ride alone and he never made it to Concord. _____

3. Since he was able to borrow a horse permitted Revere to get as far as Lexington. _____

4. By adding two other riders, William Dawes and Samuel Prescott, made it possible to get the warning to Concord. _____

5. The vigilance of a group of British soldiers on patrol overtook all three men, captured Revere, and found out who he was. _____

6. The reason minutemen reported promptly for duty was because they were warned by relays of riders who had been alerted by prearranged signals. _____

7. If Henry Wadsworth Longfellow had not written a poem about the ride forty-five years after Revere's death, so Revere might never have become famous. _____

8. Before that poem appeared, Paul Revere's name was not on any list of important people in America. _____

9. The increase in the number of times his name appeared on such lists after the poem was published was enough to make him famous. _____

10. Is fiction more powerful than fact? Is all our knowledge such a mixture of fact and fiction? _____

EXERCISE 11–4 Mixed constructions: Guided review

Edit the following paragraphs to eliminate problems with mixed constructions. Rule numbers in the margin refer to appropriate rules in section 11. The first revision has been done for you.

What did Paul Revere do when he wasn't working for the Revolution? Quite apart from his famous ride, Paul Revere made other significant contributions to American life and culture.

The basic reason for all these contributions was ~~because~~ *that* Paul Revere was an   *11c*
enterprising entrepreneur. He originally followed his father into silversmithing. Soon after the war started, he began making gunpowder. He designed and printed paper money and made the state seal that Massachusetts still uses. By carving false teeth   *11a*
from rhinoceros tusks was one of his efforts to make money; publishing hymnbooks was another. He engraved copper plates for printing. He ran a hardware store and erected barns for local farmers.

Until Revere built the first rolling mill for copper in the United States, so all   *11a*
rolled copper had to be imported. He set up the equipment to cast bronze and made cannon for the army, copper fittings for the USS *Constitution* (Old Ironsides), and bells for churches. Seventy-five of his bells still ring from New England church steeples.

As a silversmith, a very creative field, Revere displayed great talent and skill.   *11b*
His silver pieces were so beautifully designed and crafted that two hundred years later one of his punch bowls brought an offer of a hundred thousand dollars. One reason that antique lovers today search for silver objects marked "Revere" is because   *11c*
Revere's work is so graceful. Modern artisans still try to duplicate his decorated grooves and flowing lines. And shoppers admire certain smoothly curved bowls are   *11a*
known as Revere bowls whether they are made of silver or of some other metal.

Paul Revere, whether or not he rode all the way to Concord, made an indelible impression on American life and culture.

12 Repair misplaced and dangling modifiers.

Modifiers, whether they are single words, phrases, or clauses, should point clearly to the words they modify. As a rule, related words should be kept together.

 GRAMMAR CHECKERS can flag split infinitives, such as *to carefully and thoroughly sift* (12d). However, they don't alert you to other misplaced modifiers or dangling modifiers, including danglers like this one: *When a young man, my mother enrolled me in tap dance classes, hoping I would become the next Gregory Hines.*

12a Put limiting modifiers in front of the words they modify.

Limiting modifiers such as *only, even, almost, nearly,* and *just* should appear in front of a verb only if they modify the verb: *At first, I couldn't even touch my toes, much less grasp them.* If they limit the meaning of some other word in the sentence, they should be placed in front of that word.

only
► Lasers ~~only~~ destroy the target, leaving the sur-

rounding healthy tissue intact.

► Because three of its star players were injured,
even
our team didn't ~~even~~ score once.

Only limits the meaning of *the target,* not *destroy. Even* modifies *once,* not *score.*

The limiting modifier *not* is frequently misplaced, suggesting a meaning the writer did not intend.

Not all
► ~~All~~ wicker is ~~not~~ antique.

The original version means that no wicker is antique. The revision makes the writer's real meaning clear.

12b Place phrases and clauses so that readers can see at a glance what they modify.

Although phrases and clauses can appear at some distance from the words they modify, make sure your meaning is clear. When whole phrases or clauses are oddly placed, absurd misreadings can result.

MISPLACED
The king returned to the clinic where he had undergone heart surgery in 1992 in a limousine sent by the White House.

REVISED
Traveling in a limousine sent by the White House, the king returned to the clinic where he had undergone heart surgery in 1992.

The revision corrects the false impression that the king underwent heart surgery in a limousine.

On the walls
► ~~There~~ are many pictures of comedians who have

performed at Gavin's. ~~on the walls~~.

The comedians weren't performing on the walls; the pictures were on the walls.

150-pound,
► The robber was described as a six-foot-tall man

with a heavy mustache. ~~weighing 150 pounds~~.

The robber, not the mustache, weighed 150 pounds. The revision makes this clear.

Occasionally the placement of a modifier leads to an ambiguity, in which case two revisions will be possible, depending on the writer's intended meaning.

AMBIGUOUS
The exchange students we met for coffee occasionally questioned us about our latest slang.

CLEAR
The exchange students we occasionally met for coffee questioned us about our latest slang.

CLEAR
The exchange students we met for coffee questioned us occasionally about our latest slang.

In the original version, it was not clear whether the meeting or the questioning happened occasionally. The revisions eliminate the ambiguity.

12c Move awkwardly placed modifiers.

As a rule, a sentence should flow from subject to verb to object, without lengthy detours along the way. When a long adverbial element separates a subject from its verb, a verb from its object, or a helping verb from its main verb, the result is usually awkward.

▶ ~~Our son,~~ ~~after~~ doctors told him that he would
  A
  our son
never walk without a cane, began an intensive
  ^

program of rehabilitation.

There is no reason to separate the subject *Our son* from the verb *began* with a long adverb clause.

▶ ~~Oscar Lewis spent,~~ ~~in~~ researching *The Children*
  I
  Oscar Lewis spent
of Sanchez, hundreds of hours living with the
  ^

Sanchez family in a slum of Mexico City.

The *in* phrase needlessly separated the verb *spent* from its object, *hundreds of hours.*

▶ ~~Many students have,~~ ~~by~~ the time they reach their
  B
  many students have
senior year, completed all the graduation
  ^

requirements for their major.

The helping verb *have* should be closer to its main verb, *completed.*

EXCEPTION: Occasionally a writer may choose to delay a verb or an object to create suspense. In the following passage, for example, Robert Mueller inserts the *after* phrase between the subject *women* and the verb *walk* to heighten the dramatic effect.

I asked a Burmese why women, after centuries of following their men, now walk ahead. He said there were many unexploded land mines since the war.
— Robert Mueller

ESL English does not allow an adverb to appear between a verb and its object. See 31d.
  easily.
▶ Yolanda lifted ~~easily~~ the fifty-pound weight.✓

12d Do not split infinitives needlessly.

An infinitive consists of *to* plus a verb: *to think, to breathe, to dance.* When a modifier appears between *to* and the verb, an infinitive is said to be "split": *to carefully balance.* If a split infinitive is obviously awkward, it should be revised.

  If possible, the
▶ ~~The~~ patient should try to, ~~if possible,~~ avoid
  ^

going up and down stairs.

Usage varies when a split infinitive is less awkward than the preceding one. To be on the safe side, however, you should not split such infinitives, especially in formal writing.

▶ The candidate decided to ~~formally~~ launch her
  formally
campaign.
  ^

When a split infinitive is more natural and less awkward than alternative phrasing, most readers find it acceptable: *We decided to actually enforce the law* is a perfectly natural construction in English. *We decided actually to enforce the law* is not.

12e Repair dangling modifiers.

A dangling modifier fails to refer logically to any word in the sentence. Dangling modifiers are usually introductory word groups (such as verbal phrases) that suggest but do not name an actor. When a sentence opens with such a modifier, readers expect the subject of the following clause to name the actor. If it doesn't, the modifier dangles.

DANGLING MODIFIERS

Deciding to join the navy, the recruiter enthusiastically pumped Joe's hand. [*Participial phrase*]

Upon seeing the barricade, our car screeched to a halt. [*Preposition followed by a gerund phrase*]

To please the children, some fireworks were set off a day early. [*Infinitive phrase*]

Though only sixteen, UCLA accepted Martha's application. [*Elliptical adverb clause with an understood subject and verb*]

Checking for dangling modifiers

First look for the most common trouble spots:

SENTENCES OPENING WITH A VERBAL

There are three kinds of verbals (see also 49c):

-ing verb forms such as *walking* (present participles)

-ed, -d, -en, -n, or *-t* verb forms such as *planted, eaten, taught* (past participles)

to verb forms such as *to become* (infinitives)

▶ Excited about winning the championship, a rau- *we held*

  cous celebration ~~was held~~ in the locker room.

SENTENCES OPENING WITH A WORD GROUP CONTAINING A VERBAL

I swam

▶ After ~~swimming~~ across the lake, the lifeguard

  scolded me for risking my life.

SENTENCES OPENING WITH AN ELLIPTICAL CLAUSE (A CLAUSE WITH OMITTED WORDS)

I was

▶ Although only four years old, my father insisted

  that I learn to read.

Next test your sentences for dangling modifiers:

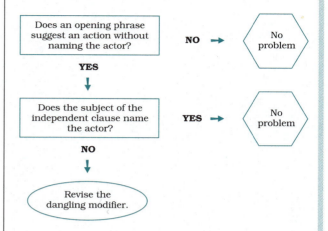

If you find a dangling modifier, revise the sentence in one of two ways:

1. Change the subject of the independent clause so that it names the actor implied by the modifier.
2. Turn the modifier into a word group that includes the actor.

These dangling modifiers falsely suggest that the recruiter decided to join the navy, that the car saw the barricade, that the fireworks intended to please the children, and that UCLA is only sixteen years old.

To repair a dangling modifier, you can revise the sentence in one of two ways:

1. Name the actor immediately following the introductory modifier or
2. turn the modifier into a word group that includes the actor.

I noticed

▶ Upon entering the doctor's office, a skeleton.

  ~~caught my attention.~~

As I entered

▶ ~~Upon entering~~ the doctor's office, a skeleton

  caught my attention.

A dangling modifier cannot be repaired simply by moving it: *A skeleton caught my attention upon entering the doctor's office.* The sentence still suggests—absurdly—that the skeleton entered the doctor's office.

When the driver opened

▶ ~~Opening~~ the window to let out a huge bumble-

  bee, the car accidentally swerved into an oncom-

  ing car.

The car didn't open the window; the driver did. The writer has revised the sentence by putting the driver in the opening modifier.

women have often been denied

▶ After completing seminary training, ~~women's~~

  access to the pulpit. ~~has often been denied.~~

The women (not their access to the pulpit) complete seminary training. The writer has revised the sentence by making *women* (not *women's access*) the subject.

EXERCISE 12–1 Misplaced and dangling modifiers: Guided practice

Edit the following paragraphs to eliminate misplaced and dangling modifiers. Rule numbers in the margin refer to appropriate rules in section 12. The first revision has been done for you, and a suggested revision of this exercise appears in the back of the book.

people usually think of

Hearing the name Karl Marx, Russia. ~~is usually the first thought that comes~~ ~~to mind.~~ Marx never lived in Russia at all. Actually, he almost spent all of his adult life in England. He was a political exile for the last half of his life. *12e* *12a*

Marx lived first in Germany. Born of Jewish parents, his university studies were completed with a Ph.D. at the University of Jena. His favorite professor tried to get Marx an appointment to teach at the university. When that professor was fired, Marx gave up hope of teaching at Jena or any other German university. Marx, because he was denied a university position, had to earn his living as a journalist. He worked briefly as a newspaper editor in Germany. *12e* *12c*

Next came France, Belgium, and a return to Germany. First Marx and his new bride moved to Paris, where Marx worked for a radical journal and became friendly with Friedrich Engels. When the journal ceased publication, Marx moved to Brussels, Belgium, and then back to Cologne, Germany. He did not hold a regular job, so he tried desperately to at least earn enough money to feed his family. *12d*

Marx decided after living in Paris and Brussels he would settle in London. He and his family lived in abject poverty while Marx earned what little income he could by writing for an American newspaper, the *New York Tribune*. *12b*

EXERCISE 12–2 Misplaced modifiers

Circle the letter of the more effective sentence in each pair. Example:

    a. Marx almost spent all his time writing, using every waking moment to get his ideas down on paper.

   (b.) Marx spent almost all his time writing, using every waking moment to get his ideas down on paper.

1a. Between 1852 and 1862, Marx just wrote more than three hundred articles for the *New York Tribune.*

  b. Between 1852 and 1862, Marx wrote more than three hundred articles just for the *New York Tribune.*

2a. During his lifetime, Marx did not receive much attention. But people all over the world paid attention to what he had written after his death.

  b. During his lifetime, Marx did not receive much attention. But after his death, people all over the world paid attention to what he had written.

3a. He wanted only one thing for himself: recognition of the importance of his ideas.

  b. He only wanted one thing for himself: recognition of the importance of his ideas.

4a. Capitalist scholars tend to usually say that Marx's work is "illogical" and "uninformed."

  b. Capitalist scholars usually tend to say that Marx's work is "illogical" and "uninformed."

5a. However, most capitalists agree that as a student of social organization, he was brilliant.

  b. However, most capitalists agree that he, as a student of social organization, was brilliant.

EXERCISE 12–3 Misplaced and dangling modifiers

Circle the letter of the more effective sentence in each pair. Be prepared to explain your choice. Example:

    a. **Deciding that there were two classes of people in the world, they were named the "bourgeoisie" and the "proletariat."**

    (b.) **Deciding that there were two classes of people in the world, Marx named them the "bourgeoisie" and the "proletariat."**

1a. Convinced that one major difference divided the people of the world into two groups, ownership of property was declared the basis for this division.

  b. Convinced that one major difference divided the people of the world into two groups, Marx declared that ownership of property was the basis for this division.

2a. Marx defined anyone who owned property as bourgeois.

  b. Owning property of any kind, the property defined its owner as bourgeois.

3a. Marx defined the proletariat as those who owned no property but labored to always produce wealth for the bourgeoisie.

  b. Marx defined the proletariat as those who owned no property but always labored to produce wealth for the bourgeoisie.

4a. After finishing his study of economic history, Marx concluded that history is progressive and maybe even inevitable.

  b. Marx, after finishing his study of economic history, concluded that history is progressive and maybe even inevitable.

5a. Denying God any role in human affairs, economic history was seen as a natural evolution in the world.

  b. Denying God any role in human affairs, Marx saw economic history as a natural evolution in the world.

EXERCISE 12–4 Misplaced and dangling modifiers: Guided review

Edit the following paragraphs to eliminate misplaced and dangling modifiers. Rule numbers in the margin refer to appropriate rules in section 12. The first revision has been done for you.

The Communist Manifesto, Marx's most famous work, was written in collaboration with Friedrich Engels, Marx's best friend, just before the German revolution of 1848. It had three sections with distinct characteristics.

In the first part, Marx tries to ~~accurately~~ define terms *accurately* and to state his basic   12d
assumptions. He traces the class systems of earlier times and concludes that there are only two classes in his day, the bourgeoisie and the proletariat. The bourgeoisie are the property-owning capitalists; the proletariat are the working class. Marx asserts that as the bourgeoisie increase their economic power, they work toward their own eventual downfall.

Set up in question-and-answer format, Marx made the second section of his   12e
Communist Manifesto resemble a debate with a bourgeois sympathizer. Of course, Marx only sees one side of the debate as being correct. After "defeating" his oppo-   12a
nent on major questions, Marx presents his own ten-point program in clear, easy-to-understand, persuasive language.

Marx, after developing the second part in detail, moves on to the final sec-   12c
tion of the *Manifesto*. He shows how Communists and other reform groups work toward the same goals. Reminding workers that they "have nothing to lose but their chains," Marx calls on them to zealously work together. Marx utters the slogan that   12d
can still be heard today in ringing tones: "Workers of the world, unite!"   12b

13 Eliminate distracting shifts.

 GRAMMAR CHECKERS do not flag the shifts discussed in this section: shifts in point of view; shifts in verb tense, mood, or voice; and shifts between direct and indirect questions or quotations. Even the most obvious errors like this one will slip right past most grammar checkers: *My three-year-old fell into the pool and to my surprise she swims to the shallow end.*

13a Make the point of view consistent in person and number.

The point of view of a piece of writing is the perspective from which it is written: first person (*I* or *we*), second person (*you*), or third person (*he/she/it/one* or *they*). The *I* (or *we*) point of view, which emphasizes the writer, is a good choice for informal letters and writing based primarily on personal experience. The *you* point of view, which emphasizes the reader, works well for giving advice or explaining how to do something. The third-person point of view, which emphasizes the subject, is appropriate in formal academic and professional writing.

 Writers who are having difficulty settling on an appropriate point of view sometimes shift confusingly from one to another. The solution is to choose a suitable perspective and then stay with it.

▶ One week our class met in a junkyard to practice

 rescuing a victim trapped in a wrecked car. We

 learned to dismantle the car with the essential

 tools. ~~You~~ *We* were graded on ~~your~~ *our* speed and ~~your~~ *our*

 skill in extricating the victim.

The writer should have stayed with the *we* point of view. *You* is inappropriate because the writer is not addressing readers directly. *You* should not be used in a vague sense meaning "anyone." (See 23d.)

▶ *You*
~~Everyone~~ should purchase a lift ticket unless

 you plan to spend most of your time walking or

 crawling up a steep hill.

Here *you* is an appropriate choice because the writer is giving advice directly to readers.

▶ *Police officers are*
~~A police officer is~~ often criticized for always being

 there when they aren't needed and never being

 there when they are.

Although the writer might have changed *they* to *he* or *she* (to match the singular *officer*), the revision in the plural is more concise. (See also 17f and 22a.)

13b Maintain consistent verb tenses.

Consistent verb tenses clearly establish the time of the actions being described. When a passage begins in one tense and then shifts without warning and for no reason to another, readers are distracted and confused.

▶ There was no way I could fight the current and win.
 jumped
 Just as I was losing hope, a stranger ~~jumps~~ off a
 swam
 passing boat and ~~swims~~ toward me.

 Writers often encounter difficulty with verb tenses when writing about literature. Because fictional events occur outside the time frames of real life, the past and the present tenses may seem equally appropriate. The literary convention, however, is to describe fictional events consistently in the present tense.

▶ The scarlet letter is a punishment sternly placed

 upon Hester's breast by the community, and yet it
 is
 ~~was~~ an extremely fanciful and imaginative product

 of Hester's own needlework.

13c Make verbs consistent in mood and voice.

Unnecessary shifts in the mood of a verb can be as distracting as needless shifts in tense. There are three moods in English: the *indicative,* used for facts, opinions, and questions; the *imperative,* used for orders or advice; and the *sub-*

junctive, used for wishes or conditions contrary to fact (see 28b).

The following passage shifts confusingly from the indicative to the imperative mood.

> The officers warned us not to allow anyone
>   *They also suggested that we*
> into our homes without proper identification. ~~Also,~~
>   ^
> alert neighbors to vacation schedules.

Since the writer's purpose was to report the officers' advice, the revision puts both sentences in the indicative.

A verb may be in either the active voice (with the subject doing the action) or the passive voice (with the subject receiving the action). (See 28c.) If a writer shifts for no reason from one to the other, readers may be left wondering why.

> When the tickets are ready, the travel agent
>   *lists each ticket*
> notifies the client/, ~~Each ticket is then listed~~ on a
>   ^
>   *files*
> daily register form, and a copy of the itinerary. ~~is~~
>   ^   ^
> ~~filed.~~

The passage began in the active voice (*agent notifies*) and then switched to the passive (*ticket is listed, copy is filed*). Because the active voice is clearer and more direct, the writer changed all the verbs to the active voice.

13d   Avoid sudden shifts from indirect to direct questions or quotations.

An indirect question reports a question without asking it: *We asked whether we could take a swim.* A direct question asks directly: *Can we take a swim?* Sudden shifts from indirect to direct questions are awkward. In addition, sentences containing such shifts are impossible to punctuate because indirect questions must end with a period and direct questions must end with a question mark. (See 38b.)

> I wonder whether the sister knew of the theft and,
>   *whether she reported*
> if so, ~~did she report~~ it to the police.
>   ^

The revision poses both questions indirectly. The writer could also ask both questions directly: *Did the sister know of the theft and, if so, did she report it to the police?*

An indirect quotation reports someone's words without quoting word for word: *Annabelle said that she is a Virgo.* A direct quotation presents the exact words of a speaker or writer, set off with quotation marks: *Annabelle said, "I am a Virgo."* Unannounced shifts from indirect to direct quotations are distracting and confusing, especially when the writer fails to insert the necessary quotation marks, as in the following example.

> Mother said that she would be late for dinner and
>   *asked me not to*
> ~~please do not~~ leave for choir practice until Dad
> ^
> *came*
> ~~comes~~ home.
> ^

The revision reports the mother's words. The writer could also quote directly: *Mother said, "I will be late for dinner. Please do not leave for choir practice until Dad comes home."*

EXERCISE 13–1 Distracting shifts: Guided practice

Edit the following paragraphs to eliminate distracting shifts. Rule numbers refer to appropriate rules in section 13. The first revision has been done for you, and a suggested revision of this exercise appears in the back of the book.

Do you know how slavery began in America or how *it ended?* ~~did it end~~? When the   *13d*
Mayflower landed in September 1620, slaves were already in America. A Dutch ship
had unloaded and sold twenty Africans in Jamestown, Virginia, the year before.

But slavery in America began long before that. Many early explorers brought
slaves with them to the new land, and some historians claim that one of the men in
Christopher Columbus's crew was a slave. From the 1500s to the 1800s, slave ships
brought ten million African slaves across the ocean.

Most of the slaves stayed in Latin America and the West Indies, but the southern part of the United States receives about six percent of them. Few northerners   *13b*
owned slaves, and opposition to slavery was evident by the time of the American
Revolution. Rhode Island prohibited the importation of slaves even before the Revolutionary War. After the war, six northern states abolished slavery at once. Others
passed laws to phase out slavery, and even Virginia enacted legislation encouraging
you to emancipate your slaves.   *13a*

But it took a war, a tricky political situation, and a very clever former slave
to free all slaves. History gives Lincoln the credit for liberating the slaves during the
Civil War, and he deserves some credit, but emancipation was not his idea. Originally, no one in government seriously considered emancipation because they were   *13a*
so focused on winning the war to save the Union. But then a very important black
man talks to Lincoln and gives him the idea and the reason. This man said that free-   *13b*
ing slaves would be good for the war effort and would Lincoln agree to do it? Who   *13d*
was this man? He was Frederick Douglass, fugitive slave and newspaper editor.

EXERCISE 13–2 Distracting shifts

A. Edit the following sentences to eliminate distracting pronoun shifts. If a sentence is correct, mark it "OK." Example:

> Frederick Douglass was born a slave, but he was lucky because his owner's wife did not
>
> *her*
> know that it was against the law for ~~you~~ to teach a slave to read and write.
>   ^

1. A slave who learned to read and write gained self-confidence, so they were harder to oversee than illiterate slaves.

2. When he had learned enough to study on his own, the slave Frederick Douglass did so; he used what he had learned to escape from his owner.

3. The master had told his slaves that all escape routes were blocked and that you would have no chance whatever at success.

4. Douglass used a simple but dangerous method of escape; he sailed from Baltimore to New York as a working sailor.

5. A listener could not learn anything about escape routes from Douglass's stories because Douglass told them nothing that would endanger other fugitives.

B. Edit the following sentences to eliminate distracting shifts in verb tense. If a sentence is correct, mark it "OK." Example:

>   *describes*
> Douglass's narrative tells about his own life as a child and ~~described~~ his torturous beatings
>   ^
> by a professional "slave breaker."

6. Douglass had few ties to his mother and never meets his father.

7. Even when Douglass worked "out" for his master, his master got his wages.

8. His master sometimes allowed him to keep one percent (six cents out of six dollars); the master thought the money would encourage Douglass to work harder.

9. Douglass escapes by pretending to be someone else; he borrowed the identification papers of a freed black sailor.

10. Frederick Douglass used several different names as he escaped slavery; an abolitionist friend suggests "Douglass" to him and Frederick uses it from that time on.

EXERCISE 13–3 Distracting shifts

Edit the following sentences to eliminate shifts between direct and indirect quotation or question. Example:

whether he

When Frederick was told to choose a new name, he asked ~~could~~ could ~~he~~ keep "Frederick" and take a new last name.

1. When a friend suggested "Douglass" as a last name, Frederick asked whether it was a satisfactory name and did it fit well with "Frederick"?

2. People frequently asked Douglass how did he feel when he found himself in a free state.

3. Lonely and frightened at the time, he said, "I can trust no man" and that he saw every white man as an enemy, every black man as a cause for distrust.

4. Douglass was befriended by David Ruggles, an abolitionist who asked him what did he plan to do.

5. Douglass married Anna and told her that they would move to New Bedford and don't worry because he would surely get a job there.

EXERCISE 13–4 Distracting shifts: Guided review

Edit the following paragraphs to eliminate any distracting shifts. Rule numbers in the margin refer to appropriate rules in section 13. The first revision has been done for you.

Frederick Douglass, who was born a slave and became a much sought after lecturer and writer, was a man of strong will and convictions.

Douglass never hesitated to defend the choices he ~~makes~~ *made* for himself and his   13b
family. On trains he sat in cars reserved for "whites only" until security officers
dragged him away. He walked out of a church when it was realized that none of his   13c
people could participate in the service until the white people were through.

Wherever he lived, Douglass fought slavery. When he published his autobiography, *Narrative of the Life of Frederick Douglass*, in 1845, he was still a fugitive
slave. He and his wife moved to England the same year because he feared that his
book would reveal his identity as a fugitive slave. Also, some of his other writings
had aroused so much animosity that he fears for his life. From England, he wrote   13b
letters and worked to gain support for freeing the slaves. After friends in England
raised enough money to buy his freedom for him, he was even more determined
to help others gain their freedom. (Slaves used to say that a free black was never
there when you needed help, but no one could ever say that about Frederick   13a
Douglass.)

Douglass was outspoken in his support for the causes he believed in. When
the Civil War broke out, Douglass comes back to the United States to help recruit   13b
African Americans to fight. "This war is for you and your children," he told them.
Douglass also supported women's suffrage, and he defended the right of members
of different races to marry if they wished. When Douglass married his second wife,
a white woman, critics complained. He answered them by saying, "My first wife was
the color of my mother" and that the second was the color of his father, so he was   13d
not playing favorites.

14 Emphasize your point.

Within each sentence, emphasize your point by expressing it in the subject and verb, the words that receive the most attention from readers. As a rule, choose an active verb and pair it with a subject that names the person or thing doing the action.

Within longer stretches of prose, you can draw attention to ideas deserving special emphasis by using a variety of techniques, usually involving an unusual twist or some element of surprise.

14a Prefer active verbs.

Active verbs express meaning more emphatically and vigorously than their weaker counterparts—forms of the verb *be* or verbs in the passive voice. Forms of the verb *be* (*be, am, is, are, was, were, being, been*) lack vigor because they convey no action. Verbs in the passive voice lack strength because their subjects receive the action instead of doing it (see 28c and 48c). Although the forms of *be* and passive verbs have legitimate uses, if an active verb can carry your meaning, use it.

> **BE VERB**
> A surge of power *was* responsible for the destruction of the pumps.

> **PASSIVE**
> The pumps *were destroyed* by a surge of power.

> **ACTIVE**
> A surge of power *destroyed* the coolant pumps.

Even among active verbs, some are more active—and therefore more vigorous and colorful—than others. Carefully selected verbs can energize a piece of writing.

> ► The goalie crouched low, ~~reached~~ out his stick, *swept*
> and ~~sent~~ the rebound away from the net. *hooked*

When to replace *be* verbs

Not every *be* verb needs replacing. The forms of *be* (*be, am, is, are, was, were, being, been*) work well when you want to link a subject to a noun that clearly renames it or to an adjective that

describes it: *History is a bucket of ashes. Scoundrels are always sociable.* And when used as helping verbs before present participles (*is flying, are disappearing*) to express ongoing action, *be* verbs are fine: *Derrick was plowing the field when his wife went into labor.* (See 29a.)

If using a *be* verb makes a sentence needlessly wordy, however, consider replacing it. Often a phrase following the verb will contain a word (such as *destruction*) that suggests a more vigorous, active alternative (*destroyed*).

> ► Burying nuclear waste in Antarctica would ~~be in violation of~~ an international treaty. *violate*

> *Violate* is less wordy and more vigorous than *be in violation of.*

> ► Escaping into the world of drugs, I ~~was rebellious about~~ every rule set down by my parents. *rebelled against*

> *Rebelled against* is more active than *was rebellious about.*

When to replace passive verbs

In the active voice, the subject of the sentence does the action; in the passive, the subject receives the action.

> **ACTIVE**
> Hernando *caught* the fly ball.

> **PASSIVE**
> The fly ball *was caught* by Hernando.

In passive sentences, the actor (in this case *Hernando*) frequently disappears from the sentence: *The fly ball was caught.*

In most cases, you will want to emphasize the actor, so you should use the active voice. To replace a passive verb with an active alternative, make the actor the subject of the sentence.

> ► ~~The transformer was struck by a bolt of lightning,~~ plunging us into darkness. *A bolt of lightning struck the transformer,*

> The active verb (*struck*) makes the point more forcefully than the passive verb (*was struck*).

The passive voice is appropriate when you wish to emphasize the receiver of the action or to minimize the importance of the actor. For example, in the sentence about the fly ball, you would choose the active voice if you wanted to emphasize the actor, Hernando: *Hernando caught the fly ball.* But you would choose the passive voice if you wanted to emphasize the ball and the catch: *The fly ball was caught by Hernando.* (See 28c.)

Some speakers of English as a second language avoid the passive voice even when it is appropriate. For advice on appropriate uses of the passive, see 28c.

GRAMMAR CHECKERS are fairly good at flagging passive verbs, such as *were given* (14a), but some passive verbs slip past these programs. Two words of caution are in order, however. First, because passive verbs are sometimes appropriate, you—not the computer program—must decide whether to make a passive verb active. (See 14a and 28c for guidelines on choosing active or passive verbs.)

Second, grammar checkers sometimes incorrectly flag verbs as passive. It's not surprising that a computer program can't distinguish between a true passive, such as *is managed*, and a *be* verb followed by a past participle functioning as an adjective, such as *are indebted.*

14b   **As a rule, choose a subject that names the person or thing doing the action.**

In weak, unemphatic prose, both the actor and the action may be buried in sentence elements other than the subject and the verb. In the following sentence, for example, the actor and the action both appear in prepositional phrases, word groups that do not receive much attention from readers.

> **WEAK**
> Exposure to Dr. Martinez's excellent teaching had the effect of inspiring me to major in education.

> **EMPHATIC**
> Dr. Martinez's excellent teaching inspired me to major in education.

Consider the subjects and verbs of the two versions—*exposure had* versus *teaching inspired.* Clearly the latter expresses the writer's point more emphatically.

14c   **Experiment with techniques for gaining special emphasis.**

By experimenting with certain techniques, usually involving some element of surprise, you can draw attention to ideas that deserve special emphasis. Use such techniques sparingly, however, or they will lose their punch. The writer who tries to emphasize everything ends up emphasizing nothing.

Using sentence endings for emphasis

You can highlight an idea simply by withholding it until the end of a sentence. The technique works something like a punch line. In the following example, the sentence's meaning is not revealed until its very last word.

> The only completely consistent people are the dead.
> —Aldous Huxley

Two types of sentence that withhold information until the end deserve special mention: the inversion and the periodic sentence. The *inversion* reverses the normal subject-verb order, placing the subject at the end, where it receives unusual emphasis. (Also see 15c.)

> In golden pots are hidden the most deadly poisons.
> —Thomas Draxe

The *periodic* sentence opens with a pile-up of modifiers and withholds the subject and verb until the end. It draws attention to itself because it contrasts with the cumulative sentence, which is used more frequently. A *cumulative* sentence begins with the subject and verb and adds modifying elements at the end.

> **PERIODIC**
> Twenty-five years ago, at the age of thirteen, while hiking in the mountains near my hometown of Vancouver, Washington, I came face to face with the legendary Goat Woman of Livingston Mountain.   — Tom Weitzel, student

CUMULATIVE

A metaphysician is one who goes into a dark cellar at midnight without a light, looking for a black cat that is not there.
———Baron Bowan of Colwood

Using parallel structure for emphasis

Parallel grammatical structure draws special attention to paired ideas or to items in a series. (See 9.) When parallel ideas are paired, the emphasis falls on words that underscore comparisons or contrasts, especially when they occur at the end of a phrase or clause.

> We must *stop talking* about the *American dream* and *start listening* to the *dreams of Americans.*
> ———Reubin Askew

In a parallel series, the emphasis falls at the end, so it is generally best to end with the most dramatic or climactic item in the series.

> Sister Charity enjoyed passing out writing punishments: translate the Ten Commandments into Latin, type a thousand-word essay on good manners, copy the New Testament with a quill pen.
> ———Marie Visosky, student

Using punctuation for emphasis

Obviously the exclamation point can add emphasis, but you should not overuse it. As a rule, the exclamation point is more appropriate in dialogue than in ordinary prose.

> I oozed a glob of white paint onto my palette, whipped some medium into it, loaded my brush, and announced to the class, "Move over, Michelangelo. Here I come!"
> ———Carolyn Goff, student

A dash or a colon may be used to draw attention to word groups worthy of special attention. (See 35a, 35b, and 39a.)

> The middle of the road is where the white line is—and that's the worst place to drive.
> ———Robert Frost

> I turned to see what the anemometer read: The needle had pegged out at 106 knots.
> ———Jonathan Shilk, student

Occasionally, a pair of dashes may be used to highlight a word or an idea.

> [My friend] was a gay and impudent and satirical and delightful young black man—a slave—who daily preached sermons from the top of his master's woodpile, with me for sole audience.
> ———Mark Twain

Using an occasional short sentence for emphasis

Too many short sentences in a row will fast become monotonous (see 8a), but an occasional short sentence, when played off against longer sentences in the same passage, will draw attention to an idea.

> The great secret, known to internists and learned early in marriage by internists' wives [or husbands], but still hidden from the general public, is that most things get better by themselves. Most things, in fact, are better by morning.
> ———Lewis Thomas

EXERCISE 14–1 Sentence emphasis: Guided practice

The following paragraph contains no grammar or punctuation errors. It does have some sentences that could be more emphatic. Revise those sentences. Rule numbers in the margin refer to appropriate revision strategies in section 14. The first revision has been made for you, and a suggested revision of this exercise appears in the back of the book.

Frederick Douglass immensely enjoyed
~~Imagining~~ his favorite fantasy about slave owners. ~~was something that Frederick Douglass enjoyed immensely.~~ In Douglass's dream, everyone conspired against   **14a**

the slave owners. No hint of an impending escape was given by slaves still in   **14a**

bondage. People who helped escaping slaves never indicated that they did so. Slaves

who escaped successfully never revealed how they got away. Owners were told noth-   **14a**

ing at all by slaves they recaptured. Even some white southerners who sympathized

with the slaves gave no information to their slave-owning friends. The part of his   **14b**

fantasy that Douglass enjoyed the most was the final part. In it, slave owners were   **14a**

imagined by Douglass as being too afraid to hunt escaping slaves. The owners were   **14a**

distrustful of their slaves, their enemies, and even their friends.

EXERCISE 14–2 Sentence emphasis

Half of the following sentences contain passive verbs or verbs that are a form of *be*. Find them and change them to active verbs. You may need to invent a subject for some verbs, and you may need to make major revisions in some sentences. If a sentence already contains only active verbs, mark it "active." Example:

> *P*
> ~~Frederick Douglass was annoyed by~~ people who spoke openly of helping on the
> *annoyed Frederick Douglass.*
> underground railroad⁄

1. Douglass said that by talking openly about it, these people had turned the "underground railroad" into an "upperground railroad."

2. Although these people were deserving of praise, their open talk endangered escaping slaves.

3. Such talk alerted slave owners to possible escape routes.

4. Escaping slaves would often be caught by professional slave hunters at the houses of those who talked openly.

5. All slaves were threatened by any information that increased the slave owners' knowledge.

6. Whenever slave owners suspected some of the escape routes, the courage of the slaves was lost.

7. Frederick Douglass understood the slaves' fears very well; his first attempt to escape had failed.

8. Professional slave breakers beat and tortured runaway slaves until the slaves submitted or died.

9. His own treatment at the hands of the slave breakers left Douglass with severe, disfiguring scars all over his back.

10. Years later, northerners were convinced by those scars that Douglass spoke the truth about slavery.

EXERCISE 14–3 Sentence emphasis

In each sentence, experiment with techniques for gaining special emphasis by following the directions in brackets. Example:

> *After what happened to him the first time,*
> Frederick Douglass almost did not try a second time to escape slavery/after what happened
>
> to him the first time. [Use a periodic sentence beginning with *After.*]

1. Douglass would be unable to try again if he failed the second time. [Start the sentence with *If.*]

2. In addition to beatings, failure could bring death, imprisonment, sale to a sadistic owner, or broken bones. [Rearrange the series to put the most dramatic or climactic item last.]

3. Douglass could already hear in his mind the baying of the dogs and the slave hunter's shout: "Good dogs. Go get him." [Use attention-getting punctuation for the slave hunter's words.]

4. A tremendous fear rose in his imagination, but it was not only a fear for his physical safety. [Use an inversion starting with *In his imagination rose.*]

5. Frederick Douglass also dreaded leaving behind all the things he had grown to love, the warm winters, the music, the friends of a lifetime. [Use attention-getting punctuation after the word *love.*]

Name _____ Section _____ Date _____

EXERCISE 14–4 Sentence emphasis: Guided review

Edit the following paragraph so that each verb is active and each subject names the person or thing doing the action. Rule numbers in the margin refer to appropriate revision strategies in section 14. The first revision has been done for you.

changed some of his

~~Some of~~ Frederick Douglass's ideas about the North ~~were changed~~ after his   14a

successful escape from slavery. The assumption that Douglass had always made   14b

was that northerners had no money and no culture. This assumption was based on   14a

his observations of southerners who did not own slaves. In Douglass's experience,

only poor people owned no slaves. Poor people also owned no lovely homes, no pi-

anos, no art, and often no books. When he first saw New Bedford, Massachusetts,

Douglass was doubtful of his own eyesight. He saw no dilapidated houses or naked   14a

children or barefoot women in New Bedford. Instead, the beautiful homes with

equally beautiful furniture and gardens were an indication of considerable wealth.   14a

Expensive merchandise was handled by laborers on the wharves and in the stores.   14a

When he saw all of this, Douglass happily changed his ideas about the North.

15   Provide some variety.

When a rough draft is filled with too many same-sounding sentences, try injecting some variety — as long as you can do so without sacrificing clarity or ease of reading.

> **GRAMMAR CHECKERS** are of little help with sentence variety. It takes a human ear to know when and why sentence variety is needed.
>
> Some programs tell you when you have used the same word to open several sentences, but sometimes it is a good idea to do so — if you are trying to highlight parallel ideas, for example (see pp. 74–75).

15a   Vary your sentence openings.

Most sentences in English begin with the subject, move to the verb, and continue along to the object, with modifiers tucked in along the way or put at the end. For the most part, such sentences are fine. Put too many of them in a row, however, and they become monotonous.

Adverbial modifiers, being easily movable, can often be inserted ahead of the subject. Such modifiers might be single words, phrases, or clauses. (See 49.)

▶ *Eventually a*
A few drops of sap ~~eventually~~ began to trickle into the bucket.

Like most adverbs, *eventually* does not need to appear close to the verb it modifies (*began*).

▶ *Just as the sun was coming up, a*
A pair of black ducks flew over the blind. ~~just as the sun was coming up.~~

The adverb clause, which modifies the verb *flew*, is as clear at the beginning of the sentence as it is at the end.

Adjectives and participial phrases can frequently be moved to the beginning of a sentence.

▶ *Dejected and withdrawn,*
Edward, ~~dejected and withdrawn,~~ nearly gave up his search for a job.

▶ *A   John and I*
~~John and I,~~ anticipating a peaceful evening, sat down at the campfire to brew a cup of coffee.

CAUTION: When beginning a sentence with an adjective or a participial phrase, make sure that the subject of the sentence names the person or thing described in the introductory phrase. If it doesn't, the phrase will dangle. (See 12e.)

15b   Use a variety of sentence structures.

A writer should not rely too heavily on simple and compound sentences, for the effect tends to be both monotonous and choppy. (See 8a and 8b.) Too many complex or compound-complex sentences, however, can be equally monotonous. If your style tends to one or the other extreme, try to achieve a better mix of sentence types.

The major sentence types are illustrated in the following sentences, all taken from Flannery O'Connor's "The King of the Birds," an essay describing the author's pet peafowl.

SIMPLE
Frequently the cock combines the lifting of his tail with the raising of his voice.

COMPOUND
Any chicken's dusting hole is out of place in a flower bed, but the peafowl's hole, being the size of a small crater, is more so.

COMPLEX
The peacock does most of his serious strutting in the spring and summer when he has a full tail to do it with.

COMPOUND-COMPLEX
The cock's plumage requires two years to attain its pattern, and for the rest of his life, this chicken will act as though he designed it himself.

For a fuller discussion of sentence types, see 50a.

15c Try inverting sentences occasionally.

A sentence is inverted if it does not follow the normal subject-verb-object pattern. (See 48c.) Many inversions sound artificial and should be avoided except in the most formal contexts. But if an inversion sounds natural, it can provide a welcome touch of variety.

▶ *Opposite the produce section is a*
A refrigerated case of mouth-watering cheeses;

~~is opposite the produce section;~~ a friendly

attendant will cut off just the amount you want.

The revision inverts the normal subject-verb order by moving the verb, *is*, ahead of its subject, *case*.

▶ *Set at the top two corners of the stage were huge*
Huge lavender hearts outlined in bright white

lights. ~~were set at the top two corners of the stage.~~

In the revision the subject, *hearts*, appears after the verb, *were set*. Notice that the two parts of the verb are also inverted—and separated from one another—without any awkwardness or loss of meaning.

Inverted sentences are used for emphasis as well as for variety. (See 14c.)

15d Consider adding an occasional question or quotation.

An occasional question can provide a welcome change of pace, especially at the beginning of a paragraph, where it engages the reader's interest.

> Virginia Woolf, in her book *A Room of One's Own*, wrote that in order for a woman to write fiction she must have two things, certainly: a room of her own (with key and lock) and enough money to support herself.
> *What then are we to make of Phillis Wheatley, a slave, who owned not even herself?...* [Italics added.]   —Alice Walker

Quotations can also provide variety, for they add other people's voices to your own. These other voices might be bits of dialogue:

> When we got back upstairs, Dr. Haney and Captain Shiller, the head nurse, were waiting for us by the elevator. As the nurse hurried off, pushing Todd, the doctor explained to us what would happen next.
> "Mrs. Barrus," he began, "this last test is one we do only when absolutely necessary. It is very painful and hard on the patient, but we have no other choice." Apologetically, he went on. "I cannot give him an anesthetic." He waited for the statement to sink in.
>   —Celeste L. Barrus, student

Or they might be quotations from written sources:

> Even when she enters the hospital on the brink of death, the anorexic will refuse help from anyone and will continue to deny needing help, especially from a doctor. At this point, reports Dr. Steven Levenkron, the anorexic is most likely "a frightened, cold, lonely, starved, and physically tortured, exhausted person—not unlike an actual concentration camp inmate" (29). In this condition she is ultimately force-fed through a tube inserted in the chest.
>   —Jim Drew, student

Notice that the quotation from a written source is documented with a citation in parentheses.

EXERCISE 15–1 Sentence variety: Guided practice

The following paragraph is grammatically correct but dull. Revise it to add variety. You may need to combine some sentences. Rule numbers in the margin refer to appropriate revision strategies in section 15. The first revision has been done for you, and a suggested revision of this exercise appears in the back of the book.

> *After studying*
> Everyone has heard of Martin Luther King, Jr. ~~He studied~~ for the ministry at   *15b, 15a (See also 8b.)*
> *earning*
> Boston University and ~~earned~~ a doctorate in theology, ~~and then~~ he went home to the
> South to work as a minister. He started working in civil rights and became the most
> influential leader of that cause in America. When he died, the victim of an assas-
> sin's bullet, his name was almost synonymous with "civil rights." Historians and bi-
> ographers have recorded his leadership in the fight to gain basic civil rights for all
> Americans. Many people who know of his civil rights work, however, are not aware
> of his skill as a writer. King produced other important writing in addition to his care-   *15a*
> fully crafted and emotional speeches.
>
> King's "Letter from a Birmingham Jail" is among his most famous writings.   *15c*
> He wrote it to answer a statement published by eight Alabama ministers that King's   *15b, 15a (See also 8b.)*
> work was "unwise and untimely," and the letter shows King to be a man who had
> great patience with his critics. King is eager to get these ministers to accept his point   *15a (See also 8b.)*
> of view, so he reminds them that they are ministers. Their goodwill, he says, should
> help them see that his views hold value. He does not attack them personally. He an-   *15a (See also 8a.)*
> alyzes their arguments. Then he presents his own views. Does he use many of the
> emotional appeals for which he is justly famous? No, in this letter King depends on
> logic and reasoning as the tools to win his argument.

EXERCISE 15–2 Sentence variety

Edit each of the following sentences in at least two ways, to provide varied openings and varied sentence structures. You may need to change other parts of the sentence as well. Example:

a. ~~Martin Luther King, Jr., was in~~ *In* jail awaiting a hearing, *Martin Luther King, Jr.,* he read a newspaper article attacking his work.

b. *When* Martin Luther King, Jr., was in jail awaiting a hearing, he read a newspaper article attacking his work.

1a.   King didn't have much to write on in the jail, so he started writing on the margins of the newspaper in which the article appeared.

  b.   King didn't have much to write on in the jail, so he started writing on the margins of the newspaper in which the article appeared.

2a.   A black trusty, wanting to help King, was able to get some scraps of paper for him after a while.

  b.   A black trusty, wanting to help King, was able to get some scraps of paper for him after a while.

3a.   His attorneys were later allowed to give him a pad of paper. King, fired up by the newspaper article, quickly filled the pad.

  b.   His attorneys were later allowed to give him a pad of paper. King, fired up by the newspaper article, quickly filled the pad.

4a.   King chose to write his response to the newspaper article in letter form, so he seemed like the biblical Paul to some people.

  b.   King chose to write his response to the newspaper article in letter form, so he seemed like the biblical Paul to some people.

5a.   How were King and Paul alike? Paul, a preacher of the Christian faith like King, wrote his famous letters from a prison cell.

  b.   How were King and Paul alike? Paul, a preacher of the Christian faith like King, wrote his famous letters from a prison cell.

EXERCISE 15–3 Sentence variety: Guided review

The following paragraph is grammatically correct but dull. Revise it to add variety. You may need to combine some sentences. Rule numbers in the margin refer to appropriate revision strategies in section 15. The first revision has been done for you.

Martin Luther King's famous "Letter from a Birmingham Jail" has a clearly
                                    Beginning
thought out structure. ~~Dr. King begins~~ with the statement that any nonviolent cam-
                                          --
paign has to go through four distinct stages, ~~He says these stages are~~ fact finding,   *15a or 15b*
                                    --Dr. King
negotiation, self-purification, and direct action, ~~He~~ says that he and his fellow cam-

paigners have gone through all these steps in Birmingham. King tries to reach his   *15a*

readers after that beginning by asking them how to answer his children's questions

about why they cannot go to the amusement park advertised on TV. Then the letter   *15a or 15b*
                                                                                          (See also
discusses the difference between just and unjust laws, and it emphasizes the need   *8b.)*

for nonviolent direct action to dramatize the unjust ones. Next King mentions the

"white moderates." He expresses his disappointment with white religious leaders and   *15a or 15b*
                                                                                          (See also
white churches who have failed to join the civil rights movement, but he praises the   *8b.)*

few who have helped. He describes the mistreatment he and his friends have suf-   *15a or 15b*
                                                                                          (See also
fered at the hands of the local police, and he gives thanks for the courage of the peo-   *8a.)*

ple involved in sit-ins and bus strikes. Dr. King writes finally of his faith. He has   *15a*

faith that the movement will survive and prosper and that racial prejudice will soon

pass away.

Unit review (8–15): Clear sentences

Edit the following paragraphs, referring to the section numbers in the margin for suggested revision techniques. The first revision has been done for you.

One of the men who greatly influenced Martin Luther King, Jr., was Mahatma

Gandhi, ~~and he~~ *who* introduced nonviolent techniques in Africa and India. Gandhi is   *8b*

called the father of his country, and he helped India gain its freedom from England.   *8b*

Gandhi's nonviolent method was based on three principles: courage, being truthful,   *9a*

and you had to have endurance. By using nonviolent techniques is how Gandhi   *11a*

helped Indians in Africa and India.

After studying law in London, he attempts to practice law in India but is not   *13b*

very successful. He then went to South Africa to do legal work in 1893. He was   *8a or 15b*

abused in South Africa because he was an Indian who also claimed the rights of a

British subject. Although he had planned to stay in Africa one year, he was there

for twenty-one years. Fighting injustice in South Africa, the principle of *satyagraha*   *12e*

(nonviolent protest) was developed by Gandhi during those years.

After working in South Africa, the Indian movement for independence made   *12e*

Gandhi return to India to lead it. While in India, he led hundreds of his followers on

a march to the sea, where they made salt from seawater to protest a law that re-

quired them to buy all their salt from the government. He also began programs of

hand weaving and spinning among the poor that exist to this day.   *12b*

Although Gandhi believed and lived by the nonviolent principle of *satya-*   *10a*

graha, he died a violent death. In 1948 he was assassinated by a high-caste Hindu

fanatic. This man feared Gandhi's tolerance for all creeds and religions. Neverthe-   *8a*

less, Gandhi's nonviolent methods have survived to this day in people like Martin

Luther King, Jr.

Word Choice

16 Tighten wordy sentences.

17 Choose appropriate language.

18 Find the exact words.

16 Tighten wordy sentences.

Long sentences are not necessarily wordy, nor are short sentences always concise. A sentence is wordy if it can be tightened without loss of meaning.

> **GRAMMAR CHECKERS** can flag some, but not all, wordy constructions. Most programs alert you to common redundancies, such as *true fact,* and empty or inflated phrases, such as *in my opinion* or *in order that.* In addition, they alert you to wordiness caused by passive verbs, such as *is determined* (see also 14a). They are less helpful in identifying sentences with needlessly complex structures.

16a Eliminate redundancies.

Redundancies such as *cooperate together, close proximity, basic essentials,* and *true fact* are a common source of wordiness. There is no need to say the same thing twice.

▶ Mr. Barker still hasn't paid last month's rent. ~~yet.~~

▶ Black slaves were ~~called or~~ stereotyped as lazy even though they were the main labor force of the South.

works

▶ Daniel ~~is now employed~~ at a private rehabilitation center ~~working~~ as a registered physical therapist.

Though modifiers ordinarily add meaning to the words they modify, occasionally they are redundant.

▶ Sylvia ~~very hurriedly~~ scribbled her name and address on the back of a greasy napkin.

▶ Joel was determined ~~in his mind~~ to lose weight.

The words *scribbled* and *determined* already contain the notions suggested by the modifiers *very hurriedly* and *in his mind.*

16b Avoid unnecessary repetition of words.

Though words may be repeated deliberately, for effect, repetitions will seem awkward if they are clearly unnecessary. When a more concise version is possible, choose it.

▶ Our fifth patient, in room six, is ~~a~~ mentally ill. ~~patient.~~

137

Reviewing your writing for wordy sentences

Look especially for these common trouble spots:

REDUNDANCIES (16a)

▶ Passive euthanasia is the ~~act or~~ practice of allowing terminally ill patients to die.

▶ The colors of the reproductions were ~~precisely~~ exact.

UNNECESSARY REPETITION OF WORDS (16b)

▶ ~~The quilt that was~~ *T*he highlight of Grandmother's collection was a crazy quilt dating from 1889.

EMPTY OR INFLATED PHRASES (16c)

▶ Although ~~it seemed that~~ it was unlikely that the call was for me, I was so excited that I ran to the phone.

▶ The ring costs ~~in the neighborhood of~~ *about* sixty dollars.

NEEDLESSLY INDIRECT STRUCTURES (16d)

▶ The institute was established to ~~provide training~~ *train* for highway agency employees.

▶ ~~There was a~~ *A* deranged vagrant *was* pestering the persons in line, spouting biblical quotations one minute and shouting obscenities the next.

▶ ~~It is imperative that~~ *A*ll police officers *must* follow strict procedures when apprehending a suspect.

▶ Last summer, a horse~~.~~ *my parents gave me* ~~was given to me by my parents.~~

NEEDLESSLY COMPLEX STRUCTURES (16e)

▶ We visited Charlottesville, ~~which is~~ the home of the historic University of Virginia.

▶ Our landlord was an elderly bachelor, *who taught us* ~~and it was through his guidance that we were able~~ to appreciate country life.

▶ When I approached the window, the guard took the form~~.~~ ~~He~~ asked me a few questions, and then ~~he~~ told me to see another guard, who would do a physical search.

▶ The best teachers help each student to ~~become a~~ *grow* ~~better student~~ both academically and emotionally.

16c Cut empty or inflated phrases.

An empty phrase can be cut with little or no loss of meaning. Common examples are introductory word groups that apologize or hedge: *in my opinion, I think that, it seems that, one must admit that,* and so on.

▶ ~~In my opinion, our~~ *Our* current immigration policy is misguided on several counts.

▶ ~~It seems that~~ *Lonesome Dove* is one of Larry McMurtry's most ambitious novels.

Readers understand without being told that they are hearing the writer's opinion or educated guess.

Inflated phrases can be reduced to a word or two without loss of meaning.

INFLATED	CONCISE
along the lines of	like
at this point in time	now
by means of	by
due to the fact that	because
for the purpose of	for

INFLATED	CONCISE
for the reason that	because
in order to	to
in spite of the fact that	although, though
in the event that	if
in the final analysis	finally
in the neighborhood of	about
until such time as	until

► We will file the appropriate papers ~~in the event~~ *if*

~~that~~ we are unable to meet the deadline.

► ~~Due to the fact that~~ the guest of honor is ill, the *Because*

party is being postponed until next Saturday.

16d Simplify the structure.

If the structure of a sentence is needlessly indirect, try simplifying it. Look for opportunities to strengthen the verb.

► The financial analyst claimed that because of

volatile market conditions she could not ~~make an~~

estimate ~~of~~ the company's future profits.

The verb *estimate* is more vigorous and more concise than *make an estimate of.*

The colorless verbs *is, are, was,* and *were* frequently generate excess words.

► The secretary ~~is responsible for monitoring and~~ *monitors and balances*

~~balancing~~ the budgets for travel, contract

services, and personnel.

The revision is more direct and concise. Actions originally appearing in subordinate structures have become verbs replacing *is.*

The expletive constructions *there is* and *there are* (or *there was* and *there were*) can also generate excess words. The same is true of expletive constructions beginning with *it.* (See 48c.)

► ~~There is~~ another module ~~that~~ tells the story of *A*

Charles Darwin and introduces the theory of

evolution.

► ~~It is important that~~ hikers remain inside the park *H must*

boundaries.

Expletive constructions do have legitimate uses, however. For example, they are appropriate when a writer has a good reason for delaying the subject. (See 48c.)

Finally, verbs in the passive voice may be needlessly indirect. When the active voice expresses your meaning as well, use it. (See 14a and 28c.)

► All too often, athletes with marginal academic *our coaches have recruited*

skills ~~have been recruited by our coaches~~.

16e Reduce clauses to phrases, phrases to single words.

Word groups functioning as modifiers can often be made more compact. Look for any opportunities to reduce clauses to phrases or phrases to single words.

► We took a side trip to Monticello, ~~which was~~ the

home of Thomas Jefferson.

► For her birthday we gave Jess a stylish vest ~~made~~ *silk*

~~of silk.~~

EXERCISE 16–1 Wordy sentences: Guided practice

Edit the following paragraph to make any wordy sentences as short as possible without changing their meaning. Rule numbers in the margin refer to appropriate strategies in section 16. The first two revisions have been made for you, and a suggested revision of this exercise appears in the back of the book.

Adam Smith, the founder of modern economics, proposed a theory in the eighteenth century that has made him controversial ever since. This ~~British~~ econo-   *16a*
mist, ~~who was~~ born in Scotland and educated in England, wrote the first complete   *16e*
study of political economy. *The Wealth of Nations* was published in the same year
that Americans declared their independence from England—that was in 1776.   *16e*
Smith's book pointed out and directed attention to the interdependence of freedom   *16a*
and order, economic processes, and free trade laws. Although Smith's thinking did
not really affect economic policies significantly during his lifetime, its influence in
the next century was considerable. Among economists, "the invisible hand" and
"laissez-faire" are synonymous with Smith's name. History has only made Smith's
ideas more controversial. Say "Adam Smith" to conservative businesspeople, and
those same people will smile and make a response with words like "He was a good   *16b, 16d*
man—really understood how business works!" Say "Adam Smith" to liberal reformers, and they will grimace and mutter something along the lines of "He was an   *16c*
evil man—really sold the average citizen down the river." Both of these reactions
are extreme, but such responses indicate that the controversy aroused by Smith's
ideas is still alive.

EXERCISE 16–2 Wordy sentences

Tighten the following sentences by eliminating redundancies, unnecessary repetition, and empty phrases. The number in parentheses at the end of each sentence is a suggested maximum number of words for your revision. You may have fewer than that number, but try not to exceed it. Example:

> ~~It is a fact that~~ Adam Smith wanted to find a theory ~~that would~~ _{to} explain how the economic world functions. (14)

1. It seems that after many years of study and then years of writing, he published a book that was called *The Wealth of Nations*. (16)

2. This lengthy, protracted book had in the neighborhood of a thousand pages, and those pages included a sixty-three-page index. (12)

3. The full and complete title of his book indicates the comprehensive, all-inclusive scope of the book: *An Inquiry into the Nature and Causes of the Wealth of Nations*. (20. Do not shorten the twelve-word title.)

4. Smith believed that there were certain basic, essential economic laws in existence and that these laws would work to the benefit of everyone if people would "let the market alone." (19)

5. He believed that something along the lines of an "invisible hand" guided economics. (10)

EXERCISE 16–3 Wordy sentences

Tighten the following sentences by simplifying structure and reducing clauses to phrases or phrases to single words. Do not change the meaning of any sentence. The number in parentheses at the end of each sentence is a suggested maximum number of words for your revision. Example:

> Adam Smith saw the market as ~~something that was~~ "self-regulating" ~~as long as~~ everyone left
> *if*
> it alone. (12)

1. Adam Smith said that there were two laws that governed the field of economics. (8)

2. The first basic, important, essential law that governed the field of economics was self-interest. (5, but can you do it in 3?)

3. The one who is employed wants a higher wage; the one who employs the worker wants a higher profit. (12)

4. The second law, which is the law of competition, works only if there is no manipulation of the market by anyone. (12)

5. Because people will buy the gloves that cost the least, a manufacturer of gloves cannot raise prices for gloves too much without bringing about the result that people who buy gloves go to competitors who sell gloves for a lower price. (25)

6. The term that has been given to Smith's "let the market alone" policy by economists is "laissez-faire." (9)

7. Adam Smith urged governments to practice the policy of laissez-faire with the resulting effect that would allow "the invisible hand" to regulate the marketplace. (16)

8. Smith assumed that there was a "law of accumulation" that worked by requiring industrialists to add buildings and machinery, to hire more workers, and to produce more goods. (23)

9. There was another law that he called the "law of population" that would supply the workers that were necessary. (11)

10. In the long run, said Smith, those who did the work would be paid, the industrialists who employed those who did the work would make a fair profit, and the landlords who rented space to the industrialists would have many tenants. (22)

EXERCISE 16–4 Wordy sentences: Guided review

Edit the following paragraph to make any wordy sentences as short as possible without changing their meaning. Rule numbers in the margin refer to appropriate strategies in section 16. The first wordy sentence has been revised for you.

Adam Smith was convinced ~~in his mind~~ that if people would "let the market   *16a*

alone," all would be well. The true facts about how the market operated during the   *16a*

next century would have distressed him. The industrialists chose Smith as the pa-

tron saint for industrialists. Working to make sure that the government "let the mar-   *16b*

ket alone," they opposed even laws that forbade shackling children to the machines

that were operated by them. By means of agreements that were secret, they agreed   *16d, 16e*

to charge identical prices. Similarly, workers agreed to demand the same wages from

every employer. Neither employers nor employees followed Adam Smith's injunction

to let the market alone. There is no doubt that Adam Smith would be disappointed   *16c*

in the way his economic theories have been used—and misused.

17   Choose appropriate language.

Language is appropriate when it suits your subject, engages your audience, and blends naturally with your own voice.

To some extent, your choice of language will be governed by the conventions of the genre in which you are writing. When in doubt about the conventions of a particular genre—lab reports, informal essays, business memos, and so on—take a look at models written by experts in the field.

17a   Stay away from jargon.

Jargon is specialized language used among members of a trade, profession, or group. Use jargon only when readers will be familiar with it; even then, use it only when plain English will not do as well.

Sentences filled with jargon are likely to be long and lumpy. To revise such sentences, you must rewrite them, usually in fewer words.

JARGON

For years the indigenous body politic of South Africa attempted to negotiate legal enfranchisement without result.

REVISED

For years the native population of South Africa negotiated in vain for the right to vote.

Though a political scientist might feel comfortable with the original version, jargon such as *body politic* and *legal enfranchisement* is needlessly complicated for ordinary readers.

Broadly defined, jargon includes puffed-up language designed more to impress readers than to inform them. The following are common examples from business, government, higher education, and the military, with plain English translations in parentheses.

ameliorate (improve)
commence (begin)
components (parts)
endeavor (try)
exit (leave)
facilitate (help)
factor (consideration, cause)
impact (v.) (affect)
indicator (sign)
optimal (best, most favorable)
parameters (boundaries, limits)
peruse (read, look over)
prior to (before)
utilize (use)
viable (workable)

Sentences filled with jargon are hard to read, and they are often wordy as well.

▶ All ~~employees functioning in the capacity of~~ *must prove that they are* work-study students ~~are required to give~~ *currently enrolled.* ~~evidence of current enrollment.~~

▶ Mayor Summers will ~~commence~~ *begin* his term of *improving* office by ~~ameliorating~~ living conditions in *poor neighborhoods.* ~~economically deprived zones.~~

17b   Avoid pretentious language, most euphemisms, and "doublespeak."

Some writers think that using large words and flowery phrases make them sound intelligent or poetic, but such language in fact sounds pretentious. In addition, it often hides the writer's real thoughts.

▶ When our ~~progenitors reach their silver-haired~~ *parents become old,* ~~and golden years,~~ we frequently ~~ensepulcher~~ *entomb* *old-age homes* them in ~~homes for senescent beings~~ as if they *dead.* were already among the ~~deceased.~~

The writer of the original sentence had turned to a thesaurus (a dictionary of synonyms and antonyms) in an attempt to sound educated. When such a writer gains enough confidence to speak in his or her own voice, pretentious language disappears.

Related to pretentious language are euphemisms, nice-sounding words or phrases substituted for words thought to sound harsh or ugly. Like pretentious language, euphemisms are wordy and indirect. Unlike pretentious language, they are sometimes appropriate. It is our social custom, for example, to use euphemisms when speaking or writing about death (*Her sister passed on*), excretion (*I have to go to the bathroom*), sexual intercourse (*They did not sleep together until they were married*), and the like. We may also use euphemisms out of concern for someone's feelings. Telling parents, for example, that their daughter is "unmotivated" is more sensitive than saying she's lazy. Tact or politeness, then, can justify an occasional euphemism.

Most euphemisms, however, are needlessly evasive or even deceitful. Like pretentious language, they obscure the intended meaning.

EUPHEMISM	PLAIN ENGLISH
adult entertainment	pornography
preowned automobile	used car
economically deprived	poor
selected out	fired
negative savings	debts
strategic withdrawal	retreat or defeat
revenue enhancers	taxes
chemical dependency	drug addiction
downsize	lay off
correctional facility	prison

The term *doublespeak*, coined by George Orwell in his novel *1984*, applies to any deliberately evasive or deceptive language, including euphemisms. Doublespeak is especially common in politics, where missiles are named "Peacekeepers," airplane crashes are termed "uncontrolled contact with the ground," and a military retreat is described as "tactical redeployment." Business also gives us its share of doublespeak. When the manufacturer of a pacemaker writes that its product "may result in adverse health consequences in pacemaker-dependent patients as a result of sudden 'no output' failure," it takes an alert reader to grasp the message: The pacemaker might suddenly

 GRAMMAR CHECKERS can be helpful in identifying jargon and pretentious language. For example, they commonly advise against using words such as *utilize*, *finalize*, *facilitate*, and *effectuate*. You may find, however, that a program advises you to "simplify" language that is not jargon or pretentious language and may in fact be appropriate in academic writing. Sometimes you can direct the program to change the style level from standard to formal.

stop functioning and cause a heart attack or even death.

17c   Avoid obsolete, archaic, and invented words.

Obsolete words are words found in the writing of the past that have dropped out of use entirely. Archaic words are old words that are still used, but only in special contexts such as literature or advertising. Although dictionaries list obsolete words such as *recomfort* and *reechy* and archaic words such as *anon* and *betwixt*, these words are not appropriate for current use.

Invented words (also called *neologisms*) are words too recently created to be part of standard English. Many invented words fade out of use without becoming standard. *Palimony, technobabble,* and *infomercial* are neologisms that may not last. *Printout, flextime,* and *Internet* are no longer neologisms; they have become standard English. Avoid using invented words in your writing unless they are given in the dictionary as standard or unless no other word expresses your meaning.

17d   In most contexts, avoid slang, regional expressions, and nonstandard English.

Slang is an informal and sometimes private vocabulary that expresses the solidarity of a group such as teenagers, rock musicians, or football fans. It is subject to more rapid change than standard English. For example, the slang teenagers use to express approval changes every few years; *cool, groovy, neat, wicked, awesome,* and *stylin'* have replaced one another within the last three decades. Sometimes slang becomes so widespread that it is accepted as standard vocabulary. *Jazz,* for example, started out as slang but is now generally accepted to describe a style of music.

Although slang has a certain vitality, it is a code that not everyone understands, and it is very informal. Therefore, it is inappropriate in most written work.

▶ If we don't begin studying for the final, a whole
   will be wasted.
semic's work ~~is going down the tubes.~~
                 ^

▶ The government's "filth" guidelines for food will
    disgust you.
    ~~gross you out.~~
    ^

Regional expressions are common to a group in a geographical area. *Let's talk with the bark off* (for *Let's speak frankly*) is an expression used in the southern United States, for example. Regional expressions have the same limitations as slang and are therefore inappropriate in most writing.

▶ John was four blocks from the house before he
                                                    turn on
    remembered to ~~cut~~ the headlights ~~on.~~
                        ^   ^

▶ I'm not ~~for~~ sure, but I think the dance has been

    postponed.

As you probably know, many people speak two varieties of English—standard English, used in academic and business situations, and a nonstandard dialect, spoken with close acquaintances who share a regional or social heritage. In written English, a dialect may be used in dialogue, to reflect actual speech, but in most other contexts it is out of place. Like slang and regionalisms, nonstandard English is a language shared by a select group. Standard English, by contrast, is accessible to all.

If you speak a nonstandard dialect, try to identify the ways in which your dialect differs from standard English. Look especially for the following features of nonstandard English, which commonly cause problems in writing.

Misuse of verb forms such as *began* and *begun* (See 27a.)

Omission of *-s* endings on verbs (See 27c.)

Omission of *-ed* endings on verbs (See 27d.)

Omission of necessary verbs (See 27e.)

Double negatives (See 26d.)

17e   Choose an appropriate level of formality.

In deciding on a level of formality, consider both your subject and your audience. Does the subject demand a dignified treatment, or is a relaxed tone more suitable? Will readers be put off if you assume too close a relationship with them, or might you alienate them by seeming too distant?

For most college and professional writing, some degree of formality is appropriate. In a letter applying for a job, for example, it is a mistake to sound too breezy and informal.

TOO INFORMAL
I'd like to get that receptionist's job you've got in the paper.

MORE FORMAL
I would like to apply for the receptionist's position listed in the *Peoria Journal Star.*

Informal writing is appropriate for private letters, articles in popular magazines, and business correspondence between close associates. Like spoken conversation, it allows contractions (*don't, I'll*) and colloquial words (*kids, buddy*). Vocabulary and sentence structure are rarely complex.

In choosing a level of formality, above all be consistent. When a writer's voice shifts from one level of formality to another, readers receive mixed messages.

▶ Once a pitcher for the Cincinnati Reds, Bob

    shared with me the secrets of his trade. His
                        began
    lesson ~~commenced~~ with his famous curveball,
    thrown
    ~~implemented~~ by tucking the little finger behind
    ^

    the ball instead of holding it straight out. Next
                    revealed
    he ~~elucidated~~ the mysteries of the sucker pitch,
        ^

    a slow ball coming behind a fast windup.

Words such as *commenced* and *elucidated* are inappropriate for the subject matter, and they clash with informal terms such as *sucker pitch* and *fast windup.*

 GRAMMAR CHECKERS can flag slang and some informal language. Be aware, though, that they tend to be conservative on the matter of using contractions. If your ear tells you that a contraction such as *isn't* or *doesn't* strikes the right tone, stay with it.

Avoiding sexist language

Avoid occupational stereotypes.

▶ After the nursing student graduates, ~~she~~ *he or she* must

     face a difficult state board examination.

When naming and identifying men and women, be consistent.

▶ Running for city council are Jake Stein, an

     attorney, and ~~Mrs.~~ Cynthia Jones, a professor of

     English~~, and mother of three~~.

Do not write to an audience of men alone.

▶ If you are a senior government official, your

     spouse
     ~~wife~~ is required to report any gifts ~~she~~ *he or she* receives

     that are valued at more than $100.

Avoid using *he* to mean "he or she" or *him* to mean "him or her."

     (For a variety of revision strategies, see the chart on p. 198.)

     All applicants want   *they*
▶ ~~Every applicant wants~~ to know how much ~~he~~

     will make.

Avoid using *-man* words to refer to persons of either sex.

     firefighter
▶ A ~~fireman~~ must always be on call, even when ~~he~~

     ~~is~~ off duty.

17f   Avoid sexist language.

Sexist language is language that stereotypes or demeans men or women, usually women. Some sexist language reflects genuine contempt for women: referring to a woman as a "broad," for example, or calling a lawyer a "lady lawyer," or saying in an advertisement, "If our new sports car were a lady, it would get its bottom pinched."

Other forms of sexist language, while they may not suggest conscious sexism, reflect stereotypical thinking: referring to nurses as women and doctors as men, using different terms when naming or identifying women and men, or assuming that all of one's readers are men. (See the chart at the top of this page.)

Still other forms of sexist language result from outmoded traditions. The pronouns *he, him,* and *his,* for instance, were traditionally used to refer indefinitely to persons of either sex.

TRADITIONAL
A journalist is stimulated by *his* deadline.

Today, however, such usage is widely viewed as sexist because it excludes women and encourages sex-role stereotyping—the view that men are somehow more suited than women to be journalists, doctors, and so on.

One option, of course, is to substitute *his or her* for *his: A journalist is stimulated by his or her deadline.* This strategy is fine in small doses, but it becomes wordy and awkward when repeated throughout an essay. A better strategy, many writers have discovered, is simply to write in the plural.

REVISED
Journalists are stimulated by *their* deadlines.

Yet another strategy is to rewrite the sentence so that the problem does not arise:

REVISED
A journalist is stimulated by *a* deadline.

When sexist language occurs throughout an essay, it is sometimes possible to adjust the essay's point of view. If the essay might be appropriately rewritten from the *I,* the *we,* or the *you* point of view, the problem of sexist English will not arise. (See 3b.)

Like the pronouns *he, him,* and *his,* the nouns *man* and *men* were once used indefinitely to refer to persons of either sex. Current usage demands gender-neutral terms for references to both men and women.

INAPPROPRIATE	APPROPRIATE
chairman	chairperson, moderator, chair, head
clergyman	member of the clergy, minister, pastor
congressman	member of Congress, representative, legislator
fireman	firefighter
foreman	supervisor
mailman	mail carrier, postal worker, letter carrier
mankind	people, humans
manpower	personnel
policeman	police officer
salesman	salesperson, sales associate, salesclerk, sales representative
to man	to operate, to staff
weatherman	weather forecaster, meteorologist
workman	worker, laborer

GRAMMAR CHECKERS are good at flagging sexist words, such as *mankind,* but they may also flag words, such as *girl* and *woman,* when they aren't being used in a sexist manner. It's sexist to call a woman a girl or a doctor a woman doctor, but you don't need to avoid the words *girl* and *woman* entirely and replace them with needlessly abstract terms like *female* and *individual.* All in all, just use your common sense. It's usually easy to tell when a word is offensive—and when it is not.

Although grammar checkers can flag sexist words, they cannot flag other kinds of sexist language, such as inconsistent treatment of men and women.

EXERCISE 17–1 Appropriate language: Guided practice

A. The writer of the following paragraph used language that is too informal for the audience — an educated group of nonexperts. Revise the paragraph by replacing slang, regional expressions, nonstandard English, and sexist language. Rule numbers in the margin refer to appropriate rules in section 17. The first revision has been done for you, and a suggested revision of this exercise appears in the back of the book.

In the 1800s, an ~~English dude~~ *Englishman* named Thomas Robert Malthus became   **17d**
involved in economics. He was really psyched about predicting how many more   **17d**
people would be in the world eventually and how much food would be available for
them. What he figured out was gross. He said people kept having children faster   **17d**
than men could produce enough to feed them. There was no way to avoid it. Hard   **17f**
times and wars would do most people in. According to Malthus, famine, plagues,   **17d**
and even wars were necessary to knock off some excess people so the remainder   **17d**
could have enough food.

B. The writer of the following paragraph, unlike the previous writer, used too much puffed-up language for the same audience — educated nonexperts. Revise the paragraph, replacing jargon, pretentious language, obsolete words, and sexist language. Rule numbers in the margin refer to appropriate rules in section 17. The first revision has been made for you, and a suggested revision of this exercise appears in the back of the book.

Robert Malthus proved that *population grows faster than food supplies.* ~~the progression of population is exponential~~   **17b**
~~while the amplification of foodstuffs proceeds mathematically.~~ His cerebrations led   **17b**
him to oppose any help for economically deprived people. He believed that by re-   **17b**
lieving the immediate problems of the poor, the government actually made it harder
for everyone to feed his family. Malthus said that if the government subsidized their   **17f**
basic needs, people would only have more children, thus increasing the population
even more. Then the inevitable famine or drought would have to eliminate even more
people to facilitate the survival of a few. Everyone from worker to foreman was   **17a, 17f**
caught in the same predicament. It is no wonder that when the English historian
Thomas Carlyle finished reading Malthus's theories, he pronounced economics "the
dismal science."

EXERCISE 17–2 Appropriate language

Change the italicized words and phrases in the following sentences to more appropriate language for an educated audience of nonexperts. Consult the dictionary if necessary. Do not change the meaning of a sentence. Example:

> *could not*
> David Ricardo was another nineteenth-century economist who thought people ~~had to stay~~
> *improve their social position.*
> ~~put in their social class.~~

1. Ricardo and Malthus were *tight, close buddies*, but they argued constantly.

2. They did agree on one thing: The future looked *inauspicious* for humanity.

3. Ricardo didn't *figure it all out* just by calculating population growth.

4. He accumulated statistical *corroboration* for the validity of his theory of economics.

5. His theory predicted that workers would always be *lowest on the totem pole*, that industrialists would barely be able to *hang in there*, and that the landowners would always be wealthy and powerful.

6. His theory made the landowners the *bad guys*.

7. In those days, landowners were called "landlords"; they rented land to tenant *agriculturists*.

8. Landlords collected rents; but since their land also supplied food for the country, they held *humongous* power.

9. Landlords would *as lief* die as give up their power.

10. When landlords *upped* land-rent fees, workers had to pay more for bread and the industrialists had to pay higher wages without getting any increase in production.

EXERCISE 17–3 Appropriate language

Circle the letter of the more appropriately worded sentence in each pair. Assume an educated audience of nonexperts, and be prepared to explain your choices. Example:

a. **Malthus did not come up with any suggestions for ameliorating the lot of the common man.**

b. **Malthus did not suggest any way to make life better for ordinary people.**

1a. Malthus opposed loans to the poor because he did not believe poor families would ever have enough income to deal with negative savings.

 b. Malthus opposed loans to the poor because he saw no way for poor people to increase their income enough to pay off debts.

2a. Every member of society found that his life was impacted by Malthus's "laws" and their parameters.

 b. No one escaped the consequences of Malthus's "laws": rich and poor both suffered the consequences of overpopulation.

3a. Malthus saw hope only in limiting marriages; he believed that if marriages were restrained, there would be fewer eventual workers and wages would go up.

 b. The one bright idea Malthus had was to put a brake on marriages; fewer weddings meant fewer kids and eventually fewer workers and higher wages.

4a. Ricardo said that the value added to a product by a man's labor was often greater than the wages paid to the laborer.

 b. Ricardo said that the value workers added to a product was not reflected in those workers' wages.

5a. In Ricardo's view, there was no viable system workers could utilize to improve their lot; they would always be stuck between a rock and a hard place.

 b. Ricardo said that workers had almost no hope of improving their lives.

EXERCISE 17–4 Appropriate language: Guided review

Revise the following paragraph using standard English free of slang, jargon, and pretentious, obsolete, and sexist language. Rule numbers in the margin refer to appropriate rules in section 17. The first sentence has been revised for you.

~~The relation between the~~ *The* theories of economists Thomas Malthus and David
Ricardo *show certain similarities, but one did not cause the other.* ~~is associative rather than causal.~~ Their visions of the future are quite sim-   **17a**

milar, but each arrived at his conclusions on his own. Ricardo predicted a dreary

future; he said that future workers would not have enough bread to buy bread. It   **17d**

was not exactly the same picture Malthus painted, but it was equally dismal. A mod-

ern scholar, Robert Heilbroner, once said that these two men "changed the world

from an optimistic to a pessimistic one." Before them, most people believed that the

world would just naturally get groovier. After them, the natural world seemed to be   **17d**

an enemy of the world's people. Although both Malthus and Ricardo studied the

problem, neither of them could render intelligible the reasons for the recurring fluc-   **17b**

tuations in the country's economic well-being. Nor could any other economist who

offered his theories on the subject. Malthus and Ricardo saw only a gloomy image   **17f**

of future life. Scrupulously honest, they reported that vision but offered no solu-

tions to the problems they predicted. For many people, economics continues to be

a dismal attempt to elucidate the reasons for behavior of phenomena in the market.   **17b**

18   Find the exact words.

Two reference works will help you find words to express your meaning exactly: a good dictionary (see 43a) and a book of synonyms and antonyms such as *Roget's International Thesaurus.*

> **GRAMMAR CHECKERS** can flag some nonstandard idioms, such as *comply to,* and many clichés, such as *leave no stone unturned.* In addition, they can flag commonly confused words such as *principal* and *principle* or *affect* and *effect,* although you must decide which word is correct in your context. Grammar checkers are less helpful with the other problems discussed in section 18: choosing words with appropriate connotations, using concrete language, and using figures of speech appropriately.

18a   Select words with appropriate connotations.

In addition to their strict dictionary meanings (or *denotations*), words have *connotations,* emotional colorings that affect how readers respond to them. The word *steel* denotes "made of or resembling steel," but it also calls up a cluster of images associated with steel, such as the sensation of touching it. These associations give the word its connotations—cold, smooth, unbending.

If the connotation of a word does not seem appropriate for your purpose, your audience, or your subject matter, you should change the word. When a more appropriate synonym does not come quickly to mind, consult a dictionary or a thesaurus.

>   *slender*
> ▶ The model was ~~skinny~~ and fashionable.

The connotation of the word *skinny* is too negative when paired with the more positive word *fashionable.*

> ▶ As I covered the boats with marsh grass, the
>   *sweat*
> ~~perspiration~~ I had worked up evaporated in
>
> the wind.

The term *perspiration* is too dainty for the context, which suggests vigorous exercise.

18b   Prefer specific, concrete nouns.

Unlike general nouns, which refer to broad classes of things, specific nouns point to definite and particular items. *Film,* for example, names a general class, *science fiction film* names a narrower class, and *Jurassic Park* is more specific still. Other examples: *team, football team, Denver Broncos; music, symphony, Beethoven's Ninth; work, carpentry, cabinet-making.*

Unlike abstract nouns, which refer to qualities and ideas (*justice, beauty, realism, dignity*), concrete nouns point to immediate, often sensory experience and to physical objects (*steeple, asphalt, lilac, stone, garlic*).

Specific, concrete nouns express meaning more vividly than general or abstract ones. Although general and abstract language is sometimes necessary to convey your meaning, ordinarily prefer specific, concrete alternatives.

> ▶ The senator spoke about the challenges of the
>   *of famine, pollution, dwindling*
> future: problems ~~concerning the environment~~
> *resources, and terrorism.*
> ~~and world peace.~~

Nouns such as *thing, area, aspect, factor,* and *individual* are especially dull and imprecise.

> ▶ A career in transportation management offers
>   *rewards.*
> many ~~things.~~

>   *experienced technician.*
> ▶ Try pairing a trainee with an ~~individual with~~
>
> ~~technical experience.~~

18c   Do not misuse words.

If a word is not in your active vocabulary, you may find yourself misusing it, sometimes with embarrassing consequences. Imagine the chagrin of the young woman who wrote that the "aroma of pumpkin pie and sage stuffing acted as an *aphrodisiac*" when she learned that aphrodisiacs are drugs or foods stimulating sexual desire. Such blunders are easily prevented: When in doubt, check the dictionary.

▶ The fans were ~~migrating~~ *climbing* up the bleachers in search of seats.

▶ Mrs. Johnson tried to fight but to no ~~prevail~~ *avail*.

▶ Drugs have so ~~diffused~~ *permeated* our culture that they touch all segments of society.

Be especially alert for misused word forms — using a noun such as *absence, significance,* or *persistence,* for example, when your meaning requires the adjective *absent, significant,* or *persistent.*

▶ Most dieters are not ~~persistence~~ *persistent* enough to make a permanent change in their eating habits.

18d Use standard idioms.

Idioms are speech forms that follow no easily specified rules. The English say "Maria went *to hospital,*" an idiom strange to American ears, which are accustomed to hearing *the* in front of *hospital.* Native speakers of a language seldom have problems with idioms, but prepositions sometimes cause trouble, especially when they follow certain verbs and adjectives. When in doubt, consult a good desk dictionary.

UNIDIOMATIC	IDIOMATIC
abide with (a decision)	abide by (a decision)
according with	according to
agree to (an idea)	agree with (an idea)
angry at (a person)	angry with (a person)
capable to	capable of
comply to	comply with
desirous to	desirous of
different than (a person or thing)	different from (a person or thing)
intend on doing	intend to do
off of	off
plan on doing	plan to do
preferable than	preferable to
prior than	prior to
superior than	superior to
sure and	sure to
try and	try to
type of a	type of

ESL Because idioms follow no particular rules, you must learn them individually. You may find it helpful to keep a list of idioms that you frequently encounter in conversation and in reading.

18e Avoid worn-out expressions (clichés).

The frontiersman who first announced that he had "slept like a log" probably amused his companions with a fresh and unlikely comparison. Today, however, that comparison is a cliché, a saying that has lost its dazzle from overuse. No longer can it surprise.

To see just how dully predictable clichés are, put your hand over the right-hand column below and then finish the phrases on the left.

cool as a	cucumber
beat around	the bush
blind as a	bat
busy as a	bee, beaver
crystal	clear
dead as a	doornail
out of the frying pan and	into the fire
light as a	feather
like a bull	in a china shop
playing with	fire
nutty as a	fruitcake
selling like	hotcakes
starting out at the bottom	of the ladder
water under the	bridge
white as a	sheet, ghost
avoid clichés like the	plague

The cure for clichés is usually simple: Just delete them. When this won't work, try adding some element of surprise. One student, for example, who had written that she had butterflies in her stomach, revised her cliché like this:

> If all of the action in my stomach is caused by butterflies, there must be a horde of them, with horseshoes on.

The image of butterflies wearing horseshoes is fresh and unlikely, not dully predictable like the original cliché.

18f Use figures of speech with care.

A figure of speech is an expression that uses words imaginatively (rather than literally). Most often, figures of speech compare two seemingly unlike things to reveal surprising similarities. For example, Richard Selzer compares an aging surgeon who has lost his touch to an old lion whose claws have become blunted.

Although figures of speech are useful devices, writers sometimes use them without thinking through the images they evoke. This can result in a *mixed metaphor,* the combination of two or more images that don't make sense together.

▶ Crossing Utah's salt flats in his new Corvette, my
     at jet speed.
father flew ~~under a full head of steam.~~

> *Flew* suggests an airplane, while *under a full head of steam* suggests a steamboat or a train. To clarify the image, the writer should stick with one comparison or the other.

▶ Our office had decided to put all controversial

issues on a back burner. ~~in a holding pattern.~~

> Here the writer is mixing stoves and airplanes. Simply deleting one of the images corrects the problem.

EXERCISE 18–1 Exact words: Guided practice

In the following paragraph, improve word choices by replacing general words with specific ones and revising clichés and mixed figures of speech. Be sure that connotations are appropriate, that idioms are used properly, and that words are not misused. Rule numbers in the margin refer to appropriate rules in section 18. The first revision has been made for you, and a suggested revision of this exercise appears in the back of the book.

dominated

Economics is not totally ~~domineered~~ by men. Even in the 1800s, when   *18c*

Thomas Malthus and David Ricardo were the experts, one leading writer about

economics was a woman, Jane Marcet. Marcet wrote for the popular press. One of

her favorite things to write about was political economy. In her book *Conversations*   *18b*

in Political Economy, Marcet summarized economic doctrines before 1800. Her aim

was different than that of either Malthus or Ricardo. Rather than propounding a   *18d*

new theory of her own, she was happy as a lark to popularize theories of other   *18e*

people. Twentieth-century women have done more than write about theories that

men have proposed. Some of them have taken the bull by the horns and charged   *18f*

full steam ahead. Sally Herbert Frankel, for example, made the first official calcula-

tions of the Union of South Africa's national income. She is only one of the increas-

ing number of ladies who make careers in economics.   *18a*

EXERCISE 18–2 Exact words

A. In each of the following sentences, circle the more specific word or phrase in parentheses. (See 18b if necessary.) Example:

> **Alice Mitchell Rivlin was an important (person, (economist)) in the federal government.**

1. Rivlin worked for (an important government office, the U.S. Congressional Budget Office), where she (secured an important position, became director of that office).

2. She received her B.A. from (Bryn Mawr College, a prestigious eastern women's college) and her (Ph.D., highest degree) from Radcliffe College.

3. Rivlin's first job, at (Brookings Institution, a think tank) in Washington, D.C., lasted (for some time, from 1957 to 1966).

4. Most of her (publications, books) have been (put out, published) by Brookings Institution.

5. Rivlin's interest in government finances carried over into the educational world when she became (a teacher, a professor of public policy) at (George Mason University near Washington, D.C., a university in northern Virginia).

B. Edit the following sentences to correct inappropriate connotations. (Consult 18a, the Glossary of Usage [p. 415], or a dictionary if necessary.) Example:

> *perceptive*
> **Alice Rivlin was ~~crafty~~ enough to understand the interrelatedness of individual budget items.**

6. She planned to execute a thorough analysis of every part of the federal budget.

7. Rivlin did not claim that federal government services were cheap.

8. What she pushed was the idea that legislators should have easy access to information they needed.

9. She allowed herself no alibi for incomplete work.

10. Rivlin's work has proved conclusively that ladies can be extremely competent in financial matters.

EXERCISE 18–3 Exact words

A. Circle the correct word or expression in the parentheses. (Consult 18c, 18d, the Glossary of Usage [p. 415], or a dictionary if necessary.) Example:

> Alice Rivlin had the skill and (patients, (patience)) to analyze the federal budget; she (planned on doing, (planned to do)) a thorough job.

1. She wanted her work to have one specific (effect, affect) and she was determined to (try and, try to) succeed.

2. She planned (on making, to make) the budget, that (incredible, incredulous) mass of material, more available to Congress before Congress actually needed it.

3.   She had no (allusions, illusions) about the difficulty of the task; luckily for Congress, she proved (capable to do, capable of doing) it.

4. When voting on the budget becomes (eminent, imminent, immanent), members of Congress need some (type of a, type of) clear, easy-to-understand document.

5. That document must be easily (assessable, accessible) to any representatives who (plan on voting, plan to vote).

B. Edit the following sentences to correct any misused words or idioms. Mark the one correct sentence "OK." (See 18c, 18d, the Glossary of Usage [p. 415], or a dictionary if necessary.) Example:

> *complement*
> The work of a government budget office should ~~compliment~~ the work of Congress.

6. Members of Congress have been known to get very angry at a budget director whose work was not satisfactory.

7. Sometimes the Budget Office must try and please a representative.

8. The director of the Budget Office, however, must maintain that office's independents from members of Congress.

9. Perhaps Alice Rivlin's style was different than that of some other budget officers, for she got the job done without making too many enemies.

10. In fact, Rivlin's performance at the Budget Office may account for her becoming deputy director of the Office of Management and Budget in 1993.

EXERCISE 18–4 Exact words

Edit the following sentences to delete or replace clichés and to clarify mixed figures of speech. Mark the two correct sentences "OK." (See 18e and 18f if necessary.) Example:

> *be undertaking too much*
> Would an economist ~~bite off more than she could chew~~ if she tried to find out why better
>   ^
> *fail to materialize?*
> financial rewards for women so often ~~hang fire?~~
>   ^

1. Rivlin has had more than one iron in the fire; besides her budget work, she has au-
    thored several books and taught public policy at George Mason University.

2. Rivlin did not sweep problems under the rug to take root there and come unraveled;
    she dealt with them before they became bigger problems.

3. When Rivlin was chosen as a MacArthur Foundation fellow, it was crystal clear that
    her talents and dedication had been recognized.

4. Rivlin is not the only modern woman to choose economics for her specialty.

5. Looking for such women is no longer like hunting for a needle in a haystack.

6. It goes without saying that women's roles in the labor market have changed
    radically.

7. It is a crying shame that the economic status of women has not kept pace with these
    changes. Why?

8. She may be playing with fire, but Cynthia Lloyd wants to get her feet wet dealing
    with that question.

9. In so doing, she has made the study of women in the labor market an integral and
    accepted part of economic analysis.

10. Her studies don't claim that money grows on trees but ask why women's efforts to
    get their share are always put on the back burner.

EXERCISE 18–5 Exact words: Guided review

The following paragraph contains six examples of word choice problems discussed in section 18. Edit the paragraph by replacing words that have inappropriate connotations, imprecise and misused words, unidiomatic expressions and clichés, and mixed figures of speech. The first revision has been made for you; find and correct the other five problems.

                                         from

Women economists are no different ~~than~~ men economists in the range of their   *18d*
interests. Jane Marcet was interested in writing about economics for the popular
press, not in developing theorems of her own. Cynthia Lloyd's primary concern is   *18c*
for improved economic status for women in the labor market. Alice Rivlin stays busy   *18e*
as a bee as vice-chair of the Board of Governors of the Federal Reserve System, a
position to which she was appointed in 1996. Sally Herbert Frankel's interest is
finance, particularly South African national income. Because she believes that cities
significantly influence national economies, Jane Jacobs concentrates on cities. She
claims that only cities can maintain or effect a nation's economic life enough to cause   *18c*
real change. Phyllis Deane intends on studying developing countries. She keeps her   *18d*
shoulder to the wheel as she digs deep to find ways to understand the economies of   *18f*
these countries.

Unit review (16–18): Word choice

Edit the following essay for problems with word choice. Rule numbers in the margin refer to appropriate rules in sections 16–18. The first revision has been made for you.

Economics, ~~which is~~ a branch of social science, deals with the production,   *16e*

distribution, and consumption of goods and services. However, you'd better believe   *17e*

it's not an exact science, though economists strive to make it so.

Economists have several aggravating habits. One of the worst is the habit of   *18c*

"two-handedness." An economist will say, "On the one hand, interest rates may rise

and. . . ." In the next breath, he will say, "On the other hand, interest rates may fall   *17f*

and. . . ." Harry Truman used to get angry at advisers who talked like that. He once   *18d*

said that what he really needed was a one-handed economist.

If the current volume of *Who's Who in Economics* fell off of its library shelf,   *18d*

this 935-page book would dent the floor. Hundreds of names are in that volume, but

the same few keep rising to the top and surfacing. Whenever people discuss eco-   *16a*

nomics, they nearly always refer to Malthus, Ricardo, Veblen, or Keynes. But time   *18e*

after time, the same name heads the list. Just as cream always rises to the top of   *18f*

the ladder of success, Adam Smith's name has led all the rest for two centuries.

Pretend you are the host of a current TV show about money. Pretend also

that you write books with titles like *The Money Game* and *Supermoney*. What type

of a name would you choose for your nom de plume? You would want an easily rec-   *18d, 17b*

ognized name. You might do just what George Jerome W. Goodman did when he

started a successful TV show about managing money—he called himself "Adam

Smith."

Grammatical Sentences

19 Repair sentence fragments.

20 Revise run-on sentences.

21 Make subjects and verbs agree.

22 Make pronouns and antecedents agree.

23 Make pronoun references clear.

24 Distinguish between pronouns such as *I* and *me*.

25 Distinguish between *who* and *whom*.

26 Choose adjectives and adverbs with care.

27 Choose standard English verb forms.

28 Use verbs in the appropriate tense, mood, and voice.

19 Repair sentence fragments.

A sentence fragment is a word group that pretends to be a sentence. Sentence fragments are easy to recognize when they appear out of context, like these:

> On the old wooden stool in the corner of my grandmother's kitchen.

> And immediately popped their flares and life vests.

When fragments appear next to related sentences, however, they are harder to spot.

> On that morning I sat in my usual spot. On the old wooden stool in the corner of my grandmother's kitchen.

> The pilots ejected from the burning plane, landing in the water not far from the ship. And immediately popped their flares and life vests.

Recognizing sentence fragments

To be a sentence, a word group must consist of at least one full independent clause. An independent clause has a subject and a verb, and it either stands alone or could stand alone.

To test a word group for sentence completeness, use the flow chart on page 168. For example, by using the flow chart, you can see exactly why *On the old wooden stool in the corner of my grandmother's kitchen* is a fragment: It lacks both a subject and a verb. *And immediately popped their flares and life vests* is a fragment because it lacks a subject.

ESL

Unlike some languages, English does not allow omission of subjects (except in imperative sentences); nor does it allow omission of verbs. See 31a and 29e.

GRAMMAR CHECKERS can flag as many as half of the sentence fragments in a sample; but that means, of course, that they miss half or more of them. If fragments are a serious problem for you, you will still need to proofread for them.

Sometimes you will get "false positives," sentences that have been flagged but are not fragments. For example, one program flagged this complete sentence as a possible fragment: *I bent down to crawl into the bunker.* When a program spots a possible fragment, you should check to see if it is really a fragment. You can do this by using the flow chart on page 168.

Repairing sentence fragments

You can repair most fragments in one of two ways: Either pull the fragment into a nearby sentence or turn the fragment into a sentence.

▶ On that morning I sat in my usual spot, ~~On~~ *on* the old wooden stool in the corner of my grandmother's kitchen.

▶ The pilots ejected from the burning plane, landing in the water not far from the ship. ~~And~~ *They* immediately popped their flares and life vests.

19a   Attach fragmented subordinate clauses or turn them into sentences.

A subordinate clause is patterned like a sentence, with both a subject and a verb, but it begins with a word that marks it as subordinate.

The following words commonly introduce subordinate clauses:

after	even though	so that	when	whom
although	how	than	where	whose
as	if	that	whether	why
as if	in order that	though	which	
because	rather than	unless	while	
before	since	until	who	

Subordinate clauses function within sentences as adjectives, as adverbs, or as nouns. They cannot stand alone. (See 49b.)

Most fragmented clauses beg to be pulled into a sentence nearby.

▶ Jane will address the problem of limited on-campus parking, ~~If~~ *if* she is elected special student adviser.

If introduces a subordinate clause that modifies the verb *will address*. (For punctuation of subordinate clauses appearing at the end of a sentence, see 33f.)

▶ Although we seldom get to see wildlife in the city, ~~At~~ *at* the zoo we can still find some of our favorites.

Although introduces a subordinate clause that modifies the verb *can find*. (For punctuation of subordinate clauses appearing at the beginning of a sentence, see 32b.)

If a fragmented clause cannot be attached to a nearby sentence or if you feel that attaching it would be awkward, try rewriting it. The simplest way to turn a subordinate clause into a sentence is to delete the opening word or words that mark it as subordinate.

▶ Population increases and uncontrolled development are taking a deadly toll on the environment. ~~So that~~ *I*n many parts of the world, fragile ecosystems are collapsing.

19b   Attach fragmented phrases or turn them into sentences.

Like subordinate clauses, phrases function within sentences as adjectives, as adverbs, or as nouns. They cannot stand alone. Fragmented phrases are often prepositional or verbal phrases; sometimes they are appositives, words or word groups that rename nouns or pronouns. (See 49a, 49c, and 49d.)

Often a fragmented phrase may simply be pulled into a nearby sentence.

▶ The panther lay quite motionless behind the
  rock/, ~~Waiting~~ silently for its prey.
    waiting

Waiting silently for its prey is a verbal phrase. (For punctuation of verbal phrases, see 32e.)

▶ Mary is suffering from agoraphobia/, ~~A~~ fear of
    a

  the outside world.

A fear of the outside world is an appositive renaming the noun *agoraphobia*. (For punctuation of appositives, see 32e.)

If a fragmented phrase cannot be pulled into a nearby sentence effectively, turn the phrase into a sentence. You may need to add a subject, a verb, or both.

▶ In the computer training session, Eugene

  explained how to install our new software.
  He also taught us
  ~~Also~~ how to organize our files, connect to the

  Internet, and back up our hard drives.

The word group beginning *Also how to organize* is a fragmented verbal phrase.

19c Attach other fragmented word groups or turn them into sentences.

Other word groups that are commonly fragmented include parts of compound predicates, lists, and examples introduced by *such as, for example,* or similar expressions.

Parts of compound predicates

A predicate consists of a verb and its objects, complements, and modifiers (see 48b). A compound predicate includes two or more predicates joined by a coordinating conjunction such as *and, but,* or *or.* Because the parts of a compound predicate share the same subject, they should appear in the same sentence.

▶ The woodpecker finch carefully selects a twig
    and
  of a certain size and shape./~~And~~ then uses

  this tool to pry out grubs from trees.

Notice that no comma appears between the parts of a compound predicate. (See 33a.)

Lists

When a list is mistakenly fragmented, it can often be attached to a nearby sentence with a colon or a dash. (See 35a and 39a.)

▶ It has been said that there are only three
    musical
  indigenous American art forms/: ~~Musical~~ comedy,

  jazz, and soap opera.

Examples introduced by *such as, for example,* or similar expressions

Expressions that introduce examples (or explanations) can lead to unintentional fragments. Although you may begin a sentence with some of the following words or phrases, make sure that what you have written is a sentence, not a fragment.

also	for instance	or
and	in addition	such as
but	like	that is
especially	mainly	
for example	namely	

Sometimes fragmented examples can be attached to the preceding sentence.

▶ The South has produced some of our greatest
    such
  twentieth-century writers/, ~~Such~~ as Flannery

  O'Connor, William Faulkner, Alice Walker,

  Tennessee Williams, and Thomas Wolfe.

At times however, it may be necessary to turn the fragment into a sentence.

▶ If Eric doesn't get his way, he goes into a fit of
    he lies
  rage. For example, ~~lying~~ on the floor screaming
  opens   *slams*
  or ~~opening~~ the cabinet doors and then ~~slamming~~

  them shut.

Checking for sentence fragments

First look for the most common trouble spots:

WORDS INTRODUCING SUBORDINATE CLAUSES (19a)

although	even though	that	where	who
as if	how	though	whether	whom
because	if	unless	which	whose
before	so that	when	while	why

▶ Pat could not come skiing with us/ ~~Because~~ *because*

she had broken her leg.

PHRASES (19b)

▶ The air force sent me to Chanute, Illinois/, *home*
~~Home~~ of the USAF Fire Academy.

PARTS OF COMPOUND PREDICATES (19c)

▶ Pressing the gun to my shoulder, I laid my *and*
cheek to the stock/ ~~And~~ sighted the target.

WORDS INTRODUCING LISTS OR EXAMPLES (19c)

for example	like	namely
for instance	mainly	such as

▶ You already know some gestures in sign *such*
language/, ~~Such~~ as a wave for "hello" and a

shake of the head for "no."

Next test possible fragments for sentence completeness:

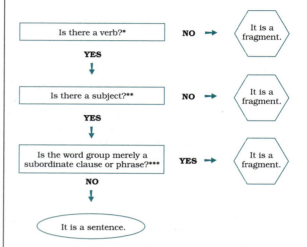

* Do not mistake verbals for verbs. (See 49c.)
** The subject of a sentence may be *you*, understood. (See 48a.)
*** A sentence may open with a subordinate clause, but the sentence must also include an independent clause. (See 49b.)

If you find any fragments, try one of these methods of revision:

1. Attach the fragment to a nearby sentence.
2. Turn the fragment into a sentence.

The writer corrected this fragment by adding a subject—*he*—and substituting verbs for the verbals *lying*, *opening*, and *slamming*.

19d Exception: Occasionally a fragment may be used deliberately, for effect.

Skilled writers occasionally use sentence fragments for the following special purposes.

FOR EMPHASIS
Following the dramatic Americanization of their children, even my parents grew more publicly confident. *Especially my mother.*
—Richard Rodriguez

TO ANSWER A QUESTION
Are these new drug tests 100 percent reliable? *Not in the opinion of most experts.*

AS A TRANSITION
And now the opposing arguments.

EXCLAMATIONS
Not again!

IN ADVERTISING
Fewer calories. Improved taste.

Although fragments are sometimes appropriate, writers and readers do not always agree on when they are appropriate. Therefore you will find it safer to write in complete sentences.

EXERCISE 19-1 Sentence fragments: Guided practice

Edit the following paragraphs to eliminate sentence fragments. Rule numbers in the margin refer to appropriate rules in section 19. The first revision has been done for you, and a suggested revision of this exercise appears in the back of the book.

Four
~~How four~~ young Englishmen added a word to the world's vocabulary in the   **19a**

1960s. A word that became synonymous with the 1960s. Especially with the music   **19b, 19c**

of that time. That word was, of course, "Beatles." The Beatles became the most fa-

mous popular musical group of the twentieth century. And may still hold that title   **19c**

when the twentieth century is over.

The Beatles were popular in Liverpool, England, and in Hamburg, Germany.

Before they came to America on tour and became world-famous. Liverpool and Ham-   **19a**

burg loved the four young men and their music. The Beatles' favorite club was the

Cavern in Liverpool. Where they hung out together, played day and night, and at-   **19a**

tracted many fans. A Liverpool disk jockey first called attention to them, and a Liv-

erpool music critic and record store owner became their first manager. The disk

jockey called them "fantastic." Saying that they had "resurrected original rock 'n'   **19b**

roll." The music critic who became their manager, Brian Epstein, made them shape

up as a group. Promoting them, arranging club dates for them, and badgering record   **19b**

companies for them. He intended to win a recording contract for this exciting new

group.

In England, the record buying led to the publicity. In America, the publicity

led to the record buying. Everyone wanted copies of the original singles. "Love Me   **19c**

Do," "Please, Please Me," and "From Me to You." In America, audiences made so

much noise that no one could hear the music. Crowds of screaming teenagers sur-

rounded the Beatles wherever they went. Determined to touch one or more of these   **19b**

famous music makers. Reporters observing the conduct of fans at Beatles' concerts

found that they had to invent another word. To describe the wild, almost insane be-   **19b**

havior of the fans. They called it "Beatlemania."

EXERCISE 19–2 Sentence fragments

Each of the following word groups includes a subordinating word. One word group in each pair contains a fragment. Mark each complete sentence "OK" and write "frag" after each fragment. Example:

a. John Lennon lived with his Aunt Mimi until he was grown. Because his parents had separated and his mother had given John to Mimi. *frag*

b. His father took him from Mimi when John was about five. Because his mother returned him to Mimi, he grew up as Mimi's child. *OK*

1a. When John Lennon was a teenager, his mother, Julia, began to pay attention to him.

 b. When Julia, John Lennon's mother, bought him a guitar and let him stay with her instead of his Aunt Mimi.

2a. Although he studied art in college, he soon became more interested in music.

 b. Although Julia encouraged his music and put up with the boyish pranks that annoyed Aunt Mimi.

3a. His mother died before he was full grown. While John was still in college, in fact.

 b. Mimi's husband, his uncle, had died while John still lived with them.

4a. John asked Paul McCartney to join his group, and later Paul brought in George Harrison, and all three asked Ringo Starr to join them. Before they cut their first record.

 b. In their early days, the Beatles copied people like Elvis Presley and Little Richard. Before these English boys even visited America, they sang with American accents.

5a. The Beatles gave one reason for quitting their tours in 1966. That the tours were wrecking their playing.

 b. Stopping the tours gave the Beatles an opportunity to do something they had never done. That was to learn to read musical notes and write their own music.

EXERCISE 19–3 Sentence fragments

Underline each fragment in the following paragraphs. (Consult the chart on p. 168 if necessary.) Do not correct the errors, but be prepared to discuss possible revision strategies for
each fragment. The first fragment is underlined for you.

Paul McCartney wrote many of the Beatles' songs. A good student who learned quickly,
he began composing songs when he was about fourteen.

Paul said that sometimes a song just came to him, like "Eleanor Rigby." <u>One of his
most famous and moving songs.</u> The song is about a lonely woman who can't connect with
other people. Paul was sitting at the piano not working on anything special. Just fooling
around with melodies and rhythms. Then some notes played themselves in his head and so
did some words. Like "Daisy Hawkins picks up the rice in the church where a wedding has
been." Later Paul saw the name "Rigby" on a shop in Bristol. And decided he liked that name
better than "Hawkins," especially with "Eleanor" instead of "Daisy." He and John Lennon finished the song together.

Paul wrote "Hey, Jude" in an effort to help John's son, Julian, who was upset over his
parents' separation. Paul wanted the boy not to be sad. "To take a sad song and make it better." He decided to change "Julian" to "Jude" after he finished the song. Because he wanted
the song to have a country and western feel.

All of the Beatles wrote songs, and often they collaborated on one, but Paul McCartney and John Lennon wrote most of the songs the Beatles sang.

EXERCISE 19–4 Sentence fragments

Correct the fragments in the following paragraphs. The first revision has been done for you. Find and revise ten more fragments.

George Harrison was known in school for two things*/.* ~~His~~ *his* sharp clothes and his love of the guitar. His mother said he sometimes practiced the guitar for hours. Not stopping until his fingers were bleeding. When George met John Lennon, he found another guitar lover. Although they went to the same school, they did not meet there. Because George was two years younger and they had no classes together. Instead, they met on the school bus. After they became friends, they spent most of their time at George's house, playing their guitars.

When George, John, Paul McCartney, and Ringo Starr formed a group, the four experimented with all kinds of things. From melodies and sounds to drugs. George, however, began to want more out of life. To find answers to the big questions he had about war and loneliness and reasons for living. The others agreed to search with him, and George Harrison became their guide.

Later, George and his wife went to India. Where a religious festival they attended impressed them deeply. When George returned to England, he read many books about meditation. And went to hear Indian holy teachers. He shared what he read and heard with the other Beatles. Who were just as interested as George was. When George learned that a holy man called the Maharishi was going to speak on transcendental meditation, he told his friends. They all went to listen to him. To learn whatever they could that would help them.

The Beatles were headed in a new direction. A direction that was obvious in their next album, *Sgt. Pepper's Lonely Hearts Club Band.* The album had innovative lyrics and an amazing musical background. A forty-one-piece orchestra, guitar, sitar, doubled voices, a comb-and-paper instrument, and all kinds of electronic and percussion tricks. The Beatles were no longer copycat rock 'n' rollers.

EXERCISE 19–5 Sentence fragments

Half of the following word groups are complete sentences. The other half contain fragments. Correct the fragments, and mark the complete sentences "OK." Example:

> As a child and a teenager, Ringo Starr spent a total of three years in the hospital/~~Because~~ of two severe health problems. *because*

1. Ringo Starr's first hospitalization lasted for a year. After his appendix burst when he was only six years old.

2. Doctors had to perform several operations; Ringo could not attend school at all that year.

3. His babysitter taught him to read and write, so he did not fall too far behind in his schoolwork.

4. When he was thirteen, Ringo had to go back into the hospital. And stay there for two years while doctors treated a lung condition.

5. Now fifteen, he worked at various jobs. But what he really liked best was playing the drums for his many fans.

6. Teaching himself on drums he bought on the installment plan, he played with different musical groups in Liverpool, including the Beatles.

7. When Ringo joined the Beatles, not everyone was sure that he could handle the job. For example, George Martin, who invited them to London to record.

8. Martin insisted on a standby drummer as insurance. Someone to step in just in case Ringo was not good enough.

9. Ringo's many devoted fans were not surprised when he handled the job and became a full-fledged Beatle, making new friends at every engagement.

10. Many people considered him the most likable member of the group. Because of his easy smile and his open approach to life.

EXERCISE 19–6 Sentence fragments: Guided review

Find and correct the sentence fragments in the following paragraphs. Rule numbers in the margin refer to appropriate rules in section 19. The first revision has been done for you.

Many people influenced the Beatles in their career. For example, Bob Waller, *19c*

a disk jockey in Liverpool/ ~~He~~ first called attention to them in one of his articles.

"They resurrected original rock 'n' roll," he wrote. When he first heard them in 1961. *19a*

From Stu Sutcliffe, a talented musician who sometimes played with them, the Bea-

tles copied several things. Their hairstyle, their dress, and much of their philoso- *19c*

phy. George Martin, who produced their records, advised them how to improve after

their early records. And taught them how to use tapes. *19c*

The person who influenced them most, however, was Brian Epstein. Owner *19b*

of some record stores and reviewer of new records. When a customer asked for a

record by a group Epstein had never heard of, he went from club to club. Looking *19b*

for a group calling itself "The Beatles." By the end of 1961, he had become the group's

manager. Convinced that he had found talented and original musicians. His con- *19b*

tract said that he was to promote the Beatles and arrange their tours and club dates.

His other duty was really the most important. To get record contracts for them. *19b*

Epstein did far more than his contract called for. He made the young men

wear suits every time they performed. Until their gray, collarless outfits became a *19a*

symbol of the Beatles. He made another demand of them. That they be on time for *19a*

appearances. He even made them quit chewing gum on the stage. And by the time

he had done all these things, he had also gotten them a recording date. Why were

the Beatles so devastated by Epstein's death? When Brian Epstein was found dead

of an accidental drug overdose in 1967. The Beatles lost far more than a good man- *19a*

ager. They lost a close friend and mentor.

20   Revise run-on sentences.

Run-on sentences are independent clauses that have not been joined correctly. An independent clause is a word group that can stand alone as a sentence. (See 50.) When two independent clauses appear in one sentence, they must be joined in one of these ways:

—with a comma and a coordinating conjunction (*and, but, or, nor, for, so, yet*)

—with a semicolon (or occasionally a colon or a dash)

Recognizing run-on sentences

There are two types of run-on sentences. When a writer puts no mark of punctuation and no coordinating conjunction between independent clauses, the result is called a *fused sentence.*

FUSED

┌──────── INDEPENDENT CLAUSE ────────┐
Gestures are a means of communication for
┌─ INDEPENDENT CLAUSE ─┐
everyone they are essential for the hearing

impaired.

A far more common type of run-on sentence is the *comma splice*—two or more independent clauses joined by a comma without a coordinating conjunction. In some comma splices, the comma appears alone.

COMMA SPLICE
Gestures are a means of communication for everyone, they are essential for the hearing impaired.

In other comma splices, the comma is accompanied by a joining word that is *not* a coordinating conjunction. There are only seven coordinating conjunctions in English: *and, but, or, nor, for, so,* and *yet.* Notice that all of these words are short—only two or three letters long.

COMMA SPLICE
Gestures are a means of communication for everyone, however, they are essential for the hearing impaired.

However is a transitional expression, not a coordinating conjunction (see 20b).

To review your writing for possible run-on sentences, use the chart on page 177.

GRAMMAR CHECKERS can flag only about 20 to 50 percent of the run-on sentences in a sample. The programs tend to be cautious, telling you that you "may have" a run-on sentence; you will almost certainly get a number of "false positives," sentences that have been flagged but are not run-ons. For example, a grammar checker flagged the following acceptable sentence as a possible run-on: *They believe that requiring gun owners to purchase a license is sufficient.*

If you have a problem with run-ons, you will need to proofread for them even after using a grammar checker. Also, if your program spots a "possible" run-on, you will need to check to see if it is in fact a run-on, perhaps by using the flow chart on page 177.

Revising run-on sentences

To revise a run-on sentence, you have four choices:

1. Use a comma and a coordinating conjunction (*and, but, or, nor, for, so, yet*).

▶ Gestures are a means of communication for
    but
everyone, they are essential for the hearing

impaired.

2. Use a semicolon (or, if appropriate, a colon or a dash). A semicolon may be used alone; it can also be accompanied by a transitional expression.

▶ Gestures are a means of communication for

everyone; they are essential for the hearing

impaired.

▶ Gestures are a means of communication for
    ; however,
everyone, they are essential for the hearing

impaired.

3. Make the clauses into separate sentences.

> Gestures are a means of communication for
> *They*
> everyone, ~~they~~ are essential for the hearing
>
> impaired.

4. Restructure the sentence, perhaps by sub-ordinating one of the clauses.

> *Although gestures*
> ~~Gestures~~ are a means of communication for
>
> everyone, they are essential for the hearing
>
> impaired.

One of these revision techniques usually works better than the others for a particular sentence. The fourth technique, the one requiring the most extensive revision, is often the most effective.

20a Consider separating the clauses with a comma and a coordinating conjunction.

There are seven coordinating conjunctions in English: *and, but, or, nor, for, so,* and *yet.* When a coordinating conjunction joins independent clauses, it is usually preceded by a comma. (See 32a.)

> *and*
> The paramedic asked where I was hurt, as soon
>
> as I told him, he cut up the leg of my favorite
>
> pair of jeans.

> Many government officials privately admit that
> *yet*
> the polygraph is unreliable, ~~however,~~ they
>
> continue to use it as a security measure.
>
> *However* is a transitional expression, not a coordinating conjunction, so it cannot be used with only a comma to join independent clauses. (See 20b.)

20b Consider separating the clauses with a semicolon (or, if appropriate, with a colon or a dash).

When the independent clauses are closely related and their relation is clear without a coordinating conjunction, a semicolon is an acceptable method of revision. (See 34a.)

> Tragedy depicts the individual confronted with
>
> the fact of death; comedy depicts the adaptability
>
> and ongoing survival of human society.

A semicolon is required between independent clauses that have been linked with a transitional expression (such as *however, therefore, moreover, in fact,* or *for example*). For a longer list, see the chart on page 177. (See also 34b.)

> The timber wolf looks much like a large German
>
> shepherd; however, the wolf has longer legs,
>
> larger feet, a wider head, and a long, bushy tail.

> Everyone in my outfit had a specific job; as a
>
> matter of fact, most of the officers had three or
>
> four duties.

If the first independent clause introduces the second or if the second clause summarizes or explains the first, a colon or a dash may be an appropriate method of revision. (See 35b and 39a.) In formal writing, the colon is usually preferred to the dash.

> *: This*
> Nuclear waste is hazardous ~~this~~ is an
>
> indisputable fact.

20c Consider making the clauses into separate sentences.

> Why should we spend money on expensive space
> *We*
> exploration? ~~we~~ have enough underfunded
>
> programs here on earth.
>
> Since one independent clause is a question and the other is a statement, they should be separate sentences.

> I gave the necessary papers to the police officer.
> *Then*
> ~~then~~ he said I would have to accompany him
>
> to the police station, where a counselor would
>
> talk with me and call my parents.
>
> Because the second independent clause is quite long, a sensible revision is to use separate sentences.

Checking for run-on sentences

First look for the most common trouble spots:

TRANSITIONAL EXPRESSIONS

also	in addition	now
as a result	in fact	of course
besides	in other words	on the other hand
consequently	in the first place	otherwise
finally	meanwhile	still
for example	moreover	then
for instance	nevertheless	therefore
furthermore	next	thus
however		

▶ We usually think of children as innocent and

guileless*;* however, they are often cruel and

unjust.

EXAMPLE OR EXPLANATION IN SECOND CLAUSE

▶ Martin looked out the window in astonishment*:*
He
~~he~~ had never seen snow before.

CLAUSES EXPRESSING CONTRAST

▶ Most of his contemporaries had made plans
but
for their retirement*,* Tom had not.

PRONOUN AS SUBJECT OF SECOND CLAUSE

who
▶ Claudia*,* was full of energy and enthusiasm,

~~she~~ tackled the job at once.

Next test your sentences for correctness:

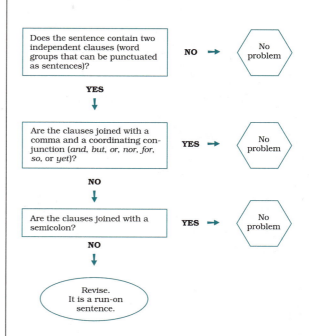

Does the sentence contain two independent clauses (word groups that can be punctuated as sentences)? — **NO** → No problem

YES ↓

Are the clauses joined with a comma and a coordinating conjunction (*and, but, or, nor, for, so,* or *yet*)? — **YES** → No problem

NO ↓

Are the clauses joined with a semicolon? — **YES** → No problem

NO ↓

Revise. It is a run-on sentence.

If you find an error, choose an effective method of revision. See 20a–d for specific revision strategies.

20d **Consider restructuring the sentence, perhaps by subordinating one of the clauses.**

If one of the independent clauses is less important than the other, turn it into a subordinate clause or phrase. (For more about subordination, see 8, especially the chart on the bottom of p. 85.)

▶ Of the many geysers in Yellowstone National
which
Park, the most famous is Old Faithful, ~~it~~

sometimes reaches 150 feet in height.

When the
▶ ~~The~~ new health plan was explained to the

employees in my division, everyone agreed to

give it a try.

▶ Saturday afternoon Julie came running into the

house*,* ~~she wanted~~ to get permission to go to

the park.

Minor ideas in these sentences are now expressed in subordinate clauses or phrases.

EXERCISE 20–1 Run-on sentences: Guided practice

Edit the following paragraphs to eliminate run-on sentences. Each rule number in the margin indicates a problem and suggests an effective method of revision. The first sentence has been done for you, and a suggested revision of this exercise appears in the back of the book.

Have you ever heard of the Wobblies/? ~~not~~ *Not* many people have these days.   *20c*

That's a shame they did at least two things for which they should be remember-   *20d*

ed. Thay probably saved the labor movement in America, they definitely gave Amer-   *20a*

ican folk music some of its most unforgettable songs. No one really knows how they

got their nickname almost everyone knows a song or two that they inspired.   *20a*

The Wobblies were the members of the Industrial Workers of the World (IWW),   *20d*

this union was a small but militant coalition of radical labor groups. The Wobblies

could not get along with the major union groups of the day, in fact, they alienated   *20b*

most of those groups.

The major unions disliked the Wobblies immensely, nevertheless they   *20d*

learned some valuable lessons from them. The first lesson was to avoid getting in-

volved in politics. If there was one thing the Wobblies hated more than capitalism,

it was politics. The Wobblies avoided politics for one good reason, they believed that   *20b*

political affiliation caused the death of unions. What else did the major unions learn,   *20c*

they learned to deal realistically with workers' problems. Major unions learned new

recruiting techniques from the Wobblies. In addition, they copied the Wobblies in

devoting their energy to nuts-and-bolts issues affecting the workers.

The major unions never recognized their debt to the Wobblies, the debt was   *20a*

still there for later historians to see. Historians began to compile the story of the

American labor unions, then they finally recognized the contributions of the   *20d*

Wobblies.

EXERCISE 20–2 Run-on sentences

One sentence in each of the following pairs is a run-on sentence. Find and correct the error, using an effective revision strategy. Mark the correct sentence "OK." Example:

        Although
a.   ^Joe Hill may not have been the first martyr of the labor movement, ~~however,~~ he was certainly its most skillful worker with words and music.

b.   Before his arrest in 1914 for killing a grocer in Salt Lake City, Joe Hill was simply the Swedish immigrant Joseph Hillstrom; no one knew or cared much about him. *OK*

1a.   Ralph Chaplin was the only person who wrote anything about Joe Hill before Hill's execution, he jotted down just a few notes based on an interview with a drunken sailor.

  b.   Serious historical research has not confirmed or denied those notes because researchers have turned up quite different stories.

2a.   All the evidence introduced at Hill's trial was circumstantial; furthermore, the dead man's son, who had witnessed the murder, refused to identify Hill as the gunman.

  b.   Did the state hide evidence it certainly seemed that way.

3a.   One Wobbly told the police that he had been with Joe Hill in another location on the night of the murder, he also told a detective he could prove Hill's innocence.

  b.   That man was promptly arrested and held in jail for the duration of the trial.

4a.   At the end of the trial the man was released and ordered to get out of the state.

  b.   Hill's own attorneys did not do much to help him their attitude was as negative as that of the prosecutors.

5a.   Because of their negative attitude, Hill discharged both of the attorneys who were supposed to be defending him.

  b.   "I have three prosecutors here, I intend to get rid of two of them," he said.

6a.   The state never showed a motive for the murder; furthermore, much evidence that Hill's attorneys could have used was never introduced.

  b.   How did Hill get that bullet wound in his chest, he told the doctor he had gotten it in a fight over a woman.

7a. The doctor who treated Hill was not asked to testify about medical aspects of the case, as a matter of fact, his testimony would probably have prevented Hill's conviction.

   b. Protests about Hill's conviction came from all over the world, but they were ignored.

8a. Important political figures tried to help Hill, hoping until the last minute that they could save him.

   b. The Swedish consul pleaded for him, President Wilson sent telegrams to the governor of Utah.

9a. Legend has it that Hill's last words before the firing squad were "Don't mourn for me; organize," in fact, he said, "Yes, aim! Let her go! Fire!"

   b. If Joe Hill is known at all today, it is probably because of Joe Glazer, his guitar, and the song "Joe Hill."

10a. Glazer was not the composer of "Joe Hill" its composers were Earl Robinson and Alfred Hayes.

   b. Glazer, however, made the song known across America, singing it at banquets as well as on picket lines.

EXERCISE 20–3 Run-on sentences

Correct each run-on sentence using the method of revision suggested in brackets. Example:

> *with whom*
> In his death cell, Joe Hill sent a letter to Big Bill Haywood, he had worked ~~with Haywood~~
> in the early days of the IWW. [*Restructure the sentence;* see 20d.]

1. Joe Hill's final letter to Big Bill Haywood had only five sentences, it contained one line about his death, one admonition to Haywood, and three comments related to Hill's burial. [*Use a colon;* see 20b.]

2. He commented briefly about his death he said, "I die like a true rebel." [*Restructure the sentence;* see 20d.]

3. Hill told Haywood, "Don't waste time mourning for me, organize instead." [*Use a semicolon;* see 20b.]

4. Hill, in prison in Utah, did not want to be buried in that state, he asked Haywood to haul his body into Wyoming, a hundred miles away. [*Use a coordinating conjunction;* see 20a.]

5. Hill gave only one reason for requesting burial in Wyoming, he said, "I don't want to be found dead in Utah." [*Make two sentences;* see 20c.]

6. On the night before his execution, he wrote a final poem, in it he made two requests. [*Restructure the sentence;* see 20d.]

7. He wanted his body to be cremated, he wanted his ashes to be allowed to blow freely around the earth. [*Use a coordinating conjunction;* see 20a.]

8. Here's how he said it in his poem,

   Let the merry breezes blow
   My dust to where some flowers grow.
   Perhaps some fading flower then
   Would come to life and bloom again. [*Use a colon;* see 20b.]

9. Obviously, Joe Hill was not a great poet, however, he was clever with rhymes. [*Use a semicolon;* see 20b.]

10. Even in his will he managed to fit in a humorous rhyme.

    This is my last and final will.
    Good luck to all of you.
        Joe Hill [*Use a colon;* see 20b.]

EXERCISE 20–4 Run-on sentences

Revise each of the following run-on sentences in the way you think is most effective. Example:

Joe Hill was not buried in Utah; he was not buried in Wyoming either.

1. After Joe Hill's death, his body was sent to Chicago, a large auditorium was secured for the funeral services.

2. More than thirty thousand people overflowed the auditorium, they jammed the streets as they followed the funeral train to the cemetery.

3. Very few of these mourners knew Joe Hill personally, nevertheless, he was a true hero to them.

4. On that Thanksgiving Day of 1915, they knew that other people mourned him too they heard eulogies to him in nine different languages.

5. Those mourners and thousands like them sang his songs, because they did, Joe Hill's name lived on.

6. Hill's satirical, angry songs often had a surprising tenderness, it is no wonder that he was named poet laureate of the Wobbly movement.

7. In some ways, Joe Hill's death freed him, in other ways, he remains a prisoner.

8. Joe Hill did get part of his deathbed wish, his body was cremated.

9. He was cremated at the cemetery afterward his ashes were put in thirty envelopes and sent all over the world.

10. The IWW kept one envelope, the Department of Justice confiscated it in 1918 for use in a trial. Since the envelope was never returned, part of Joe Hill is still "in prison."

EXERCISE 20–5 Run-on sentences: Guided review

Revise each run-on sentence in the following paragraphs, using the method of revision suggested by the rule number in the margin. The first sentence has been revised for you.

    Although he
~~He~~ never calls them by name, John Steinbeck immortalizes the Wobblies in   *20d*

The Grapes of Wrath. The novel is about the life of the Joad family. The Joads have

lost their farm during the Depression, the family has come to California seeking   *20d*

work. There is no permanent work for anyone, moreover, the money earned by pick-   *20b*

ing crops is not enough to feed the family.

    Union organizers have talked to the workers about organizing and striking.

Tom, the oldest Joad son, has listened to them, however, he has not yet joined them.   *20a*

Tom is in hiding because he has accidentally killed a man in a fight. He spends all

his daylight hours alone, he has lots of time to think about his family's situation.   *20a*

Tom becomes convinced that life is unfair for his people, he decides to leave the fam-   *20d*

ily, find the union men, and work with them.

    He is inarticulate when he tries to explain to Ma what he hopes to do he   *20c*

gropes for words to express his frustration and his hope. Ma asks him how she will

know about him, she worries that he might get killed and she would not know. Tom's   *20c*

reassurances are almost mystical: "Wherever they's a fight so hungry people can eat,

I'll be there an' when our folks eat the stuff they raise an' live in the houses they

build, I'll be there."

    If Tom had had a copy of the Wobblies' "little red song book," he could have

found less mystical words. Every copy of the book contained the Wobblies' Pre-

amble, the first sentence in the Preamble was unmistakably clear "The working class   *20d, 20b*

and the employing class have nothing in common." Tom would have understood

those words he would have believed them too.   *20b*

21 Make subjects and verbs agree.

Native speakers of standard English know by ear that *he talks, she has,* and *it doesn't* (not *he talk, she have,* and *it don't*) are standard subject-verb combinations. For such speakers, problems with subject-verb agreement arise only in certain tricky situations, which are detailed in 21b–21k.

If you don't trust your ear—perhaps because you speak English as a second language, perhaps because you speak or hear nonstandard English in your community—you will need to learn the standard forms explained in 21a. Even if you do trust your ear, take a quick look at 21a to see what "subject-verb agreement" means.

21a Consult this section for standard subject-verb combinations.

In the present tense, verbs agree with their subjects in number (singular or plural) and in person (first, second, or third). The present-tense ending *-s* (or *-es*) is used on a verb if its subject is third-person singular; otherwise the verb takes no ending. Consider, for example, the present-tense forms of the verb *love,* given at the beginning of the chart at the top of page 188.

The verb *be* varies from this pattern; unlike any other verb, it has special forms in *both* the present and the past tense. These forms appear at the end of the top chart on page 188.

If you aren't confident that you know the standard forms, use the charts on page 188 as you proofread for subject-verb agreement. You may also want to take a look at 27c, which discusses the matter of *-s* endings in some detail.

 GRAMMAR CHECKERS attempt to flag faulty subject-verb agreement, but they have mixed success. They fail to flag many problems; in addition, they flag a number of correct sentences, usually because they have misidentified the subject, the verb—or both.

If you are good at identifying subjects and verbs and seeing whether they agree, the grammar checker can be of some use to you, since you will be able to tell when a flagged sentence really has a problem and when it doesn't. Even so, bear in mind that the program won't catch all problems.

If you are not confident of your ability to identify subjects and verbs and see whether they agree, the grammar checker can do you serious harm. Writing center tutors report that some bizarre errors result when students don't have the confidence to reject the computer program's incorrect advice—or don't stop to think before accepting it. For example, without thinking first, one student changed *is* to *am* in this sentence because the computer said that the subject *I* agreed with the verb *am,* not with *is*: *Eating raw limpets, I found out, am like trying to eat art gum erasers.* You can imagine this student's embarrassment upon reading this sentence later. Slow down before taking the computer's advice. And when in doubt, rely on your handbook and your own good sense, not on the grammar checker.

21b Make the verb agree with its subject, not with a word that comes between.

Word groups often come between the subject and the verb. Such word groups, usually modifying the subject, may contain a noun that at first appears to be the subject. By mentally stripping away such modifiers, you can isolate the noun that is in fact the subject.

The *tulips* in the pot on the balcony *need* watering.

▶ High levels of air pollution causes damage to the respiratory tract.

The subject is *levels,* not *pollution.* Strip away the phrase *of air pollution* to hear the correct verb: *levels cause.*

▶ The slaughter of pandas for their pelts has~~have~~ caused the panda population to decline drastically.

The subject is *slaughter,* not *pandas* or *pelts.*

NOTE: Phrases beginning with the prepositions *as well as, in addition to, accompanied by, together with,* and *along with* do not make a singular subject plural.

Subject-verb agreement at a glance

PRESENT-TENSE FORMS OF *LOVE* (A TYPICAL VERB)

	SINGULAR		PLURAL	
FIRST PERSON	I	love	we	love
SECOND PERSON	you	love	you	love
THIRD PERSON	he/she/it	loves	they	love

PRESENT-TENSE FORMS OF *HAVE*

	SINGULAR		PLURAL	
FIRST PERSON	I	have	we	have
SECOND PERSON	you	have	you	have
THIRD PERSON	he/she/it	has	they	have

PRESENT-TENSE FORMS OF *DO*

	SINGULAR		PLURAL	
FIRST PERSON	I	do/don't	we	do/don't

PRESENT-TENSE FORMS OF *DO* (CONT.)

	SINGULAR		PLURAL	
SECOND PERSON	you	do/don't	you	do/don't
THIRD PERSON	he/she/it	does/doesn't	they	do/don't

PRESENT-TENSE AND PAST-TENSE FORMS OF *BE*

	SINGULAR		PLURAL	
FIRST PERSON	I	am/was	we	are/were
SECOND PERSON	you	are/were	you	are/were
THIRD PERSON	he/she/it	is/was	they	are/were

When to use the -s (or -es) form of a present-tense verb

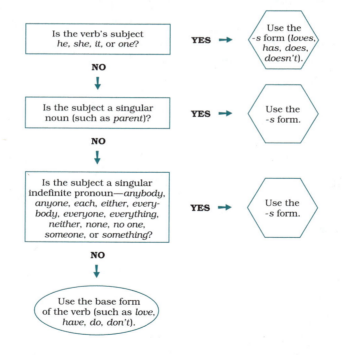

Is the verb's subject *he, she, it,* or *one*? — **YES** → Use the -s form (*loves, has, does, doesn't*).

NO ↓

Is the subject a singular noun (such as *parent*)? — **YES** → Use the -s form.

NO ↓

Is the subject a singular indefinite pronoun—*anybody, anyone, each, either, everybody, everyone, everything, neither, none, no one, someone,* or *something*? — **YES** → Use the -s form.

NO ↓

Use the base form of the verb (such as *love, have, do, don't*).

EXCEPTION: Choosing the correct present-tense form of *be* (*am, is,* or *are*) is not quite so simple. See the chart at the top of this page for both present- and past-tense forms of *be*.

ESL CAUTION: Do not use the -s form of a verb that follows a helping verb such as *can, must,* or *should*. (See 29a.)

▶ The governor, as well as his press secretary, ~~were~~ *was*

shot.

To emphasize that two people were shot, the writer could use *and* instead: *The governor and his press secretary were shot.*

21c Treat most subjects joined with *and* as plural.

A subject with two or more parts is said to be compound. If the parts are connected by *and,* the subject is nearly always plural.

Leon and Jan often *jog* together.

▶ Jill's natural ability and her desire to help others *have* ~~has~~ led to a career in the ministry.

Ability and desire is a plural subject, so its verb should be *have.*

EXCEPTIONS: When the parts of the subject form a single unit or when they refer to the same person or thing, treat the subject as singular.

Strawberries and cream was a last-minute addition to the menu.

Sue's friend and adviser was surprised by her decision.

When a compound subject is preceded by *each* or *every,* treat it as singular.

Each tree, shrub, and vine needs to be sprayed.

Every car, truck, and van is required to pass inspection.

This exception does not apply when a compound subject is followed by *each: Alan and Marcia each have different ideas.*

21d With subjects joined with *or* or *nor* (or by *either . . . or* or *neither . . . nor*), make the verb agree with the part of the subject nearer to the verb.

A driver's *license* or credit *card is* required.

A driver's *license* or two credit *cards are* required.

▶ If a relative or neighbor ~~are~~ *is* abusing a child, notify

the police immediately.

▶ Neither the lab assistant nor the students ~~was~~ *were*

able to download the information.

The verb must be matched with the part of the subject closer to it: *neighbor is* in the first sentence, *students were* in the second.

NOTE: If one part of the subject is singular and the other is plural, put the plural one last to avoid awkwardness.

21e Treat most indefinite pronouns as singular.

Indefinite pronouns are pronouns that do not refer to specific persons or things. The following commonly used indefinite pronouns are singular:

anybody	either	neither	somebody
anyone	everybody	nobody	someone
anything	everyone	none	something
each	everything	no one	

Many of these words appear to have plural meanings, and they are often treated as such in casual speech. In formal written English, however, they are nearly always treated as singular.

Everyone on the team *supports* the coach.

▶ Each of the furrows ~~have~~ *has* been seeded.

▶ Everybody who signed up for the ski trip ~~were~~ *was*

taking lessons.

The subjects of these sentences are *Each* and *Everybody.* These indefinite pronouns are third-person singular, so the verbs must be *has* and *was.*

The indefinite pronouns *none* and *neither* are considered singular when used alone.

None is immune to this disease.

Neither is able to attend.

When these pronouns are followed by prepositional phrases with a plural meaning, however, usage varies. Some experts insist on treating the pronouns as singular, but many writers disagree. It is safer to treat them as singular.

> *None* of these trades *requires* a college education.

> *Neither* of those pejoratives *fits* Professor Brady.

A few indefinite pronouns (*all, any, some*) are singular or plural depending on the noun or pronoun they refer to.

> *Some* of the *lemonade has* disappeared.

> *Some* of the *rocks were* slippery.

21f Treat collective nouns as singular unless the meaning is clearly plural.

Collective nouns such as *jury, committee, audience, crowd, class, troop, family,* and *couple* name a class or a group. In American English, collective nouns are nearly always treated as singular: They emphasize the group as a unit. Occasionally, when there is some reason to draw attention to the individual members of the group, a collective noun may be treated as plural. (Also see 22b.)

SINGULAR

The *class respects* the teacher.

PLURAL

The *class are* debating among themselves.

To underscore the notion of individuality in the second sentence, many writers would add a clearly plural noun such as *members:*

PLURAL

The class *members are* debating among themselves.

> ▸ The scout troop ~~meet~~ *meets* in our basement on
>
> Tuesdays.

The troop as a whole meets in the basement; there is no reason to draw attention to its individual members.

> ▸ A young couple ~~was~~ *were* arguing about politics while
>
> holding hands.

The meaning is clearly plural. Only individuals can argue and hold hands.

NOTE: The phrase *the number* is treated as singular, *a number* as plural.

SINGULAR

The number of school-age children *is* declining.

PLURAL

A number of children *are* attending the wedding.

NOTE: When units of measurement are used collectively, treat them as singular; when they refer to individual persons or things, treat them as plural.

SINGULAR

Three-fourths of the pie *has* been eaten.

PLURAL

One-fourth of the drivers *were* drunk.

21g Make the verb agree with its subject even when the subject follows the verb.

Verbs ordinarily follow subjects. When this normal order is reversed, it is easy to become confused. Sentences beginning with *there is* or *there are* (or *there was* or *there were*) are inverted; the subject follows the verb.

> There *are* surprisingly few *children* in our neighborhood.

> ▸ There ~~was~~ *were* a social worker and a crew of twenty
>
> volunteers at the scene of the accident.

The subject *worker and crew* is plural, so the verb must be *were.*

Occasionally you may decide to invert a sentence for variety or effect. When you do so, check to make sure that your subject and verb agree.

> *are*
> At the back of the room ~~is~~ a small aquarium and
> an enormous terrarium.

The subject *aquarium and terrarium* is plural, so the verb must be *are*. If the correct sentence seems awkward, begin with the subject: *A small aquarium and an enormous terrarium are at the back of the room.*

21h Make the verb agree with its subject, not with a subject complement.

One basic sentence pattern in English consists of a subject, a linking verb, and a subject complement: *Jack is a securities lawyer.* Because the subject complement names or describes the subject (*Jack*), it is sometimes mistaken for the subject. (See 48b on subject complements.)

> These *problems are* a way to test your skill.

> *are*
> A tent and a sleeping bag ~~is~~ the required equip-
> ment for all campers.

Tent and bag is the subject, not *equipment*.

> *is*
> A major force in today's economy ~~are~~ women—
> as earners, consumers, and investors.

Force is the subject, not *women*. If the corrected version seems awkward, make *women* the subject: *Women are a major force in today's economy—as earners, consumers, and investors.*

21i *Who, which,* and *that* take verbs that agree with their antecedents.

Like most pronouns, the relative pronouns *who, which,* and *that* have antecedents, nouns or pronouns to which they refer. Relative pronouns used as subjects of subordinate clauses take verbs that agree with their antecedents.

> Take a *suit that travels* well.

Problems can arise with the constructions *one of the* and *only one of the.* As a rule, treat *one of the* constructions as plural, *only one of the* constructions as singular.

> Our ability to use language is one of the things
> that *sets* us apart from animals.

The antecedent of *that* is *things*, not *one*. Several things set us apart from animals.

> Dr. Barker knew that Frank was the only one of
> *was*
> his sons who ~~were~~ responsible enough to
> handle the estate.

The antecedent of *who* is *one*, not *sons*. Only one son was responsible enough.

21j Words such as *athletics, economics, mathematics, physics, statistics, measles, mumps,* and *news* are usually singular, despite their plural form.

> *is*
> Statistics are among the most difficult courses
> in our program.

EXCEPTION: When they describe separate items rather than a collective body of knowledge, words such as *athletics, mathematics, physics,* and *statistics* are plural: *The statistics on school retention rates are impressive.*

21k Titles of works, company names, words mentioned as words, and gerund phrases are singular.

> *describes*
> *Lost Cities* ~~describe~~ the discoveries of many
> ancient civilizations.

> *specializes*
> Delmonico Brothers ~~specialize~~ in organic
> produce and additive-free meats.

> *is*
> *Controlled substances* ~~are~~ a euphemism for illegal
> drugs.

A gerund phrase consists of an *-ing* verb form followed by any objects, complements, or modifiers (see 49c). Treat gerund phrases as singular.

> *is*
> Encountering busy signals ~~are~~ troublesome to our
> clients, so we have hired two new switchboard
> operators.

EXERCISE 21–1 Subject-verb agreement: Guided practice

Circle the correct verb from each pair in parentheses. Rule numbers in the margin refer to appropriate rules in section 21. The first selection has been made for you, and an answer to this exercise appears in the back of the book.

Before reaching college, nearly everyone already ((knows,) know) several facts   *21e*

about fables. Most students know, for example, that fables are short stories that   *21i*

(conveys, convey) a moral. They also know that fables nearly always have animal

characters but that animal characters alone (is, are) not a signal that the story is a   *21h*

fable. They know of Aesop, to whom most familiar fables in Western culture (is, are)   *21b*

attributed. They know that there (is, are) generally only two or three characters in an   *21g*

Aesop fable, that a crowd of observers almost never (has, have) a role in his stories.   *21f*

Most adults recognize that the subject matter of Aesop's fables is nearly al-

ways the same. Once in a while, but not often, politics (is, are) highlighted in a story.   *21j*

Usually, however, Aesop's fables point out the value of common sense or make

gentle fun of human failings. Since neither foolish behavior nor human failings   *21d*

(seems, seem) to be in short supply, Aesop's stories keep on being told. Besides, they

attract a wide audience: Adults and children both (enjoy, enjoys) them. Everyone   *21c*

who has gone to school (is, are) supposed to know some of Aesop's fables. "The Fox   *21e*

and the Grapes," for instance, (is, are) familiar to many children as a story long   *21k*

before they understand its meaning.

EXERCISE 21–2 Subject-verb agreement

Verbs in the following sentences are italicized. Underline the subject (or compound subject) of each verb, and edit the sentence to make the subject and verb agree. Keep all verbs in the present tense, and do not change the three correct sentences. Example:

> *have*
> **Many** of the morals or wise sayings from fables ~~has~~ become a part of our language.

1. Phrases like "a wolf in sheep's clothing" *is used and understood* by many people.

2. The expression "a wolf in sheep's clothing" *comes* from one of Aesop's fables.

3. A flock of sheep and a hungry lion *is* the main characters in the story.

4. After killing a sheep for their supper, the shepherd and his helpers *forgets* about the skin from the sheep.

5. The wolf, finding the discarded skin, *cover* himself with it.

6. Joining the flock, he *pretends* to be a mother looking for her lamb.

7. The flock *accept* him as a sheep.

8. Neither the sheep nor the shepherd *notice* the wolf at first.

9. Daily luring a lamb from the flock, the wolf *feeds* himself very well for a while.

10. Everyone hearing the story *understand* its warning to beware of people pretending to be what they are not.

EXERCISE 21–3 Subject-verb agreement

All of the following sentences have two subjects and verbs. The subjects are italicized. Edit each sentence to make the subjects and verbs agree. Keep all verbs in the present tense. One subject-verb pair in each sentence is correct. Example:

is
"Sour grapes" ~~are~~ a common expression, but not *everyone* knows the origin of that phrase.

1. Aesop's *story* "The Fox and the Grapes" tells about a fox *who* try unsuccessfully to get some grapes.

2. There are a big *bunch* of grapes hanging over the top of a wall, and the *fox* is hot and thirsty.

3. A favorite *food* of his are grapes, and *he* leaps up to get some—without success.

4. Hoping that no *crowd* of friends are watching, the *fox* takes a running leap for the top of the wall.

5. Unsuccessful, the *fox* in the story tries again and again with the same result; neither his *cleverness nor* his high *leaps* is successful.

6. Embarrassed, the *fox* fears that *news* of his failures are going to give his friends something to tease him about.

7. The fox's *pride and* his *self-confidence* has suffered, so *he* claims not to want the grapes anyway.

8. The *fox*, stalking proudly off with his nose in the air, say the *grapes* are sour.

9. *Everyone* know that the *fox* does not believe his own words.

10. To save their pride, *people* often pretends not to want what *they* cannot get.

EXERCISE 21–4 Subject-verb agreement: Guided review

Circle the correct verb from each pair in parentheses. Rule numbers in the margin refer to appropriate rules in section 21. The first selection has been made for you.

From one of Aesop's lesser-known fables (comes, come) the question "Who's   21g
going to bell the cat?" The fable "Belling the Cat" describes the long battle between
mice and cats.

In the story, a committee of many mice is appointed to find a way to keep
the cat from killing so many mice. Everyone on the committee (tries, try) to solve the   21e
problem. There (is, are) many committee meetings and much discussion, but in the   21g
end neither the committee nor its chairperson (is, are) able to make any good sug-   21d
gestions. Finally, the time comes for the committee to make its report at a public
meeting. Embarrassed, the committee (reports, report) its failure.   21f

At first, there is only silence; no one wants to accept the committee's report
as the final word on the problem. Then a little pip-squeak among the mice (suggests,   21b
suggest) tying a bell on the cat. The young mouse makes quite a speech in favor of
his idea. According to that mouse, statistics (shows, show) that no mice have ever   21j
been captured by a noisy cat. The mouse points out that his solution would not cost
much; a bell and a string (is, are) all the equipment needed to give the mice warn-   21c
ing of the cat's approach. The mouse who makes the suggestion gets a round of ap-
plause. The committee members, who (wishes, wish) that they had thought of the   21i
idea, are silent. Then a wise old mouse asks, "Who will bell the cat?" The experienced mice and the young pip-squeak (is, are) silent.   21c

It is easy to make suggestions that other people (has, have) to carry out.   21a

22 Make pronouns and antecedents agree.

A pronoun is a word that substitutes for a noun. (See 47b.) Many pronouns have antecedents, nouns or pronouns to which they refer. A pronoun and its antecedent agree when they are both singular or both plural.

SINGULAR

Dr. Sarah Simms finished *her* rounds.

PLURAL

The *doctors* finished *their* rounds.

ESL

The pronouns *he, his, she, her, it,* and *its* must agree in gender (masculine, feminine, or neuter) with their antecedents, not with the words they modify.

Jane visited *her* [not *his*] brother in Denver.

GRAMMAR CHECKERS do not flag problems with pronoun-antecedent agreement. It takes a human eye to see that a singular noun, such as *logger,* does not agree with a plural pronoun, such as *their,* in a sentence like this: *The logger in the Northwest relies on the old forest growth for their living.*

22a Do not use plural pronouns to refer to singular antecedents.

Writers are frequently tempted to use plural pronouns to refer to two kinds of singular antecedents: indefinite pronouns and generic nouns.

Indefinite pronouns

Indefinite pronouns refer to nonspecific persons or things. Even though some of the following indefinite pronouns may seem to have plural meanings, treat them as singular in formal English.

anybody	either	neither	somebody
anyone	everybody	nobody	someone
anything	everyone	none	something
each	everything	no one	

In class *everyone* performs at *his or her* [not *their*] own fitness level.

When a plural pronoun refers mistakenly to a singular indefinite pronoun, you can usually choose one of three options for revision.

1. Replace the plural pronoun with *he or she* (or *his or her*).
2. Make the antecedent plural.
3. Rewrite the sentence so that no problem of agreement exists.

► When someone has been drinking, ~~they are~~ likely *he or she is*

   to speed.

► When ~~someone has~~ been drinking, they are likely *drivers have*

   to speed.

► When ~~someone~~ has been drinking,/~~they are~~ likely *A driver who* *is*

   to speed.

Because the *he or she* construction is wordy, often the second or third revision strategy is more effective. Be aware that the traditional use of *he* (or *his*) to refer to persons of either sex is now widely considered sexist. (See 17f.)

Generic nouns

A generic noun represents a typical member of a group, such as a typical student, or any member of a group, such as any lawyer. Although generic nouns may seem to have plural meanings, they are singular.

Every *runner* must train rigorously if *he or she wants* [not *they want*] to excel.

When a plural pronoun refers mistakenly to a generic noun, you will usually have the same three revision options as just mentioned for indefinite pronouns.

► A medical student must study hard if ~~they want~~ to *he or she wants*

   succeed.

Checking for problems with pronoun-antecedent agreement

First look for the most common trouble spots:

INDEFINITE PRONOUNS (SINGULAR) (22a)

anybody	either	neither	somebody
anyone	everybody	nobody	someone
anything	everyone	none	something
each	everything	no one	

No one will see a salary increase until *he or she has* [not *they have*] been employed for two years.

GENERIC NOUNS (SINGULAR) (22a)

A generic noun names a typical person or thing (such as a typical teacher) or any person or thing (such as any employee of a company).

An adult *panda* must consume ninety pounds of bamboo if *it is* [not *they are*] to remain healthy.

COLLECTIVE NOUNS (SINGULAR UNLESS THE MEANING IS CLEARLY PLURAL) (22b)

audience	committee	crowd	majority	team
class	couple	family	minority	troop

The *committee* selected *its* [not *their*] new chairperson last night.

Choose an effective revision strategy that avoids sexist language.

Because many readers object to sexist language, avoid the use of *he, him,* and *his* as shorthand for *he or she, him or her,* and *his or hers.* Also try to be sparing in your use of *he or she* and *his or her,* since these expressions can become awkward, especially when repeated several times in a short passage. Where possible, seek out more graceful alternatives.

USE AN OCCASIONAL *HE OR SHE* (OR *HIS OR HER*).

► In our office, everyone works at ~~their~~ own *his or her* pace.

MAKE THE ANTECEDENT PLURAL.

► *Employees* ~~An employee~~ on extended leave may continue their life insurance.

RECAST THE SENTENCE.

► The amount of annual leave a federal worker may accrue depends on ~~their~~ length of service.

► ~~If a~~ *A* child ~~is~~ born to parents who are both schizophrenic~~, they have~~ *has* a high chance of being schizophrenic.

► A year later someone finally admitted ~~that they~~ *to being* ~~were~~ involved in the kidnapping.

► I was taught that no one could escape the fires of purgatory~~. if they wanted to reach heaven.~~ *who wanted to reach heaven*

► *Medical students* ~~A medical student~~ must study hard if they want to succeed.

► A medical student must study hard ~~if they want~~ to succeed.

22b Treat collective nouns as singular unless the meaning is clearly plural.

Collective nouns such as *jury, committee, audience, crowd, class, troop, family, team,* and *couple* name a class or a group. Ordinarily the group functions as a unit, so the noun should be treated as singular; if the members of the group function as individuals, however, the noun should be treated as plural. (See also 21f.)

AS A UNIT

The *committee* granted *its* permission to build.

AS INDIVIDUALS

The *committee* put *their* signatures on the document.

► The jury has reached ~~their~~ *its* decision.

There is no reason to draw attention to the individual members of the jury, so *jury* should be treated as singular. Notice also that the writer treated the noun as singular when choosing the verb *has,* so for consistency the pronoun must be *its.*

▸ The audience shouted "Bravo" and stamped ~~its~~ *their* feet.

It is difficult to see how the audience as a unit can stamp *its* feet. The meaning here is clearly plural, requiring *their.*

22c Treat most compound antecedents connected by *and* as plural.

Joanne and John moved to the mountains, where *they* built a log cabin.

22d With compound antecedents connected by *or* or *nor* (or by *either . . . or* or *neither . . . nor*), make the pronoun agree with the nearer antecedent.

Either *Bruce* or *James* should receive first prize for *his* sculpture.

Neither the *mouse* nor the *rats* could find *their* way through the maze.

NOTE: If one of the antecedents is singular and the other plural, as in the second example, put the plural one last to avoid awkwardness.

EXCEPTION: If one antecedent is male and the other female, do not follow the traditional rule. The sentence *Either Bruce or Ann should receive the blue ribbon for her sculpture* makes no sense. The best solution is to recast the sentence: *The blue ribbon for best sculpture should go to Bruce or Ann.*

EXERCISE 22–1 Pronoun-antecedent agreement: Guided practice

Edit the following paragraphs for problems with pronoun-antecedent agreement. Rule numbers in the margin refer to appropriate rules in section 22. The first revision has been done for you, and a suggested revision of this exercise appears in the back of the book.

Everyone has heard of Dorothy and Toto and their tornado "flight" from

Everyone also knows

Kansas to Oz. ~~They also know~~ that the Oz adventure was pure fantasy and that it   **22a**

ended happily. But another girl from Kansas took real flights all around the real world.

Whenever she landed safely after setting one of her many records, everyone rejoiced

and sent their congratulations to her. When she disappeared on her last flight, the   **22a**

whole world mourned. Not every pilot can claim they have that kind of following.

Neighbors knew that Amelia Earhart would not be a typical "lady." A child   **22a**

as curious, daring, and self-confident as Amelia was bound to stand out among

peers. When she and her sister Muriel were young, girls were supposed to play with

dolls. If a girl played baseball or collected worms, they were called "tomboys" and   **22a**

were often punished. Boys and girls even had different kinds of sleds—the girls'

sleds were lightweight, impossible-to-steer box sleds.

But the Earhart family lived by their own rules. Amelia's father, whom she   **22b**

depended on for approval, bought her the boy's sled she longed for. Many fast trips

down steep hills gave Amelia a foretaste of flying with the wind in her face.

The closest Amelia came to flying was on a homemade roller coaster. She and

her friends built it, using an old woodshed for the base of the ride. They started eight

feet off the ground and tried to sled down the slope without falling off. No one was

successful on their first attempt, but Amelia kept trying until she had a successful   **22a**

ride. Satisfied at last, she declared that the ride had felt "just like flying."

EXERCISE 22–2 Pronoun-antecedent agreement

Five of the following word groups contain a problem with pronoun-antecedent agreement. Mark the correct sentences "OK," and edit the incorrect ones to eliminate the problem. Example:

> During World War I, Amelia Earhart listened to wounded pilots' tales of adventure. ~~A pilot~~ *Pilots* would describe a particularly daring wartime adventure and joke about their ability to beat the odds.

1. After World War I, Amelia Earhart took flying lessons. She learned quickly, but the lessons cost her most of her salary.

2. She wanted those lessons, so she worked two jobs to pay for them: She clerked for the telephone company and drove a dump truck for a sand and gravel company.

3. Members of her family pooled their funds to buy a gift—a little yellow biplane—for her twenty-fourth birthday celebration; it was the perfect gift.

4. Amelia Earhart soon learned that when someone owns a plane, they need a lot of money.

5. She sometimes executed dangerous maneuvers before her teacher was sure Amelia could handle it.

6. At first everyone could not believe their eyes when she deliberately put her plane into a spin.

7. Each spectator would gasp when they heard her cut the engine off in a spin.

8. But Amelia Earhart repeatedly pulled the plane out of its spin and landed safely, delighting everyone.

9. When an aviator wants to break records, they will work very hard.

10. Aviation record keepers had to make a new entry in the record books: They had seen Amelia Earhart fly 14,000 feet high.

EXERCISE 22–3 Pronoun-antecedent agreement

In each set of sentences, circle the letter of the sentence that has a problem with pronoun-antecedent agreement. Which of the other two sentences (both correct) do you prefer? Put a check mark next to that sentence. Example:

(a.) A college dropout often gets little respect for their choosing to leave school.

b. College dropouts often get little respect for their choosing to leave school.

√ c. A college dropout often gets little respect for choosing to leave school.

1a. Not everyone who drops out of college ruins their life.

b. Not all students who drop out of college ruin their lives.

c. Not all college dropouts ruin their lives.

2a. Students sometimes discover that they don't like their chosen field.

b. A student sometimes discovers that he or she doesn't like their chosen field.

c. Students may lose interest in their chosen field.

3a. Amelia had always loved planes, so her family was not surprised when she quit school to learn to fly.

b. Amelia had always loved planes, so her family were not surprised when she quit school to learn to fly.

c. Knowing that Amelia had always loved planes, her family was not surprised when she quit school to learn to fly.

4a. In their catalog, Columbia University offered a wide range of courses, but Flying Airplanes was not among them.

b. Flying Airplanes was not among the wide range of courses offered in Columbia University's catalog.

c. In its catalog, Columbia University offered a wide range of courses, but Flying Airplanes was not among them.

5a. Amelia Earhart became a dropout any university would be proud to claim.

b. Amelia Earhart became one of those dropouts any university would be proud to claim as theirs.

c. Amelia Earhart became a dropout all universities would be proud to claim.

EXERCISE 22–4 Pronoun-antecedent agreement: Guided review

Edit the following paragraphs for problems with pronoun-antecedent agreement. Rule numbers in the margin refer to appropriate rules in section 22. The first revision has been done for you.

When Amelia Earhart became the first woman to cross the Atlantic in a plane,
she got no money; she did get a free ride, fame, and job offers. Not ~~every flier~~ *all fliers* would   22a
think these rewards were enough for their time and trouble on the trip, but Amelia
Earhart was delighted with the whole experience. Afterward, a book she wrote about
that flight brought her another first: a publisher, a shrewd business manager, and
a husband—all in one man, George Putnam. (Putnam also understood her fierce independence—not every man would sign a prenuptial agreement saying their wife   22a
could have a divorce anytime she asked!)

The first national organization for "flying women," formed by Amelia Earhart
and a friend, recruited their members in the belief that every woman should follow   22b
her own interest. After all, who had made the first solo flight from Honolulu to the
United States? From Los Angeles to Mexico City? And from Mexico City to New Jersey? It was she, Amelia Earhart. No woman ever did more to prove that they could   22a
handle jobs traditionally reserved for men.

Amelia Earhart's last "first" was never completed. When she tried to become
the first pilot to fly around the world at the equator, she disappeared somewhere
over the Pacific. The government searched more than 265,000 miles of air and sea   22a
space, but they found nothing.

In 1994, fifty-seven years after Amelia Earhart's disappearance, twelve-
year-old Vicki Van Meter became the youngest female pilot to fly across the Atlantic.
She took off from Augusta, Maine, from the very spot where Amelia Earhart had
started her flight across the Atlantic. When Van Meter landed safely in Glasgow,
everyone offered their congratulations, and Van Meter felt a special kinship with her   22a
predecessor, Amelia Earhart.

23 Make pronoun references clear.

Pronouns substitute for nouns; they are a kind of shorthand. In a sentence like *After Andrew intercepted the ball, he kicked it as hard as he could*, the pronouns *he* and *it* substitute for the nouns *Andrew* and *ball*. The word a pronoun refers to is called its *antecedent*.

> GRAMMAR CHECKERS do not flag problems with faulty pronoun reference. Although a computer program can identify pronouns, it has no way of knowing which words, if any, they refer to. For example, grammar checkers miss the fact that the pronoun *it* has an ambiguous reference in the following sentence: *The thief stole the woman's purse and her car and then destroyed it.* Did the thief destroy the purse or the car? It takes human judgment to realize that readers might be confused.

23a Avoid ambiguous or remote pronoun reference.

Ambiguous pronoun reference occurs when the pronoun could refer to two possible antecedents.

> *The pitcher broke when Gloria set it*
> ▶ ~~When Gloria set the pitcher~~ on the glass-topped
> table,/it ~~broke.~~

> ▶ Tom told James, *"You have* ~~that he had~~ won the lottery*."*

What broke—the table or the pitcher? Who won the lottery—Tom or James? The revisions eliminate the ambiguity.

Remote pronoun reference occurs when a pronoun is too far away from its antecedent for easy reading.

> ▶ After the court ordered my ex-husband to pay
>
> child support, he refused. Approximately eight
>
> months later, we were back in court. This time
>
> the judge ordered him to make payments

directly to the Support and Collections Unit,

which would in turn pay me. For the first six

months I received regular payments, but then
my ex-husband
they stopped. Again ~~he~~ was summoned to appear

in court; he did not respond.

The pronoun *he* was too distant from its antecedent, *ex-husband*, which appeared several sentences earlier.

23b Generally, avoid broad reference of *this, that, which,* and *it.*

For clarity, the pronouns *this, that, which,* and *it* should ordinarily refer to specific antecedents rather than to whole ideas or sentences. When a pronoun's reference is needlessly broad, either replace the pronoun with a noun or supply an antecedent to which the pronoun clearly refers.

> ▶ More and more often, especially in large cities,
>
> we are finding ourselves victims of serious crimes.
> *our fate*
> We learn to accept ~~this~~ with minor gripes and
>
> groans.

For clarity the writer substituted a noun (*fate*) for the pronoun *this*, which referred broadly to the idea expressed in the preceding sentence.

> ▶ Romeo and Juliet were both too young to have
> *a fact*
> acquired much wisdom, which accounts for their
>
> rash actions.

The writer added an antecedent (*fact*) that the pronoun *which* clearly refers to.

EXCEPTION: Many writers view broad reference as acceptable when the pronoun refers clearly to the sense of an entire clause.

> If you pick up a starving dog and make him prosperous, he will not bite you. This is the principal difference between a dog and a man.
> —Mark Twain

23c Do not use a pronoun to refer to an implied antecedent.

A pronoun should refer to a specific antecedent, not to a word that is implied but not present in the sentence.

▶ After braiding Ann's hair, Sue decorated ~~them~~ *the braids*

with ribbons.

The pronoun *them* referred to Ann's braids (implied by the term *braiding*), but the word *braids* did not appear in the sentence.

Modifiers, such as possessives, cannot serve as antecedents. A modifier may strongly imply the noun that the pronoun might logically refer to, but it is not itself that noun.

▶ In ~~Euripides'~~ *Medea,* ~~he~~ *Euripides* describes the plight of a

woman rejected by her husband.

The pronoun *he* cannot refer logically to the possessive modifier *Euripides'.* The revision substitutes the noun *Euripides* for the pronoun *he,* thereby eliminating the problem.

23d Avoid the indefinite use of *they, it,* and *you.*

Do not use the pronoun *they* to refer indefinitely to persons who have not been specifically mentioned. *They* should always refer to a specific antecedent.

▶ Sometimes a list of ways to save energy is
included with the gas bill. For example, ~~they~~ *the gas company suggests*

~~suggest~~ setting a moderate temperature for the

hot water heater.

The word *it* should not be used indefinitely in constructions such as "It is said on television . . ." or "In the article it says that. . . ."

▶ In ~~t~~The report ~~it~~ points out that lifting the ban on

Compound 1080 would prove detrimental, possi-

bly even fatal, to the bald eagle.

The pronoun *you* is appropriate when the writer is addressing the reader directly: *Once*

you have kneaded the dough, let it rise in a warm place for at least twenty-five minutes. (See p. 26.) Except in informal contexts, however, the indefinite *you* (meaning "anyone in general") is inappropriate.

▶ In Ethiopia ~~you don't~~ *one doesn't* need much property to be

considered well-off.

If the pronoun *one* seems too stilted, the writer might recast the sentence: *In Ethiopia a person doesn't need much property to be considered well-off.*

23e To refer to persons, use *who, whom,* or *whose,* not *that* or *which.*

In most contexts, use *who, whom,* or *whose* to refer to persons, *that* or *which* to refer to animals or things. Although *that* is occasionally used to refer to persons, it is more polite to use a form of *who. Which* is reserved only for animals or things, so it is impolite to use it to refer to persons.

▶ When he heard about my seven children, four of
~~which~~ *whom* continue to live at home, Vincent smiled

and said, "I love children."

▶ Fans wondered how an out-of-shape old man ~~that~~ *who*

walked with a limp could play football.

NOTE: Occasionally *whose* may be used to refer to animals and things to avoid the awkward *of which* construction.

▶ A major corporation, ~~the name of which~~ *whose* name will be

in tomorrow's paper, has been illegally dumping

toxic waste in the harbor for years.

EXERCISE 23–1 Pronoun reference: Guided practice

Edit the following paragraphs to correct errors in pronoun reference. Rule numbers in the margin refer to appropriate rules in section 23. The first revision has been made for you, and a suggested revision of this exercise appears in the back of the book.

George and Mary Jones lived in Memphis during the Civil War. They were sympathetic to the Union, but the city definitely favored the Confederates. *Being caught in the middle* ~~This~~ made the war years especially hard on them. They looked forward to a much better life after the war. *23b*

At first, it seemed that they were going to have that better life. George got a job as a labor organizer, and Mary stayed at home to care for their four healthy children. Then came yellow fever. In nine months, Mary went from a happy wife and mother to a despondent widow that had no children. She had to find work. Because *23e* you must have some meaning for living, she needed work that she could care *23d* strongly about.

By 1900, Mary had become involved in union activities all over the United States. She found her calling among the coal miners and their wives, a calling she followed for the next thirty years. Making friends with the workers and outwitting private detectives, she held secret meetings to help them organize and plan strat- *23a* egy. In the newspaper, it often reported her ability to outwit and outlast mine bosses *23d* and lawyers as well as to reawaken courage in disconsolate workers.

Mary Jones spent many nights in jail, but often her jailers did not know what to do with this attractive, gray-haired woman whom the workers called "Mother." The jailers' confusion simply amused Mary, who was far more used to jail than they *23c* could imagine.

EXERCISE 23–2 Pronoun reference

Six of the following sentences contain faulty pronoun references. Find the faulty references and fix them. Mark the correct sentences "OK." Example:

> *and this job*
> Mother Jones got a job working in the textile mills, ~~which~~ made her conscious of how
> women workers were mistreated.

1. When Mother Jones started working in the textile mills at the turn of the century, she saw "the little gray ghosts," the child laborers which worked from sunup to sundown.

2. Children as young as six scooted along the floor oiling and cleaning the huge whirring looms, which often devoured a child's fingers or hand.

3. Mother Jones once led a delegation of three hundred children from Philadelphia to New York to dramatize their plight; in some of the newspapers they called her "the greatest female agitator in the country."

4. The speeches Mother Jones made about child labor were among her best: they called for legislation to forbid labor practices dangerous to children's health.

5. When Mother Jones asked for permission to bring three of the children and meet with President Theodore Roosevelt in New York, she was refused. It saddened her because she had hoped for the president's help.

6. Mother Jones asked again and was again refused. This second one saddened her even more, but she still did not consider the trip a failure.

7. She told the children and their parents that they had been successful.

8. Public awareness, which she felt would help the children, gradually began to increase.

9. Thousands of people had learned about the children's plight, which was bound to affect their thinking about child labor laws.

10. Mother Jones's optimism had another basis as well: The children would remember— and they would grow up.

EXERCISE 23–3 Pronoun reference

Problem pronouns are italicized in the following paragraphs. Edit the paragraphs to eliminate any misunderstandings these pronouns might cause. You may need to restructure some sentences. Example:

> *workers*
> In the mines, ~~you~~ didn't get much chance at the good life.

Mother Jones was determined to change the intolerable working conditions in the mines. After digging coal for twelve- to fourteen-hour shifts, *they* found in their miners' pay envelopes not U.S. currency but scrip, paper money that was honored only by the mining company. Local merchants had no use for the scrip, so *they* couldn't use it to buy food, clothes, or anything else. Workers, therefore, had to rent their homes from the company and buy their supplies at company stores. In company-run schools, the workers' children were taught by teachers *that* were hired by the company. *Their* families listened to company-paid ministers in company-owned churches.

Songwriter Merle Travis may have broken a pronoun reference rule, but he certainly summed *it* up neatly in one of his songs:

> You load sixteen tons, what do you get?
>
> Another day older and deeper in debt.
>
> St. Peter, don't you call me 'cause I can't go,
>
> I owe my soul to the company store.

[What pronoun does Travis use in a way that would be inappropriate in formal written English?]

EXERCISE 23–4 Pronoun reference: Guided review

Edit the following paragraphs to correct errors in pronoun reference. Rule numbers in the margin refer to appropriate rules in section 23. The first revision has been made for you.

Coal miners' struggles turned into actual war in the Kanawha Valley of West Virginia, where ~~they~~ *miners* were striking. The mine owners dominated the courts and the newspapers; they did not need to worry about the law or public opinion. Although the miners did not want to accept this, they were often forced to face it. Guards used violent tactics to maintain the mine owners' control, once spraying strikers' tent colonies with machine-gun fire and kicking a pregnant woman so hard that her unborn child died in the womb.

23c

23b

Mother Jones urged the miners to fight while she tried to gain the ear of the governor, the federal lawmakers, and the public. In records of the fight, it says that two thousand miners came from outside the valley to help in the battle. The state militia was called in, but the owners got control of it soon after it arrived. En route to the state legislature to ask them for help, Mother Jones was kidnapped by soldiers, held incommunicado, put in solitary confinement, and tried by a military court. When the new governor of West Virginia, Henry D. Hatfield, investigated, he found a soldier guarding an eighty-year-old pneumonia-ridden woman that had a 104-degree fever.

23d

23c

23e

Word about the Kanawha situation got out, but Governor Hatfield acted first. Out of his work came the Hatfield Agreement. This document, which historians of the labor movement consider a major advance for workers in the United States, forced the companies to recognize the union and to shorten the workday. Even more important, it stipulated that companies must pay wages in U.S. currency. He also guaranteed civilians the right to civil, not military, trials and dismissed all sentences the military court had imposed—including the twenty-year prison term it had set for Mother Jones.

23a

24 Distinguish between pronouns such as *I* and *me*.

The personal pronouns in the following chart change what is known as case form according to their grammatical function in a sentence. Pronouns functioning as subjects (or subject complements) appear in the *subjective* case; those functioning as objects appear in the *objective* case; and those showing ownership appear in the *possessive* case.

SUBJECTIVE CASE	OBJECTIVE CASE	POSSESSIVE CASE
I	me	my
you	you	your
he/she/it	him/her/it	his/her/its
we	us	our
you	you	your
they	them	their

Pronouns in the subjective and objective cases are frequently confused. Most of the rules in this section specify when to use one or the other of these cases (*I* or *me, he* or *him,* and so on). Rule 24g details a special use of pronouns and nouns in the possessive case.

> **GRAMMAR CHECKERS** can flag some incorrect pronouns and explain the rules for using *I* or *me, he* or *him, she* or *her, we* or *us,* and *they* or *them.* For example, grammar checkers correctly flagged *we* in the following sentence, suggesting that *us* should be used as the object of the preposition *for: I say it is time for we parents to revolt.*
>
> You should not assume, however, that a computer program will catch all incorrect pronouns. For example, grammar checkers did not flag *more than I* in this sentence, where the writer's meaning requires *me: I get a little jealous that our dog likes my neighbor more than I.*

24a Use the subjective case (*I, you, he, she, it, we, they*) for subjects and subject complements.

When personal pronouns are used as subjects, ordinarily your ear will tell you the correct pronoun. Problems sometimes arise, however, with compound word groups containing a pronoun, so it is not always safe to trust your ear.

> ▶ Joel ran away from home because his stepfather
>   *he*
> and ~~him~~ had quarreled.

His stepfather and he is the subject of the verb *had quarreled.* If we strip away the words *his stepfather and,* the correct pronoun becomes clear: *he had quarreled* (not *him had quarreled*).

When a pronoun is used as a subject complement (a word following a linking verb), your ear may mislead you, since the incorrect form is frequently heard in casual speech. (See subject complement, 48b.)

> *she.*
> ▶ Sandra confessed that the artist was ~~her.~~

The pronoun *she* functions as a subject complement with the linking verb *was.* In formal, written English, subject complements must be in the subjective case. If your ear rejects *artist was she* as too stilted, try rewriting the sentence: *Sandra confessed that she was the artist.*

24b Use the objective case (*me, you, him, her, it, us, them*) for all objects.

When a personal pronoun is used as a direct object, an indirect object, or the object of a preposition, ordinarily your ear will lead you to the correct pronoun. When an object is compound, however, you may occasionally become confused.

> ▶ Janice was indignant when she realized that the
>   *her.*
> salesclerk was insulting her mother and ~~she.~~

Her mother and her is the direct object of the verb *was insulting.* Strip away the words *her mother and* to hear the correct pronoun: *was insulting her* (not *was insulting she*).

> *me*
> ▶ Geoffrey went with my family and ~~I~~ to King's
> Dominion.

Me is the object of the preposition *with.* We would not say *Geoffrey went with I.*

When in doubt about the correct pronoun, some writers try to avoid making the choice by using a reflexive pronoun such as *myself.* Such evasions are nonstandard, even though they are used by some educated persons.

▶ The Egyptian cab driver gave my husband and
me
~~myself~~ some good tips on traveling in North Africa.
^

My husband and me is the indirect object of the
verb *gave*. For correct uses of *myself*, see the Glossary of Usage.

24c Put an appositive and the word to which it refers in the same case.

Appositives are noun phrases that rename
nouns or pronouns. A pronoun used as an appositive has the same function (usually subject
or object) as the word(s) the appositive renames.

▶ At the drama festival, two actors, Christina and
I,
~~me,~~ were selected to do the last scene of *King*
^

Lear.

The appositive *Christina and I* renames the subject,
actors.

▶ The college interviewed only two applicants for
me.
the job, Professor Stevens and ~~I~~.
^

The appositive *Professor Stevens and me* renames
the direct object *applicants.*

24d Following *than* or *as*, choose the pronoun that expresses your meaning.

When a comparison begins with *than* or *as,*
your choice of a pronoun will depend on your
intended meaning. Consider, for example, the
difference in meaning between these sentences:

My husband likes football better than I.

My husband likes football better than me.

Finish each sentence mentally and its meaning
becomes clear: *My husband likes football better
than I [do]. My husband likes football better
than [he likes] me.*

▶ Even though he is sometimes ridiculed by the
they.
other boys, Norman is much better off than ~~them.~~
^

They is the subject of the verb *are,* which is understood: *Norman is much better off than they [are].*

If the correct English seems too formal, you can always add the verb.

her.
▶ We respected no other candidate as much as ~~she.~~
^

This sentence means that we respected no other
candidate as much as *we respected her. Her* is the
direct object of an understood verb.

24e When deciding whether *we* or *us* should precede a noun, choose the pronoun that would be appropriate if the noun were omitted.

We
▶ ~~Us~~ tenants would rather fight than move.
^

us
▶ Management is short-changing ~~we~~ tenants.
^

No one would say *Us would rather fight than move*
or *Management is short-changing we.*

24f Use the objective case for subjects and objects of infinitives.

An infinitive is the word *to* followed by the base
form of a verb. (See 49c.) Subjects of infinitives
are an exception to the rule that subjects must
be in the subjective case. Whenever an infinitive has a subject, it must be in the objective
case. Objects of infinitives also are in the objective case.

me
▶ The crowd expected Chris and ~~I~~ to defeat Tracy
him
and ~~he~~ in the doubles championship.
^

Chris and me is the subject of the infinitive *to defeat; Tracy and him* is the direct object of the infinitive.

24g Use the possessive case to modify a gerund.

A pronoun that modifies a gerund or a gerund
phrase should appear in the possessive case
(*my, our, your, his/her/its, their*). A gerund is a
verb form ending in *-ing* that functions as a
noun. Gerunds frequently appear in phrases,
in which case the whole gerund phrase functions as a noun. (See 49c.)

our
▶ My father always tolerated ~~us~~ talking after the
^

lights were out.

Checking for problems with pronoun case

Look for the most common trouble spots; where possible, apply a test for the correct pronoun.

COMPOUND WORD GROUPS (24a, 24b)

Test: Mentally strip away the rest of the compound word group.

> While diving for pearls, [Ikiko and] *she* found a treasure chest full of gold bars.

> The most traumatic experience for [her father and] *me* occurred long after her operation.

PRONOUN AFTER IS, ARE, WAS, OR WERE (24a)

In formal English, remember to use the subjective-case pronouns *I, he, she, we,* and *they* after the linking verbs *is, are, was,* and *were.*

> The panel was shocked to learn that the undercover agent was *she.*

APPOSITIVES (24c)

Test: Mentally strip away the word group that the appositive renames.

> [The chief strategists], Dr. Bell and *I,* could not agree on a plan.

> The company could afford to send only [one of two researchers], Dr. Davis or *me,* to Paris.

PRONOUN AFTER THAN OR AS (24d)

Test: Mentally complete the sentence.

> The supervisor claimed that she was much more experienced than *I* [was].

> Gloria admitted that she liked Greg's twin better than [she liked] *him.*

WE OR US BEFORE A NOUN (24e)

Test: Mentally delete the noun.

> *We* [women] really have come a long way.

> Sadly, discrimination against *us* [women] occurs in most cultures.

PRONOUN BEFORE OR AFTER AN INFINITIVE (24f)

Remember that both subjects and objects of infinitives take the objective case.

> Ms. Wilson asked John and *me* to drive the senator and *her* to the airport.

PRONOUN OR NOUN BEFORE A GERUND (24g)

Remember to use the possessive case when a pronoun modifies a gerund.

> There is only a small chance of *his* bleeding excessively because of this procedure.

The possessive pronoun *our* modifies the gerund *talking.*

Nouns as well as pronouns may modify gerunds. To form the possessive case of a noun, use an apostrophe and an *-s* (*a victim's rights*) or just an apostrophe (*victims' rights*). (See 36a.)

> ▶ We had to pay a fifty-dollar fine for ~~Brenda~~ driving
> ^*Brenda's*
>
> without a permit.

The possessive noun *Brenda's* modifies the gerund phrase *driving without a permit.*

EXERCISE 24–1 Pronoun and noun case: Guided practice

Circle the correct pronoun from each pair in parentheses. Rule numbers in the margin refer to appropriate rules in section 24. The first selection has been made for you, and an answer to this exercise appears in the back of the book.

When union organizer Mother Jones went to Colorado in 1913, no one worked harder than (she, her) to help the miners. (They, Them) and their families *24d, 24a* lived in company houses that the company's own reports called unfit for human habitation. Mine owners refused to discuss the problem. Mother Jones could see no way to get the two groups, the owners and (they, them), together. *24c*

Mother Jones did not give up. When threatening posters went up all over town, she just laughed and encouraged the miners with slogans like "We can win this one" and "(We, Us) miners have got to stick together." When Mother Jones ap- *24e* pealed to the governor for help, no one really expected the governor and (she, her) *24f* to agree, but many people hoped he would help somehow. Instead, he simply or- dered her out of the state.

The miners were evicted from their houses. (They, them) and their families *24a* moved into tents. Because company guards raked the tents with machine-gun fire, the miners dug pits under the tents. The pits were deep enough to protect (they, *24b* them) and their families from gunfire, but at Ludlow, guards set fire to the tents. Whole families were roasted to death in the pits. When word of the massacre got out, workers from all over the state swarmed to Ludlow. No one was ever as angry as (they, them). They set fire to company buildings, fought the state and company *24d* troops, and took over the nearby mines and towns.

Mother Jones went to Washington to ask President Wilson for help. Athough she and (he, him) did not agree on all points, he did establish a review board and *24a* send in federal troops to restore order. The companies did not like the (president, president's) sending in troops and absolutely refused to accept the findings of the *24g* review board. Eventually, the miners went back to work under almost the same con- ditions as before. Disappointed as they were, they knew that it was (she, her), Mother *24a* Jones, who was the most disappointed of all.

EXERCISE 24–2 Pronoun and noun case

Six of the following sentences have errors in pronoun or noun case. Find and fix the errors. Mark "OK" next to the sentences that have no errors. Example:

> *he*
> Mother Jones liked to discuss union affairs with her friend Terence Powderly; she and ~~him~~ could argue for hours about the best approach to a problem.

1. People all over the world knew about Mother Jones. Wherever she went, she was invited into their homes and their workplaces.

2. Once when she was traveling with Fred Mooney in Mexico, a crowd stopped the train and urged Mooney and she to open the train window.

3. Mooney and she were not sure whether they should open the window, but they decided to do so. When they did, she and him both were covered with red carnations and blue violets.

4. Although the people gave the flowers to both him and her, the flowers were meant as gifts in honor of "Madre Yones."

5. The trip to Mexico was exhausting, but it was she, over ninety, who never ran out of energy.

6. When Mooney fretted about her health, it was her who laughed and proposed that they get on with their sightseeing.

7. No one was more excited than her about the idea of a Pan-American Federation of Labor, an organization that would unite workers from Canada to South America.

8. The president of Mexico was as pleased as her at the idea of bringing together all the working people in the hemisphere.

9. "This is the beginning of a new day for us working people," exclaimed Mother Jones.

10. It was a day Mother Jones long remembered; years later it brought happy smiles to she and her friends whenever they saw carnations and violets or thought of that day's events.

EXERCISE 24–3 Pronoun and noun case

Some of the personal pronouns in this passage are italicized; six of them are not in the correct case. The first one has been corrected for you. Find and correct the other five.

 Though *she* ~~her~~ and a friend would occasionally work together on the friend's campaign, Mother Jones avoided politics most of the time. *She*, the agitator, had no more interest in politics and political science than *her*, the labor organizer, had in economic theory. Mother Jones understood one kind of economics, the kind that dealt with wages, benefits, and the cost of bread and housing. The here-and-now problems of the poor called to Mother Jones so strongly that *she* had to do what *she* could to stop the injustice *she* saw around *her*.

 Surprisingly, Mother Jones was not a supporter of women's suffrage. When the fight to win women's right to vote came along, it was not *her* who supported it. *Herself* and her people were the working classes, both men and women, and neither *she* nor *them* had much patience for the "society women" who led the movement. As far as Mother Jones was concerned, well-dressed women parading down the city streets carrying placards and banners did not help working men and women obtain a decent life. Mother Jones objected to *them* spending time and energy and money on activities that would not help her kind of people. Nor was *she* interested in helping a cause that would benefit only women; her concern was for all workers, regardless of gender. *She* seemed not to understand that the votes of the miners' wives might do as much to help the working men as *her* agitating and organizing did.

EXERCISE 24–4 Pronoun and noun case: Guided review

Circle the correct pronoun from each group in parentheses. Rule numbers in the margin refer to appropriate rules in section 24. The first selection has been made for you.

Eventually, labor organizer Mother Jones began to think about her death. She wrote her autobiography and made plans for her burial, but she could not have dreamed how her name would be kept alive many years after her death.

(She,) Her) and an editor friend began her autobiography when Mother Jones   *24a*
was ninety-two. Even with her friend working as hard as (she, her), Mother Jones found   *24d*
writing to be a grinding, demanding chore. Annoyed with her (friend, friend's) trying to   *24g*
make her remember details of her youth, she covered the first thirty years of her life in a few paragraphs. She had trouble remembering even the later years, confusing names and occasionally mixing up dates. She was never confused, however, about her conviction that working people were being unfairly treated. Nor did she doubt the necessity for (she, her) and her friends to help redress the wrongs done to working people.   *24f*

Mother Jones planned to be buried in a place special to her. Back in 1898, four miners had been killed during a strike in Mount Olive, Illinois, and no cemetery in town would allow the bodies of these men to be buried on its land. So the union bought its own cemetery to bury them and others like them. For Mother Jones, burial in Miners Cemetery, Mount Olive, Illinois, was a way to say "(We, Us) work-   *24e*
ing people have got to stick together" even after her death.

She would have been puzzled by two memorials honoring her work. The first was a statue of her in the Department of Labor building in Washington, D.C. It is now gone. Then in the mid-twentieth century, some writers decided to publish a magazine devoted to exposing fraud and injustice in society. (They, Them) and their   *24a*
friends named this new publication *Mother Jones*. Mother Jones might not have appreciated the accolades it won or its citation by the *American Journalism Review* as "best in the business for investigative reporting," but she would have recognized at once the woman first listed under the journal's masthead: "Mother Jones (1830–1930)— Orator, Union Organizer, and Hellraiser."

25 Distinguish between *who* and *whom.*

The choice between *who* and *whom* (or *whoever* and *whomever*) occurs primarily in subordinate clauses and in questions. *Who* and *whoever*, subjective-case pronouns, are used for subjects and subject complements. *Whom* and *whomever*, objective-case pronouns, are used for objects. (For more about pronoun case, see 24.)

 GRAMMAR CHECKERS can flag some sentences with a misused *who* or *whom* and explain the nature of the error. For example, grammar checkers flagged the subject pronoun *who* in the following sentence, suggesting correctly that the context calls for the object pronoun *whom*: *One of the women who Martinez hired became the most successful lawyer in the agency.*

However, at times the programs skip past a misused *who* or *whom*, as they did with this sentence: *Now that you have studied with both musicians, whom in your opinion is the better teacher?* The programs could not tell that the object pronoun *whom* functions as the subject of the verb *is.*

25a In subordinate clauses, use *who* and *whoever* for subjects or subject complements, *whom* and *whomever* for all objects.

When *who* and *whom* (or *whoever* and *whomever*) introduce subordinate clauses, their case is determined by their function *within the clause they introduce.* To choose the correct pronoun, you must isolate the subordinate clause and then decide how the pronoun functions within it. (See subordinate clauses, 49b.)

In the following two examples, the pronouns *who* and *whoever* function as the subjects of the clauses they introduce.

> who
▶ The prize goes to the runner ~~whom~~ collects the
      ^

most points.

The subordinate clause is *who collects the most points.* The verb of the clause is *collects,* and its subject is *who.*

> whoever
▶ He tells that story to ~~whomever~~ will listen.
      ^

The writer selected the pronoun *whomever,* thinking that it was the object of the preposition *to.* However, the object of the preposition is the entire subordinate clause *whoever will listen.* The verb of the clause is *will listen,* and its subject is *whoever.*

Who occasionally functions as a subject complement in a subordinate clause. Subject complements occur with linking verbs (usually *be, am, is, are, was, were, being,* and *been*). (See 48b.)

> who
▶ **The receptionist knows ~~whom~~ you are.**
          ^

The subordinate clause is *who you are.* Its subject is *you,* and its subject complement is *who.*

When functioning as an object in a subordinate clause, *whom* (or *whomever*) appears out of order, before both the subject and the verb. To choose the correct pronoun, you must mentally restructure the clause.

> ▶ **You will work with our senior industrial engineers,**
> whom
> ~~who~~ **you will meet later.**
>   ^

The subordinate clause is *whom you will meet later.* The subject of the clause is *you,* the verb is *will meet,* and *whom* is the direct object of the verb. This becomes clear if you mentally restructure the clause: *you will meet whom.*

When functioning as the object of a preposition in a subordinate clause, *whom* is often separated from its preposition.

> whom
▶ **The tutor ~~who~~ I was assigned to was very**
          ^

supportive and helpful.

Whom is the object of the preposition *to.* In this sentence, the writer might choose to drop *whom*: *The tutor I was assigned to was very supportive and helpful.*

NOTE: Inserted expressions such as *they know, I think,* and *she says* should be ignored in determining whether to use *who* or *whom.*

Checking for problems with who *and* whom

Look for common trouble spots; where possible, apply a test for correct usage.

IN A SUBORDINATE CLAUSE

Isolate the subordinate clause. Then read its subject, verb, and any objects, restructuring the clause if necessary. Some writers find it helpful to substitute *he* for *who* and *him* for *whom*.

> Samuels hoped to become the business partner of (whoever/whomever) found the treasure.
>
> Test: . . . *whoever* found the treasure. [. . . *he* found the treasure.]
>
> Ada always seemed to be bestowing a favor on (whoever/whomever) she worked for.

Test: . . . she worked for *whomever*. [. . . she worked for *him*.]

IN A QUESTION

Read the subject, verb, and any objects, rearranging the sentence structure if necessary.

> (Who/Whom) conferred with Roosevelt and Stalin at Yalta in 1945?
>
> Test: *Who* conferred . . . ?
>
> (Who/Whom) did the committee nominate?
>
> Test: The committee did nominate *whom*?

▶ All of the show-offs, bullies, and tough guys in school want to take on a big guy ~~whom~~ *who* they know will not hurt them.

Who is the subject of *will hurt*, not the object of *know*.

25b In questions, use *who* and *whoever* for subjects, *whom* and *whomever* for all objects.

When *who* and *whom* (or *whoever* and *whomever*) are used to open questions, their case is determined by their function within the question. In the following example, *who* functions as the subject of the question.

▶ ~~Whom~~ *Who* was responsible for creating that computer virus?

When *whom* functions as the object of a verb or the object of a preposition in a question, it appears out of normal order. To choose the correct pronoun, you must mentally restructure the question.

▶ ~~Who~~ *Whom* did the committee select?

Whom is the direct object of the verb *did select*. To choose the correct pronoun, restructure the question: *The committee did select whom?*

▶ ~~Who~~ *Whom* did you enter into the contract with?

Whom is the object of the preposition *with*, as is clear if you recast the question: *You did enter into the contract with whom?*

USAGE NOTE: In spoken English, *who* is frequently used to open a question even when it functions as an object: *Who did Joe replace?* Although some readers will accept such constructions in informal written English, it is safer to use *whom*: *Whom did Joe replace?*

EXERCISE 25–1 *Who* and *whom*: Guided practice

Circle the correct pronoun from each pair in parentheses. Rule numbers in the margin refer to appropriate rules in section 25. The first selection has been made for you, and an answer to this exercise appears in the back of the book.

Have you ever heard of George Leroy Parker? You probably have; you just don't think so because you don't know (who, whom) George Leroy Parker really was. **25a**
He was born on a Utah ranch in 1867. There were several cowhands on the place, and some of them had other jobs as well. One or two did a bit of farming, others went in for gambling, and one was a horse thief and cattle rustler. Of them all, (who, **25b**
whom) did young George find most attractive? George never had any question about (who, whom) he admired most on the ranch. (Who, Whom) else would it be but Mike, **25a, 25b**
the horse thief and cattle rustler? George was so impressed by Mike that years later he would tell stories about Mike's exploits to (whoever, whomever) would listen. Mike **25a**
was the man George was eternally grateful to because he taught George how to ride and shoot. George was so grateful, in fact, that he took that man's last name for his own. He wanted to honor Mike Cassidy, the man (who, whom) he admired above all **25a**
others.

[*Note:* Sometimes the pronoun *whom* may be dropped without loss of clarity. Are there any *whom*s in this paragraph that you might choose to drop?]

EXERCISE 25–2 *Who* and *whom*

One sentence in each of the following pairs uses *who* and *whom* correctly and the other does not. Put "OK" after the correct sentence and correct the other one. Example:

    a. People who deliberately change their last names do so for specific reasons. *OK*

                                                  whom

    b. Sometimes they are hiding from people ~~who~~ they have harmed.

1a.   It is unusual for a man to change his last name to honor someone who he admires.

  b.   George Leroy Parker became George Cassidy when he named himself for the man who had taught him the most.

2a.   One day George said good-bye to Mike Cassidy, who was leaving for Mexico.

  b.   The lawmen who Mike planned to outwit did not catch up with him this time.

3a.   George decided to join up with whoever he could find to try a train robbery.

  b.   He found the McCarty brothers and Matt Warner, to whom a robbery sounded like a good idea.

4a.   The gang underestimated who they would be dealing with.

  b.   The guard whom they threatened refused to open the safe.

5a.   The gang then voted on whether to rob the passengers, whom they had not originally intended to disturb.

  b.   The "no" votes won, so the gang left the passengers to wonder whom these vote-taking train robbers were.

[*Note:* Sometimes the pronoun *whom* may be dropped without loss of clarity. Are there any *whom*s in the preceding sentences that you might choose to drop?]

EXERCISE 25–3 *Who* and *whom*

Edit the following sentences to eliminate errors in the use of *who* and *whom*. Mark correct sentences "OK." Example:

George Cassidy, who was later known as Butch, robbed his first bank in 1889. *OK*

1. George Cassidy, who had already decided to rob the First National Bank of Denver, had a problem: Who could he find as a partner?

2. Maybe one of his old buddies who now lived in Star Valley, an almost perfect hideout, would be a partner on whom he could depend.

3. Whom else could it be but Tom McCarty, with whom George had tried his first train robbery?

4. When the robbers threatened the bank president with a bottle they said contained nitroglycerin, others said it was only water. The bank president didn't know who to believe because he couldn't tell whom was lying.

5. Actually, it was water, but who could have been sure of that?

EXERCISE 25–4 *Who* and *whom*: Guided review

Circle the correct pronoun from each pair in the parentheses. Rule numbers in the margin refer to appropriate rules in section 25. The first selection has been made for you.

George Cassidy got his nickname Butch from the people he served during one of the few times he earned an honest living. The people George Cassidy worked for from 1890 to 1892 knew him as an honest worker. The available records don't show (who, whom) trained him for his job—butchering sheep, hogs, and steers.   *25a*

(Whoever, Whomever) had trained him had done it well. It was obvious to (whoever,   *25a, 25a*

whomever) looked at his work that George Cassidy knew how to handle a knife. His customers, (who, whom) he may well have robbed later, were satisfied with his work.   *25a*

They probably did not realize how famous—or infamous—their butcher was to become. Even if Butch didn't know which townspeople had given him his name, obviously he liked it; he used it for the rest of his life. (Who, Whom) today hasn't heard   *25b*

of Butch Cassidy? (Who, Whom) did the movie industry choose as the hero of one   *25b*

of its most popular films?

26 Choose adjectives and adverbs with care.

Adjectives ordinarily modify nouns or pronouns; occasionally they function as subject complements following linking verbs. Adverbs modify verbs, adjectives, or other adverbs. (See 47d and 47e.)

Many adverbs are formed by adding *-ly* to adjectives (*normal, normally; smooth, smoothly*). But don't assume that all words ending in *-ly* are adverbs or that all adverbs end in *-ly.* Some adjectives end in *-ly* (*lovely, friendly*) and some adverbs don't (*always, here, there*). When in doubt, consult a dictionary.

ESL In English, adjectives are not pluralized to agree with the words they modify: *The red* [not *reds*] *roses were a wonderful surprise.*

GRAMMAR CHECKERS can flag a number of problems with adjectives and adverbs: some misuses of *bad* or *badly* and *good* or *well*; some double comparisons, such as *more meaner;* some absolute comparisons, such as *most unique;* and some double negatives, such as *can't hardly.* However, the programs slip past more problems than they find. Programs ignored errors like these: *could have been handled more professional* and *hadn't been bathed regular.*

26a Use adverbs, not adjectives, to modify verbs, adjectives, and adverbs.

When adverbs modify verbs (or verbals), they nearly always answer the question When? Where? How? Why? Under what conditions? How often? or To what degree? When adverbs modify adjectives or other adverbs, they usually qualify or intensify the meaning of the word they modify. (See 47e.)

The incorrect use of adjectives in place of adverbs to modify verbs occurs primarily in casual or nonstandard speech.

> ▶ The arrangement worked out ~~perfect~~ for everyone.
>   *perfectly*

> ▶ The manager must see that the office runs
>   ~~smooth~~ and ~~efficient.~~
>   *smoothly   efficiently.*

The adverb *perfectly* modifies the verb *worked out;* the adverbs *smoothly* and *efficiently* modify the verb *runs.*

The incorrect use of the adjective *good* in place of the adverb *well* is especially common in casual and nonstandard speech.

> ▶ We were surprised to hear that Louise had done
>   so ~~good~~ on the CPA exam.
>   *well*

The adverb *well* (not the adjective *good*) should be used to modify the verb *had done.*

NOTE: The word *well* is an adjective when it means "healthy," "satisfactory," or "fortunate": *I am very well, thank you. All is well. It is just as well.*

Adjectives are sometimes used incorrectly to modify adjectives or adverbs.

> ▶ For a man eighty years old, Joe plays golf ~~real~~
>   well.
>   *really*

> ▶ We were ~~awful~~ sorry to hear about your uncle's
>   death.
>   *awfully*

Only adverbs can be used to modify adjectives or other adverbs. *Really* intensifies the meaning of the adverb *well,* and *awfully* intensifies the meaning of the adjective *sorry.* The writers could substitute other intensifiers: *very well, terribly sorry.*

ESL Placement of adjectives and adverbs can be a tricky matter for second language speakers. See 31d.

26b Use adjectives, not adverbs, as complements.

Adjectives ordinarily precede nouns, but they can also function as subject complements or as object complements.

Subject complements

A subject complement follows a linking verb and completes the meaning of the subject. (See 48b.) When an adjective functions as a subject complement, it describes the subject.

Justice is *blind*.

Problems can arise with verbs such as *smell, taste, look,* and *feel,* which sometimes, but not always, function as linking verbs. If the word following one of these verbs describes the subject, use an adjective; if it modifies the verb, use an adverb.

ADJECTIVE
The detective looked *cautious*.

ADVERB
The detective looked *cautiously* for fingerprints.

The adjective *cautious* describes the detective; the adverb *cautiously* modifies the verb *looked*.
   Linking verbs suggest states of being, not actions. Notice, for example, the different meanings of *looked* in the preceding examples. To look cautious suggests the state of being cautious; to look cautiously is to perform an action in a cautious way.

▶ The lilacs in our backyard smell especially
   sweet
   ~~sweetly~~ this year.
   ^

   good
▶ Lori looked ~~well~~ in her new raincoat.
   ^

   The verbs *smell* and *looked* suggest states of being, not actions. Therefore, they should be followed by adjectives, not adverbs. (Contrast with action verbs: *We smelled the flowers. Lori looked for her raincoat.*)

Object complements

An object complement follows a direct object and completes its meaning. (See 48b.) When an adjective functions as an object complement, it describes the direct object.

Sorrow makes us *wise*.

Object complements occur with verbs such as *call, consider, create, find, keep,* and *make.* When a modifier follows the direct object of one of these verbs, check to see whether it functions as an adjective describing the direct object or as an adverb modifying the verb.

ADJECTIVE
The referee called the plays *perfect*.

ADVERB
The referee called the plays *perfectly*.

The first sentence means that the referee considered the plays to be perfect; the second means that the referee did an excellent job of calling the plays.

                                             equal.
▶ God created all men and women ~~equally.~~
                                             ^

   The adjective *equal* is an object complement describing the direct object *men and women*.

26c Use comparatives and superlatives with care.

Most adjectives and adverbs have three forms: the positive, the comparative, and the superlative.

POSITIVE	COMPARATIVE	SUPERLATIVE
soft	softer	softest
fast	faster	fastest
careful	more careful	most careful
bad	worse	worst
good	better	best

Comparative versus superlative

Use the comparative to compare two things, the superlative to compare three or more.

▶ Which of these two brands of toothpaste
   better?
   is ~~best?~~
      ^

▶ Though Shaw and Jackson are impressive,
                       most
   Hobbs is the ~~more~~ qualified of the three
                       ^
   candidates running for mayor.

Form of comparatives and superlatives

To form comparatives and superlatives of most one- and two-syllable adjectives, use the endings *-er* and *-est: smooth, smoother, smoothest; easy, easier, easiest.* With longer adjectives, use *more* and *most* (or *less* and *least* for downward comparisons): *exciting, more exciting, most exciting; helpful, less helpful, least helpful.*

Some one-syllable adverbs take the endings *-er* and *-est* (*fast, faster, fastest*), but longer adverbs and all of those ending in *-ly* form the comparative and superlative with *more* and *most* (or *less* and *least*).

The comparative and superlative forms of the following adjectives and adverbs are irregular: *good, better, best; well, better, best; bad, worse, worst; badly, worse, worst.*

> *most talented*
> ▶ The Kirov is the ~~talentedest~~ ballet company we
>
> have seen.

> *worse*
> ▶ Lloyd's luck couldn't have been ~~worser~~ than
>
> David's.

Double comparatives or superlatives

Do not use double comparatives or superlatives. When you have added *-er* or *-est* to an adjective or adverb, do not also use *more* or *most* (or *less* or *least*).

> ▶ Of all her family, Julia is the ~~most~~ happiest
>
> about the move.

> *inane*
> ▶ That is the most ~~inanest~~ joke I have ever heard.

Absolute concepts

Avoid expressions such as *more straight, less perfect, very round,* and *most unique.* Either something is unique or it isn't. It is illogical to suggest that absolute concepts come in degrees.

> *unusual*
> ▶ That is the most ~~unique~~ wedding gown I have
>
> ever seen.

> *valuable*
> ▶ The painting would have been even more ~~priceless~~
>
> had it been signed.

26d **Avoid double negatives.**

Standard English allows two negatives only if a positive meaning is intended: *The orchestra was not unhappy with its performance.* Double negatives used to emphasize negation are nonstandard.

Negative modifiers such as *never, no,* and *not* should not be paired with other negative modifiers or with negative words such as *neither, none, no one, nobody,* and *nothing.*

> *anything*
> ▶ Management is not doing ~~nothing~~ to see that the
>
> trash is picked up.

> *ever*
> ▶ George won't ~~never~~ forget that day.

> ▶ I enjoy living alone because I don't have to
> *anybody.*
> answer to ~~nobody~~.

The double negatives *not . . . nothing, won't never,* and *don't . . . nobody* are nonstandard.

The modifiers *hardly, barely,* and *scarcely* are considered negatives in standard English, so they should not be used with negatives such as *not, no one,* or *never.*

> *can*
> ▶ Maxine is so weak she ~~can't~~ hardly climb stairs.

EXERCISE 26–1 Adjectives and adverbs: Guided practice

Edit the following paragraphs for correct use of adjectives and adverbs. Rule numbers in the margin refer to appropriate rules in section 26. The first revision has been done for you, and an answer to this exercise appears in the back of the book.

Novelists have often used their storytelling talents to influence people's thinking. Charles Dickens did it in nineteenth-century England. From *David Copperfield* to *Oliver Twist*, book after book depicted the plight of the poor and other ~~real~~ *really* unfortunate members of society. Harriet Beecher Stowe did it in nineteenth-century America, but with not hardly as many books. Her *Uncle Tom's Cabin* depicted slavery so well that the book was very influential in causing the Civil War.

26a

26d

Harriet Beecher Stowe considered slavery sinful and wanted her book to help end slavery quick and peaceful. People first read parts of the novel ten years before the beginning of the war. An abolitionist magazine published it a few chapters at a time, hoping the effect of the story would make readers feel so badly about slavery that they would rally to the abolitionist cause. Many people, reading *Uncle Tom's Cabin* installment by installment, did become convinced that nothing could be worser than living in slavery on a southern plantation.

26a

26b

26c

None of the abolitionists, who devoted their energy to abolishing slavery, expected a more perfect world when the book itself was published in 1852. But they certainly hoped that the book would be influential. It was. Of all the novels published that year, it was the best seller on both sides of the Atlantic. Its popularity was good news for the abolitionists. Harriet Beecher Stowe's wish came true.

26c

EXERCISE 26–2 Adjectives and adverbs

Both sentences in each of the following pairs are grammatically correct. The sentences mean different things because one uses an adjective, the other an adverb. Read both sentences carefully to understand their meaning. Then circle the letter of the sentence that answers the question and be prepared to explain what the other sentence means. Example:

Which sentence means that southerners thought the book itself was dishonest?

(a.) Many southerners did not consider *Uncle Tom's Cabin* honest.

b. Many southerners did not consider *Uncle Tom's Cabin* honestly.

1. In which sentence did the people do a poor job of judging?

   a. Those people judged Mrs. Stowe's depiction of slave life inaccurate.

   b. Those people judged Mrs. Stowe's depiction of slave life inaccurately.

2. Which sentence says that the slaves had trouble finding the escape routes?

   a. Most slaves did not find their escape routes easy.

   b. Most slaves did not find their escape routes easily.

3. In which sentence do northerners think Stowe herself was honest?

   a. Most northerners believed Mrs. Stowe honest.

   b. Most northerners believed Mrs. Stowe honestly.

4. In which sentence did the law not consider one person to have just as many rights as another?

   a. Southern judges did not consider all people equal.

   b. Southern judges did not consider all people equally.

5. Which sentence says that the overseers were looking scared?

   a. Rumors of escaping slaves made overseers look anxious in the fields and forests.

   b. Rumors of escaping slaves made overseers look anxiously in the fields and forests.

EXERCISE 26–3 Adjectives and adverbs

Six of the adjectives and adverbs in the following paragraphs are not used correctly. The first one has been corrected. Find and correct the other five.

                             really
      Uncle Tom's Cabin was ~~real~~ popular, even though it was a very long book. When it was published as a serial in the abolitionist magazine *National Era* in 1851 and 1852, people probably read all of it. But when the novel was published as a book, many people did not have enough time to read it. Since it had been a best-seller, enterprising publishers brought out new, abridged copies for more faster reading. By the end of the Civil War, many people knew the story of *Uncle Tom's Cabin* only from these shorter versions of it—both novels and plays.

      Unfortunately, their knowledge was not only incomplete; it was distorted. Publishers left out important sections of this most priceless story. For example, in the book, Uncle Tom works for three different owners, two of whom treat him fairly good. But in the shortened versions of the story, Tom works for only one owner, who treats him very cruel. Even insensitive readers rightly found that cruel owner, Simon Legree, vicious, and they judged all slave owners by that one. What had been a subplot in the novel—the story of George, Eliza, their baby, and the family's attempted escape to freedom in Canada—became a major portion of the story. Playwrights favored such dramatic subplots and incidents because they were easily dramatized.

      Modern readers are often real surprised when they read the entire novel, a book that American critic Edmund Wilson called "a much more remarkable book than one had ever been allowed to suspect."

EXERCISE 26–4 Adjectives and adverbs: Guided review

Edit the following paragraph for correct use of adjectives and adverbs. Rule numbers in the margin refer to appropriate rules in section 26. The first revision has been done for you.

Playwrights often find popular novels suitable for the stage. Produced as a
play, *Uncle Tom's Cabin* was the ~~successfulest~~ *most successful* stage play of the 1800s. The play used   *26c*

only the real dramatic portions of the novel and therefore somewhat slanted its basic   *26a*

message. Even worse than the plays were the "Tom Shows" that toured small towns

all over the North; these shows didn't have scarcely anything but the violent scenes.   *26d*

Audiences felt very badly when they watched George and Eliza's desperate escape   *26b*

over the ice with their baby. Dramatists played on their viewers' sympathy with the

plight of this slave family. Viewers hoped until the very end that the family's escape

would work out perfect. Distortion was bad in both the plays and the Tom Shows,   *26a*

but it was worse in the Tom Shows, which turned this most unique story of slavery   *26c*

in the South into little more than propaganda. Particularly moving scenes from the

story continue to be used in plays and musicals. *The King and I* made use of sev-

eral. If a modern movie is ever made from *Uncle Tom's Cabin*, the movie will no doubt

reflect the same distortions present in the old plays and the Tom Shows—and will

probably be just as popular.

27   Choose standard English verb forms.

In nonstandard English, spoken by those who share a regional or cultural heritage, verb forms sometimes differ from those of standard English. In writing, use standard English verb forms unless you are quoting nonstandard speech or using nonstandard forms for literary effect. (See 17d.)

Except for the verb *be,* all verbs in English have five forms. The following chart lists the five forms and provides a sample sentence in which each might appear.

BASE FORM	Usually I (*walk, ride*).
PAST TENSE	Yesterday I (*walked, rode*).
PAST PARTICIPLE	I have (*walked, ridden*) many times before.
PRESENT PARTICIPLE	I am (*walking, riding*) right now.
-S FORM	He/she/it (*walks, rides*) regularly.

Both the past-tense and past-participle forms of regular verbs end in *-ed* (*walked, walked*). Irregular verbs form the past tense and past participle in other ways (*rode, ridden*).

The verb *be* has eight forms instead of the usual five: *be, am, is, are, was, were, being, been.*

 GRAMMAR CHECKERS can flag some misused irregular verbs, such as *had drove* or *Lucia swum,* but they miss about twice as many errors as they find.

27a   Use the correct forms of irregular verbs.

For all regular verbs, the past-tense and past-participle forms are the same (ending in *-ed* or *-d*), so there is no danger of confusion. This is not true, however, for irregular verbs, such as the following.

BASE FORM	PAST TENSE	PAST PARTICIPLE
go	went	gone
fight	fought	fought
fly	flew	flown

The past-tense form, which never has a helping verb, expresses action that occurred entirely in the past. The past participle is used with a helping verb—either with *has, have,* or *had* to form one of the perfect tenses or with *be, am, is, are, was, were, being,* or *been* to form the passive voice.

PAST TENSE	Last July, we *went* to Paris.
PAST PARTICIPLE	We have *gone* to Paris twice.

When you aren't sure which verb form to choose (*went* or *gone, began* or *begun,* and so on), consult the list of common irregular verbs that starts on the next page. Choose the past-tense form if the verb in your sentence doesn't have a helping verb; choose the past-participle form if it does.

In nonstandard English speech, the past-tense and past-participle forms may differ from those of standard English, as in the following sentences.

>   *saw*
> ► Yesterday we ~~seen~~ an unidentified flying object.

>   *sank*
> ► The reality of the situation finally ~~sunk~~ in.

The past-tense forms *saw* and *sank* are required because there are no helping verbs.

>   *stolen*
> ► The truck was apparently ~~stole~~ while the driver
>
> ate lunch.

>   *done*
> ► The teacher asked Dwain if he had ~~did~~ his
>
> homework.

Because of the helping verbs, the past-participle forms are required: *was stolen, had done.*

When in doubt about the standard English forms of irregular verbs, consult the following list or look up the base form of the verb in the dictionary, which also lists any irregular forms. (If no additional forms are listed in the dictionary, the verb is regular, not irregular.)

Common irregular verbs

BASE FORM	PAST TENSE	PAST PARTICIPLE
arise	arose	arisen
awake	awoke, awaked	awaked, awoke
be	was, were	been
beat	beat	beaten, beat
become	became	become
begin	began	begun
bend	bent	bent
bite	bit	bitten, bit
blow	blew	blown
break	broke	broken
bring	brought	brought
build	built	built
burst	burst	burst
buy	bought	bought
catch	caught	caught
choose	chose	chosen
cling	clung	clung
come	came	come
cost	cost	cost
deal	dealt	dealt
dig	dug	dug
dive	dived, dove	dived
do	did	done
drag	dragged	dragged
draw	drew	drawn
dream	dreamed, dreamt	dreamed, dreamt
drink	drank	drunk
drive	drove	driven
eat	ate	eaten
fall	fell	fallen
fight	fought	fought
find	found	found
fly	flew	flown
forget	forgot	forgotten, forgot
freeze	froze	frozen
get	got	gotten, got
give	gave	given
go	went	gone
grow	grew	grown
hang (suspend)	hung	hung
hang (execute)	hanged	hanged
have	had	had
hear	heard	heard
hide	hid	hidden
hurt	hurt	hurt
keep	kept	kept
know	knew	known
lay (put)	laid	laid
lead	led	led
lend	lent	lent
let (allow)	let	let
lie (recline)	lay	lain
lose	lost	lost

BASE FORM	PAST TENSE	PAST PARTICIPLE
make	made	made
prove	proved	proved, proven
read	read	read
ride	rode	ridden
ring	rang	rung
rise (get up)	rose	risen
run	ran	run
say	said	said
see	saw	seen
send	sent	sent
set (place)	set	set
shake	shook	shaken
shoot	shot	shot
shrink	shrank	shrunk
sing	sang	sung
sink	sank	sunk
sit (be seated)	sat	sat
slay	slew	slain
sleep	slept	slept
speak	spoke	spoken
spin	spun	spun
spring	sprang	sprung
stand	stood	stood
steal	stole	stolen
sting	stung	stung
strike	struck	struck, stricken
swear	swore	sworn
swim	swam	swum
swing	swung	swung
take	took	taken
teach	taught	taught
throw	threw	thrown
wake	woke, waked	waked, woken
wear	wore	worn
wring	wrung	wrung
write	wrote	written

27b Distinguish among the forms of *lie* and *lay*.

Writers and speakers frequently confuse the various forms of *lie* (meaning "to recline or rest on a surface") and *lay* (meaning "to put or place something"). *Lie* is an intransitive verb; it does not take a direct object: *The tax forms lie on the table.* The verb *lay* is transitive; it takes a direct object: *Please lay the tax forms on the coffee table.* (See 48b.)

In addition to confusing the meaning of *lie* and *lay*, writers and speakers are often unfamiliar with the standard English forms of these verbs.

BASE FORM	PAST TENSE	PAST PARTICIPLE	PRESENT PARTICIPLE
lie	lay	lain	lying
lay	laid	laid	laying

▶ Sue was so exhausted that she ~~laid~~ *lay* down for a

nap.

The past-tense form of *lie* ("to recline") is *lay.*

▶ The patient had ~~laid~~ *lain* in an uncomfortable

position all night.

The past-participle form of *lie* ("to recline") is *lain.* If the correct English seems too stilted, recast the sentence: *The patient had been lying in an uncomfortable position all night.*

▶ Mary ~~lay~~ *laid* the baby on my lap.

The past-tense form of *lay* ("to place") is *laid.*

▶ My mother's letters were ~~laying~~ *lying* in the corner of

the chest.

The present participle of *lie* ("to rest on a surface") is *lying.*

27c Use -*s* (or -*es*) endings on present-tense verbs that have third-person singular subjects.

All singular nouns (*child, tree*) and the pronouns *he, she,* and *it* are third-person singular; indefinite pronouns such as *everyone* and *neither* are also third-person singular. When the subject of a sentence is third-person singular, its verb takes an -*s* or -*es* ending in the present tense. (See also 21.)

	SINGULAR		PLURAL	
FIRST PERSON	I	know	we	know
SECOND PERSON	you	know	you	know
THIRD PERSON	he/she/it	knows	they	know
	child	knows	parents	know
	everyone	knows		

In nonstandard speech, the -*s* ending required by standard English is sometimes omitted.

▶ Ellen taught him what he ~~know~~ *knows* about the

software.

▶ Sulfur dioxide ~~turn~~ *turns* leaves yellow, ~~dissolve~~ *dissolves* marble,

and ~~eat~~ *eats* away iron and steel.

The subjects *he* and *sulfur dioxide* are third-person singular, so the verbs must end in -*s.*

CAUTION: Do not add the -*s* ending to the verb if the subject is not third-person singular.

The writers of the following sentences, knowing they sometimes dropped -*s* endings from verbs, overcorrected by adding the endings where they don't belong.

▶ I prepares program specifications and logic

diagrams.

The writer mistakenly concluded that the -*s* ending belongs on present-tense verbs used with *all* singular subjects, not just *third-person* singular subjects. The pronoun *I* is first-person singular, so its verb does not require the -*s.*

▶ The dirt floors requires continual sweeping.

The writer mistakenly thought that the -*s* ending on the verb indicated plurality. The -*s* goes on present-tense verbs used with third-person *singular* subjects.

Has *versus* have

In the present tense, use *has* with third-person singular subjects; all other subjects require *have.*

	SINGULAR		PLURAL	
FIRST PERSON	I	have	we	have
SECOND PERSON	you	have	you	have
THIRD PERSON	he/she/it	has	they	have

In some dialects, *have* is used with all subjects. But standard English requires *has* for third-person singular subjects.

▶ This respected musician almost always ~~have~~ *has* a

message to convey in his work.

▶ As for the retirement income program, it ~~have~~ *has*

finally been established.

The subjects *musician* and *it* are third-person singular, so the verb should be *has* in each case.

CAUTION: Do not use *has* if the subject is not third-person singular. The writers of the following sentences were aware that they often wrote *have* when standard English requires *has*. Here they are using what appears to them to be the "more correct" form, but in an inappropriate context.

> *have*
> ► My business law classes ~~has~~ helped me to
>
> understand more about contracts.

> *have*
> ► I ~~has~~ much to be thankful for.

The subjects of these sentences—*classes* and *I*—are third-person plural and first-person singular, so standard English requires *have*. *Has* is used with third-person singular subjects only.

Does *versus* do *and* doesn't *versus* don't

In the present tense, use *does* and *doesn't* with third-person singular subjects; all other subjects require *do* and *don't*.

	SINGULAR		PLURAL	
FIRST PERSON	I	do/don't	we	do/don't
SECOND PERSON	you	do/don't	you	do/don't
THIRD PERSON	he/she/ it	does/ doesn't	they	do/don't

The use of *don't* instead of the standard English *doesn't* is a feature of many dialects in the United States. Use of *do* for *does* is rarer.

> *doesn't*
> ► Grandfather really ~~don't~~ have a place to call home.

> *Does*
> ► ~~Do~~ she know the correct procedure for setting
>
> up the experiment?

Grandfather and *she* are third-person singular, so the verbs should be *doesn't* and *does*.

Am, is, *and* are; was *and* were

The verb *be* has three forms in the present tense (*am, is, are*) and two in the past tense (*was, were*). Use *am* and *was* with first-person singular subjects; use *is* and *was* with third-person singular subjects. With all other subjects, use *are* and *were*.

	SINGULAR		PLURAL	
FIRST PERSON	I	am/was	we	are/were
SECOND PERSON	you		are/were you	are/were
THIRD PERSON	he/she/it	is/was	they	are/were

> *was*
> ► Judy wanted to borrow Tim's notes, but she ~~were~~
>
> too shy to ask for them.

The subject *she* is third-person singular, so the verb should be *was*.

> *were*
> ► Did you think you ~~was~~ going to drown?

The subject *you* is second-person singular, so the verb should be *were*.

> **GRAMMAR CHECKERS** can catch some missing *-s* endings on verbs and some misused *-s* forms of the verb. Unfortunately, they flag quite a few correct sentences, so you need to know how to interpret what the programs tell you. (See the grammar checker advice on p. 187 for more detailed information.)

27d Do not omit *-ed* endings on verbs.

Speakers who do not fully pronounce *-ed* endings sometimes omit them unintentionally in writing. Failure to pronounce *-ed* endings is common in many dialects and in informal speech even in standard English. In the following frequently used words and phrases, for example, the *-ed* ending is not always fully pronounced.

advised	developed	prejudiced	supposed to
asked	fixed	pronounced	used to
concerned	frightened	stereotyped	

When a verb is regular, both the past tense and the past participle are formed by adding *-ed* to the base form of the verb. (See 27a.)

Past tense

Use an *-ed* or *-d* ending to express the past tense of regular verbs. The past tense is used when the action occurred entirely in the past.

> *fixed*
> ► Over the weekend, Ed ~~fix~~ his brother's skateboard
>
> and tuned up his mother's 1955 Thunderbird.

> *advised*
> ► Last summer my counselor ~~advise~~ me to ask my
>
> chemistry instructor for help.

Past participles

Past participles are used in three ways: (1) following *have, has,* or *had* to form one of the perfect tenses; (2) following *be, am, is, are, was, were, being,* or *been* to form the passive voice; and (3) as adjectives modifying nouns or pronouns. The perfect tenses are listed on pages 243–44, and the passive voice is discussed in 28c. For a discussion of participles functioning as adjectives, see 49c.

> *asked*
> ► Robin has ~~ask~~ me to go to California with her.

> *Has asked* is present perfect tense (*have* or *has* followed by a past participle).

> ► Though it is not a new phenomenon, domestic
> *publicized*
> violence is ~~publicize~~ more frequently than before.

> *Is publicized* is a verb in the passive voice (a form of *be* followed by a past participle).

> ► All aerobics classes end in a cool-down period to
> *tightened*
> stretch ~~tighten~~ muscles.

> The past participle *tightened* functions as an adjective modifying the noun *muscles.*

GRAMMAR CHECKERS can catch some missing *-ed* endings, but they tend to slip past as many as they catch. For example, although programs flagged *was accustom,* they ignored *has change* and *was pass.*

27e Do not omit needed verbs.

Although standard English allows some linking verbs and helping verbs to be contracted, at least in informal contexts, it does not allow them to be omitted.

Linking verbs, used to link subjects to subject complements, are frequently a form of *be: be, am, is, are, was, were, being, been.* (See 48b.) Some of these forms may be contracted (*I'm, she's, we're, you're, they're*), but they should not be omitted altogether.

> *are*
> ► When we out there in the evening, we often hear
>
> the helicopters circling above.

> *is*
> ► Alvin a man who can defend himself.

Helping verbs, used with main verbs, include forms of *be, do,* and *have* or the words *can, will, shall, could, would, should, may, might,* and *must.* (See 47c.) Some helping verbs may be contracted (*he's leaving, we'll celebrate, they've been told*), but they should not be omitted altogether.

> *have*
> ► We been in Chicago since last Thursday.

> *would*
> ► Do you know someone who be good for the job?

ESL Speakers of English as a second language sometimes have problems with omitted verbs and correct use of helping verbs. See 29e and 29a.

GRAMMAR CHECKERS are fairly good at flagging omitted verbs, but they do not catch all of them. For example, programs caught the missing verb in this sentence: *He always talking.* But in the following, more complicated sentence, they did not catch the missing verb: *We often don't know whether he angry or just talking.*

EXERCISE 27–1 Verb forms: Guided practice

Correct any nonstandard verb forms in the following paragraphs. Rule numbers in the margin refer to appropriate rules in section 27. The first revision has been made for you, and an answer to this exercise appears in the back of the book.

    What Hollywood film director ~~get~~ *gets* credit for some of the scariest movies ever   *27c*

made, for some of the most incredible special effects anyone has ever dream of, and   *27d*

for one of the most popular children's movies ever made? If your answer is Steven

Spielberg, you're right. *Jaws* and *Jurassic Park* have frighten millions of viewers,   *27d*

Raiders of the Lost Ark and *Close Encounters of the Third Kind* continue to intrigue

how-to-do-it fans, and *E.T.* have won the hearts of children and adults throughout   *27c*

the world.

    What kind of person is the creator of these widely different films? He a man   *27e*

who has been in love with a movie camera all of his life. His family claims that when

Spielberg's father tried to take the first home movies of his young son, Spielberg got

up and walked directly toward the camera, as if he already knowed how an actor   *27a*

should respond to the lens. As a child, he set up two electric trains going full speed

toward each other so that he could film the resulting crash. Once he even talk his   *27d*

mother into boiling a cherry dessert in a pressure cooker until it exploded — so he

could film the explosion and the sticky red mess that laid on top of all the counters   *27b*

afterward.

    Those events were stage for the fun and information they provided the boy.   *27d*

But he found other uses for his camera as well. His moviemaking given this nonaca-   *27a*

demic, nonathletic schoolboy something to do with his after-school hours and pro-

vided him with a little bit of popularity and even protection: Other children liked to

be in his movies, and the bully who been picking on him ceased his harassment   *27e*

after having a role in one of them.

EXERCISE 27–2 Verb forms

Edit the following paragraphs for missing *-ed* endings and incorrect forms of irregular verbs. The first revision has been made for you. You should make ten more.

From the day Steven Spielberg got his first movie camera, it ~~become~~ *became* his best friend. Spielberg was given that movie camera when he was a Boy Scout. He earn a merit badge for a three-minute film he made as a scouting project. When he got to high school, Spielberg join the drama club and begun making longer films. One of them, a two-and-a-half-hour science fiction story, was even showed one night in a local theater and netted the theater owner a hundred-dollar profit. Spielberg wanted to study filmmaking in college. Not having good enough grades to get into UCLA or USC, he went to a state college in Long Beach, California. Even in college, he spent most of his time making movies.

Spielberg's love affair with the camera was match by his bravado. He was not afraid to put on an act of his own to get what he wanted. On one of his summer vacations, he went on a group tour of Universal Studios. Spielberg slip away from the guided tour and gone off on his own, scouting out the lot. The next day, dress carefully in a suit and tie and carrying a briefcase, he walked briskly onto the lot right past a guard and headed for an empty office he had found the day before. Then he somehow got the telephone switchboard operator to list him and give him calls. Spielberg work there the whole summer, managed to meet the studio president, and persuaded him to view one of his films. The president was impress; he gave Spielberg a contract.

EXERCISE 27–3 Verb forms

Edit the following paragraphs for problems with *-s* and *-ed* verb forms. The first revision has been made for you. You should make ten more.

                                         get

People often ask filmmakers where they ~~gets~~ ideas for their stories. Many of Steven Spielberg's ideas come from his own life, particularly his childhood.

In *Raiders of the Lost Ark*, Indiana Jones survives one narrow escape after another. The idea of those escapes sprang from the old Saturday serials Spielberg had love as a child. He even updated a scene he remembered from one of them for *Raiders*. In the serial, the good guy crawls between the hooves of a stagecoach team of horses and work his way up the back of the stagecoach. In *Raiders*, Indiana Jones crawl between the wheels of the truck that is suppose to kill him and works his way up the back of the truck.

Several scenes in *Poltergeist* reflects Spielberg's own life. The dark closet and the scary tree in the film are the same closet and tree that terrified him as a child in his New Jersey home. Spielberg have said that *Poltergeist* caught the feeling of his childhood nightmares.

E.T. also reflects part of Spielberg's life — a particularly embarrassing childhood memory that the movie turn into a hilarious joke. In school, Spielberg's biology class was assign the task of dissecting a frog. Not only was Spielberg unable to dissect the frog — he could not even watch. He raced from the classroom and vomited in the playground. The frogs hopping everywhere in *E.T.* have exorcise that old memory.

When Spielberg talk about his childhood memories, it is not difficult to believe his statement that "*Poltergeist* is what I fear, and *E.T.* is what I love."

EXERCISE.27−4 Verb forms: Guided review

Correct any nonstandard verb usage in the following paragraphs. Rule numbers in the margin refer to appropriate rules in section 27. The first revision has been made for you.

    Steven Spielberg is renowned for his ability to get an audience to believe in

his films. One technique Spielberg ~~use~~ *uses* is to require viewers to do much of the work.   **27c**

    Spielberg withholds visual information, knowing that viewers will imagine

what is most frightening to them. Their own images will be more terrifying than any

Spielberg could stage. When he made *Jaws*, Spielberg made no effort to film the

shark attacks in detail; he simply shown scene after scene of water in various stages   **27a**

of agitation. He used the same technique in *Close Encounters of the Third Kind*, ex-

cept that he focus on the sky instead of the ocean.   **27d**

    In *E.T.*, Spielberg withholds information and also restricts the angle of the

camera shooting the scenes. *E.T.* tells the story of a lonely, shy little boy name El-   **27d**

liot and an equally lonely and shy space creature whose name, E.T., is a shorten   **27d**

form of the boy's. Elliot is visible at once, but E.T. is not. In one scene, the space

creature obviously following a trail of candy laying on the ground. Viewers see Elliot   **27e, 27b**

put the candy on the ground, and they see the candy disappear, but they do not see

E.T. Viewers must imagine this creature from outer space long before seeing him;

thirty minutes into the film, his face, part green and part gray and very much like

a turtle's, have not appeared.   **27c**

    By also keeping the angle of the camera low, Spielberg lets the audience see

E.T. much as Elliot do. When grown-ups appear, the low camera angle reveals only   **27c**

feet, legs, and shadows, so the audience must imagine faces and facial expressions.

    By forcing viewers to do so much imaginative work, Spielberg succeed in   **27c**

making the film seem real—even more real than if he had devise explicit visuals.   **27d**

28 Use verbs in the appropriate tense, mood, and voice.

28a Choose the appropriate verb tense.

Tenses indicate the time of an action in relation to the time of the speaking or writing about that action.

The most common problem with tenses—shifting confusingly from one tense to another—is discussed in 13. Other problems with tenses are detailed in this section, after the following survey of tenses.

GRAMMAR CHECKERS do not flag the problems with tense discussed in this section. Although some programs may tell you that *had had* is incorrect, in fact it is often correct. See "perfect tenses" on this page.

Survey of tenses

English has three simple tenses (present, past, and future) and three perfect tenses (present perfect, past perfect, and future perfect). In addition, there is a progressive form of each of these six tenses.

SIMPLE TENSES   The simple present tense is used primarily to describe habitual actions (*Jane walks to work*) or to refer to actions occurring at the time of speaking (*I see a cardinal in our maple tree*). It is also used to state facts or general truths and to describe fictional events in a literary work (see p. 244). The present tense may even be used to express future actions that are to occur at some specified time (*The semester begins tomorrow*).

The simple past tense is used for actions completed entirely in the past (*Yesterday Jane walked to work*).

The simple future tense is used for actions that will occur in the future (*Tomorrow Jane will walk to work*) or for actions that are predictable, given certain causes (*Meat will spoil if not properly refrigerated*).

In the following chart, the simple tenses are given for the regular verb *walk*, the irregular verb *ride*, and the highly irregular verb *be*.

SIMPLE PRESENT

SINGULAR

I	walk, ride, am
you	walk, ride, are
he/she/it	walks, rides, is

PLURAL

we	walk, ride, are
you	walk, ride, are
they	walk, ride, are

SIMPLE PAST

SINGULAR

I	walked, rode, was
you	walked, rode, were
he/she/it	walked, rode, was

PLURAL

we	walked, rode, were
you	walked, rode, were
they	walked, rode, were

SIMPLE FUTURE

I, you, he/she/it, we, they	will walk, ride, be

PERFECT TENSES   More complex time relations are indicated by the perfect tenses (which consist of a form of *have* plus the past participle). The present perfect tense is used for an action that began in the past and is still going on in the present (*Jane has walked to work for years*) or an action that began in the past and is finished by the time of speaking or writing (*Jane has discovered a new restaurant on Elm Street*).

The past perfect tense is used for an action already completed by the time of another past action (*Jane hailed a cab after she had walked several blocks in the rain*) or for an action already completed at some specific past time (*By 8:30, Jane had walked two miles*). (See also p. 245.)

The future perfect tense is used for an action that will be completed before or by a certain future time (*Jane will have left Troy by the time Jo arrives*).

PRESENT PERFECT

I, you, we, they	have walked, ridden, been
he/she/it	has walked, ridden, been

PAST PERFECT

I, you, he/she/it, we, they	had walked, ridden, been

FUTURE PERFECT

I, you, he/she/it, we, they	will have walked, ridden, been

PROGRESSIVE FORMS The simple and perfect tenses already discussed have progressive forms that describe actions in progress. The present progressive form is used for actions currently in progress (*Jane is writing a letter*) or for future actions that are to occur at some specified time (*Jane is leaving for Chicago on Monday*).

The past progressive is used for past actions in progress (*Jane was writing a letter last night*).

The future progressive is used for future actions in progress (*Jane will be traveling next week*).

PRESENT PROGRESSIVE

I	am walking, riding, being
he/she/it	is walking, riding, being
you, we, they	are walking, riding, being

PAST PROGRESSIVE

I, he/she/it	was walking, riding, being
you, we, they	were walking, riding, being

FUTURE PROGRESSIVE

I, you, he/she/it, we, they	will be walking, riding, being

Like the simple tenses, the perfect tenses have progressive forms. The perfect progressive forms express the length of time an action is, was, or will be in progress. *Jane has been walking to work for five years* (present perfect progressive). *Jane had been walking to work until she was mugged* (past perfect progressive). *Jane will have been walking to work for five*

years by the end of this month (future perfect progressive).

PRESENT PERFECT PROGRESSIVE

I, you, we, they	have been walking, riding, being
he/she/it	has been walking, riding, being

PAST PERFECT PROGRESSIVE

I, you, he/she/it, we, they	had been walking, riding, being

FUTURE PERFECT PROGRESSIVE

I, you, he/she/it, we, they	will have been walking, riding, being

ESL The progressive forms are not normally used with mental activity verbs such as *believe*. See page 256.

Special uses of the present tense

Use the present tense when writing about events in a literary work, when expressing general truths, and when quoting, summarizing, or paraphrasing an author's views.

When writing about a work of literature, you may be tempted to use the past tense. The convention, however, is to describe fictional events in the present tense. (See also 13b.)

> *reaches*
> ► In Masuji Ibuse's *Black Rain*, a child ~~reached~~
>   for a pomegranate in his mother's garden,
>   *is*
>   and a moment later he ~~was~~ dead, killed by the
>   blast of the atomic bomb.

Scientific principles or general truths should appear in the present tense, unless such principles have been disproved.

> *revolves*
> ► Galileo taught that the earth ~~revolved~~ around
>   the sun.

Since Galileo's teaching has not been discredited, the verb should be in the present tense. The following sentence, however, is acceptable: *Ptolemy taught that the sun revolved around the earth.*

When you are quoting, summarizing, or paraphrasing the author of a nonliterary work, use present-tense verbs such as *writes*, *reports*, *asserts*, and so on. This convention is usually followed even when the author is dead (unless a date specifies the time of writing).

▶ Baron Bowan of Colwood ~~wrote~~ *writes* that a

metaphysician is "one who goes into a dark

cellar at midnight without a light, looking

for a black cat that is not there."

E. Wilson (1996) reported that positive reinforcement alone was a less effective teaching technique than a mixture of positive reinforcement and constructive criticism.

The past perfect tense

The past perfect tense consists of a past participle preceded by *had* (*had worked, had gone, had had*). (See pp. 243–44.) This tense is used for an action already completed by the time of another past action or for an action already completed at some specific past time.

Everyone *had spoken* by the time I arrived.

Everyone *had spoken* by 10:00 A.M.

Writers sometimes use the simple past tense when they should use the past perfect.

▶ We built our cabin high on a pine knoll, forty
feet above an abandoned quarry that ~~was~~ *had been*

flooded in 1920 to create a lake.

The building of the cabin and the flooding of the quarry both occurred in the past, but the flooding was completed before the time of building.

▶ By the time we arrived at the party, the guest
of honor *had* left.

The past perfect tense is needed because the action of leaving was completed at a specific past time (*by the time we arrived*).

Some writers tend to overuse the past perfect tense. Do not use the past perfect if two past actions occurred at the same time.

▶ When we arrived in Paris, Pauline ~~had~~ met

us at the train station.

Sequence of tenses with infinitives and participles

An infinitive is the base form of a verb preceded by *to*. (See 49c.) Use the present infinitive to show action at the same time as or later than the action of the verb in the sentence.

▶ The club had hoped to ~~have~~ *raise* ~~raised~~ a thousand

dollars by April 1.

The action expressed in the infinitive (*to raise*) occurred later than the action of the sentence's verb (*had hoped*).

Use the perfect form of an infinitive (*to have* followed by the past participle) for an action occurring earlier than that of the verb in the sentence.

▶ Dan would like to ~~join~~ *have joined* the navy, but he did not

pass the physical.

The liking occurs in the present; the joining would have occurred in the past.

Like the tense of an infinitive, the tense of a participle is also governed by the tense of the sentence's verb. Use the present participle (ending in *-ing*) for an action occurring at the same time as that of the sentence's verb.

Hiking the Appalachian Trail in early spring, we spotted many wildflowers.

Use the past participle (such as *given* or *helped*) or the present perfect participle (*having* plus the past participle) for an action occurring before that of the verb.

Discovered off the coast of Florida, the *Atocha* yielded many treasures.

Having worked her way through college, Melanie graduated debt-free.

28b Use the subjunctive mood in the few contexts that require it.

There are three moods in English: the *indicative*, used for facts, opinions, and questions;

the *imperative,* used for orders or advice; and the *subjunctive,* used in certain contexts to express wishes, requests, or conditions contrary to fact. Of these moods, only the subjunctive causes problems for writers.

Forms of the subjunctive

In the subjunctive mood, present-tense verbs do not change form to indicate the number and person of the subject (see 21). Instead, the subjunctive uses the base form of the verb (*be, drive, employ*) with all subjects.

> It is important that you *be* [not *are*] prepared for the interview.

> We asked that she *drive* [not *drives*] more slowly.

Also, in the subjunctive mood, there is only one past-tense form of *be: were* (never *was*).

> If I *were* [not *was*] you, I'd proceed more cautiously.

Uses of the subjunctive

The subjunctive mood appears only in a few contexts: in contrary-to-fact clauses beginning with *if* or expressing a wish; in *that* clauses following verbs such as *ask, insist, recommend, request,* and *suggest;* and in certain set expressions.

IN CONTRARY-TO-FACT CLAUSES BEGINNING WITH *IF*
When a subordinate clause beginning with *if* expresses a condition contrary to fact, use the subjunctive mood.

> ► If I ~~was~~ a member of Congress, I would vote for
>   ^were^
>
> that bill.

> ► We could be less cautious if Jake ~~was~~ more
>   ^were^
>
> trustworthy.

The verbs in these sentences express conditions that do not exist: The writer is not a member of Congress, and Jake is not trustworthy.

Do not use the subjunctive mood in *if* clauses expressing conditions that exist or may exist.

If Dana *wins* the contest, she will leave for Barcelona in June.

IN CONTRARY-TO-FACT CLAUSES EXPRESSING A WISH
In formal English, the subjunctive is used in clauses expressing a wish or desire; in informal speech, however, the indicative is more common.

> **FORMAL**
> I wish that Dr. Kurtinitis *were* my professor.

> **INFORMAL**
> I wish that Dr. Kurtinitis *was* my professor.

IN *THAT* CLAUSES FOLLOWING VERBS SUCH AS *ASK, INSIST, RECOMMEND, REQUEST,* AND *SUGGEST* Because requests have not yet become reality, they are expressed in the subjunctive mood.

> ► Professor Moore insists that her students ~~are~~
>   ^be^
>
> on time.

> ► We recommend that Lambert ~~files~~ form 1050 soon.
>   ^file^

IN CERTAIN SET EXPRESSIONS   The subjunctive mood, once more widely used in English, remains in certain set expressions: *Be* that as it may, as it *were, come* rain or shine, far *be* it from me, and so on.

 GRAMMAR CHECKERS rarely flag problems with the subjunctive mood. They may at times question your correct use of the subjunctive, since your correct use will seem to violate the rules of subject-verb agreement (see 21). For example, one program suggested using *was* instead of *were* in the following correct sentence: *This isn't my dog; if it were, I would feed it.* Because the sentence describes a condition contrary to fact, the subjunctive form *were* is correct.

28c   Use the active voice unless you have a good reason for choosing the passive.

Transitive verbs (verbs that take a direct object) appear in either the active or the passive voice. (See 48c.) In the active voice, the subject of the sentence does the action; in the passive, the subject receives the action. Although both voices are grammatically correct, the active voice is usually more effective because it is simpler, more direct, and less wordy.

ACTIVE
The committee *reached* a decision.

PASSIVE
A decision *was reached* by the committee.

To transform a sentence from the passive to the active voice, make the actor the subject of the sentence.

▶ For the opening flag ceremony, ~~a dance was~~ *choreographed a dance* ~~choreographed by~~ Mr. Martins to the song "Two Hundred Years and Still a Baby."

The revision emphasizes Mr. Martins by making him the subject.

▶ *We did not take down the* ~~The~~ Christmas decorations ~~were not taken down~~ until Valentine's Day.

Very often the actor does not even appear in a passive-voice sentence. To turn such a sentence into the active voice, the writer must decide on an appropriate subject, in this case *We*.

The passive voice is appropriate if you wish to emphasize the receiver of the action or to minimize the importance of the doer.

APPROPRIATE PASSIVES
Many native Hawaiians *are forced* to leave their beautiful beaches to make room for hotels and condominiums.

As the time for harvest approaches, the tobacco plants *are sprayed* with a chemical to retard the growth of suckers.

The writer of the first sentence wished to emphasize the receivers of the action, Hawaiians. The writer of the second sentence wished to focus on the tobacco plants, not on the people spraying them.

Some speakers of English as a second language tend to avoid the passive voice even when it is appropriate. For advice on transforming an active-voice sentence to the passive, see 48c.

GRAMMAR CHECKERS can flag many, but not all, passive verbs, and in some cases they flag verbs that aren't passive. Be aware, however, that passive verbs are sometimes appropriate, so you must decide whether to use an active verb instead. (For more detailed information, see the grammar checker advice on p. 124.)

EXERCISE 28–1 Verb tense, mood, and voice: Guided practice

Correct any tense or mood errors in the following paragraphs and change all passive verbs to active. Rule numbers in the margin refer to appropriate rules in section 28. The first revision has been made for you, and a suggested revision of this exercise appears in the back of the book.

    Almost everyone has heard about Aesop's fables, but most people know very little about Aesop himself. Most of what we know about Aesop is a mixture of hearsay and conjecture. We do know that he was a slave in Greece. One theory is that before he came to Greece he *had* lived in Ethiopia for most of his life and that "Aesop" is a much-shortened form of "the Ethiopian."   28a

    Aesop was not a storyteller then, though he would have loved to have spoken well enough to tell a good story. He stuttered so badly that he did not even try to talk. In one story we learn, however, that he could communicate. A gift of figs was brought to Aesop's master by a neighbor. Greatly pleased, the master planned to enjoy the figs after his bath and directed that they be put in a cool place until he was ready. While the master was bathing, the overseer and his friends ate the figs. When the master discovered the loss of his figs, the other slaves placed the blame on Aesop. They knew that if Aesop was able to speak, he could defend himself, but they did not fear this stammering slave.   28a / 28c / 28b

    The master ordered that Aesop be flogged. Aesop got the master to delay punishment briefly. Aesop drank a glass of warm water, ran his fingers down his throat, and vomited only water. Pointing at the overseer, he made gestures that the overseer and his friends should do as he had done. They drank the water, ran their fingers down their throats—and vomited figs.

    Although Aesop's cleverness saved him from a flogging, it also made an enemy of the overseer. A basic truth about life was discovered by Aesop: Being right didn't always help one to make friends.   28c / 28a

EXERCISE 28–2 Verb tense, mood, and voice

One sentence in each of the following pairs is correct: the other contains an error discussed in section 28. Circle the letters of the correct sentences, and edit the incorrect ones. Example:

(a.) Aesop was sent to work in the farthest field because he had made an enemy of the overseer.

b. Maybe the overseer ~~hope~~ *hoped* Aesop would run away, or maybe he had forgotten that the field was next to a major road.

1a. One day a caravan that had lost its way came by the field where Aesop was working.

b. The caravan driver requested that Aesop shows him the route to Cairo.

2a. Aesop, who was unable to speak, wanted to have helped him, so he walked with the caravan until it was on the correct road.

b. Grateful for Aesop's help and wanting to show his appreciation, the leader offered Aesop a reward.

3a. Aesop silently refused the reward; he had given his help without expecting anything in return.

b. The caravan leader wanted to leave at once because he lost valuable time on his trip to Cairo.

4a. When the caravan leader said good-bye, he asked the gods to bless Aesop.

b. As the caravan moved out of sight, Aesop had decided to take a nap.

5a. While Aesop slept, the gods restored his speech, proving that good deeds were sometimes rewarded.

b. When Aesop awoke and could speak, he rejoiced that the gods help those who befriend strangers.

EXERCISE 28–3 Verb tense, mood, and voice

Some of the italicized verbs in the following sentences are correct; others are in the wrong mood. Mark the correct sentences "OK" and change any incorrect verbs. Example:

> In ancient Greek culture, an overseer usually tried to sell a troublesome slave; if the slave *was* sold, the overseer's life would be easier. *OK*

1. When his Greek slave owner ordered that Aesop *be* sold, it was hard to find a buyer for him because he was so ugly.

2. Finally Aesop requested that he *be* allowed to sell himself.

3. Aesop knew that if he *was* not so ugly, many buyers would be glad to get him.

4. If he *was* going to find a buyer, Aesop would need to be clever.

5. One day a caravan that *was* in the slave-trading business stopped at Aesop's master's house.

6. The caravan driver requested that the slave owner *sells* him at least one strong slave.

7. The driver *saw* that Aesop's muscles were strong, but Aesop's hunched back and ugly face discouraged him.

8. Aesop realized that his chances of getting away *were* slim.

9. "If I *was* handsome, I would not be useful as a bogeyman to scare any misbehaving children," he said.

10. If he *were* afraid, the caravan owner did not show it; he laughed at Aesop—and bought him.

EXERCISE 28–4 Verb tense, mood, and voice

The verbs in the following sentences are italicized. Label each verb "A" if it is in the active voice or "P" if it is in the passive voice. Example:

                                    A   P

    a. Whenever a new slave *joined* the caravan, the slaves' burdens *were reassigned* by

       the caravan driver.

                                  A   A

    b. Whenever a new slave *joined* the caravan, the caravan driver *reassigned* the slaves'

       burdens.

  1a.   In ancient Greece, new slaves *were allowed* by the caravan driver to choose their

        burdens.

    b.   In ancient Greece, the caravan driver *allowed* new slaves to choose their burdens.

  2a.   Aesop *chose* the heavy breadbasket, full to overflowing.

    b.   The heavy breadbasket, full to overflowing, *was chosen* by Aesop.

  3a.   He *was mocked* by all the other slaves for choosing such a heavy load.

    b.   All the other slaves *had expected* him not to choose such a heavy load.

  4a.   After a few days of travel, however, his choice no longer *amused* the other slaves.

    b.   After a few days of travel, however, the other slaves *were* no longer *amused* by his

        choice.

  5a.   At each meal many loaves of bread *were taken* from the basket.

    b.   Entering Cairo, Aesop *carried* an empty basket.

EXERCISE 28–5 Verb tense, mood, and voice: Guided review

Correct any errors in verb tense or mood in the following paragraphs. Also change all passive verbs to active. Rule numbers in the margin refer to appropriate rules in section 28. The first revision has been made for you. You need to make ten more.

Aesop's death illustrated the implied moral of his last fable: When two ene-
mies fight each other, it ~~was~~ *is* wise to watch for a larger enemy of both. Aesop's death   28a
came some years after one of his owners gave him his freedom. His former owner   28a
would have liked Aesop to have stayed in the same town, but Aesop became an ad-   28a
viser at the court of several kings.

Aesop was sent to Delphi by one of those kings, Croessus, to distribute some   28c
gifts. The people of Delphi demanded that he gives them the gifts at once. Aesop re-   28b
fused, having discovered that the people of Delphi had lied to Croessus about their
activities. The angry people decided that if Aesop was dead, they could distribute the   28b
gifts as they pleased. He was thrown over a cliff to his death by these people, but   28c
not before Aesop told one more story.   28a

In the story, a frog invites a rat to dinner. To help the rat across the river to
the frog's house, the frog ties one of the rat's legs to one of his own. Midstream, the
frog tried to drown the rat. The rat puts up such a fight that an eagle flying over-   28a
head sees the commotion and promptly they are both eaten by him.   28c

"You will succeed in killing me," said Aesop to the people of Delphi, "but a
larger enemy will kill you as well." After Aesop's death, terrible plagues devastated
the city. People believed that the plagues came because of what they did to Aesop.   28a
To this day, the expression "blood of Aesop" refers to an innocent person whose
death someone has avenged.

Unit review (19–28): Grammatical sentences

Edit the following paragraphs to eliminate grammatical errors. Rule numbers in the margin refer to appropriate rules in sections 19–28. First try to find and correct the error on your own. Then look up the rule if you need to. The first revision has been done for you.

represent
The fables of Aesop ~~represents~~ the Western root of fable, but there are two   *21a*
strong Eastern roots of fable also: the Panchatantra and the Jataka tales.

The Panchatantra is a collection of stories designed to teach a first prince
and his brothers how to rule over a kingdom. (Until a tutor taught the first prince
with these stories, him and his brothers would never stay in the schoolroom. The   *24a*
boys listened eagerly to this new tutor who their father had found.) They are usu-   *25a, 23a*
ally longer than Western fables and have people as well as animals for characters.
Their tone sounds differently, too. Aesop's fables make gentle fun of people's foibles,   *26b, 20b*
Panchatantra fables teach lessons in how to achieve and hold power. This difference
is easily recognize in the moral to one of the Panchatantra fables: "Do not strike an   *27d*
enemy of iron with a fist of flesh. Wait until your enemy is stranded at the bottom
of a well. Then throw stones upon him."

The stories that carry the name "Jataka" tells about the Buddha and the ad-   *21a*
ventures he had when he came to earth in various incarnations. In these stories,
the Buddha appeared as an animal. Or sometimes simply as a "wise old man." Like   *28a, 19b*
the Panchatantra stories, the Jataka tales often depict people's foibles and short-
comings, but the Jataka tales are not satiric. They promote compassion rather than
power.

In one story, for example, monkeys try to help their friend, the gardener, by
watering newly planted trees for him. In doing so, they pull each tree out of the
ground to see how long their roots are. Of course the trees die. The Buddha com-   *22a*
ments, "The ignorant and foolish, even when they desire to do good, often do ill."

Putting all three traditions of fable together, any reader can choose from a
rich combination of small stories that carry large messages.

ESL Trouble Spots

Sections 29–31 have a special audience: speakers of English as a second language (ESL) who have learned English but continue to have problems in a few trouble spots.

---

29 Be alert to special problems with verbs.

Both native and nonnative speakers of English encounter the following problems with verbs, which are treated elsewhere in this workbook:

> problems with subject-verb agreement (21)
> misuse of verb forms (27)
> problems with tense, mood, and voice (28)

This section focuses on features of the English verb system that cause special problems for second language speakers.

29a Match helping verbs and main verbs appropriately.

Only certain combinations of helping verbs and main verbs are allowed in English. The correct combinations are discussed in this section, after the following review of helping verbs and main verbs.

Review of helping verbs and main verbs

Helping verbs always appear before main verbs. (See 47c.)

>   **HV** **MV**   **HV**
> We *will leave* for the picnic at noon. *Do* you
>   **MV**
> *want* a ride?

Some helping verbs — *have*, *do*, and *be* — change form to indicate tense; others, known as modals, do not.

> **FORMS OF *HAVE, DO,* AND *BE***
> have, has, had
> do, does, did
> be, am, is, are, was, were, being, been
>
> **MODALS**
> can, could, may, might, must, shall, should, will, would (*also* ought to)

Every main verb has five forms (except *be*, which has eight forms). The following list shows these forms for the regular verb *help* and the irregular verb *give*. (See 27a for a list of common irregular verbs.)

BASE FORM	help, give
PAST TENSE	helped, gave
PAST PARTICIPLE	helped, given
PRESENT PARTICIPLE	helping, giving
-S FORM	helps, gives

Modal + base form

After the modals *can, could, may, might, must, shall, should, will,* and *would,* use the base form of the verb.

▶ My cousin will sends us photographs from her

wedding.

          speak
▶ We could ~~spoke~~ Spanish when we were young.

CAUTION: Do not use *to* in front of a main verb that follows a modal. (*Ought to* is an exception.)

▶ Gina can ~~to~~ drive us home if we miss the bus.

Do, does, or did + base form

After helping verbs that are a form of *do,* use the base form of the verb.

The helping verbs *do, does,* and *did* are used in three ways: (1) to express a negative meaning with the adverb *not* or *never,* (2) to ask a question, and (3) to emphasize a main verb used in a positive sense.

▶ Mariko does not wants any more dessert.

          buy
▶ Did Janice ~~bought~~ the gift for Katherine?

          hope
▶ We do ~~hoping~~ that you will come to the party.

Have, has, or had + past participle (perfect tenses)

After the helping verb *have, has,* or *had,* use the past participle to form one of the perfect

tenses. (See 28a.) Past participles usually end in *-ed, -d, -en, -n,* or *-t.* (See 49c.)

          offered
▶ On cold nights many churches in the city have
  ~~offer~~ shelter to the homeless.

          spoken
▶ An-Mei has not ~~speaking~~ Chinese since she was

a child.

The helping verbs *have, has,* and *had* are sometimes preceded by a modal helping verb such as *will: By nightfall, we will have driven five hundred miles.* (See also perfect tenses, 28a.)

Form of be + present participle (progressive forms)

After the helping verb *be, am, is, are, was, were,* or *been,* use the present participle to express a continuing action. (See progressive forms, 28a.)

          building
▶ Carlos is ~~build~~ his house on a cliff overlooking

the ocean.

          driving
▶ Uncle Roy was ~~driven~~ a brand-new red Corvette.

The helping verb *be* must be preceded by a modal (*can, could, may, might, must, shall, should, will,* or *would*): *Edith will be going to Germany soon.* The helping verb *been* must be preceded by *have, has,* or *had: Andy has been studying English for five years.* (See also progressive forms, 28a.)

CAUTION: Certain verbs are not normally used in the progressive sense in English. In general, these verbs express a state of being or mental activity, not a dynamic action. Common examples are *appear, believe, belong, contain, have, hear, know, like, need, see, seem, taste, think, understand,* and *want.*

          want
▶ I ~~am wanting~~ to see August Wilson's *Fences* at

Arena Stage.

Some of these verbs, however, have special uses in which progressive forms are normal. (*We are thinking about going to the Bahamas.*)

You will need to make a note of exceptions as you encounter them.

Form of *be* + *past participle (passive voice)*

When a sentence is written in the passive voice, the subject receives the action instead of doing it: *Melissa was given a special award.* (See 28c.)

To form the passive voice, use *be, am, is, are, was, were, being,* or *been* followed by a past participle (usually ending in *-ed, -d, -en, -n,* or *-t*).

> **written**
> ▶ *Bleak House* was ~~write~~ by Charles Dickens.

> **honored**
> ▶ The scientists were ~~honor~~ for their work with
>
> dolphins.

When the helping verb is *be, being,* or *been,* it must be preceded by another helping verb. *Be* must be preceded by a modal such as *will: Senator Dixon will be defeated. Being* must be preceded by *am, is, are, was,* or *were: The child was being teased. Been* must be preceded by *have, has,* or *had: I have been invited to a party.*

CAUTION: Although they may seem to have passive meanings, verbs such as *occur, happen, sleep, die,* and *fall* may not be used to form the passive voice because they are intransitive. Only transitive verbs, those that take direct objects, may be used to form the passive voice. (See transitive and intransitive verbs, 48b.)

> ▶ The earthquake ~~was~~ occurred last Wednesday.

GRAMMAR CHECKERS can catch some mismatches of helping and main verbs. They can tell you, for example, that the base form of the verb should be used after certain helping verbs, such as *did* and *could,* in incorrect sentences like these: *Did you understood my question? Could Alan comes with us?*

Programs can also catch some, but not all, problems with main verbs following forms of *have* or *be.* For example, grammar checkers flagged *have spend,* explaining that the past participle *spent* is required, and they flagged *are expose,* suggesting that either *exposed* or *exposing* is required. However, programs failed to flag problems in many sentences, such as these: *Sasha has change her major three times. The provisions of the contract were broke by both parties.*

29b   In conditional sentences, choose verbs with care.

Conditional sentences state that one set of circumstances depends on whether another set of circumstances exists. Choosing verbs in such sentences can be tricky, partly because two clauses are involved: usually an *if* or a *when* or an *unless* clause and an independent clause.

Three kinds of conditional sentences are discussed in this section: factual, predictive, and speculative.

Factual

Factual conditional sentences express factual relationships. These relationships might be scientific truths, in which case the present tense is used in both clauses.

> If water *cools* to 32°, it *freezes.*

Or they might be present or past relationships that are habitually true, in which case the same tense is used in both clauses.

> When Sue *bicycles* along the canal, her dog *runs* ahead of her.

> Whenever the coach *asked* for help, I *volunteered.*

Predictive

Predictive conditional sentences are used to predict the future or to express future plans or possibilities. In such a sentence, an *if* or *unless* clause contains a present-tense verb; the verb in the independent clause usually consists of the modal *will, can, may, should,* or *might* followed by the base form of the verb.

> If you *practice* regularly, your tennis game *will improve.*

> We *will lose* our remaining wetlands unless we *act* now.

Speculative

Speculative conditional sentences are used for three purposes: (1) to speculate about unlikely possibilities in the present or future, (2) to speculate about events that did not happen in the past, and (3) to speculate about conditions that are contrary to fact. Each of these purposes requires its own combination of verbs.

UNLIKELY POSSIBILITIES   Somewhat confusingly, English uses the past tense in an *if* clause to speculate about a possible but unlikely condition in the present or future. The verb in the independent clause consists of *would*, *could*, or *might* plus the base form of the verb.

> If I *had* the time, I *would travel* to Senegal.

> If Stan *studied* harder, he *could master* calculus.

In the *if* clause, the past-tense form *were* is used with subjects that would normally take *was*: *Even if I were* [not *was*] *invited, I wouldn't go to the picnic.* (See also 28b.)

EVENTS THAT DID NOT HAPPEN   English uses the past perfect tense in an *if* clause to speculate about an event that did not happen in the past or to speculate about a state of being that was unreal in the past. (See past perfect tense, 28a.) The verb in the independent clause consists of *would have*, *could have*, or *might have* plus the past participle.

> If I *had saved* enough money, I *would have traveled* to Senegal last year.

> If Aunt Grace *had been* alive for your graduation, she *would have been* very proud.

CONDITIONS CONTRARY TO FACT   To speculate about conditions that are currently unreal or contrary to fact, English usually uses the past-tense verb *were* (never *was*) in an *if* clause. (See 28b.) The verb in the independent clause consists of *would*, *could*, or *might* plus the base form of the verb.

> If Grandmother *were* alive today, she *would be* very proud of you.

> I *would make* children's issues a priority if I *were* president.

 GRAMMAR CHECKERS do not flag problems with conditional sentences. The programs miss even obvious errors, such as this one: *Whenever I washed my car, it rains.*

29c   Become familiar with verbs that may be followed by gerunds or infinitives.

A gerund is a verb form that ends in *-ing* and is used as a noun: *sleeping, dreaming.* (See 49c.) An infinitive is the base form of the verb preceded by the word *to*: *to sleep, to dream.* The word *to* is not a preposition in this use but an infinitive marker. (See 49c.)

A few verbs may be followed by either a gerund or an infinitive; others may be followed by a gerund but not by an infinitive; still others may be followed by an infinitive (either directly or with a noun or pronoun intervening) but not by a gerund.

Verb + gerund or infinitive

These commonly used verbs may be followed by a gerund or an infinitive, with little or no difference in meaning:

begin	hate	love
can't stand	like	start
continue		

> I love *skiing.*

> I love *to ski.*

With a few verbs, however, the choice of a gerund or infinitive changes the meaning dramatically:

forget	remember	stop	try

> She stopped *speaking* to Lucia. [She no longer spoke to Lucia.]

> She stopped *to speak* to Lucia. [She paused so that she could speak to Lucia.]

Verb + gerund

These verbs may be followed by a gerund but not by an infinitive:

admit	discuss	imagine	put off	risk
appreciate	enjoy	miss	quit	suggest
avoid	escape	postpone	recall	tolerate
deny	finish	practice	resist	

> Have you finished *decorating* [not *to decorate*] the tree?

> Bill enjoys *playing* [not *to play*] the piano.

Verb + infinitive

These verbs may be followed by an infinitive but not by a gerund:

agree	decide	manage	pretend	want
ask	expect	mean	promise	wish
beg	have	offer	refuse	
claim	hope	plan	wait	

> We plan *to visit* [not *visiting*] the Yucatan next week.

> Jill has offered *to water* [not *watering*] the plants while we are away.

Verb + noun or pronoun + infinitive

With certain verbs, a noun or pronoun must come between the verb and the infinitive that follows it. The noun or pronoun usually names a person who is affected by the action.

advise	command	have	persuade	tell
allow	convince	instruct	remind	urge
cause	encourage	order	require	warn

> The dean encourages *you to apply* for the scholarship.

> The class asked *Luis to tell* the story of his escape.

A few verbs may be followed either by an infinitive directly or by an infinitive preceded by a noun or pronoun.

ask	expect	need	want	would like

> We asked *to speak* to the congregation.

> We asked *Rabbi Abrams to speak* to our congregation.

Verb + noun or pronoun + unmarked infinitive

An unmarked infinitive is an infinitive without *to*. A few verbs (known as "causative verbs") may be followed by a noun or pronoun and an unmarked (but not a marked) infinitive.

have ("cause")	let ("allow")	make ("force")

> Absence makes *the heart grow* [not *to grow*] fonder.

> Please let *me pay* [not *to pay*] for the tickets.

> **GRAMMAR CHECKERS** can flag some, but not all, problems with gerunds and infinitives following verbs. For example, programs flagged many sentences with misused infinitives, such as these: *Have you finished to weed the garden? Chris enjoys to play tennis.* Programs were less successful at flagging sentences with misused present participles, skipping past incorrect sentences like this one: *We want traveling to Hawaii next spring.*

29d Become familiar with commonly used two-word verbs.

Many verbs in English consist of a verb followed by a preposition or adverb known as a *particle.* (See 47c.) A two-word verb (also known as a *phrasal verb*) often expresses an idiomatic meaning that cannot be understood literally. Consider the verbs in the following sentences, for example:

> We *ran across* Professor Magnotto on the way to the bookstore.

> Calvin *dropped in* on his adviser this morning.

> Regina told me to *look* her *up* when I got to Seattle.

As you probably know, *ran across* means "encountered," *dropped in* means "paid an unexpected visit," and *look up* means "get in touch with." When you were first learning English, however, these two-word verbs must have suggested strange meanings.

Some two-word verbs are intransitive; they do not take direct objects. (See 48b.)

> This morning I *got up* at dawn.

Transitive two-word verbs (those that take direct objects) have particles that are either separable or inseparable. Separable particles may be separated from the verb by the direct object.

> Lucy *called* the wedding *off.*

When the direct object is a noun, a separable particle may also follow the verb immediately.

> At the last minute, Lucy *called off* the wedding.

When the direct object is a pronoun, however, the particle must be separated from the verb.

Why was there no wedding? Lucy *called* it *off* [not *called off* it].

Inseparable particles must follow the verb immediately. A direct object cannot come between the verb and the particle.

The police will *look into* the matter [not *look the matter into*].

The following list includes common two-word verbs. If a particle can be separated from the verb by a direct object, a pronoun is shown between the verb and the particle: *ask (someone) out*. When in doubt about the meaning of a two-word verb, consult the dictionary.

COMMON TWO-WORD VERBS

ask (someone) out
break down
bring (something or someone) up
burn (something) down
burn down
burn (something) up
burn up
call (something) off
call (someone) up
clean (something) up
clean up
come across
cut (something) up
do (something) over
drop in (on someone)
drop (someone or something) off
drop out (of something)
fill (something) out
fill (something) up
get along (with someone)
get away (with something)
get up
give (something) away
give (something) back
give in
give up
go out (with someone)
go over (something)
grow up
hand (something) in
hand (something) out
hang (something) up
help out
help (someone) out
keep on (doing something)

keep up (with someone or something)
leave (something) out
look into (something)
look (something) over
look (something) up
make (something) up
pick (something) out
pick (someone) up
pick (something) up
play around
point (something) out
put (something) away
put (something) back
put (something) off
put (something) on
put (something) out
put (something) together
put up (with someone or something)
quiet down
run across (someone or something)
run into (someone or something)
run out (of something)
see (someone) off
shut (something) off
speak to (someone)
speak up
stay away (from someone or something)
stay up
take care of (someone or something)
take off
take (something) off

COMMON TWO-WORD VERBS

take (someone) out
take (something) over
think (something) over
throw (something) away
throw (something) out
try (something) on
try (something) out

turn (something) down
turn (something) on
turn up
wake up
wake (someone) up
wear out
wrap (something) up

29e Do not omit needed verbs.

Some languages allow the omission of the verb when the meaning is clear without it; English does not.

▶ Jim *is* exceptionally intelligent.

▶ Many streets in San Francisco *are* very steep.

EXERCISE 29–1 Special problems with verbs: Guided practice

Edit the following paragraphs to correct problems with verbs. Rule numbers in the margin refer to appropriate rules in section 29. The first revision has been done for you, and a suggested revision of this exercise appears in the back of the book.

       Immigrants have *come* ~~came~~ to the United States from all over the world. Initially,   *29a*
new settlers were mostly European, Irish, or English. By the twentieth century,
many Asians had took the frightening boat trip across the Pacific. Usually the men   *29a*
came first. After they had made enough money for passage, their wives and children
were bring over. All were in search of the same good life that earlier European im-   *29a*
migrants had sought. Unable to live comfortably in their homelands, a large number of Chinese and Japanese gave up them and settled in the western part of the   *29d*
United States.

       These new immigrants worked on the railroads and in the mines. American
businesses recruited Chinese labor because it was difficult to find American workers who would accept the wages that were paying. Why did workers decided to come   *29a, 29a*
to America anyway? Somehow the idea got started that America was a "golden
mountain," where people could pick up gold nuggets after an easy climb. Once they
got here, most immigrants worked hard because they hoped making enough money   *29c*
to bring relatives over to America too.

       Before and during World War II, many Germans who had been persecuted
by Hitler escaped to America. After the war, thousands of "displaced persons" were
welcome by the United States. Later, refugees from Asia, Africa, Latin America, and   *29a*
the Caribbean wanted being accepted. Franklin D. Roosevelt once said, "All of our   *29c*
people all over the country, except the pure-blooded Indians, are immigrants or descendants of immigrants." If Roosevelt were alive today, he will know that his state-   *29b*
ment still true.   *29e*

EXERCISE 29–2 Helping verbs and main verbs

A. Edit the italicized verb or verb phrase in each of the following sentences to correct the error in the use of helping verbs or main verbs. Example:

> In the early twentieth century, so many immigrants wanted to enter the United States that a
>   *built*
> special center *was ~~build~~* to process them.
>   ^

1. That center, Ellis Island, *had built* to handle five thousand people a day, but often ten thousand people were processed in one day.

2. All immigrants *were check* by a doctor, and an immigrant's coat was marked with a code if a problem was suspected.

3. Everyone knew that if an immigrant *was gave* an "X," the immigrant had practically no chance to enter America; an "X" meant "possible mental problems."

4. Sometimes families were divided because one child was rejected for some reason; often the child *would sent* back alone.

5. Although it was the entrance to a new life for many people, "Ellis Island" *was translate* as "Isle of Tears" in many European languages.

B. Four of the following sentences have incorrect helping verbs or main verbs. Find and correct them. Mark "OK" next to the one correct sentence. Example:

>   *come*
> Where did most immigrants to the United States in the 1980s ~~came~~ from?
>   ^

6. Eighty percent of the immigrants who were allow to come to the United States in the 1980s were Asian or Latin American.

7. The number of Asians who were lived in the United States more than doubled between 1970 and 1980.

8. People from the Philippines, China, and Korea been regular immigrants to the United States.

9. Since 1975, a rush of immigrant refugees been arriving in the United States.

10. In less than a seven-year period, 600,000 refugees from Vietnam, Laos, and Cambodia came to the United States.

EXERCISE 29-3 Helping verbs, main verbs, and omitted verbs

A. In the following sentences, underline the correct phrase in the parentheses. Example:

(Haven't you hear, <u>Haven't you heard</u>) of Eckeo Kounlavong?

1. Eckeo Kounlavong (was born, had born) in Laos, lived in a refugee camp in Thailand, and later settled in Nashville, Tennessee.

2. Many people (do not knew, do not know) that in Laos, Eckeo was the leader of the Royal Laotian Classical Dance Troupe.

3. Before him, the troupe (had been directed, had been directing) by his father and grandfather.

4. In those days in Laos, the law said that the families of all the dancers (must living, must live) in the palace.

5. They (could not to dance, could not dance) for anyone except the king and his guests.

B. Four of the following sentences have omitted or incorrect helping verbs or main verbs. Find and correct them. Mark "OK" next to the one correct sentence. Example:

           changed
The dancers' lives were ~~change~~ drastically when the Communists gained power in Laos.

6. Eckeo and his mother escaped from Laos to the Nongkhai refugee camp in Thailand.

7. The troupe was resettled in Nashville, Tennessee; they been in Nashville ever since.

8. Since 1980, Nashville has attract many Laotians.

9. Nashville has long been knowing as the country music capital of the United States.

10. Now Nashville can claims it is the capital for country music and for classical Laotian music.

EXERCISE 29-4 Helping verbs and main verbs

Insert appropriate helping verbs in the following sentences. Sometimes several answers are possible. Example:

Do (or Did) you know many musicians?

1. Immigrants _____ brought much music to the United States.

2. _____ you heard of Seiji Ozawa, the conductor of the Boston Symphony Orchestra?

3. _____ you know that he is from Japan?

4. Eileen Farrell, who _____ known internationally as a Metropolitan Opera star, is the daughter of the Irish "Singing O'Farrells."

5. Americans _____ been awed by Chinese cellist Yo-Yo Ma.

6. Chuing Chou, a Chinese American composer, _____ awarded a Guggenheim Fellowship.

7. Yi Knei Sze, a Chinese American singer, _____ won international fame.

8. _____ the name Myung Whun Chung mean anything to you?

9. Many critics think that this young Korean who studied at Juilliard _____ become one of America's outstanding pianists and composers.

10. Mischa Elman, Jascha Heifetz, and Nathan Milstein, all famous American violinists, _____ born in Russia and immigrated to the United States.

EXERCISE 29–5 Helping verbs and main verbs

Turn each of the following sentence openings into a complete sentence using the correct main verb form. Choose from these verbs: *give, name, take, buy, offer.* Example:

I did not _*take my children to the concert.*_____

1. Did you _____

2. He could not _____

3. An award was _____

4. She has already _____

5. They do _____

6. Immigrants have _____

7. Does your father _____

8. My uncle could _____

9. The house is _____

10. I have been _____

EXERCISE 29–6 Conditional verbs

Edit the following paragraph for problems with conditional verbs. The first revision has been made for you. You should make five more.

> If my grandfather had immigrated today, instead of eighty years ago, he probably *would* ~~will~~ have traveled by jet. He came from Croatia to the United States just before the First World War. In those days, when you left your native country, you usually do so forever. My grandfather missed Croatia, but he liked America very much. He always said that America was a country where if you work hard, you would be successful. My grandfather, who will be ninety-five years old if he were alive today, was not as successful as he had hoped. If he has earned more money, he would have gone back to Croatia to visit. I'm sure my grandfather will have enjoyed that trip if he had ever had the chance to make it.

EXERCISE 29–7 Verbs followed by gerunds or infinitives

A. The gerunds and infinitives are italicized in the following sentences. Only one in each sentence is correct; correct the other one. Example:

Among the many Laotian refugees in Thailand's Nongkhai refugee camp were some

members of the Royal Laotian Classical Dance Troupe. They wanted *~~continuing~~* *to continue* their

dancing and discussed *finding* ways that they could stay together.

1. In the refugee camp in Thailand, the dance troupe began *to think* about *to resettle* together.

2. They enjoyed *to work* together on their music and liked *to perform* for others.

3. Someone suggested *discussing* the idea with resettlement officials who might help them *staying* together.

4. The Laotians wanted *resettling* together; they suggested *sending* the 70 dancers and their families—260 people—to one place.

5. They hardly dared *wishing* for that possibility; nevertheless, they enjoyed *thinking* about it.

B. Correct the use of gerunds and infinitives in the following sentences. Put "OK" next to the one correct sentence. Example:

The United States allowed the Laotian dancers ~~coming~~ *to come* to America together.

6. The officials let them to bring all their equipment and costumes for performing in their new country.

7. Refugee officials needed to handle thousands of pieces of paper for the dancers before they finished to process them.

8. To avoid splitting up the troupe, officials asked resettlement agencies in America finding sponsors for all of the dancers and their families in one community.

9. People in Nashville, Tennessee, offered to let the troupe settle there.

10. The Laotians wanted thanking the people of Nashville by giving a concert for the city.

EXERCISE 29–8 Two-word verbs

A. Insert the correct two-word verb in each of the following sentences. A synonym for the verb is in parentheses at the end of each sentence. Choose from these two-word verbs: *help out, keep up, make up, put on, turn down.* Example:

Nashville ___*helped*___ the Laotians ___*out*___ . (aided)

1. Laotians _____ much of Northern Telecom's work force. (constitute)

2. Telecom says that they are excellent employees and seldom _____ an opportunity for extra work. (reject)

3. They _____ their musical skill by practicing on weekends. (preserve)

4. They _____ special programs for cities in the area and for their cultural celebrations. (produce)

5. They _____ many of their cultural traditions this way. (maintain)

B. In each of the following sentences, underline the correct two-word verb. A synonym for the verb is in parentheses after the sentence. Example:

The dance troupe (<u>ran into</u>, ran out of) many difficulties. (encountered)

6. Trained as dancers, the troupe members had to (look over, look into) other ways to earn money when they settled in Nashville. (investigate)

7. Since they were the first Laotians in Nashville, they had no old friends whom they could (look over, look up, look into) in the city. (find, visit)

8. The new life in Nashville was difficult, but the Laotians did not (give up, give in) their dancing. (abandon)

9. They have (taken care of, taken off) their traditions while learning new American ones. (preserved)

10. No doubt their American friends will (pick out, pick up) some information about Laotian customs also. (learn)

EXERCISE 29–9 Special problems with verbs: Guided review

Edit the following paragraphs to correct errors in the use of verbs. Rule numbers in the margin refer to appropriate rules in section 29. The first sentence has been revised for you.

Although most refugee immigrants have ~~adapt~~ *adapted* well to life in America, some have not. Many have great difficulty learning English and accepting the customs of this land they have came to. Other newcomers find that they miss their former homes more than they thought they would. They believe that they would have been much happier if they have stayed in their native countries. Among the Laotians, the saddest stories indicate that homesickness can even cause death. Would you believe that homesickness could be so powerful? Young Laotian men with no apparent health problems have died suddenly in their sleep. Doctors can to give no reason for these deaths, but Laotians believe that the young men wanted going home too much. They say that the young men gave to their feelings in, and their bodies died so that their spirits could enjoy to go home again.

[margin: 29a, 29a, 29b, 29a, 29c, 29d, 29c]

Immigrants from Mexico, Cuba, and Puerto Rico have had problems, too. Many Mexican immigrants been forcefully repatriated because the American government considered them "illegal" immigrants. Most Cuban immigrants in the 1960s expected their stay in America to be temporary, so they did not became U.S. citizens. Because Puerto Ricans are U.S. citizens, they are not really "immigrants." They here because they are looking for a better life. They do not always find it. So many Puerto Ricans have returned to their homeland that they have been given a special name, "Neoricans."

[margin: 29a, 29a, 29e]

Most immigrants, however, have adapt to the new country, changing themselves—and it.

[margin: 29a]

30 Use the articles *a*, *an*, and *the* appropriately.

Except for occasional difficulty in choosing between *a* and *an*, native speakers of English encounter few problems with articles. To speakers whose native language is not English, however, articles can prove troublesome, for the rules governing their use are surprisingly complex. This section summarizes those rules.

The definite article *the* and the indefinite articles *a* and *an* signal that a noun is about to appear. The noun may follow the article immediately or modifiers may intervene (see 47a and 47d).

> *the candidate*, *the* exceptionally well qualified *candidate*

> *a sunset*, *a* spectacular *sunset*

> *an apple*, *an* appetizing *apple*

Articles are not the only words used to mark nouns. Other noun markers (sometimes called *determiners*) include possessive nouns (*Helen's*), numbers, and the following pronouns: *my, your, his, her, its, our, their, whose, this, that, these, those, all, any, each, either, every, few, many, more, most, much, neither, several, some.*

Usually an article is not used with another noun marker. Common exceptions include expressions such as *a few*, *the most*, and *all the*.

GRAMMAR CHECKERS can flag some missing or misused articles, pointing out, for example, that an article usually precedes a word such as *paintbrush* or *vehicle* or that the articles *a* and *an* are not usually used before a noncount noun such as *sugar* or *advice*.

However, the programs fail to flag many missing or misused articles. For example, in two paragraphs with eleven missing or misused articles, grammar checkers caught only two of the problems. In addition, the programs frequently suggest that an article is missing when it is not. For example, one program suggested that an article might be needed before *teacher* in this correct sentence: *My social studies teacher entered me in a public-speaking contest.*

30a Use *a* (or *an*) with singular count nouns whose specific identity is not known to the reader.

Count nouns refer to persons, places, or things that can be counted: *one girl, two girls; one city, three cities; one apple, four apples.* Noncount nouns refer to entities or abstractions that cannot be counted: *water, steel, air, furniture, patience, knowledge.* It is important to remember that noncount nouns vary from language to language. To see what nouns English categorizes as noncount nouns, refer to the chart on page 270.

If a singular count noun names something not known to the reader—perhaps because it is being mentioned for the first time, perhaps because its specific identity is unknown even to the writer—the noun should be preceded by *a* or *an* unless it has been preceded by another noun marker. *A* (or *an*) usually means "one among many" but can also mean "any one."

>   *a*
> ▶ Mary Beth arrived in limousine.
>   ^

>   *an*
> ▶ We are looking for apartment close to the lake.
>   ^

NOTE: *A* is used before a consonant sound: *a banana, a tree, a picture, a hand, a happy child. An* is used before a vowel sound: *an eggplant, an occasion, an uncle, an hour, an honorable person.* Notice that words beginning with *h* can have either a consonant sound (*hand, happy*) or a vowel sound (*hour, honorable*). (See also the Glossary of Usage: *a, an*.)

30b Do not use *a* (or *an*) with noncount nouns.

A (or *an*) is not used to mark noncount nouns, such as *sugar, gold, honesty,* or *jewelry.* A list of commonly used noncount nouns is given in the chart on page 270.

> ▶ Claudia asked her mother for ~~an~~ advice.

If you want to express an approximate amount, you can often use one of the following quantifiers with a noncount noun.

Commonly used noncount nouns

FOOD AND DRINK

> bacon, beef, bread, broccoli, butter, cabbage, candy, cauliflower, celery, cereal, cheese, chicken, chocolate, coffee, corn, cream, fish, flour, fruit, ice cream, lettuce, meat, milk, oil, pasta, rice, salt, spinach, sugar, tea, water, wine, yogurt

NONFOOD SUBSTANCES

> air, cement, coal, dirt, gasoline, gold, paper, petroleum, plastic, rain, silver, snow, soap, steel, wood, wool

ABSTRACT NOUNS

> advice, anger, beauty, confidence, courage, employment, fun, happiness, health, honesty, information, intelligence, knowledge, love, poverty, satisfaction, truth, wealth

OTHER

> biology (and other areas of study), clothing, equipment, furniture, homework, jewelry, luggage, lumber, machinery, mail, money, news, poetry, pollution, research, scenery, traffic, transportation, violence, weather, work

NOTE: A few noncount nouns may also be used as count nouns, especially in informal English: *Bill loves chocolate; Bill offered me a chocolate. I'll have coffee; I'll have a coffee.*

QUANTIFIER	NONCOUNT NOUN
a great deal of	candy, courage
a little	salt, rain
any	sugar, homework
enough	bread, wood, money
less	meat, violence
little (*or* a little)	knowledge, time
more	coffee, information
much (*or* a lot of)	snow, pollution
plenty of	paper, lumber
some	tea, news, work

To express a more specific amount, you can often precede a noncount noun with a unit word that is typically associated with it. Here are some common combinations.

A OR *AN* + UNIT + *OF*	NONCOUNT NOUNS
a bottle of	water, vinegar
a carton of	ice cream, milk, yogurt
an ear of	corn
a head of	cabbage, lettuce
a loaf of	bread
a piece of	meat, furniture, advice
a pound of	butter, sugar
a quart of	milk, ice cream
a slice of	bread, bacon

CAUTION: Noncount nouns do not have plural forms, and they should not be used with numbers or words suggesting plurality (such as *several, many, a few, a couple of, a number of*).

▶ We need some information~~s~~ about rain forests.

▶ Do you have ~~many~~ money with you?
  much

30c Use *the* with most nouns whose specific identity is known to the reader.

The definite article *the* is used with most nouns whose identity is known to the reader. (For exceptions, see 30d.) Usually the identity will be clear to the reader for one of the following reasons:

— The noun has been previously mentioned.

— A phrase or a clause following the noun restricts its identity.

— A superlative such as *best* or *most intelligent* makes the noun's identity specific.

— The noun describes a unique person, place, or thing.

— The context or situation makes the noun's identity clear.

▶ A truck loaded with dynamite cut in front of our van. When truck skidded a few seconds
    the

later, we almost plowed into it.

The noun *truck* is preceded by *A* when it is first mentioned. When the noun is mentioned again, it is preceded by *the* since readers now know the specific truck being discussed.

Geographical names

WHEN TO OMIT *THE*		large regions, deserts	the East Coast, the Sahara
streets, squares, parks	Ivy Street, Union Square, Denali National Park	peninsulas	the Iberian Peninsula
		oceans, seas, gulfs	the Pacific, the Dead Sea, the Persian Gulf
cities, states, counties	Miami, Idaho, Bee County	canals and rivers	the Panama Canal, the Amazon
most countries	Italy, Nigeria, China		
continents	South America, Africa	mountain ranges	the Rocky Mountains, the Alps
bays, single lakes	Tampa Bay, Lake Geneva		
single mountains, islands	Mount Everest, Crete	groups of islands	the Solomon Islands

WHEN TO USE *THE*	
united countries	the United States, the Republic of China

▶ Bob warned me that *the* gun on the top shelf of the

cupboard was loaded.

The phrase *on the top shelf of the cupboard* identifies the specific gun.

▶ Our petite daughter dated *the* tallest boy in her class.

The superlative *tallest* restricts the identity of the noun *boy*.

▶ During an eclipse, one should not look directly
at *the* sun.

There is only one sun in our solar system, so its identity is clear.

▶ Please don't slam *the* door when you leave.

Both the speaker and the listener know which door is meant.

30d Do not use *the* with plural or noncount nouns meaning "all" or "in general"; do not use *the* with most proper nouns.

When a plural or a noncount noun means "all" or "in general," it is not marked with *the*.

▶ ~~The~~ Fountains are an expensive element of

landscape design.

▶ In some parts of the world, ~~the~~ rice is preferred

to all other grains.

As you probably know, proper nouns—which name specific people, places, or things—are capitalized. Although there are many exceptions, *the* is not used with most singular proper nouns, such as *Judge Ito, Spring Street,* and *Lake Huron*. However, *the* is used with plural proper nouns, such as *the United Nations, the Bahamas,* and *the Finger Lakes*.

Geographical names create problems because there are so many exceptions to the rules. When in doubt, consult the chart at the top of this page or ask a native speaker.

EXERCISE 30-1 Articles: Guided practice

Edit the following paragraphs to correct the use of articles. Rule numbers in the margin refer to appropriate rules in section 30. The first revision has been done for you, and a suggested revision of this exercise appears in the back of the book.

The
^United States has always attracted immigrants. Modern scientists think that   *30d, 30c*

first immigrants arrived at least 25,000 years ago, probably traveling over land   *30a*

bridge just below the Arctic Circle—from Siberia to Alaska. (Of course land bridge   *30c*

is no longer there. Scientists think that such a bridge formed during the Ice Age,

when much of water in the ocean froze into tall glaciers. As it froze, it exposed large   *30c*

strips of land. Hunters probably followed animals across this land bridge.)

      Descendants of the original immigrants were still here in 1607 when settlers

from the England arrived in Virginia. These early settlers were followed by many   *30d*

more. In the hundred and forty years that followed, thousands made trip to America.   *30c*

Crowded onto small wooden boats, they left behind their kinfolk and their history and

crossed the Atlantic Ocean. Making such a trip took a bravery and faith in the future.   *30b*

      Some of the settlers came for religious reasons; others came to escape poverty

or imprisonment. But all of them came hoping for a happiness. They were followed   *30b*

by many others with same goal. Ever since those first immigrants 25,000 years ago,   *30c*

waves of the immigrants have been a common occurrence in America.   *30d*

EXERCISE 30–2 Articles

Some of the following sentences have errors in the use of articles. Mark the correct sentences "OK" and correct the others. Example:

> *a*
> European immigrants to America hoped for ~~an~~ friendly reception; some got quite a
>   ^
> surprising welcome.

1. In 1621, several Pilgrims were actually greeted by an Native American who spoke English and offered them a pleasant welcome.

2. Squanto was a member of the Pawtuxet tribe and became a real friend of the Pilgrims.

3. An explorer had taken Squanto to visit England in 1605; his visit there had turned into an lengthy one.

4. Squanto stayed in London almost a decade until a ship brought him back to America in 1614.

5. He had not been home very long when he was kidnapped and sent to Spain as slave, but he escaped and caught a ship to England.

6. In 1619, a English sea captain brought him back to a place Squanto knew, Cape Cod.

7. Squanto acted as useful interpreter and a unselfish guide for the Pilgrims.

8. The settlers wanted to grow a corn, but they had a hard time learning to farm in this new land.

9. Squanto gave the settlers an advice about planting their corn: He told them to plant a dead fish with each seed for fertilizer.

10. When Squanto died of a fever in 1622, Plymouth Colony lost an unsung hero who many historians believe was responsible for the success of the colony.

EXERCISE 30–3 Articles

Each of the following sentences has one missing or misused article. Correct each sentence.
Example:

> *the*
> Not all newcomers to America have come for same reasons.
> ^

1. Whatever their reasons for coming, early immigrants to the America came of their own free will.

2. In the eighteenth and nineteenth centuries, hundreds of thousands of the Africans were brought to America by slave traders.

3. Slaves were sold primarily to southern farmers, who wanted a cheap labor.

4. Hundreds of thousands of Africans were brought to United States before 1861.

5. Each one was brought specifically to be an slave.

6. Some European immigrants came as indentured servants; they had borrowed cost of their voyage and had to work for their "owners" until the debt was repaid.

7. But these workers were promised the freedom after their debts had been paid.

8. The Africans had only hard work and the mistreatment.

9. Early settlers in America came primarily to North; slaves came primarily to the South.

10. America fought war to end slavery so that people would come to America only of their own free will.

EXERCISE 30–4 Articles: Guided review

Edit the following paragraphs to correct the use of articles. Rule numbers in the margin refer to appropriate rules in section 30. The first revision has been done for you.

              the
One reason people immigrated to United States was to escape poverty. Par-   *30d*

ents who could not earn enough money to take care of their children in their

native land tried to find other places to live. All during the nineteenth century,

immigrants flocked to America to escape a poverty. Unable in their own countries   *30b*

to provide for their families, they left their homes to seek their fortunes in a   *30a*

unknown land.

    Sometimes only one family member came to the new land. The father of the

family would come alone, hoping to earn enough money to send back for a mother   *30c*

and children. Other times, the whole family made the journey together to the other

side of the Atlantic. Irish and European families by the thousands settled on the

East Coast of the United States, often bringing only the clothes on their backs. It

took a self-confidence to leave all that was familiar and start over again in new world.   *30b, 30c*

Self-confidence, hard work, and determination paid off for many immigrants. Before

long, for example, the Irish were movers and shakers in the politics.   *30d*

    Norwegians and Swedes came to the East Coast also, but they kept moving

until they arrived in the Minnesota. Why did they decide to settle there? They were   *30d*

attracted by price of land in Minnesota: It was free. With their own labor, families   *30c*

could turn acres of prairie grasses into fields of corn and wheat. Families could raise

enough food for themselves and have enough left over to trade for other things or to

sell for cash.

    To families who had never owned land and were escaping from poverty, the

United States offered chance to start over. It offered them their best hope for a   *30a, 30b*

happiness.

31 Be aware of other potential trouble spots.

31a Do not omit subjects or the expletive *there* or *it*.

English requires a subject for all sentences except imperatives, in which the subject *you* is understood (*Give to the poor*). (See 48a.) If your native language allows the omission of an explicit subject in other sentences or clauses, be especially alert to this requirement in English.

    I have
▶ ~~Have~~ a large collection of baseball cards.

                    she
▶ Your aunt is very energetic; seems young for

   her age.

When the subject has been moved from its normal position before the verb, English sometimes requires an expletive (*there* or *it*) at the beginning of the sentence or clause. (See 48c.) *There* is used at the beginning of a sentence or clause to draw the reader's (or listener's) attention to the location or existence of something.

    There is
▶ ~~Is~~ an apple in the refrigerator.

             there
▶ As you know, are many religious sects in India.

Notice that the verb agrees with the subject that follows it: *apple is, sects are.* (See 21g.)

    In one of its uses, the word *it* functions as an expletive, to call attention to a subject following the verb.

    It is
▶ ~~Is~~ healthy to eat fruit and grains.

    It is
▶ ~~Is~~ clear that we must change our approach.

The subjects of these sentences are *to eat fruit and grains* (an infinitive phrase) and *that we must change our approach* (a noun clause). (See 49c and 49b.)

    As you probably know, the word *it* is also used as the subject of sentences describing the weather or temperature, stating the time, indi-

cating distance, or suggesting an environmental fact.

> It is raining in the valley, and it is snowing in the mountains.

> In July, it is very hot in Arizona.

> It is 9:15 A.M.

> It is three hundred miles to Chicago.

> It gets noisy in our dorm on weekends.

> **GRAMMAR CHECKERS** can flag some sentences with a missing expletive (*there* or *it*), but they often misdiagnose the problem, suggesting that if a sentence opens with a word such as *Is* or *Are*, it may need a question mark at the end. Consider this sentence, which grammar checkers flagged: *Are two grocery stores on Elm Street.* Clearly, the sentence doesn't need a question mark. What it needs is an expletive: *There are two grocery stores on Elm Street.*

31b Do not repeat the subject of a sentence.

English does not allow a subject to be repeated in its own clause.

▶ The doctor ~~she~~ advised me to cut down on salt.

   The pronoun *she* repeats the subject *doctor*.

The subject of a sentence should not be repeated even if a word group intervenes between the subject and the verb.

▶ The car that had been stolen ~~it~~ was found.

   The pronoun *it* repeats the subject *car*.

31c Do not repeat an object or adverb in an adjective clause.

In some languages an object or an adverb is repeated later in the adjective clause in which it appears; in English such repetitions are not allowed. Adjective clauses begin with relative pronouns (*who, whom, whose, which, that*) or relative adverbs (*when, where*), and these words always serve a grammatical function within the clauses they introduce. (See 49b.) Another word in the clause cannot also serve that same grammatical function.

When a relative pronoun functions as the object of a verb or the object of a preposition, do not add another word with the same function later in the clause.

▶ **The puppy ran after the car that we were riding**

  in. ~~it.~~
       ^

> The relative pronoun *that* is the object of the preposition *in*, so the object *it* is not allowed.

Even when the relative pronoun has been omitted, do not add another word with its same function.

▶ **The puppy ran after the car we were riding in. ~~it.~~**
                                                    ^

> The relative pronoun *that* is understood even though it is not present in the sentence.

Like a relative pronoun, a relative adverb should not be echoed later in its clause.

▶ **The place where I work ~~there~~ is one hour from**

  my apartment in the city.

> The adverb *there* should not echo the relative adverb *where*.

 GRAMMAR CHECKERS can flag certain sentences with repeated subjects or objects, but they misdiagnose the problem as two independent clauses incorrectly joined. For example, programs flagged this sentence: *The roses that they brought home they cost three dollars each.* The sentence does not have two independent clauses incorrectly joined. The problem with the sentence is that *they* repeats the subject *roses*.

31d Place adjectives and adverbs with care.

Adjectives modify nouns or pronouns; adverbs modify verbs, adjectives, or other adverbs (see 47d and 47e). Both native and nonnative speakers encounter problems in the use of ad-

jectives and adverbs (see 26). For nonnative speakers, the placement of adjectives and adverbs can be troublesome.

Placement of adjectives

No doubt you have already learned that in English adjectives usually precede the nouns they modify and that they may also appear following linking verbs. (See 26b and 48b.)

> Janine wore a *new* necklace.
>
> Janine's necklace was *new*.

When adjectives pile up in front of a noun, however, you may sometimes have difficulty arranging them. English is quite particular about the order of cumulative adjectives, those not separated by commas. (See 32d.)

> Janine was wearing a *beautiful antique silver* necklace [not *silver antique beautiful* necklace].

The chart on page 279 shows the order in which cumulative adjectives ordinarily appear in front of the noun they modify. This list is just a general guide; don't be surprised when you encounter exceptions.

Placement of adverbs

Adverbs modifying verbs appear in various positions: at the beginning or end of the sentence, before or after the verb, or between a helping verb and its main verb.

> *Slowly*, we drove along the rain-slick road.
>
> Mia handled the teapot *very carefully*.
>
> Martin *always* wins our tennis matches.
>
> Christina is *rarely* late for our lunch dates.
>
> My daughter has *often* spoken of you.

An adverb may not, however, be placed between a verb and its direct object.

▶ **Mother wrapped ~~carefully~~ the gift.** *carefully.*

> The adverb *carefully* may be placed at the beginning or at the end of this sentence or before the verb. It cannot appear after the verb because the verb is followed by the direct object *the gift*.

Usual order of cumulative adjectives

ARTICLE OR OTHER NOUN MARKER

a, an, the, her, Joe's, two, many, some

EVALUATIVE WORD

attractive, dedicated, delicious, ugly, disgusting

SIZE

large, enormous, small, little

LENGTH OR SHAPE

long, short, round, square

AGE

new, old, young, antique

COLOR

yellow, blue, crimson

NATIONALITY

French, Scandinavian, Vietnamese

RELIGION

Catholic, Protestant, Jewish, Muslim

MATERIAL

silver, walnut, wool, marble

NOUN/ADJECTIVE

tree (as in *tree house*), kitchen (as in *kitchen table*)

THE NOUN MODIFIED

house, sweater, bicycle, bread, woman, priest

 GRAMMAR CHECKERS do not flag problems with the placement of adjectives and adverbs. They can, however, flag a few other problems with adjectives and adverbs. See the grammar checker advice on page 225.

31e Distinguish between present participles and past participles used as adjectives.

Both present and past participles may be used as adjectives. The present participle always ends in *-ing*. Past participles usually end in *-ed*, *-d*, *-en*, *-n*, or *-t*. (See 47c.)

PRESENT PARTICIPLES   confusing, speaking

PAST PARTICIPLES   confused, spoken

Participles used as adjectives can precede the nouns they modify; they can also follow linking verbs, in which case they describe the subject of the sentence. (See 48b.)

It was a *depressing* movie.

Jim was a *depressed* young man.

The essay was *confusing*.

The student was *confused*

A present participle should describe a person or thing causing or stimulating an experience; a past participle should describe a person or thing undergoing an experience.

The lecturer was *boring* [not *bored*].

The audience was *bored* [not *boring*].

In the first example, the lecturer is causing boredom, not experiencing it. In the second example, the audience is experiencing boredom, not causing it.

The participles that cause the most trouble for nonnative speakers are those describing mental states:

annoying / annoyed
boring / bored
confusing / confused
depressing / depressed
exciting / excited

exhausting / exhausted
fascinating / fascinated
frightening / frightened
satisfying / satisfied
surprising / surprised

At, on, in, *and* by *to show time and place*

Showing time

AT *at* a specific time: *at* 7:20, *at* dawn, *at* dinner

ON *on* a specific day or date: *on* Tuesday, *on* June 4

IN *in* a part of a 24-hour period: *in* the afternoon, *in* the daytime [but *at* night]

  in a year or month: *in* 1999, *in* July

  in a period of time: finished *in* three hours

BY *by* a specific time or date: *by* 4:15, *by* Christmas

Showing place

AT *at* a meeting place or location: *at* home, *at* the club

  at the edge of something: sitting *at* the desk
  at the corner of something: turning *at* the intersection
  at a target: throwing the snowball *at* Lucy

ON *on* a surface: placed *on* the table, hanging *on* the wall
  on a street: the house *on* Spring Street
  on an electronic medium: *on* television, *on* the Internet

IN *in* an enclosed space: *in* the garage, *in* the envelope
  in a geographic location: *in* San Diego, *in* Texas
  in a print medium: *in* a book, *in* a magazine

BY *by* a landmark: *by* the fence, *by* the flagpole

GRAMMAR CHECKERS do not flag problems with present and past participles used as adjectives. Not surprisingly, the programs have no way of knowing the meaning a writer intends. For example, both of the following sentences could be correct, depending on the writer's meaning: *My roommate was annoying. My roommate was annoyed.*

GRAMMAR CHECKERS are of little or no help with prepositions showing time and place. The conventions of preposition use do not have the kind of mathematical precision that a computer program requires.

31f Become familiar with common prepositions that show time and place.

The most frequently used prepositions in English are *at*, *by*, *for*, *from*, *in*, *of*, *on*, *to*, and *with*. Each of these prepositions has a variety of uses that must be learned gradually, in context.

Prepositions that indicate time and place can be difficult to master because the differences among them are subtle and idiomatic. The chart in this section limits itself to four troublesome prepositions that show time and place: *at*, *on*, *in*, and *by*.

Not every possible use is listed in the chart, so don't be surprised when you encounter exceptions and idiomatic uses that you must learn one at a time. For example, in English we ride *in* a car but *on* a bus, train, or subway. And when we fly *on* (not *in*) a plane, we are not sitting on top of the plane.

EXERCISE 31–1 Other potential trouble spots: Guided practice

Edit the following paragraphs to correct any misuses of subjects, expletives, adjectives, adverbs, participles, and prepositions. Rule numbers in the margin refer to appropriate rules in section 31. The first revision has been done for you, and a suggested revision of this exercise appears in the back of the book.

The Cisneros family lived out an American immigrant's dream. José Romulo Munguía y Torres could not see a way to succeed in his home country, Mexico. This young man, like many Mexicans before him, ~~he~~ crossed the Rio Grande from   **31b**
Mexico. In Texas, he found a job, worked, saved his money, bought a house, and started a family.

Two generations later, José's first grandson, Henry, was a professor in the   **31f**
University of Texas. This young professor decided to enter politics. Were many Mex-   **31a**
ican Americans in San Antonio, where he lived. The Mexican Americans in the part
of town where Henry lived there were trying to get political power in the city. It was   **31c**
not easy to do so. The white powerful people controlled the city government. The city   **31d**
may have been controlling by the white people, but the Mexican Americans had the   **31e**
most voting power. Not having an elected Mexican American in public office was discouraged to them.   **31e**

It was very difficult for everyone because neither group trusted really the   **31d**
other at all. Henry Cisneros was the Mexican Americans' first choice to run for city
council. This man, whom they had hoped to persuade him, was willing to run for   **31c**
election. Henry's friends campaigned for him as the man everyone could trust, and
the people elected Henry Cisneros to office. At twenty-eight, Cisneros became a
young dedicated city council member, the youngest that San Antonio had ever had.   **31d**
Clearly, Mexican Americans were not the only people at San Antonio who wanted to   **31f**
put Henry Cisneros in office.

EXERCISE 31–2 Omissions and needless repetitions

In the following sentences, add needed subjects or expletives and delete any repeated subjects, objects, or adverbs. Mark the one correct sentence "OK." Example:

> **Henry Cisneros was the city council candidate whom San Antonio's citizens elected** ~~**him**~~ **in 1975.**

1. After Henry Cisneros's election to the city council, was no doubt about his goal: He wanted to get people to work together.

2. The programs he thought would help people the most they were the ones he voted for.

3. Was so successful that he was reelected easily in 1977 and 1979, and more and more people looked to him for leadership.

4. By the time of the 1981 election, Henry had decided not to run for city council again; instead, he ran for mayor.

5. He wanted to be Mayor Cisneros in the city where he had spent his childhood there.

EXERCISE 31–3 Placement of adjectives

Insert the adjectives in their correct positions in the following sentences. Do not add commas. Example:

childhood, old

_____*Old*_____ ___*childhood*___ friends came to help elect Henry.

1. experienced, union

    _____ _____ leaders were happy to join the campaign.

2. young, dedicated

    _____ _____ people were particularly interested in working with him.

3. concerned, senior

    _____ _____ citizens worked happily for this young man.

4. political, seasoned

    _____ _____ workers actively promoted his campaign.

5. city, young, exciting

    In short, everyone worked together in a very hard fight to elect this

    _____ _____ _____ council member to the position

    of mayor.

EXERCISE 31–4 Use of present and past participles

Circle the letter of the sentence that answers the question. Example:

> **In which sentence do the campaigners themselves excite other people?**
>
> **a. The excited campaigners waited for the election results.**
>
> **(b.) The exciting campaigners waited for the election results.**

1. In which sentence were the campaign workers always interested?

   a. However, no one in the campaign was ever bored.

   b. However, no one in the campaign was ever boring.

2. In which sentence were the campaign workers always in a happy mood?

   a. No one ever found the campaign workers depressing.

   b. No one ever found the campaign workers depressed.

3. In which sentence do the politicians fascinate Henry?

   a. Henry found the professional politicians fascinating.

   b. Henry found the professional politicians fascinated.

4. In which sentence do the voters think that Henry Cisneros will satisfy them?

   a. Evidently the voters thought that Henry Cisneros was a satisfying candidate.

   b. Evidently the voters thought that Henry Cisneros was a satisfied candidate.

5. In which sentence was the mayor clear in his own mind about what lay ahead?

   a. On April 4, 1981, the new mayor was no longer confusing.

   b. On April 4, 1981, the new mayor was no longer confused.

Here's a tricky one just for fun. You may need to use your dictionary for this one.

6. In which sentence was there no more work to do?

   a. The work was exhausting.

   b. The work was exhausted.

EXERCISE 31–5 Other potential trouble spots: Guided review

Edit the following paragraphs to correct any misuses of subjects, expletives, adjectives, adverbs, participles, and prepositions. Do not change correct sentences. Rule numbers in the margin refer to appropriate rules in section 31. The first revision has been done for you.

Henry Cisneros ~~he~~ has had much success. When he became Mayor Cisneros   *31b*

in 1981, he rapidly concluded that San Antonio needed more places for its people

to work and began talking with possible employers about coming to San Antonio.

His recruiting efforts brought quickly new business to his city. The city leaders were   *31d*

pleased by his work, the people of the city were exciting about the city's progress,   *31e*

and Henry Cisneros's popularity increased. Many San Antonio citizens voted for him

in the next campaign. Elected him to be their mayor again in 1983.   *31a*

By now, the city where he worked was becoming famous. Delegates to the

Democratic National Convention, where he was asked to speak there, were im-   *31c*

pressed by him. Simply attending the convention was rewarding to Cisneros, but

getting the attention of Walter Mondale, a presidential candidate, was particularly

excited for Cisneros and his family. People outside Texas wanted to meet this excit-   *31e*

ing young Mexican American mayor. Mondale, eager to find a good running mate,

seriously considered this Hispanic popular politician. The person whom Mondale   *31d*

chose would play a major role in his campaign. Eventually, Mondale chose a woman.

The person whom Mondale selected her she was Geraldine Ferraro.   *31c, 31b*

In 1992 Cisneros moved to Washington, D.C., to become secretary of Hous-

ing and Urban Development. Cisneros began by trying to solve the problems of

homelessness. He went out on the streets in Washington, D.C., at night to talk to

homeless people. On very cold nights, he arranged for homeless people to spend the

night at the lobby of his agency's building, out of the cold.   *31f*

People attacked Cisneros for personal as well as political activities. But this

son of immigrant José Romulo Munguía y Torres was always positive. Said to every-   *31a*

one: "You can do it. We can do it. I have seen it done."

EXERCISE 32/33 – 4 The comma

This paragraph has eleven errors. Rule numbers in the margin refer to appropriate rules in sections 29–31. The first revision has been done for you. Find and correct ten more errors.

Immigrants have gave the United States their language, their foods, and their customs. Native Americans gave the United States the names for half of its states. *Texas* is an Indian old word for "friends," and *Idaho* means "good morning." Spanish immigrants gave the United States the longest name for any of its cities. In Spanish, is *El Pueblo de Nuestra Señora la Reina de los Angeles de Porciúncula* — Los Angeles. American cuisine now includes foods of many other traditions, from Chinese sweet-and-sour pork to Greek baklava. American children who enjoy to eat pizza or spaghetti or tacos think they are eating American food. Since the Germans brought the Christmas tree to America, every immigrant group that celebrates Christmas it has added something to American Christmas customs. Fiestas and serenades are common in the United States, and even New England children often want breaking a piñata on their birthday parties. Every summer in Washington, D.C., Americans celebrate the diversity of their culture with an excited folk festival. Groups from many different cultures in America bring an equipment to produce their own foods and festivities on the national Mall, where many other Americans can enjoy them. A alien visitor from Mars would not be able to tell which songs and stories are "American," for the food, festivals, dances, music, and folktales of immigrant groups have became part of America's own culture.

Punctuation

32 The comma

The comma was invented to help readers. Without it, sentence parts can collide into one another unexpectedly, causing misreadings.

> **CONFUSING**
> If you cook Elmer will do the dishes.

> **CONFUSING**
> While we were eating a rattlesnake approached our campsite.

Add commas in the logical places (after *cook* and *eating*), and suddenly all is clear. No longer is Elmer being cooked, the rattlesnake being eaten.

Various rules have evolved to prevent such misreadings and to speed readers along through complex grammatical structures. Those rules are detailed in this section.

GRAMMAR CHECKERS do not offer much advice about commas. They can tell you that a comma is usually used before *which* but not before *that* (see 32e), but they fail to flag most other missing or misused commas. For example, in an essay with ten missing commas and five misused commas, a grammar checker spotted only one missing comma (after the word *therefore*).

32a Use a comma before a coordinating conjunction joining independent clauses.

When a coordinating conjunction connects two or more independent clauses—word groups that could stand alone as separate sentences—a comma must precede it. There are seven coordinating conjunctions in English: *and, but, or, nor, for, so,* and *yet.*

287

A comma tells readers that one independent clause has come to a close and that another is about to begin.

▶ **Nearly everyone has heard of love at first sight, but I fell in love at first dance.**

EXCEPTION: If the two independent clauses are short and there is no danger of misreading, the comma may be omitted.

The plane took off and we were on our way.

CAUTION: As a rule, do *not* use a comma to separate coordinate word groups that are not independent clauses. (See 33a.)

▶ **A good money manager controls expenses/ and invests surplus dollars to meet future needs.**

The word group following *and* is not an independent clause; it is the second half of a compound predicate.

32b Use a comma after an introductory clause or phrase.

Common introductory word groups are clauses and phrases that function as adverbs. Such word groups usually tell when, where, how, why, or under what conditions the main action of the sentence occurred. (See 49a–49c.)

A comma tells readers that the introductory clause or phrase has come to a close and that the main part of the sentence is about to begin.

▶ **When Irwin was ready to eat, his cat jumped onto the table.**

Without the comma, readers may have Irwin eating his cat. The comma signals that *his cat* is the subject of a new clause, not part of the introductory one.

▶ **Near a small stream at the bottom of the canyon, we discovered an abandoned shelter.**

The comma tells readers that the introductory prepositional phrase has come to a close.

EXCEPTION: The comma may be omitted after a short adverb clause or phrase if there is no danger of misreading.

In no time we were at 2,800 feet.

Sentences also frequently begin with participial phrases describing the noun or pronoun immediately following them. The comma tells readers that they are about to learn the identity of the person or thing described; therefore, the comma is usually required even when the phrase is short. (See 49c.)

▶ **Knowing that he couldn't outrun a car, Sy took to the fields.**

▶ **Excited about the move, Alice and Don began packing their books.**

The commas tell readers that they are about to hear the nouns described: *Sy* in the first sentence, *Alice and Don* in the second.

NOTE: Other introductory word groups include transitional expressions and absolute phrases. (See 32f.)

32c Use a comma between all items in a series.

When three or more items are presented in a series, those items should be separated from one another with commas. Items in a series may be single words, phrases, or clauses.

At Dominique's one can order fillet of rattlesnake, bison burgers, or pickled eel.

Although some writers view the comma between the last two items as optional, most experts advise using the comma because its omission can result in ambiguity or misreading.

▶ **Uncle David willed me all of his property, houses, and warehouses.**

Did Uncle David will his property *and* houses *and* warehouses—or simply his property, consisting of houses and warehouses? If the former meaning is intended, a comma is necessary to prevent ambiguity.

32d Use a comma between coordinate adjectives not joined with *and*. Do not use a comma between cumulative adjectives.

When two or more adjectives each modify a noun separately, they are coordinate.

With the help of a therapist, Mother has become a *strong, confident, independent* woman.

Adjectives are coordinate if they can be joined with *and* (strong *and* confident *and* independent) or if they can be scrambled (an *independent, strong, confident* woman).

Adjectives that do not modify the noun separately are cumulative.

Three large gray shapes moved slowly toward us.

Beginning with the adjective closest to the noun *shapes*, these modifiers lean on one another, piggyback style, with each modifying a larger word group. *Gray* modifies *shapes*, *large* modifies *gray shapes*, and *three* modifies *large gray shapes*. We cannot insert the word *and* between cumulative adjectives (three *and* large *and* gray shapes). Nor can we scramble them (*gray three large* shapes).

COORDINATE ADJECTIVES

▶ Roberto is a warm, gentle, affectionate father.

The adjectives *warm, gentle,* and *affectionate* modify *father* separately. They can be connected with *and* (*warm and gentle and affectionate*), and they can be scrambled (an *affectionate, warm, gentle father*).

CUMULATIVE ADJECTIVES

▶ Ira ordered a rich/ chocolate/ layer cake.

Ira didn't order a cake that was rich and chocolate and layer: He ordered a *layer cake* that was *chocolate*, a *chocolate layer cake* that was *rich*. These cumulative adjectives cannot be scrambled: a *layer chocolate rich* cake.

32e Use commas to set off nonrestrictive elements. Do not use commas to set off restrictive elements.

Word groups describing nouns or pronouns (adjective clauses, adjective phrases, and appositives) are restrictive or nonrestrictive. A *restrictive* element defines or limits the meaning of the word it modifies and is therefore essential to the meaning of the sentence. Because it contains essential information, a restrictive element is not set off with commas.

RESTRICTIVE

For camp the children needed clothes *that were washable.*

If you remove a restrictive element from a sentence, the meaning changes significantly, becoming more general than you intended. The writer of the example sentence does not mean that the children needed clothes in general. The intended meaning is more limited: the children needed *washable* clothes.

A *nonrestrictive* element describes a noun or pronoun whose meaning has already been clearly defined or limited. Because it contains nonessential or parenthetical information, a nonrestrictive element is set off with commas.

NONRESTRICTIVE

For camp the children needed sturdy shoes, *which were expensive.*

If you remove a nonrestrictive element from a sentence, the meaning does not change dramatically. Some meaning is lost, to be sure, but the defining characteristics of the person or thing described remain the same as before. The children needed *sturdy shoes*, and these happened to be expensive.

Word groups describing proper nouns are nearly always nonrestrictive: *The Illinois River, which flows through our town, has reached flood stage.* Word groups modifying indefinite pronouns such as *everyone* and *something* are nearly always restrictive: *Joe whispered something that we could not hear.*

NOTE: Often it is difficult to tell whether a word group is restrictive or nonrestrictive without seeing it in context and considering the writer's meaning. Both of the following sentences are grammatically correct, but their meaning is slightly different.

The dessert made with fresh raspberries was delicious.

The dessert, made with fresh raspberries, was delicious.

In the example without commas, the phrase *made with fresh raspberries* tells readers which of two or more desserts the writer is referring to. In the example with commas, the phrase merely adds information about the particular dessert served with the meal.

Adjective clauses

Adjective clauses are patterned like sentences, containing subjects and verbs, but they function within sentences as modifiers of nouns or pronouns. They always follow the word they modify, usually immediately. Adjective clauses begin with a relative pronoun (*who, whom, whose, which, that*) or with a relative adverb (*where, when*).

Nonrestrictive adjective clauses are set off with commas; restrictive adjective clauses are not.

NONRESTRICTIVE CLAUSE

▶ Ed's house, which is located on thirteen

acres, was completely furnished with bats

in the rafters and mice in the kitchen.

The adjective clause *which is located on thirteen acres* does not restrict the meaning of *Ed's house,* so the information is nonessential.

RESTRICTIVE CLAUSE

▶ The corporation/ that hired my husband/ was

hurt by recent budget cuts.

Because the adjective clause *that hired my husband* identifies the corporation, the information is essential.

NOTE: Generally reserve *that* for restrictive clauses and *which* for nonrestrictive clauses. See the Glossary of Usage.

Phrases functioning as adjectives

Prepositional or verbal phrases functioning as adjectives may be restrictive or nonrestrictive. Nonrestrictive phrases are set off with commas; restrictive phrases are not.

NONRESTRICTIVE PHRASE

▶ The helicopter, with its 100,000-candlepower

spotlight illuminating the area, circled above.

The *with* phrase is nonessential because its purpose is not to specify which of two or more helicopters is being discussed.

RESTRICTIVE PHRASE

▶ One corner of the attic was filled with

newspapers/ dating from the turn of

the century.

Dating from the turn of the century restricts the meaning of *newspapers,* so the comma should be omitted.

Appositives

An appositive is a noun or noun phrase that renames a nearby noun. Nonrestrictive appositives are set off with commas; restrictive appositives are not.

NONRESTRICTIVE APPOSITIVE

▶ Norman Mailer's first novel, *The Naked and*

the Dead, was a best-seller.

The term *first* restricts the meaning to one novel, so the appositive *The Naked and the Dead* is nonrestrictive.

RESTRICTIVE APPOSITIVE

▶ The song/ "Fire It Up/" was blasted out of

amplifiers ten feet tall.

Once they've read *song,* readers still don't know precisely which song the writer means. The appositive following *song* restricts its meaning.

32f   Use commas to set off transitional and parenthetical expressions, absolute phrases, and elements expressing contrast.

Transitional expressions

Transitional expressions serve as bridges between sentences or parts of sentences. They include conjunctive adverbs such as *however, therefore,* and *moreover* and transitional phrases such as *for example, as a matter of fact,* and *in other words.* (For more complete lists, see 34b.)

When a transitional expression appears between independent clauses in a compound sentence, it is preceded by a semicolon and is usually followed by a comma. (See 34b.)

▶ Minh did not understand our language; more-

over, he was unfamiliar with our customs.

▶ Natural foods are not always salt free; for

example, celery contains more sodium than

most people would imagine.

When a transitional expression appears at the beginning of a sentence or in the middle of an independent clause, it is usually set off with commas.

▶ As a matter of fact, American football was

established by fans who wanted to play

a more organized game of rugby.

▶ The prospective babysitter looked very

promising; she was busy, however, throughout

the month of January.

EXCEPTION: If a transitional expression blends smoothly with the rest of the sentence, calling for little or no pause in reading, it does not need to be set off with a comma. Expressions such as *also, at least, certainly, consequently, indeed, of course, moreover, no doubt, perhaps, then,* and *therefore* do not always call for a pause.

> Alice's bicycle is broken; *therefore* you will need to borrow Sue's.

NOTE: The conjunctive adverb *however* always calls for a pause, but it should not be confused with *however* meaning "no matter how," which does not: *However hard Bill tried, he could not match his previous record.*

Parenthetical expressions

Expressions that are distinctly parenthetical should be set off with commas. Providing supplemental information, they interrupt the flow of a sentence or appear at the end as afterthoughts.

▶ Evolution, as far as we know, doesn't work

this way.

▶ The bass weighed about twelve pounds, give or

take a few ounces.

Absolute phrases

An absolute phrase, which modifies the whole sentence, usually consists of a noun followed by a participle or participial phrase. (See 49e.) Absolute phrases may appear at the beginning or at the end of a sentence. Wherever they appear, they should be set off with commas.

▶ Her tennis game at last perfected, Krista

won the cup.

▶ Brian was forced to rely on public

transportation, his car having been

wrecked the week before.

> In the first example, the absolute phrase appears at the beginning of the sentence; in the second example, it appears at the end.

CAUTION: Do not insert a comma between the noun and participle of an absolute construction.

▶ The next day/ being a school day, we turned

down the invitation.

Contrasted elements

Sharp contrasts beginning with words such as *not, never,* and *unlike* are set off with commas.

▶ Celia, unlike Robert, had no loathing for

dance contests.

▶ Jane talks to me as an adult and friend, not

as her little sister.

32g Use commas to set off nouns of direct address, the words *yes* and *no*, interrogative tags, and mild interjections.

▶ Forgive us, Dr. Spock, for reprimanding Jason.

▶ Yes, the loan will probably be approved.

► The film was faithful to the book, wasn't it?

► Well, cases like these are difficult to decide.

32h Use commas with expressions such as *he said* to set off direct quotations. (See also 37f.)

► Naturalist Arthur Cleveland Bent remarked, "In part the peregrine declined unnoticed because it is not adorable."

► "Convictions are more dangerous foes of truth than lies," wrote philosopher Friedrich Nietzsche.

32i Use commas with dates, addresses, titles, and numbers.

Dates

In dates, the year is set off from the rest of the sentence with a pair of commas.

► On December 12, 1890, orders were sent out for the arrest of Sitting Bull.

EXCEPTIONS: Commas are not needed if the date is inverted or if only the month and year are given.

The recycling plan went into effect on 15 April 1997.

January 1997 was an extremely cold month.

Addresses

The elements of an address or place name are separated by commas. A zip code, however, is not preceded by a comma.

► John Lennon was born in Liverpool, England, in 1940.

► Please send the package to Greg Tarvin at 708 Spring Street, Washington, Illinois 61571.

Titles

If a title follows a name, separate it from the rest of the sentence with a pair of commas.

► Sandra Belinsky, M.D., has been appointed to the board.

Numbers

In numbers more than four digits long, use commas to separate the numbers into groups of three, starting from the right. In numbers four digits long, a comma is optional.

3,500 [*or* 3500]
100,000
5,000,000

EXCEPTIONS: Do not use commas in street numbers, zip codes, telephone numbers, or years.

32j Use a comma to prevent confusion.

In certain contexts, a comma is necessary to prevent confusion. If the writer has omitted a word or phrase, for example, a comma may be needed to signal the omission.

► To err is human; to forgive, divine.

If two words in a row echo each other, a comma may be needed for ease of reading.

► All of the catastrophes that we had feared might happen, happened.

Sometimes a comma is needed to prevent readers from grouping words in ways that do not match the writer's intention.

► Patients who can, walk up and down the halls several times a day.

Major uses of the comma

BEFORE A COORDINATING CONJUNCTION JOINING INDEPENDENT CLAUSES (32a)

> No grand idea was ever born in a conference, but a lot of foolish ideas have died there.
> —F. Scott Fitzgerald

AFTER AN INTRODUCTORY CLAUSE OR PHRASE (32b)

> If thought corrupts language, language can also corrupt thought. —George Orwell

BETWEEN ALL ITEMS IN A SERIES (32c)

> All the things I really like to do are either immoral, illegal, or fattening.
> — Alexander Woollcott

BETWEEN COORDINATE ADJECTIVES (32d)

> There is a mighty big difference between good, sound reasons and reasons that sound good.
> —Burton Hillis

TO SET OFF NONRESTRICTIVE ELEMENTS (32e)

> Silence, which will save me from shame, will also deprive me of fame. —Igor Stravinsky

33 Unnecessary commas

Many common misuses of the comma result from an incomplete understanding of the major comma rules presented in 32. In particular, writers frequently form misconceptions about rules 32a–32e, either extending the rules inappropriately or misinterpreting them. Such misconceptions can lead to the errors described in 33a–33e; rules 33f–33h list other common misuses of the comma.

33a Do not use a comma between compound elements that are not independent clauses.

Though a comma should be used before a coordinating conjunction joining independent clauses (see 32a), this rule should not be extended to other compound word groups.

▶ Jake still doesn't realize that his illness is serious,/and that he will have to alter his diet to improve his chances of survival.

And links two subordinate clauses, each beginning with *that.*

▶ The director led the cast members to their positions on the stage,/and gave them an inspiring last-minute pep talk.

And links the two parts of a compound predicate: *led . . . and gave.*

33b Do not use a comma after a phrase that begins an inverted sentence.

Though a comma belongs after most introductory phrases (see 32b), it does not belong after phrases that begin an inverted sentence. In an inverted sentence, the subject follows the verb, and a phrase that ordinarily would follow the verb is moved to the beginning (see 48c).

▶ At the bottom of the sound,/lies a ship laden with treasure.

▶ Etched on my brother's left wrist,/was a tattoo of a dragon chasing a tiger.

33c Do not use a comma before the first or after the last item in a series.

Though commas are required between items in a series (32c), do not place them either before or after the whole series.

▶ Other causes of asthmatic attacks are/stress, change in temperature, humidity, and cold air.

▶ Ironically, this job that appears so glamorous, carefree, and easy/carries a high degree of responsibility.

33d Do not use a comma between cumulative adjectives, between an adjective and a noun, or between an adverb and an adjective.

Commas are required between coordinate adjectives (those that can be joined with *and*), but they do not belong between cumulative adjectives (those that cannot be joined with *and*). (For a full discussion, see 32d.)

▶ In the corner of the closet we found an old/maroon hatbox from Sears.

A comma should never be used between an adjective and the noun that follows it.

▶ It was a senseless, dangerous/mission.

Nor should a comma be used between an adverb and an adjective that follows it.

▶ The Hurst Home is unsuitable as a mental facility for severely/disturbed youths.

33e Do not use commas to set off restrictive or mildly parenthetical elements.

Restrictive elements are modifiers or appositives that restrict the meaning of the nouns they follow. Because they are essential to the meaning of the sentence, they are not set off with commas. (For a full discussion of both restrictive and nonrestrictive elements, see 32e.)

▶ Drivers/who think they own the road/make cycling a dangerous sport.

The modifier *who think they own the road* restricts the meaning of *Drivers* and is therefore essential to the meaning of the sentence. Putting commas around the *who* clause falsely suggests that all drivers think they own the road.

▶ Margaret Mead's book/*Coming of Age in Samoa/* stirred up considerable controversy when it was published.

Since Mead wrote more than one book, the appositive contains information essential to the meaning of the sentence.

Although commas should be used with distinctly parenthetical expressions (see 32f), do not use them to set off elements that are only mildly parenthetical.

▶ Charisse believes that the Internet is/essentially/ a bastion of advertising.

33f Do not use a comma to set off a concluding adverb clause that is essential to the meaning of the sentence.

When adverb clauses introduce a sentence, they are nearly always followed by a comma (see 32b). When they conclude a sentence, however, they are not set off by commas if their content is essential to the meaning of the earlier part of the sentence. Adverb clauses beginning with *after, as soon as, because, before, if, since, unless, until,* and *when* are usually essential.

▶ Don't visit Paris at the height of the tourist season/ unless you have booked hotel reservations.

Without the *unless* clause, the meaning of the sentence would be broader than the writer intended.

When a concluding adverb clause is nonessential, it should be preceded by a comma. Clauses beginning with *although, even though, though,* and *whereas* are usually nonessential.

▶ The lecture seemed to last only a short time, although the clock said it had gone on for more than an hour.

33g Do not use a comma to separate a verb from its subject or object.

A sentence should flow from subject to verb to object without unnecessary pauses. Commas may appear between these major sentence elements only when a specific rule calls for them.

▶ Zoos large enough to give the animals freedom to roam/are becoming more popular.

▶ Francesca explained to him/ that she was busy and would see him later.

> In the first sentence, the comma should not separate the subject, *Zoos*, from the verb, *are becoming*. In the second sentence, the comma should not separate the verb, *explained*, from its object, the subordinate clause *that she was busy and would see him later*.

33h Avoid other common misuses of the comma.

Do not use a comma in the following situations.

AFTER A COORDINATING CONJUNCTION (*AND*, *BUT*, *OR*, *NOR*, *FOR*, *SO*, *YET*)

▶ Occasionally soap operas are performed live, but/ more often they are taped.

AFTER *SUCH AS* OR *LIKE*

▶ Many shade-loving plants, such as/begonias, impatiens, and coleus, can add color to a shady garden.

BEFORE *THAN*

▶ Touring Crete was more thrilling for us/ than visiting the Greek islands frequented by rich Europeans.

AFTER *ALTHOUGH*

▶ Although/the air was balmy, the water was too cold for swimming.

BEFORE A PARENTHESIS

▶ At MCI Sylvia began at the bottom/ (with only three and a half walls and a swivel chair), but within five years she had been promoted to supervisor.

TO SET OFF AN INDIRECT (REPORTED) QUOTATION

▶ Samuel Goldwyn once said/that a verbal contract isn't worth the paper it's written on.

WITH A QUESTION MARK OR AN EXCLAMATION POINT

▶ "Why don't you try it?/" she coaxed. "You can't do any worse than the rest of us."

EXERCISE 32/33−1 The comma and unnecessary commas: Guided practice

Edit the following essay by adding commas where they are needed and removing unnecessary commas. Rule numbers in the margin refer to appropriate rules in sections 32 and 33. The first revision has been made for you, and answers to this exercise appear in the back of the book.

If a boy wanted to join the football team at Carlisle Indian School, he had to   **32b**
go through a difficult test. Any boy who wanted to be on the team had to stand at
one of the goal lines; all the first-string players stood around the field. When the ball
was punted to the new boy, he had to catch it and try to get all the way to the other
end zone with it. The team members tried to stop him before he could get very far.
Only a few players had ever gotten as far as the fifty-yard line so "Pop" Warner, coach   **32a**
at the Carlisle Indian School considered it a good test.   **32e**

One day a quiet Indian boy surprised Pop. The boy caught the ball, started
running, wheeled away from the first players who tried to stop him, shook off the
others and ran the ball all the way to the opposite goal line. Convinced that the   **32c**
player's success was an accident, the coach ordered him to run the play again.
Brusquely, the coach spoke to the players, and reminded them that this workout   **33a**
was supposed to be tackling practice. Jim, the nineteen-year-old six-footer, simply
said "Nobody tackles Jim." Then he ran the ball to the goal line a second time.   **32h**

Well, almost no one tackled Jim Thorpe successfully for many years. Life itself got him down and made him fumble more often than his football opponents did,
but, he was usually able to recover and go on. The first blow was the death of his   **33h**
twin brother while the two boys were still in grade school. This tragedy was followed
by others; by the time Jim was twenty-five, he had lost his brother, his mother, and
his father to death. They left him a Native American heritage: His father was half
Irish and half Native American and his mother was the granddaughter of a famous,   **32a, 33d**
Indian warrior named Chief Black Hawk.

Fortunately or unfortunately, along with his Native American heritage came great pride and stoicism. That pride kept him silent when the greatest blow of all came: He was forced to return the Olympic medals he had won in 1912 because he was declared to be not an amateur. He dealt stoically with his personal tragedies. When infantile paralysis struck his son Jim Thorpe disappeared for a few days to deal with the tragedy alone. His stoicism also saw him through a demotion to the minor leagues and sad years of unemployment and poverty before his death.

32b

Even death's tackle may not have been totally successful: After Jim Thorpe's death his Olympic medals were returned, and a town was named after him.

32b

EXERCISE 32/33–2 The comma

A. Insert commas where they are needed with coordinating conjunctions in the following sentences. If a sentence is correct, mark it "OK." Example:

> Coach Warner was impressed with the new player's skill, and he looked for a chance to try him in an actual game.

1. Jim passed Coach Warner's test but he did not get to play right away.

2. Then in one game a player was injured and Coach Warner sent Jim in.

3. At first, no one but Jim and the coach believed that Jim could play well enough.

4. He lost five yards the first time he got the ball but the next time he ran sixty-five yards for a touchdown.

5. His sports career began with that game and included major honors in track, lacrosse, baseball, and football.

B. Insert commas when they are needed after an introductory element, in a series, and with coordinate adjectives. If a sentence is correct, mark it "OK." Example:

> After trying to tackle Thorpe only once, Jim's most famous opponent never played football again.

6. In a game against Army, Carlisle's Thorpe had the ball.

7. One Army player tried to tackle Jim, failed, injured his knee in the process and had to be helped from the field.

8. That strong confident player said in later years, "Thorpe gained ground; he *always* gained ground."

9. Although the injured player was never able to play football again he became famous in other ways.

10. He became supreme commander of the Allied armies in Europe in World War II and thirty-fourth president of the United States—Dwight D. Eisenhower.

EXERCISE 32/33–3 The comma

A. Add commas where needed around nonrestrictive elements. If a sentence is correct, mark it "OK." Example:

> Jim Thorpe's Olympic medals, which he won in 1912 but had to forfeit, were for the
> pentathlon and the decathlon. [Thorpe won Olympic medals only in 1912.]

1. The Carlisle students who needed summer jobs often played baseball for Carolina teams. [Not all Carlisle students needed summer jobs.]

2. The players who were willing to lie used false names when they played for little-known teams; Jim did not. [Only some of the players were willing to lie.]

3. Those who had received money for playing their sport were disqualified because they were no longer "amateurs." [Only some received money.]

4. The five-sport event which is called the pentathlon is difficult. [There is only one five-sport event.]

5. The decathlon which is a ten-sport event is considered the most difficult of all Olympic events. [There is only one ten-sport event.]

B. Add commas as necessary in the following sentences. Example:

> In Stockholm, Sweden's King Gustav presented the 1912 Olympic winners with their gold
> medals; in addition, he spoke briefly to some of them.

6. As King Gustav presented Jim Thorpe's 1912 Olympic medal, he said to Jim "Sir you are the greatest athlete in the world."

7. In January 1913 however a newspaper reported that Jim had been paid for playing for the Carolina baseball teams.

8. When the Amateur Athletic Union (AAU) asked Jim said he had been paid.

9. Stating that he had not known he was doing wrong, Jim insisted that he had acted no worse than athletes who used false names.

10. Jim having presented his case, the AAU made its ruling; specifically it ruled that Jim had not been an amateur at the time of the Olympics.

Unit review (29–31): ESL trouble spots

Edit the following paragraphs to correct the use of commas. The first revision has been done for you. You should add ten more commas.

When the Amateur Athletic Union ruled that 1912 Olympic winner Jim Thorpe had not been an amateur *given* at the time he won his medals several consequences followed. Once the rul- *29a* ing was formally stated, Jim Thorpe's name was erased from the Olympic records. In addition he had to return his medals. Friends wanted him to fight the AAU ruling but he was too proud *31d* to do so.

During the next sixteen years that Jim played football was quite different from what it *31a* is today. Players then had no league, no formal schedule, no required helmets and often no salaries. Then representatives of eight concerned teams met to form a league. The organiza- *29c* tion they formed which was called the American Professional Football Association later be- came the National Football League; Jim Thorpe was its first president.

Jim's playing declined with the years until on November 30, 1929 an Associated Press *31b* story described him as "a mere shadow of his former self." No longer able to play sports Thorpe had to dig ditches in the Depression years. When the 1932 Olympics were held in Los Ange- *29c, 31f* les California he could not afford to buy a ticket. *31e*

30b

30a

29a

EXERCISE 32/33–5 Unnecessary commas

Each of the following sentences has one unnecessary comma. Delete the comma that is not needed. Example:

> **Along with other bad news about Thorpe, newspaper stories reported/that he drank too much and that drinking caused his second marriage to go wrong.**

1. After Jim Thorpe's death, his friends still worked to have his medals restored, and to get his name back on the list of Olympic winners.

2. Knowing that they would not be happy, until the AAU and the Olympic committees changed their minds, his friends made repeated appeals.

3. The AAU acted first, reversing itself some years later, (in 1973) by saying that Thorpe's titles should be restored.

4. The American Olympic Committee agreed two years later, but, it was not until 1982 that the International Olympic Committee voted to restore Jim's titles.

5. New, Olympic medals were presented to Thorpe's children in a 1983 ceremony in Los Angeles, California.

6. However, the International Olympic Committee, did not erase the names of the second-place finishers.

7. Even though Thorpe had beaten the other "winners," his friends had to accept the fact, that Jim would be listed only as a cochampion.

8. In the hearts of Jim's supporters remains the honest, firm conviction, that Jim should be listed as the sole winner.

9. They thought that the International Olympic Committee's reversing its position, restoring the titles, and awarding Thorpe's medals to his children, were not enough.

10. It is not likely that there will be any further action, such as, erasing the other winners' names.

EXERCISE 32/33–6 Unnecessary commas

One sentence in each of the following pairs is correctly punctuated. Circle the letter of the correct sentence and edit the incorrect sentence. Example:

    (a.) Jim Thorpe was a greater athlete than any other athlete of his time.

    b. In 1950, an Associated Press poll of hundreds of sportswriters indicated that Thorpe was better/than any other athlete from 1900 to 1950.

1a. According to many experts, (sportswriters, coaches, and the like), Thorpe will still be considered the best in 2000.

  b. Others think that modern knowledge of various aspects of training (nutrition, drugs, and the like) will produce even greater players by the turn of the century.

2a. People said, that Thorpe's confidence in himself was so great that he often skipped practice at the Olympics, and they told the "broad jump story" to illustrate his confidence.

  b. Observers said that he measured the broad jump distance with his eye, decided he could jump it, and lay down in a hammock for a nap, not even bothering to take a practice run at it.

3a. In his 289 games in baseball's major leagues, the only statistic that suggested trouble was his batting average of .252.

  b. It seems that the only thing that really bothered Jim, was hitting curveballs.

4a. He had a peculiar style of running, that left his football tacklers flat on the ground.

  b. He would twist his hips away from the player who was after him.

5a. He would wait until that player's head was at the exact, dangerous, height.

  b. Then he would swing his hips with full, direct force right into the player's head.

EXERCISE 32/33 – 7 The comma and unnecessary commas: Guided review

Edit the following paragraphs by adding commas where they are needed and removing commas where they are not needed. Rule numbers in the margin refer to appropriate rules in sections 32 and 33. The first revision has been done for you.

Quarrels about one of America's greatest athletes, Jim Thorpe, continue. Even though the decision about his Olympic standing has been made, other quarrels about him remain.   *32b*

After Jim Thorpe died his wife had to choose a burial place. Everyone assumed he would be buried in his home state of Oklahoma, but, his wife made other arrangements. Some people from Mauch Chunk, Pennsylvania, made her an offer. They said, that they wanted Jim buried in their town. Having his body there would make more tourists want to come to their small, Pennsylvania town. They talked of a burial place, a Jim Thorpe Museum and a hospital in his memory. They also offered to change the name of the town from Mauch Chunk to Jim Thorpe.   *32b* *33h* *33h* *33d* *32c*

Mrs. Thorpe, who wanted a memorial for Jim, agreed to these proposals, and gave Jim's body to the town. It is probable that at the core of her decision was the desire for Jim Thorpe to be remembered. After some negotiation, the agreement was concluded and the town is now on the map as "Jim Thorpe."   *33a* *32a*

Jim's wife, not his children, made the agreement. His children, seven sons and daughters, wanted his body buried in Oklahoma. They wanted the body to be given a traditional Indian burial. They wanted the town to give back their father's body. Jack Thorpe, one of the sons, said to a *Sports Illustrated* writer in 1982 "Dad's spirit is still roaming." In Jim Thorpe's family pride is still part of the Thorpe heritage. The family has not given up the struggle. Other people have also asked the townspeople to change their minds.   *32h* *32b*

Jim Thorpe lived a tough, honest, gifted, and controversial, life. Even if his records are someday broken, he will remain a legend of the American sports world.   *33c*

34 The semicolon

The semicolon is used to connect major sentence elements of equal grammatical rank.

> **GRAMMAR CHECKERS** flag some, but not all, misused semicolons (34d). In addition, they can alert you to some run-on sentences (34a). However, they miss more run-on sentences than they identify, and they sometimes flag correct sentences as possible run-ons. (See also the grammar checker advice on p. 175.)

34a Use a semicolon between closely related independent clauses not joined with a coordinating conjunction.

When related independent clauses appear in one sentence, they are ordinarily linked with a comma and a coordinating conjunction (*and, but, or, nor, for, so, yet*). The coordinating conjunction signals the relation between the clauses. If the clauses are closely related and the relation is clear without a conjunction, they may be linked with a semicolon instead.

> Injustice is relatively easy to bear; what stings is justice. —H. L. Mencken

A semicolon must be used whenever a coordinating conjunction has been omitted between independent clauses. To use merely a comma creates a kind of run-on sentence known as a comma splice. (See 20.)

▶ Grandmother's basement had walls of Mississippi

clay**;** to me it looked like a dungeon.

CAUTION: Do not overuse the semicolon as a means of revising run-on sentences. For other revision strategies, see 20a, 20c, and 20d.

34b Use a semicolon between independent clauses linked with a transitional expression.

Transitional expressions include conjunctive adverbs and transitional phrases.

CONJUNCTIVE ADVERBS
accordingly, also, anyway, besides, certainly, consequently, conversely, finally, furthermore, hence, however, incidentally, indeed, instead, likewise, meanwhile, moreover, nevertheless, next, nonetheless, otherwise, similarly, specifically, still, subsequently, then, therefore, thus

TRANSITIONAL PHRASES
after all, as a matter of fact, as a result, at any rate, at the same time, even so, for example, for instance, in addition, in conclusion, in fact, in other words, in the first place, on the contrary, on the other hand

When a transitional expression appears between independent clauses, it is preceded by a semicolon and usually followed by a comma.

▶ I learned all the rules and regulations**;** however,

I never really learned to control the ball.

When a transitional expression appears in the middle or at the end of the second independent clause, the semicolon goes *between the clauses.*

▶ Most singers gain fame through hard work and

dedication**;** Evita, however, found other means.

Transitional expressions should not be confused with the coordinating conjunctions *and, but, or, nor, for, so,* and *yet,* which are preceded by a comma when they link independent clauses. (See 32a.)

34c Use a semicolon between items in a series containing internal punctuation.

▶ Classic science fiction sagas are *Star Trek,* with

Mr. Spock and his large pointed ears**;** *Battlestar*

Galactica, with its Cylon Raiders**;** and *Star Wars,*

with Han Solo, Luke Skywalker, and Darth Vader.

Without the semicolons, the reader would have to sort out the major groupings, distinguishing between important and less important pauses according to the logic of the sentence. By inserting semicolons at the major breaks, the writer does this work for the reader.

34d Avoid common misuses of the semicolon.

Do not use a semicolon in the following situations.

BETWEEN A SUBORDINATE CLAUSE AND THE REST OF THE SENTENCE

▶ Unless you brush your teeth within ten or fifteen minutes after eating*;*‚ brushing does almost no good.

BETWEEN AN APPOSITIVE AND THE WORD IT REFERS TO

▶ Another delicious dish is the chef's special*;*‚ a roasted duck rubbed with spices and stuffed with wild rice.

TO INTRODUCE A LIST

▶ Some of my favorite film stars have home pages on the Web*;*: John Travolta, Susan Sarandon, Brad Pitt, and Emma Thompson.

BETWEEN INDEPENDENT CLAUSES JOINED BY *AND*, *BUT*, *OR*, *NOR*, *FOR*, *SO*, OR *YET*

▶ Five of the applicants had worked with spreadsheets*;*‚ but only one was familiar with database management.

EXERCISE 34-1 The semicolon: Guided practice

Edit the following paragraphs for semicolon use. Rule numbers in the margin refer to appropriate rules in section 34. The first revision has been done for you, and answers to this exercise appear in the back of the book.

When Cheryl Toussaint came in second in a race she had never planned to run⁄, she started on a road that led to the Olympics and a world record.   34d

Cheryl began running almost by accident one day when she went to watch a city-sponsored track meet in Brooklyn, New York. During the preliminaries, the officials announced an "open" race, it was a race that anyone could enter. Cheryl   34a
wanted to enter, but she was dressed in a skirt and sandals. Four things made her run: One friend traded shoes with her, another let her borrow jeans, several called her "chicken" if she didn't run, and one girl dared her to run. Coming in second in that race led this teenager to many places, including Munich, Germany, Toronto,   34c
Canada, and Montreal, Canada.

There were, however, many races to run and lessons to learn. Cheryl joined the all-female Atoms Track Club, and she began training under Coach Fred Thompson. Like most coaches, Fred had his own way of testing newcomers. He watched a new runner carefully, however, he gave her no special attention. Instead, he just   34b
gave her orders one after another. He would tell Cheryl to run laps, go through exercises, and do practice starts, but he would never comment on how she performed. If the newcomer endured the hard, time-consuming workouts without encouragement or praise, Thompson was sure she was ready for real coaching.

Cheryl quit after two months, for six more months she stayed out. During   34a
that time she thought about her attitude toward work, her poor record at school, her pleasure in running, and her lack of goals. When she returned, Thompson welcomed her back, he knew how special Cheryl was. Before he was through with Cheryl   34a
Toussaint, Coach Thompson not only convinced her she was college material, but he pushed her to achieve the highest goal of the amateur athlete—the Olympics.

EXERCISE 34–2 The semicolon

Add semicolons in the five word groups that need them; mark the other word groups "OK."
Example:

> Cheryl Toussaint's first run was an indication of her character and determination; no one
> could find fault with her effort.

1. Cheryl's first run—at a cross-country meet on Long Island—would certainly have impressed any coach every person watching was astounded by her perseverance.

2. Coach Thompson had warned her not to start too fast but to stay with the pack. "Just try to finish," he said.

3. Too excited to follow his directions, Cheryl took off at top speed at the starting gun, moreover, she did not slow down even after she was a hundred yards in front of everyone else.

4. Cheryl kept that distance for most of the run, she did not allow herself any slack.

5. Then, with only a hundred yards to go, Cheryl gave out, she collapsed and fell down.

6. Immediately, she got to her knees and started crawling. She crawled toward the finish line, not to the grassy area where runners who left the race were supposed to go.

7. She got up, staggered a little farther, and fell again. Once more she started crawling.

8. Not able to get to her feet, Cheryl continued to crawl, after all, she was nearly to the finish line.

9. She had almost reached the line when another runner passed her and won.

10. "I knew at that moment," said her coach, "that this girl was going to be something special." Her coach was right.

EXERCISE 34–3 The semicolon

Each of the following sentences has two semicolons but should have only one. Delete the incorrect one and replace it with other punctuation if necessary. Example:

> No one else had ever seen anything special in Cheryl/‸who had never shown any ambition; her teachers had labeled her a "slow learner" long before she got to high school.

1. Cheryl had to beg her teachers to allow her to take college preparatory courses; they were sure she would fail; no matter how hard she tried.

2. Coach Thompson did many things for Cheryl; including coaching track, prodding her about schoolwork, encouraging good eating habits, and insisting that she think about college; most important of all, he gave her faith in herself.

3. All of the runners knew that if they made qualifying times; Coach Thompson would see to it that they were entered in the national meets; however, they also knew that if they did not qualify, they were off the team.

4. Cheryl soon discovered that she had to schedule her time; or she would fail at school or at track or at both; thinking about Coach Thompson, she began to care.

5. By the time Cheryl graduated from high school, she was an A student; this "slow learner" received an academic scholarship to New York University; although she had thought only an athletic one was possible.

EXERCISE 34–4 The semicolon: Guided review

Edit the following paragraphs for semicolon use. Rule numbers in the margin refer to appropriate rules in section 34. The first revision has been done for you.

Every runner dreams of winning both individual and relay medals at the Olympics*/;* in 1972, Cheryl Toussaint was no exception. When she did not make the individual finals; she pinned her hopes on the relay race. Her teammates on the American team were ready: Mabel Ferguson, Madeline Jackson, and Kathy Hammond. The relay was Cheryl's last chance to win a medal, unfortunately, it seemed that everything was against her.

34a

34d

34b

Cheryl began the third leg of the qualifying heat with runners ahead of her. Then a runner in front of her fell. As Cheryl dashed around her, another runner stepped on the heel of Cheryl's left shoe, so Cheryl was running with her shoe half on and half off. She needed to stop and pull the shoe on, but she knew two things: She would lose valuable time, and this was her team's last chance to qualify for the finals. She kept running, very soon the shoe flew up in the air. Cheryl wondered whether the shoe would hit anyone, whether TV viewers could see her bare foot, and whether people in the stands had noticed. But she ran on, passing the other runners. Her team qualified for the finals that day, and in the finals, Cheryl and her teammates won silver medals.

34a

Cheryl remembered her very first run, at which she hadn't even known how to start, her first "real" race, at which she'd crawled to the finish line, and her most recent one, at which she'd failed to qualify for the 800-meter run. She could laugh about all those memories now, for she and her teammates were Olympic winners.

34c

Back home, Cheryl kept to her plans: graduating from college (with a B+ average), getting a job in the Federal Reserve Bank's management training program, and starting to train for the next Olympics. She knew that nothing would ever mean as much to her again as track, the Atoms, and Coach Thompson had meant her success was also theirs.

34a

35 The colon

The colon is used primarily to call attention to the words that follow it.

 GRAMMAR CHECKERS do not flag missing or misused colons. For example, they failed to catch the misused colon in this sentence: *Uncle Carlos left behind: his watch, his glasses, and his favorite pen.* Occasionally grammar checkers flag misused semicolons in contexts where a colon is required.

35a Use a colon after an independent clause to direct attention to a list, an appositive, or a quotation.

A LIST
The daily routine should include at least the following: twenty knee bends, fifty sit-ups, fifteen leg lifts, and five minutes of running in place.

AN APPOSITIVE
My roommate is guilty of two of the seven deadly sins: gluttony and sloth.

A QUOTATION
Consider the words of John F. Kennedy: "Ask not what your country can do for you; ask what you can do for your country."

For other ways of introducing quotations, see 37f.

35b Use a colon between independent clauses if the second summarizes or explains the first.

Faith is like love: It cannot be forced.

NOTE: When an independent clause follows a colon, it may begin with a lowercase or a capital letter.

Minds are like parachutes: They [*or* they] function only when open.

35c Use a colon after the salutation in a formal letter, to indicate hours and minutes, to show proportions, between a title and subtitle, and between city and publisher in bibliographic entries.

Dear Sir or Madam:

5:30 P.M. (or p.m.)

The ratio of women to men was 2:1.

The Glory of Hera: Greek Mythology and the Greek Family

Boston: Bedford, 1998

NOTE: In biblical references, a colon is ordinarily used between chapter and verse (Luke 2:14). The Modern Language Association recommends a period instead (Luke 2.14).

35d Avoid common misuses of the colon.

A colon must be preceded by a full independent clause. Therefore, avoid using it in the following situations.

BETWEEN A VERB AND ITS OBJECT OR COMPLEMENT

▶ Some important vitamins found in vegetables are: vitamin A, thiamine, niacin, and vitamin C.

BETWEEN A PREPOSITION AND ITS OBJECT

▶ The areas to be painted consisted of: three gable ends, trim work, sixteen windows, and a front and back porch.

AFTER *SUCH AS, INCLUDING,* OR *FOR EXAMPLE*

▶ The trees on our campus include many fine Japanese specimens such as: black pines, ginkgos, and weeping cherries.

EXERCISE 35–1 The colon: Guided practice

In the following paragraph, insert colons where they are needed and eliminate any improperly used colons. Rule numbers in the margin refer to appropriate rules in section 35. The first revision has been done for you, and answers to this exercise appear in the back of the book.

In 1951, Althea Gibson broke the color barrier in women's tennis and became admired all over the world. No one who knew her as a teenager would have predicted her success. By the time Althea Gibson reached her teens, her record showed three indications of trouble: running away from home, dropping out of **35a** school, and losing the one job she had been able to find. To survive in her neighborhood, Althea depended on: a small welfare allowance, occasional handouts, and **35d** plain old luck. She listed her skills as the following, good bowler, great two-on-two **35a** basketball player, and fast paddleball player. Even after she began playing tennis and moving in upper-class Harlem society, she resented the efforts of the society ladies to improve her. They busied themselves with tasks such as: correcting her **35d** manners and restricting her behavior. Looking back, she later summed up her attitude she said she wasn't ready to study about "how to be a fine lady." At eighteen, **35b** she finally got: a waitress job, a congenial roommate, and a good friend. **35d**

EXERCISE 35–2 The colon

In the following sentences, insert colons where they can be effectively used. Example:

> In 1957, Althea Gibson won the women's title at the most prestigious tennis tournament in
> the world: Wimbledon.

1. Althea Gibson broke the color barrier in women's tennis she was the first black female player to compete in national championships.

2. Two tennis-playing doctors opened their homes to her so she could finish high school and go to college Dr. Hubert A. Eaton of Wilmington, North Carolina, and Dr. Robert W. Johnson of Lynchburg, Virginia.

3. Her life in a southern high school was not pleasant; if she had written a book about it, she could have titled it *Misfit, A Yankee Woman in a Southern School.*

4. Besides tennis, Althea's other love was music the drums, the chorus, and especially the saxophone.

5. Her friend Sugar Ray Robinson advised her firmly to go to college "No matter what you want to do, tennis or music or what, you'll be better at it if you get some education."

EXERCISE 35–3 The colon

In the following paragraph, the italicized words indicate where two parts of a sentence come together. Decide whether the sentence needs a colon to join these parts. If so, insert it. If not, mark the spot "OK." The first spot has been done for you. HINT: You will need very few colons.

OK

Althea Gibson began playing *tennis when* she was a young teenager in the 1940s. In just over a decade, she *became one* of the world's greatest women tennis players.

The tennis world began to notice her after only a few years of amateur *play she* was winning women's singles meets one after the other. In 1950 and the years immediately *following, she* became more and more famous. By 1957–58, Althea Gibson, the rising young tennis star, was well known on both sides of the *Atlantic she* was the most respected woman player in Britain and America. In both countries she won the national women's singles title for two years in a row: 1957 and 1958. The British meet, which is *called The* Wimbledon, is generally regarded *as the* unofficial world championship meet. Gibson also played on the U.S. team at other major meets, *including the* Wightman Cup meet. That meet is a special British-American *meet that* pits U.S. women against British women. When Althea Gibson was on the U.S. team, the United States won.

Gibson's retirement from tennis in 1958 *was a* complete surprise to her fans. What reason did she give for her retirement? She had *decided to* become a professional golfer!

EXERCISE 35–4 The colon: Guided review

In the following paragraph, insert colons where they are needed and eliminate any improperly used colons. Rule numbers in the margin refer to appropriate rules in section 35. The first revision has been done for you.

When the Eatons of North Carolina invited Althea Gibson to move into their home for the school year, she hesitated. Northerner Althea had one major fear/: white **35a** southerners. She decided to go in spite of her fears. At the Eatons' house, Althea had to get used to: wearing skirts, obeying rules, and getting along with people. She **35d** was expected to listen to adult conversations and join in with well-chosen comments. At the time, Althea considered these requirements to be serious disadvantages. However, there were also advantages to life at the Eatons, such as: regular meals, a room **35d** of her own, an allowance, and unlimited use of the doctor's private tennis court. School presented one overwhelming social problem Althea could not make friends **35b** with either boys or girls. The boys may have resented her athletic prowess and her self-confidence. The girls considered her a tomboy. Years later Althea still recalled their taunts "She's no lady" and "Look at her throwing that ball just like a man." **35a** Even the singing instructor added to her woes. When he placed her in the tenor section to make the chorus sound better, the other girls in the chorus could not control their giggles. Some people even made fun of her tennis, but her tenacity paid off. Before she had finished high school, Florida A & M University had offered her a scholarship. Althea had been right to expect problems if she lived in the South, but she had not anticipated what the problems would be. If she had put those high school years into a book, she could have titled it *The Unexpected, Problems Are Not* **35c** *Always What They Seem.*

36 The apostrophe

GRAMMAR CHECKERS can flag some, but not all, missing or misused apostrophes. They can catch missing apostrophes in common contractions, such as *don't*. They can also flag some problems with possessives, although they miss others. The programs usually phrase their advice cautiously, telling you that you have a "possible possessive error" in a phrase such as *a days work* or *sled dogs feet*. Therefore, you—not the grammar checker—must decide whether to add an apostrophe and, if so, whether to put it before or after the *-s*.

36a Use an apostrophe to indicate that a noun is possessive.

Possessive nouns usually indicate ownership, as in *Tim's hat* or *the lawyer's desk*. Frequently, however, ownership is only loosely implied: *the tree's roots, a day's work*. If you are not sure whether a noun is possessive, try turning it into an *of* phrase: *the roots of the tree, the work of a day*.

When to add -'s

1. If the noun does not end in *-s*, add *-'s*.

   Roy managed to climb out on the driver's side.

   Thank you for refunding the children's money.

2. If the noun is singular and ends in *-s*, add *-'s*.

   Lois's sister spent last year in India.

EXCEPTION: If pronunciation would be awkward with the added *-'s*, some writers use only the apostrophe. Either use is acceptable.

   Sophocles' plays are among my favorites.

When to add only an apostrophe

If the noun is plural and ends in *-s*, add only an apostrophe.

   Both diplomats' briefcases were stolen.

Joint possession

To show joint possession, use *-'s* or *(-s')* with the last noun only; to show individual possession, make all nouns possessive.

   Have you seen Joyce and Greg's new camper?

   John's and Marie's expectations of marriage couldn't have been more different.

In the first sentence, Joyce and Greg jointly own one camper. In the second sentence, John and Marie individually have different expectations.

Compound nouns

If a noun is compound, use *-'s* (or *-s'*) with the last element.

   My father-in-law's sculpture won first place.

36b Use an apostrophe and -s to indicate that an indefinite pronoun is possessive.

Indefinite pronouns refer to no specific person or thing: *everyone, someone, no one, something*. (See 47b.)

   Someone's raincoat has been left behind.

   This diet will improve almost anyone's health.

36c Use an apostrophe to mark omissions in contractions and numbers.

In contractions the apostrophe takes the place of missing letters.

   It's a shame that Frank can't go on the tour.

It's stands for *it is, can't* for *cannot.*
   The apostrophe is also used to mark the omission of the first two digits of a year (*the class of '95*) or years (*the '60s generation*).

   We'll never forget the blizzard of '96.

36d Use an apostrophe and -s to pluralize numbers mentioned as numbers, letters mentioned as letters, words mentioned as words, and abbreviations.

Margarita skated nearly perfect figure 8's.

The bleachers in our section were marked with large red *J*'s.

We've heard enough *maybe*'s.

You must ask to see their I.D.'s.

Notice that the *-s* is not italicized when used with an italicized number, letter, or word.

EXCEPTION: An *-s* alone is often added to the years in a decade: *the 1980s.*

36e Avoid common misuses of the apostrophe.

Do not use an apostrophe in the following situations.

WITH NOUNS THAT ARE NOT POSSESSIVE

▶ Some ~~outpatient's~~ *outpatients* are given special parking

permits.

IN THE POSSESSIVE PRONOUNS *ITS*, *WHOSE*, *HIS*, *HERS*, *OURS*, *YOURS*, AND *THEIRS*

▶ Each area has ~~it's~~ *its* own conference room.

It's means "it is." The possessive pronoun *its* contains no apostrophe despite the fact that it is possessive.

▶ This course was taught by a professional florist ~~who's~~ *whose* technique was oriental.

Who's means "who is." The possessive pronoun is *whose.*

EXERCISE 36–1 The apostrophe: Guided practice

In the following paragraphs, add apostrophes where they are missing and delete or correct them where they have been misused. Rule numbers in the margin refer to appropriate rules in section 36. The first revision has been done for you, and answers to this exercise appear in the back of the book.

During the 1990 troubles in Panama, American television and newspaper reporters had an exciting piece of news. They reported that for the first time American female soldiers had been engaged in actual combat. Acting as her ~~soldiers~~ *soldiers'* leader,   *36a*
Captain Linda Bray led her troops into combat. Names of two additional women who were involved in combat, Staff Sergeant April Hanley and PFC Christina Proctor, were reported in the newspapers. Their's were the only names reported, although   *36e*
other women also took part.

It wasn't the first time an American woman had fought in an American battle, but its not likely that many people are aware of that fact. The Civil War had   *36c*
its female fighters too. Loreta Janeta Velazquez fought for the Confederates' in the   *36e*
Civil War after her husbands death. Like many other women whose husbands were   *36a*
killed in that war, she must have asked herself, "Whose going to take his place in   *36c*
battle?" The decision to fight was hers alone. Someone is sure to ask how that was possible, even in those days. Military I.D.s were not very sophisticated in the 1860s.   *36d*
Someones willingness to fight was that person's major qualification, and each fight-   *36b*
ing unit needed to replace it's losses as fast as possible. Velazquez simply disguised   *36e*
herself in mens clothing, found a troop needing replacements, and joined the fight.   *36a*
Loreta Janeta Velazquez was Linda Brays Civil War predecessor.   *36a*

EXERCISE 36–2 The apostrophe

A. Each of the following sentences has two words containing apostrophes. Only one of the apostrophes is used correctly in each sentence. Delete or move the other apostrophe. Example:

> Further back in American history, one woman's soldiering had made her famous; no one
>
> *hers.*
> has yet had a story to match ~~her's.~~

1. Deborah Sampson never dreamed that she would someday fight in battles' for American independence, much less that the battles' outcomes might depend on her.

2. Because her parents' income was not enough to support their children, Deborah was sent to live with relatives of her parents' in another town.

3. Later she was sent to live in a foster family with ten sons'; the sons' acceptance of her was wholehearted, and one son became her fiancé when she grew up.

4. The Revolutionary War was'nt over when news of his death reached Deborah; she wasn't long in making a major decision.

5. Using a false name, she enlisted to take his place—determined to mind her *p*s' and *q*'s so well that she would not be detected.

B. The following sentences contain no apostrophes. Add any that are needed. If a sentence is correct, mark it "OK." Example:

> *Who's*   *who's*
> ~~Whose~~ to say ~~whos~~ right about Deborah Sampson's decision?

6. If men have the right to fight for their beliefs, should women have the right to fight for theirs?

7. Its clear that Deborah Sampson thought so; she enlisted twice to fight for hers.

8. On her first attempt, Sampson enlisted almost at the end of the day—and was discovered before its end arrived.

9. Though drinking was not a habit of hers, she spent her first evening as a soldier copying other new soldiers behavior.

10. Coming to the aid of this very noisy, very drunk, and very sick "buddy" of theirs, they soon were asking, "Whose this?"

EXERCISE 36–3 The apostrophe

Circle the correct form of the word in parentheses. The first one has been done for you.

Loreta Velazquez was not the only woman (who's, (whose)) help was used during the Civil War, nor was being a foot soldier the only way women served in that war.

She was not in combat, but Mary Walker, then in her (thirties, thirty's), served in the Union army. She served with such distinction that she became the first woman to receive the Medal of Honor, the (military's, militarys') highest-ranking medal. It is awarded only to members of the armed (forces, force's) and only for gallantry in action.

Mary (Walker's, Walkers) specialty was surgery. Just as shocking as her profession — the role of military surgeon was not (everyone's, everyones') idea of the proper role for a woman in the 1860s — were Dr. Walker's opinions on how women should dress. She said that women (shouldn't, should'nt) wear tight corsets because such corsets were injurious to (women's, womens') health. She even considered long skirts unhealthy. She felt so strongly on the subject of women's attire that she herself determined to wear long pants. Army (regulations, regulations') did not permit such attire for a woman. (Who's, Whose) permission was required for her to do so? It required special permission from the U.S. Congress, but Dr. Mary Walker finally won that battle of the Civil War.

She did not live to see the ending of her final battle. After the war, she went back to her private practice of medicine and began fighting for a constitutional amendment to allow women to vote. Congress passed the Twentieth Amendment in 1920. But Mary Walker died before (its, it's) adoption.

EXERCISE 36–4 The apostrophe: Guided review

In the following paragraph, add apostrophes where they are missing and delete or correct them where they have been misused. Rule numbers in the margin refer to appropriate rules in section 36. The first revision has been done for you.

Deborah Sampson, who fought in America's Revolution, fulfilled her light infantryman duties pretending to be a private named Robert Shurtlieff. To ~~anyones~~ *anyone's*   **36b**

questions about where he was based, this private said, "West Point." Sampson's first

enlistment lasted less than a day, but her second enlistment was different. It lasted

until the wars end, and along with many others she was honorably discharged from   **36a**

the Continental Army on October 23, 1783. Throughout her service, it was every-

ones opinion that she was an excellent soldier. Her officers reports on her were al-   **36b, 36a**

ways good. Wounded twice, she outwitted the doctors and returned to her unit

undetected; but when she came down with "the fevers," a doctor discovered the se-

cret that until then had been her's alone. (Many of the distinctions among different   **36e**

illnesses that produce fevers—from typhoid to influenza—were not yet known; if

patients had a high fever and it's accompanying discomforts for very long, they were   **36e**

diagnosed as having "the fevers.") Its no surprise that when her secret was finally   **36c**

told, her superior officers wouldnt believe it. Dressed in women's clothes, she was   **36c**

escorted to separate quarters not by the M.P.s but by her superior officers. Many   **36d**

years later, at Paul Reveres' suggestion, she donned the uniform again and went on   **36a**

speaking tours' to raise much-needed money for her family and to secure a monthly   **36e**

pension from the army she had once served.

37 Quotation marks

GRAMMAR CHECKERS are good at telling you to put commas and periods inside quotation marks; they are also fairly good at flagging "unbalanced quotes," an opening quotation mark that is not balanced with a closing quotation mark. The programs can't tell you, however, when you should or shouldn't use quotation marks.

37a Use quotation marks to enclose direct quotations.

Direct quotations of a person's words, whether spoken or written, must be in quotation marks.

> In a husky voice Muhammad Ali bragged, "My opponent will be on the floor in round four. He'll take a dive in round five. In round nine he'll be all mine."

> "A foolish consistency is the hobgoblin of little minds," wrote Ralph Waldo Emerson.

CAUTION: Do not use quotation marks around indirect quotations. An indirect quotation reports someone's ideas without using that person's exact words.

> Ralph Waldo Emerson believed that consistency for its own sake is the mark of a small mind.

NOTE: In dialogue, begin a new paragraph to mark a change in speaker.

> "Mom, his name is Willie, not William. A thousand times I've told you, it's *Willie.*"
> "Willie is a derivative of William, Lester. Surely his birth certificate doesn't have Willie on it, and I like calling people by their proper names."
> "Yes, it does, ma'am. My mother named me Willie K. Mason."
> —Gloria Naylor

If a single speaker utters more than one paragraph, introduce each paragraph with quotation marks, but do not use closing quotation marks until the end of the speech.

37b Set off long quotations of prose or poetry by indenting.

When a quotation of prose runs to more than four typed lines in your paper, set it off by indenting one inch (or ten spaces) from the left margin. Quotation marks are not required because the indented format tells readers that the quotation is taken word for word from a source. Long quotations are ordinarily introduced by a sentence ending with a colon.

```
After making an exhaustive study of the
historical record, James Horan evaluates
Billy the Kid like this:

      The portrait that emerges of [the
      Kid] from the thousands of pages
      of affidavits, reports, trial
      transcripts, his letters, and his
      testimony is neither the mythical
      Robin Hood nor the stereotyped
      adenoidal moron and pathological
      killer. Rather Billy appears as
      a disturbed, lonely young man,
      honest, loyal to his friends,
      dedicated to his beliefs, and
      betrayed by our institutions and
      the corrupt, ambitious, and com-
      promising politicians of his
      time. (158)
```

The page number in parentheses is a citation handled according to the Modern Language Association style of documentation.

NOTE: When you quote more than three lines of a poem, set it off from the text by indenting ten spaces from the left margin. Use no quotation marks unless they appear in the poem itself.

37c Use single quotation marks to enclose a quotation within a quotation.

> According to Paul Eliott, Eskimo hunters "chant an ancient magic song to the seal they are after: 'Beast of the sea! Come and place yourself before me in the early morning!'"

37d Use quotation marks around the titles of short works: newspaper and magazine articles, poems, short stories, songs, episodes of television and radio programs, and chapters or subdivisions of books.

> Katherine Mansfield's "The Garden Party" provoked a lively discussion in our short-story class last night.

NOTE: Titles of books, plays, television and radio programs, and films and names of magazines and newspapers are put in italics or underlined. (See 42a.)

37e Quotation marks may be used to set off words used as words.

Although words used as words are ordinarily underlined or italicized (see 42d), quotation marks are also acceptable. Just be sure to follow consistent practice throughout a paper.

> The words "accept" and "except" are frequently confused.

> The words *accept* and *except* are frequently confused.

37f Use punctuation with quotation marks according to convention.

This section describes the conventions used by American publishers in placing various marks of punctuation inside or outside quotation marks. It also explains how to punctuate when introducing quoted material.

Periods and commas

Always place periods and commas inside quotation marks.

> "This is a stick-up," said the well-dressed young couple. "We want all your money."

This rule applies to single quotation marks as well as double quotation marks. (See 37c.) It also applies to all uses of quotation marks: for quoted material, for titles of works, and for words used as words.

Colons and semicolons

Put colons and semicolons outside quotation marks.

> Harold wrote, "I regret that I am unable to attend the fundraiser for AIDS research"; his letter, however, came with a substantial contribution.

Question marks and exclamation points

Put question marks and exclamation points inside quotation marks unless they apply to the whole sentence.

> Contrary to tradition, bedtime at my house is marked by "Mommy, can I tell you a story now?"

> Have you heard the old proverb "Do not climb the hill until you reach it"?

In the first sentence, the question mark applies only to the quoted question. In the second sentence, the question mark applies to the whole sentence.

Introducing quoted material

After a word group introducing a quotation, choose a colon, a comma, or no punctuation at all, whichever is appropriate in context.

If a quotation is formally introduced, a colon is appropriate. A formal introduction is a full independent clause, not just an expression such as *he said* or *she remarked*.

> Morrow views personal ads in the classifieds as an art form: "The personal ad is like a haiku of self-celebration, a brief solo played on one's own horn."

If a quotation is introduced with an expression such as *he said* or *she remarked*—or if it is followed by such an expression—a comma is needed.

> Robert Frost said, "You can be a little ungrammatical if you come from the right part of the country."

> "You can be a little ungrammatical if you come from the right part of the country," Robert Frost said.

When a quotation is blended into the writer's own sentence, either a comma or no punctuation is appropriate, depending on the way in which the quotation fits into the sentence structure.

> The future champion could, as he put it, "float like a butterfly and sting like a bee."

> Charles Hudson noted that the prisoners escaped "by squeezing through a tiny window eighteen feet above the floor of their cell."

If a quotation appears at the beginning of a sentence, set it off with a comma unless the quotation ends with a question mark or an exclamation point.

> "We shot them like dogs," boasted Davy Crockett, who was among Jackson's troops.

> "What is it?" I asked, bracing myself.

If a quoted sentence is interrupted by explanatory words, use commas to set off the explanatory words.

> "A great many people think they are thinking," wrote William James, "when they are merely rearranging their prejudices."

If two successive quoted sentences from the same source are interrupted by explanatory words, use a comma before the explanatory words and a period after them.

> "I was a flop as a daily reporter," admitted E. B. White. "Every piece had to be a masterpiece — and before you knew it, Tuesday was Wednesday."

37g Avoid common misuses of quotation marks.

Do not use quotation marks to draw attention to familiar slang, to disown trite expressions, or to justify an attempt at humor.

▶ Between Thanksgiving and Super Bowl Sunday, many American wives become ⁄football widows.⁊

Do not use quotation marks around indirect quotations. (See also 37a.)

▶ After leaving the scene of the domestic quarrel, the officer said that ⁄he was due for a coffee break.⁊

Do not use quotation marks around the title of your own essay.

EXERCISE 37–1 Quotation marks: Guided practice

Edit the following sentences to correct the quotation marks and punctuation used with quotation marks. Rule numbers in the margin refer to appropriate rules in section 37. Answers to this exercise appear in the back of the book. Example:

> **The parents watched as the doctor bandaged the boy's eyes. "For the love of God,**
>
> **what can we do?" asked the father?.**   *37f*

1. The doctor answered "You can do nothing but pray."   *37f*

2. When the bandages were removed and the shades were opened to let in
    the bright sunlight, the doctor asked, "What do you see"?   *37f*

3. "Nothing," said the boy. I see nothing.   *37a*

4. The village priest said "I have recently seen a remarkable school." He had   *37f*
    just returned from a trip to Paris.

5. "In this school, he added, blind students are taught to read."   *37a*

6. "You didn't say "read," did you?" asked the boy's father.   *37c*

7. The boy responded to the priest's words as if they were a trick of some
    kind "Now you are joking with me. How can such a thing be possible?"   *37f*

8. The boy, Louis, thought it would be "great fun" to visit that school   *37g*
    someday.

9. His father promised "We will go soon, Louis."   *37f*

10. And so it happened that ten-year-old Louis Braille entered the National In-
    stitute for Blind Youths and began the long effort to erase the fear people
    had of even the word blind.   *37e*

EXERCISE 37–2 Quotation marks

Change each indirect quotation into a direct quotation, using correct punctuation and deleting or changing words as necessary. Example:

The doctor told them not to look for miracles.

The doctor said, "Do not look for miracles."

_____

1. The doctor added that in all probability their son would never see again.

   _____

   _____

2. Mr. Braille exclaimed that he had seen blind students at the institute making their own clothes and shoes.

   _____

   _____

3. The inventor of the military raised-dot system of writing told Louis to experiment all he wished but not to set his hopes too high.

   _____

   _____

4. When his old friends in the village saw him with his stylus and paper, they asked him if he was still punching away at it.

   _____

   _____

5. Louis asked the government official if he was blind and if he understood what it was like not to see.

   _____

   _____

EXERCISE 37–3 Quotation marks

In the following sentences, insert needed quotation marks and punctuation used with quotation marks. If a sentence is correct, mark it "OK." Example:

> One of Braille's students wrote,"Attending his classes was a pleasure to enjoy rather than a duty to fulfill."

1. Louis Braille asked the inventor of the military raised-dot system a serious question "Do you think it would be possible to change the symbols in some way, to reduce them in size?"

2. Barbier, the inventor of the system, replied "Of course. Anything is possible."

3. "I have hoped" said the founder of the institute "that this school would be a bright torch held aloft to bring light to the blind."

4. "I am going to instruct the teachers to begin using your system in the classroom," said the institute director. "You must understand, though, that your method has not yet been proved."

5. Louis Braille wanted a system so complete that people could read and write the words and music to a song like the Marseillaise, the French national anthem.

EXERCISE 37–4 Quotation marks: Guided review

Edit the following paragraphs to correct the use of quotation marks and punctuation used with quotation marks. Rule numbers in the margin refer to appropriate rules in section 37. The first revision has been made for you.

Louis Braille entered the National Institute for Blind Youths in Paris when he was ten. At twelve, he was already experimenting with a system of raised letters known as "night-~~writing~~", *writing,"* which was used by the military. Institute teachers decided that night-writing was impractical, but Louis became proficient at it. When Charles Barbier, inventor of the system, visited the institute, Louis told him "Your symbols are too large and too complicated. Impressed, Barbier encouraged him and said that "since Louis was blind himself, he might discover the magic key that had eluded his teachers."   *37f 37f 37a 37g*

Louis Braille wanted a system that would work for everything from a textbook on science to a poem like Heinrich Heine's Loreley. At fifteen, he had worked out his own system of six dots arranged in various patterns. "Read to me," he said to one of his teachers, and I will take down your words." As the teacher read, Louis punched his paper and then read the passage back without error. The teacher exclaimed, "Remarkable"! Government officials, not impressed enough to take any action, said simply that Braille should be encouraged. "You didn't say "encouraged," did you?" asked Braille. He wanted official acceptance, not simply encouragement. "The system has proved itself," said Louis. We have been using it for five years now."   *37d 37f 37f 37c 37f*

For most people, the word Braille itself now means simply a system of reading and writing used by blind people; for blind people, it means freedom and independence. Braille himself died before his system was recognized beyond the institute. The plaque on the house of his birth, however, records the world's recognition of his work with these words: He opened the doors of knowledge to all those who cannot see.   *37e 37a*

38 End punctuation

GRAMMAR CHECKERS occasionally flag sentences beginning with words like *Why* or *Are* and suggest that a question mark may be needed. On the whole, however, grammar checkers are of little help with end punctuation. Most notably, they neglect to tell you when your sentence is missing end punctuation.

38a The period

Use a period to end all sentences except direct questions or genuine exclamations. Also use periods in abbreviations according to convention.

To end sentences

Everyone knows that a period should be used to end most sentences. The only problems that arise concern the choice between a period and a question mark or between a period and an exclamation point.

If a sentence reports a question instead of asking it directly, it should end with a period, not a question mark.

▶ Celia asked whether the picnic would be

canceled?.

If a sentence is not a genuine exclamation, it should end with a period, not an exclamation point.

▶ After years of working her way through school,

Pat finally graduated with high honors!.

In abbreviations

A period is conventionally used in abbreviations such as the following:

Mr.	B.A.	B.C.	i.e.	A.M. (or a.m.)
Mrs.	M.A.	B.C.E.	e.g.	P.M. (or p.m.)
Ms.	Ph.D.	A.D.	etc.	
Dr.	R.N.	C.E.		

A period is not used with U.S. Postal Service abbreviations for states: MD, TX, CA.

Ordinarily a period is not used in abbreviations of organization names:

NATO	IRS	SEC	IBM
TVA	NAACP	PUSH	FTC
USA (*or* U.S.A.)	UCLA	NBA	NIH
UNESCO	AFL-CIO	FCC	

Usage varies, however. When in doubt, consult a dictionary, a style manual, or a publication by the agency in question. Even the yellow pages can help.

NOTE: If a sentence ends with a period marking an abbreviation, do not add a second period to the end of the sentence.

38b The question mark

Obviously a direct question should be followed by a question mark.

What is the horsepower of a 747 engine?

If a polite request is written in the form of a question, it too is usually followed by a question mark, although usage varies.

Would you please send me your catalog of lilies?

CAUTION: Do not use a question mark after an indirect question, one that is reported rather than asked directly. Use a period instead.

▶ He asked me who was teaching the mythology

course?.

NOTE: Questions in a series may be followed by question marks even when they are not complete sentences.

We wondered where Calamity had hidden this time. Under the sink? Behind the furnace? On top of the bookcase?

38c The exclamation point

Use an exclamation point after a word group or sentence that expresses exceptional feeling or deserves special emphasis.

> When Gloria entered the room, I switched on the lights and we all yelled "Surprise!"

CAUTION: Do not overuse the exclamation point.

▶ In the fisherman's memory the fish lives on, increasing in length and weight with each passing year, until at last it is big enough to shade a fishing boat!.

This sentence doesn't need to be pumped up with an exclamation point. It is emphatic enough without it.

▶ Whenever I see Steffi lunging forward to put away an overhead smash, it might as well be me!. She does it just the way that I would!

The first exclamation point should be deleted so that the second one will have more force.

EXERCISE 38–1 End punctuation: Guided practice

Supply end punctuation as needed in the following paragraph. Rule numbers in the margin refer to appropriate rules in section 38. The first and last revisions have been made for you, and answers to this exercise appear in the back of the book.

After Louis Braille invented his new system that would allow blind people to
read and write, he tested it thoroughly. Students and faculty of the National Insti-   *38a*
tute for Blind Youths were excited at how easily they could master it and encouraged Louis to demonstrate the system to the French educational authorities, who
made the rules for the institute Louis agreed to do so   *38a, 38a*

When Louis held the demonstration, all went well What excitement he and   *38a*
his friends felt But the authorities would not recommend that the institute adopt   *38c*
Louis's new system Why didn't the French authorities recognize the advantages of   *38a*
Braille's system Did they have a vested interest in the old system of teaching the   *38b*
blind Or a real doubt about the system Whatever their reasons, they delayed the   *38b, 38b*
pleasures of reading for thousands of people In addition, a new director, Dr. Pignier,   *38a*
even outlawed the use of the system at the institute for four years   *38a*

Although unhappy and disheartened, Braille never gave up; he knew his system would enable the blind to read.

EXERCISE 38–2 End punctuation

Supply end punctuation—period, question mark, or exclamation point—for each of the following sentences. At least one sentence of each pair is a question. Example:

    a. Louis asked if he could demonstrate his technique at the institute.

    b. Louis asked, "May I demonstrate my technique at the ~~institute~~ *institute?"*

1a.   What Louis had figured out was a new code

  b.   What had Louis figured out

2a.   What should I do about teaching it

  b.   What to do about teaching it was the next decision to make

3a.   Who could help him test the system was another question

  b.   Who could help him test the system

4a.   How extraordinary it was that a leather worker's son should have such talent

  b.   How was it that he had such extraordinary talent

5a.   Why did he never give up, either as a child or as an adult

  b.   Why he never gave up, either as a child or as an adult, puzzled many of his friends

EXERCISE 38-3 End punctuation: Guided review

Supply appropriate end punctuation in the following paragraphs. Rule numbers in the margin refer to appropriate rules in section 38. The first revision has been made for you.

Braille's system depended on a group of six dots. He called this group a "cell." He conceived of the cell as three rows with space for two dots on each row. But he did not have to put two dots on each row, and he did not have to use all three rows. **38a** Figuring it this way, Braille counted sixty-three possible arrangements for the dots. Using these possibilities, Braille worked out an alphabet. Then he added punctuation marks and numerals. But he still was not satisfied. There was something else that he wanted to do.

Braille knew very well that blindness does not keep someone from becoming proficient at a particular skill. Like many other blind people, Braille himself was an accomplished musician. As a young boy at the National Institute for Blind Youths, he had learned to play several instruments. But he could play only by ear Louis **38a** Braille wanted to be able to read music, play what he read, and then write music that other musicians could read and play.

When Braille was only fifteen, he devised a way to write music using his six-dot cell. As soon as he knew it was workable, he wanted a piano of his own to try it on. By saving his small salary, he was able to buy a piano. Next he wanted lessons **38a** Paris had many good music teachers. Braille took lessons from some of the best and then began to teach piano and violoncello at the institute. He also gave frequent piano recitals throughout Paris.

When he knew he was good on the piano, Braille said it was time to play something else "God's music," the church organ, was what he wanted to learn. With **38a** great effort he learned to manage the foot pedals, the double keyboard, and the rows of stops St. Nicholas-des-Champs Church hired him as organist. However, Braille **38a** found himself so busy thinking about stops and pedals that he couldn't keep up with the service at first. Did he resign Of course not Braille simply became so fa- **38b, 38c** miliar with the music that he did not have to think about it and could follow the

church service as it went along Louis Braille may have been the first blind organist   *38a*
in Paris, but he was not the last. In Braille's lifetime, the institute's music director
placed more than fifty blind organists in the city.

Many people have wondered where Braille got the idea of adapting the Braille
system to music. Did it come from one of his teachers Or one of his friends Or from   *38b, 38b*
his own mind Whichever way it happened, the Braille system was adapted for music,   *38b*
and again Braille opened a new world to the blind. What an extraordinary gift was
this Except for sight itself, could anyone have given blind musicians a greater gift   *38c, 38b*

39   Other punctuation marks: the dash, parentheses, brackets, the ellipsis mark, the slash

 GRAMMAR CHECKERS rarely flag problems with the punctuation marks in this section: the dash, parentheses, brackets, the ellipsis mark, and the slash.

39a   The dash

When typing, use two hyphens to form a dash (--). Do not put spaces before or after the dash. (If your word processing program has what is known as an "em-dash," you may use it instead, with no space before or after it.) Dashes are used for the following purposes.

To set off parenthetical material that deserves emphasis

> Everything that went wrong—from the peeping Tom at her window last night to my head-on collision today—was blamed on our move.

To set off appositives that contain commas

An appositive is a noun or noun phrase that renames a nearby noun. Ordinarily most appositives are set off with commas (see 32e), but when the appositive contains commas, a pair of dashes helps the readers see the relative importance of all the pauses.

> In my hometown the basic needs of people—food, clothing, and shelter—are less costly than in Los Angeles.

To prepare for a list, a restatement, an amplification, or a dramatic shift in tone or thought

> Along the wall are the bulk liquids—sesame seed oil, honey, safflower oil, and that half-liquid "peanuts only" peanut butter.

> Consider the amount of sugar in the average person's diet—104 pounds per year, 90 percent more than that consumed by our ancestors.

> Everywhere we looked there were little kids—a box of Cracker Jacks in one hand and mommy or daddy's sleeve in the other.

> Kiere took a few steps back, came running full speed, kicked a mighty kick—and missed the ball.

In the first two examples, the writer could also use a colon. (See 35a.) The colon is more formal than the dash and not quite as dramatic.

CAUTION: Unless there is a specific reason for using the dash, avoid it. Unnecessary dashes create a choppy effect.

▶ Insisting that students use computers as instructional tools ⫽ for information retrieval ⫽ makes good sense. Herding them ⫽ sheeplike ⫽ into computer technology does not.

39b   Parentheses

Use parentheses to enclose supplemental material, minor digressions, and afterthoughts.

> After taking her temperature, pulse, and blood pressure (routine vital signs), the nurse made Becky as comfortable as possible.

> The weights James was first able to move (not lift, mind you) were measured in ounces.

Use parentheses to enclose letters or numbers labeling items in a series.

> Regulations stipulated that only the following equipment could be used on the survival mission: (1) a knife, (2) thirty feet of parachute line, (3) a book of matches, (4) two ponchos, (5) an *E* tool, and (6) a signal flare.

CAUTION: Do not overuse parentheses. Rough drafts are likely to contain more afterthoughts than necessary. As writers head into a sentence, they often think of additional details, occasionally working them in as best they can with parentheses. Usually such sentences should be revised so that the additional details no longer seem to be afterthoughts.

from ten to fifty million

▶ Researchers have said that ~~ten million (estimates~~
   ^
~~run as high as fifty million)~~ Americans have

hypoglycemia.

39c   Brackets

Use brackets to enclose any words or phrases
that you have inserted into an otherwise word-
for-word quotation.

> *Audubon* reports that "if there are not enough
> young to balance deaths, the end of the
> species [California condor] is inevitable."

The sentence quoted from the *Audubon* article
did not contain the words *California condor*
(since the context made clear what species was
meant), so the writer needed to add the name
in brackets.

The Latin word *sic* in brackets indicates
that an error in a quoted sentence appears in
the original source.

> According to the review, k. d. lang's
> performance was brilliant, "exceding [*sic*] the
> expectations of even her most loyal fans."

Do not overuse *sic*, however, since calling attention to others' mistakes can appear snob-
bish. The preceding quotation, for example,
might have been paraphrased instead: *According to the review, even k. d. lang's most loyal
fans were surprised by the brilliance of her performance.*

39d   The ellipsis mark

The ellipsis mark consists of three spaced periods. Use an ellipsis mark to indicate that you
have deleted words from an otherwise word-
for-word quotation.

> Reuben reports that "when the amount of cho-
> lesterol circulating in the blood rises
> over . . . 300 milligrams per 100, the chances
> of a heart attack increase dramatically."

If you delete a full sentence or more in the
middle of a quoted passage, use a period before
the three ellipsis dots.

"Most of our efforts," writes Dave Erikson, "are
directed toward saving the bald eagle's wintering habitat along the Mississippi River. . . . It's
important that the wintering birds have a
place to roost, where they can get out of the
cold wind and be undisturbed by man."

CAUTION: Do not use the ellipsis mark at the beginning of a quotation; do not use it at the end
of a quotation unless you have cut some words
from the final sentence quoted.

39e   The slash

Use the slash to separate two or three lines of
poetry that have been run in to your text. Add
a space both before and after the slash.

> In the opening lines of "Jordan," George
> Herbert pokes gentle fun at popular poems of
> his time: "Who says that fictions only and false
> hair / Become a verse? Is there in truth no
> beauty?"

More than three lines of poetry should be handled as an indented quotation. (See 37b.)

The slash may occasionally be used to separate paired terms such as *pass/fail* and *pro-
ducer/director.* Do not use a space before or
after the slash.

> Roger, the producer/director, announced a
> casting change.

Be sparing, however, in this use of the slash.
In particular, avoid the use of *and/or, he/she,*
and *his/her.*

NOTE: For all the exercises in section 39, you will need to refer to the following poem.

The New Colossus

by Emma Lazarus

Not like the brazen giant of Greek fame,
With conquering limbs astride from land to land;
Here at our sea-washed, sunset gates shall stand
A mighty woman with a torch, whose flame
Is the imprisoned lightning, and her name
Mother of Exiles. From her beacon hand
Glows world-wide welcome; her mild eyes command
The air-bridged harbor that twin cities frame.
"Keep, ancient lands, your storied pomp!" cries she
With silent lips. "Give me your tired, your poor,
Your huddled masses yearning to breathe free,
The wretched refuse of your teeming shore,
Send these, the home-less, tempest-tost to me,
I lift my lamp beside the golden door."

EXERCISE 39–1 Other punctuation marks: Guided practice

Edit the following paragraphs for correct use of the dash, parentheses, brackets, ellipsis mark, and slash. Refer to the poem "The New Colossus" (p. 339) as necessary. Rule numbers in the margin refer to appropriate rules in section 39. The first revision has been made for you, and answers to this exercise appear in the back of the book.

The most famous woman in America is Miss Liberty͵a 450,000-pound, 154-   *39a*

foot resident of New York City. For people all over the world, the Statue of Liberty

symbolizes America. Yet the idea for the statue did not come from America, England,

or even New York itself, but from France. Three men can claim the credit for con-   *39a*

struction of Miss Liberty: 1. Frédéric-Auguste Bartholdi, sculptor; 2. Alexandre-   *39b*

Gustave Eiffel, structural engineer; and 3. Richard Morris Hunt, architect. France

gave the statue to the United States and the United States provided the pedestal—   *39a*

on which it stands.

Two Americans contributed significantly to the statue. The first was Joseph

Pulitzer, then owner and publisher of the *New York World* (and a Russian immigrant).   *39b*

He led several fundraising efforts and urged every American to give what he/she   *39e*

could to help build the pedestal. The second American who contributed significantly

was Emma Lazarus. She wrote the famous lines on the bronze plaque inside the

statue. Her three-word title "The New Colossus" (huge statue) alludes to a statue

built in the harbor of Rhodes in ancient Greece. The most quoted lines from "The

New Colossus" are probably these: "Give me your tired, your poor, / Your huddled

masses yearning to breathe free."

EXERCISE 39–2 Other punctuation marks

Edit the following sentences by using the punctuation indicated in brackets. Refer to the poem "The New Colossus" (p. 339) as necessary. Example:

Bartholdi's Statue of Liberty better known in France as *Liberty Enlightening the World* celebrated ideals that France and America shared. [Dashes]

1. America's Revolution celebrated liberty. The French added two more words to form the battle cry of the French Revolution, "Liberty, Equality, and Fraternity." [Dash]

2. Emma Lazarus understood Bartholdi's desire to demonstrate this common interest. In her opening line, "Not like the brazen giant of Greek fame" (the Colossus of Rhodes), she alludes to an ancient statue one hundred feet high. [Brackets]

3. Bartholdi was determined to build "A mighty woman—Mother of Exiles" and place her in New York Harbor. [Ellipsis mark]

4. He traveled all over America, to Boston, Chicago, Denver, Salt Lake City, and many other places, to promote his idea. [Dashes]

5. He was amazed at the country's size, industry, and enthusiasm for creating things, buildings, that is, not art. [Parentheses]

6. Bartholdi discovered that money, the enthusiasm of U.S. citizens, and political support, all necessary for his project, were hard to get. [Parentheses]

7. He decided on a novel, hands-on approach, allowing people to climb into completed parts of the statue. [Dash]

8. Three cities were chosen: [1] In Philadelphia, the hand and torch attracted Centennial Exhibition visitors; [2] in New York, the same exhibit drew people downtown; and [3] in Paris, visitors explored the head and shoulders. [Parentheses]

9. When more money was needed, wealthy newspaper publisher Joseph Pulitzer, an immigrant himself, turned to nonwealthy Americans, working-class men, women, and children, and it was their small gifts that paid for the statue's pedestal. [Dashes]

10. Their gifts allowed Miss Liberty's torch to shine out over the water to say, "Send these, the homeless, tempest-tost to me, I lift my lamp beside the golden door." [Slash]

EXERCISE 39–3 Other punctuation marks

The dashes, parentheses, brackets, ellipsis marks, and slashes in the following sentences are not well used. Edit the sentences to be more effective by deleting punctuation marks, replacing them with other marks, or restructuring the sentences. Refer to "The New Colossus" (p. 339) as necessary. Example:

> On October 29, 1886 —, one hundred and ten years after the Declaration of Independence, — Miss Liberty was formally dedicated.

1. Miss Liberty was the only woman at her dedication (except for two Frenchwomen who came with the sculptor).

2. On that day, the Lady who was such a contrast to the "brazen giant of Greek fame" [the Colossus of Rhodes] was almost obscured from view by rain and wind.

3. Also, the crowds of people pushing and shoving resembled the ". . . huddled masses" Emma Lazarus wrote about.

4. The crowd—crushed together—trying to listen to the main speaker—he was William M. Evarts—could hear other voices too.

5. Women who were angry about being excluded from the ceremony had sailed in close to the island (they had chartered a boat) and were yelling their protests.

6. With all of the noise from the crowd and/or the women, the speaker paused.

7. He paused so long that an aide thought the speech was over. The aide signaled Bartholdi (who had been waiting inside the statue).

8. Bartholdi saw the signal and unveiled the statue . . . an hour early.

9. The plaque with Emma Lazarus's poem on it was not on the statue at this time; it was added later—in 1903—without any special attention.

10. It is still there today for all visitors to read/ponder as they meet America's most beloved lady.

EXERCISE 39–4 Other punctuation marks: Guided review

Edit the following paragraphs for most effective use of the dash, parentheses, brackets, ellipsis mark, and slash. Refer to "The New Colossus" (p. 339) as necessary. Rule numbers in the margin refer to appropriate rules in section 39. The first revision has been done for you.

fourteen-line

The sonnet is a poem —of fourteen lines—with a particular pattern to its   39a
rhymes; it is often used to compare or contrast two items. Emma Lazarus's poem
"The New Colossus" is a sonnet. Lazarus uses its fourteen lines to contrast two
statues. One, the ancient Colossus of Rhodes (which was male) represented the sun   39b
god; the other, the new Colossus, was female and represented Liberty. The Rhodes
Colossus symbolized what Lazarus calls "storied pomp." The French-made American one stood for freedom and opportunity.

In her first line, "Not like the brazen (bronze) giant of Greek fame," Lazarus   39c
refers to the material of which the old Colossus was made. Bronze, a valuable metal
when the Colossus of Rhodes was erected in 280 B.C., was available only to the
wealthy. Miss Liberty was made of copper, a material available to all classes of
people. When Miss Liberty was erected in 1898, America's least valuable coin—the   39a
one-cent piece, was made from copper. Miss Liberty was for everyone, not just the
wealthy.

The major contrast Lazarus sets up is in the attitudes of the two statues. The
old Colossus is powerful, not caring about the ". . . wretched refuse" of its "teeming   39d
shore." The new one welcomes all: "Send these, the homeless, tempest-tost to me, I
lift my lamp beside the golden door."   39e

Unit review (32–39): Punctuation

Edit the following paragraphs to correct errors in punctuation or to use more effective punctuation. A rule number in the margin indicates a problem or a suggested revision in the adjacent line. The first revision has been done for you.

The outside of the Statue of Liberty is made of copper‸ but what is inside the   *32a*

statue. Inside the statue are: iron braces and staircases. The thin copper plates that   *38b, 35d*

form the outside of the statue are bolted to a network of iron braces. There are

several staircases allowing workers and tourists to climb all the way into the head

and the torch. (This intricate network of braces and stairways was designed by

Alexandre-Gustave Eiffel; the same man who designed the famous Eiffel Tower in   *34d*

Paris.)

For some years, the lighting equipment for Miss Libertys torch was also in-   *36a*

side. Soon after the statue was set up for example engineers tried Edison's new in-   *32f*

vention, the electric lightbulb. They cut holes in the torch's copper sheets and hung

lightbulbs inside. Later, the copper sheets came down and glass windows went up.

Giving Miss Liberty a light that everyone would recognize as hers, challenged engi-   *33g*

neers and designers for sixty more years. When the statue was restored in the 1980s   *32b*

part of the lighting equipment went outside. Floodlights were installed on the torch's

balcony, and focused on thin gold sheets that form the torch "... whose flame / Is   *33a, 39d*

the imprisoned lightning. Miss Liberty will be able to welcome newcomers for many   *37a*

years.

Mechanics

40 Abbreviations
41 Numbers
42 Italics (underlining)
43 Spelling
44 The hyphen
45 Capital letters

---

40 Abbreviations

 GRAMMAR CHECKERS can flag a few inappropriate abbreviations, such as *Xmas* and *e.g.*, but do not assume that a program will catch all problems with abbreviations.

40a Use standard abbreviations for titles immediately before and after proper names.

TITLES BEFORE PROPER NAMES	TITLES AFTER PROPER NAMES
Mr. Rafael Zabala	William Albert, Sr.
Ms. Nancy Linehan	Thomas Hines, Jr.
Mrs. Edward Horn	Anita Lor, Ph.D.
Dr. Margaret Simmons	Robert Simkowski, M.D.
the Rev. John Stone	William Lyons, M.A.
St. Joan of Arc	Margaret Chin, LL.D.
Prof. James Russo	Polly Stein, D.D.S.

Do not abbreviate a title if it is not used with a proper name.

>   *professor*
> ▶ My history prof. was an expert on America's
>
> use of the atomic bomb in World War II.

Avoid redundant titles such as *Dr. Amy Day, M.D.* Choose one title or the other: *Dr. Amy Day* or *Amy Day, M.D.*

40b Use abbreviations only when you are sure your readers will understand them.

Familiar abbreviations, often written without periods, are acceptable:

CIA	FBI	AFL-CIO	NAACP
IBM	UPI	CBS	USA (or U.S.A.)

While in Washington the schoolchildren toured the FBI.

NOTE: When using an unfamiliar abbreviation (such as CBE for Council of Biology Editors) throughout a paper, write the full name followed by the abbreviation in parentheses at the first mention of the name. Then use the abbreviation throughout the rest of the paper.

40c Use B.C., A.D., A.M., P.M., No., and $ only with specific dates, times, numbers, and amounts.

The abbreviation B.C. ("before Christ") follows a date, and A.D. ("*anno Domini*") precedes a date. Acceptable alternatives are B.C.E. ("before the common era") and C.E. ("common era").

40 B.C. (or B.C.E.)	4:00 A.M. (or a.m.)
A.D. 44 (or C.E.)	6:00 P.M. (or p.m.)
No. 12 (or no. 12)	$150

Avoid using A.M., P.M., No., or $ when not accompanied by a specific figure.

▶ We set off for the lake early in the ~~A.M.~~ *morning.*

40d Be sparing in your use of Latin abbreviations.

Latin abbreviations are acceptable in footnotes and bibliographies and in informal writing for comments in parentheses.

cf. (Latin *confer,* "compare")

e.g. (Latin *exempli gratia,* "for example")

et al. (Latin *et alii,* "and others")

etc. (Latin *et cetera,* "and so forth")

i.e. (Latin *id est,* "that is")

N.B. (Latin *nota bene,* "note well")

Harold Simms et al., *The Race for Space*

Alfred Hitchcock directed many classic thrillers (e.g., *Psycho, Rear Window,* and *Vertigo*).

In formal writing use the appropriate English phrases.

▶ Many obsolete laws remain on the books, ~~e.g.,~~ *for example,* a law in Vermont forbidding an unmarried man and woman to sit closer than six inches apart on a park bench.

40e Avoid inappropriate abbreviations.

In formal writing, abbreviations for the following are not commonly accepted: personal names, units of measurement, days of the week, holidays, months, courses of study, divisions of written works, states, and countries (except in addresses and except Washington, D.C.). Do not abbreviate *Company* and *Incorporated* unless their abbreviated forms are part of an official name.

PERSONAL NAME
Charles (not Chas.)

UNITS OF MEASUREMENT
pound (not lb.)

DAYS OF THE WEEK
Monday (not Mon.)

HOLIDAYS
Christmas (not Xmas)

MONTHS
January, February, March (not Jan., Feb., Mar.)

COURSES OF STUDY
political science (not poli. sci.)

DIVISIONS OF WRITTEN WORKS
chapter, page (not ch., p.)

STATES AND COUNTRIES
Massachusetts (not MA or Mass.)

PARTS OF A BUSINESS NAME
Adams Lighting Company (not Adams Lighting Co.); Kim and Brothers, Inc. (not Kim and Bros., Inc.)

▶ Eliza promised to buy me one ~~lb.~~ *pound* of Godiva chocolate for my birthday, which was last ~~Fri.~~ *Friday.*

41 Numbers

41a Spell out numbers of one or two words or those that begin a sentence. Use figures for numbers that require more than two words to spell out.

> *eight*
> ► Now, some ~~8~~ years later, Muffin is still with us.

> *176*
> ► I counted ~~one hundred seventy-six~~ CD's on
>
> the shelf.

If a sentence begins with a number, spell out the number or rewrite the sentence.

> *One hundred fifty*
> ► ~~150~~ children in our program need expensive
>
> dental treatment.

> Rewriting the sentence will also correct the error and may be less awkward if the number is long: *In our program 150 children need expensive dental treatment.*

EXCEPTIONS: In technical and some business writing, figures are preferred even when spellings would be brief, but usage varies.

When several numbers appear in the same passage, many writers choose consistency rather than strict adherence to the rule.

When one number immediately follows another, spell out one and use figures for the other: three 100-meter events, 125 four-poster beds.

GRAMMAR CHECKERS can tell you to spell out certain numbers, such as *thirty-three* and numbers that begin a sentence, but they won't help you understand when it is acceptable to use figures.

41b Generally, figures are acceptable for dates, addresses, percentages, fractions, decimals, scores, statistics and other numerical results, exact amounts of money, divisions of books and plays, pages, identification numbers, and the time.

DATES
July 4, 1776, 56 B.C., A.D. 30

ADDRESSES
77 Latches Lane, 519 West 42nd Street

PERCENTAGES
55 percent (or 55%)

FRACTIONS, DECIMALS
½, 0.047

SCORES
7 to 3, 21–18

STATISTICS
average age 37, average weight 180

SURVEYS
4 out of 5

EXACT AMOUNTS OF MONEY
$105.37, $106,000

DIVISIONS OF BOOKS
volume 3, chapter 4, page 189

DIVISIONS OF PLAYS
act 3, scene 3 (or act III, scene iii)

IDENTIFICATION NUMBERS
serial number 10988675

TIME OF DAY
4:00 P.M., 1:30 A.M.

> *$255,000*
> ► Several doctors put up ~~two hundred fifty-five~~
>
> ~~thousand dollars~~ for the construction of a
>
> golf course.

NOTE: When not using A.M. or P.M., write out the time in words (*two o'clock in the afternoon, twelve noon, seven in the morning*).

42 Italics (underlining)

Italics, a slanting typeface used in printed material, can be produced by some word processing programs. In handwritten or typed papers, this typeface is indicated by <u>underlining</u>. Some instructors prefer underlining even if their students can produce italics.

NOTE: Current e-mail systems do not allow for italics or underlining. Many people indicate words that should be italicized by preceding and ending them with underscore marks or asterisks. Punctuation should follow the coding.

```
I am planning to write my senior thesis on
_Anna Karenina_.
```

In less formal e-mail messages, normally italicized words aren't marked at all.

```
I finally finished reading Anna Karenina--
what a masterpiece!
```

 GRAMMAR CHECKERS do not flag problems with italics or underlining.

42a Underline or italicize the titles of works according to convention.

Titles of the following works should be underlined or italicized.

TITLES OF BOOKS
The Great Gatsby, A Distant Mirror

MAGAZINES
Time, Scientific American

NEWSPAPERS
the *St. Louis Post-Dispatch*

PAMPHLETS
Common Sense, Facts about Marijuana

LONG POEMS
The Waste Land, Paradise Lost

PLAYS
King Lear, A Raisin in the Sun

FILMS
Casablanca, Independence Day

TELEVISION PROGRAMS
Friends, 60 Minutes

RADIO PROGRAMS
All Things Considered

MUSICAL COMPOSITIONS
Gershwin's *Porgy and Bess*

CHOREOGRAPHIC WORKS
Twyla Tharp's *Brief Fling*

WORKS OF VISUAL ART
Rodin's *The Thinker*

COMIC STRIPS
Dilbert

SOFTWARE
WordPerfect

ONLINE MEDIA
Barron's Online, ESPNET SportsZone

The titles of other works, such as short stories, essays, episodes of radio and television programs, songs, and short poems, are enclosed in quotation marks. (See 37d.)

NOTE: Do not use underlining or italics when referring to the Bible, titles of books in the Bible (Genesis, not *Genesis*), or titles of legal documents (the Constitution, not *Constitution*). Do not underline the title of your own paper.

42b Underline or italicize the names of spacecraft, aircraft, ships, and trains.

Challenger, Spirit of St. Louis, Queen Elizabeth II, Silver Streak

▶ The success of the Soviets' <u>Sputnik</u> galvanized the U.S. space program.

42c Underline or italicize foreign words used in an English sentence.

▶ Although Joe's method seemed to be successful, I decided to establish my own <u>modus operandi</u>.

EXCEPTION: Do not underline or italicize foreign words that have become a standard part of the English language—"laissez-faire," "fait accompli," "habeus corpus," and "per diem," for example.

42d Underline or italicize words mentioned as words, letters mentioned as letters, and numbers mentioned as numbers.

▶ Tim assured us that the howling probably came from his bloodhound, Hill Billy, but his probably stuck in our minds.

▶ Sarah called her father by his given name, Johnny, but she was unable to pronounce J.

▶ A big 3 was painted on the door.

NOTE: Quotation marks may be used instead of underlining or italics to set off words mentioned as words. (See 37e.)

42e Avoid excessive underlining or italics for emphasis.

Underlining or italicizing to emphasize words or ideas is distracting and should be used sparingly.

▶ Tennis is a sport that has become an addiction.

EXERCISE 40/41/42–1 Abbreviations, numbers, and italics: Guided practice

Correct any error in abbreviations, numbers, and italics in the following paragraphs. Rule numbers in the margin refer to appropriate rules in sections 40, 41, and 42. The first revision has been done for you, and a suggested revision of these paragraphs appears in the back of the book.

Everyone has heard of Christopher Columbus, but not many people know much about him. Most people learn that he discovered America in ~~1492 A.D.~~ *A.D. 1492.* Some **40c** people know that he had three ships, and they might be able to name them. (The ships were the "Niña," the "Pinta," and the "Santa María.") A few people might even **42b** remember that Columbus thought he had found the Indies. And those with great self-confidence might be willing to guess at the number of trips he made to his India. (It was 4.) Probably no one would be familiar with his favorite word, adelante. **41a, 42d**

If they were asked what Columbus was trying to prove with his expensive journey, most people would reply that he was trying to prove the world is round. They would be wrong. If they were asked what Columbus meant by "the Indies," they would probably say "India." They would be wrong again. If they were asked what Columbus's rank was, they would most likely say "captain." They would be wrong again. If they were asked what his sailors feared most, a no. of them would reply, **40e** "They feared that the boats would fall off the edge of the earth." And they would be wrong *again.* **42e**

Isn't it strange that people can be so ignorant about a well-known man like Columbus?

EXERCISE 40/41/42–2 Abbreviations and numbers

A. Edit the following sentences to correct errors in the use of abbreviations. Mark the one correct sentence "OK." Example:

> **The sailors who went with Columbus had the same four directions sailors still use:**
> *north, south, east, and west.*
> ~~N, S, E, and W.~~
> ^

1. Sailors in A.D. 1492 knew the world was round; they were not afraid of sailing off the edge of the world.

2. They worried about more serious things, e.g., whether the wind would blow both ways so they could get back home to Spain.

3. They also weren't sure about distances; however, one famous Italian prof., Dr. Toscanelli, thought he knew.

4. He was willing to estimate the distance from Lisbon, Port., to Japan.

5. He said that the exact no. of miles between the two places was three thousand nautical miles.

B. Edit the following sentences to correct errors in the use of numbers. Mark the one correct sentence "OK." Example:

> *three*
> **Dr. Toscanelli set the distance at ~~3~~ thousand nautical miles.**
> ^

6. In twelve ninety-eight, Marco Polo had written a book about his travels to the Indies.

7. 7,448 islands were in the Indies, according to Marco Polo's book, as well as India, China, the East Indies, and Japan.

8. Columbus was 41 when he convinced Queen Isabella to send him to find those islands.

9. As part of the contract, Columbus demanded ten % of the treasure he brought back to Spain.

10. At 8:00 A.M. on August 3, 1492, Columbus set out from Spain for the Indies.

EXERCISE 40/41/42–3 Italics

Edit the following sentences to correct the use of italics (underlining). Example:

Marco Polo's book was named <u>Description of the World</u>.

1. On the "Niña," the "Pinta," and the "Santa María" Columbus had one hundred men, all kinds of supplies, and enough cats to control the rat population.

2. Columbus always spoke the same word to his men—Adelante! (That means "Forward!" or "Sail on!")

3. Marco Polo's book Description of the World had not prepared the men for seeing the same horizon week after week.

4. To every fear or complaint, Columbus simply replied "Forward!" and that word forward began to get on the sailors' nerves.

5. Columbus offered a special reward—a silk jacket—to the first man who spotted *land*.

EXERCISE 40/41/42–4 Abbreviations, numbers, and italics: Guided review

Correct any errors in the use of abbreviations, numbers, and italics in the following paragraphs. Rule numbers in the margin refer to appropriate rules in sections 40, 41, and 42. The first revision has been done for you.

        Columbus's first voyage, in 1492 *A.D.* ~~A.D.~~, was successful. Pleased with the gifts   *40c*
he had brought and impressed by his reports, King Ferdinand and Queen Isabella
quickly ordered him to organize another voyage. Columbus was delighted to do so.
At first his luck held. Led by the flagship Mariagalante, a fleet of 17 ships and a   *42b, 41a*
thousand men who wanted to colonize the new land made the second trip in twenty-
one days. Columbus's good fortune, however, did not last. Life went downhill for the
Italian sailor from that time on.

        The so-called Admiral of the Ocean Sea (a title Columbus had given himself)
had one disastrous experience after another. When he got back to the recently settled new town he had left, the whole settlement had been destroyed, and the 39 men   *41a*
he had left there were all dead. Columbus quickly found a new spot for his new
colony, the first European colony in America. The new site had serious drawbacks,
e.g., bad water and many mosquitoes. Embarrassed, Columbus had to send Queen   *40d*
Isabella's ships back for help; he loaded them not with gold but with pepper, san-
dalwood, and a no. of exotic birds.   *40e*

        Other voyages followed, but each turned out worse than the one before it.
Not even his favorite word, *adelante,* seemed to work for Columbus anymore. His
first voyage had definitely been the most successful.

43   Spelling

You learned to spell from repeated experience with words in both reading and writing, but especially writing. Words have a look, a sound, and even a feel to them as the hand moves across the page. As you proofread, you can probably tell if a word doesn't look quite right. In such cases, the solution is obvious: Look up the word in the dictionary.

SPELL CHECKERS AND GRAMMAR CHECKERS are useful alternatives to a dictionary, but only to a point. A spell checker will not tell you how to spell words not listed in its dictionary; nor will it help you catch words commonly confused, such as *accept* and *except*, or some typographical errors, such as *own* for *won*. You will still need to proofread, and for some words you may need to turn to the dictionary.

Grammar checkers can flag commonly confused words such as *accept* and *except* or *principal* and *principle*, but they often do this when you have used the correct word. You will still need to think about the meaning you intend.

43a   Become familiar with your dictionary.

A good desk dictionary—such as *The American Heritage Dictionary of the English Language, The Random House College Dictionary,* or *Merriam-Webster's Collegiate Dictionary* or *New World Dictionary of the American Language*—is an indispensable writer's aid.

A sample dictionary entry, taken from *The American Heritage Dictionary*, appears on page 356. Labels show where various kinds of information about a word can be found in that dictionary.

Spelling, word division, pronunciation

The main entry (*re•gard* in the sample entry) shows the correct spelling of the word. When there are two correct spellings of a word (as in *collectible, collectable,* for example), both are given, with the preferred spelling usually appearing first.

The main entry also shows how the word is divided into syllables. The dot between *re* and *gard* separates the word's two syllables and indicates where the word should be divided if it

can't fit at the end of a line of type (see 44f). When a word is compound, the main entry shows how to write it: as one word (*crossroad*), as a hyphenated word (*cross-stitch*), or as two words (*cross section*).

The word's pronunciation is given just after the main entry. The accents indicate which syllables are stressed; the other marks are explained in the dictionary's pronunciation key. In some dictionaries this key appears at the bottom of every page or every other page.

Word endings and grammatical labels

When a word takes endings to indicate grammatical functions (called *inflections*), the endings are listed in boldface, as with *-garded, -garding,* and *-gards* in the sample entry.

Labels for the parts of speech and for other grammatical terms are abbreviated. The most commonly used abbreviations are these:

n.	noun	**adj.**	adjective
pl.	plural	**adv.**	adverb
sing.	singular	**pron.**	pronoun
v.	verb	**prep.**	preposition
tr.	transitive verb	**conj.**	conjunction
intr.	intransitive verb	**interj.**	interjection

Meanings, word origin, synonyms, and antonyms

Each meaning for the word is given a number. Occasionally a word's use is illustrated in a quoted sentence.

Sometimes a word can be used as more than one part of speech (*regard*, for instance, can be used as either a verb or a noun). In such a case, all the meanings for one part of speech are given before all the meanings for another, as in the sample entry. The entry also gives idiomatic uses of the word.

The origin of the word, called its *etymology*, appears in brackets after all the meanings (in some dictionaries it appears before the meanings).

Synonyms, words similar in meaning to the main entry, are frequently listed. In the sample entry, the dictionary draws distinctions in meaning among the various synonyms. Antonyms, which do not appear in the sample

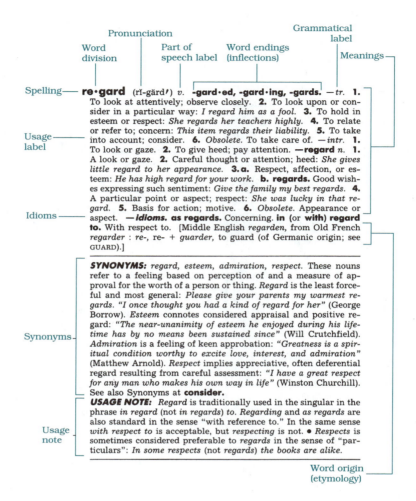

Pronunciation

Grammatical label

Word division

Part of speech label

Word endings (inflections)

Meanings

Spelling——— **re·gard** (rĭ-gärd′) *v.* **-gard·ed, -gard·ing, -gards.** —*tr.* **1.** To look at attentively; observe closely. **2.** To look upon or consider in a particular way: *I regard him as a fool.* **3.** To hold in esteem or respect: *She regards her teachers highly.* **4.** To relate or refer to; concern: *This item regards their liability.* **5.** To take into account; consider. **6.** *Obsolete.* To take care of. —*intr.* **1.** To look or gaze. **2.** To give heed; pay attention. —**regard** *n.* **1.** A look or gaze. **2.** Careful thought or attention; heed: *She gives little regard to her appearance.* **3. a.** Respect, affection, or esteem: *He has high regard for your work.* **b. regards.** Good wishes expressing such sentiment: *Give the family my best regards.* **4.** A particular point or aspect; respect: *She was lucky in that regard.* **5.** Basis for action; motive. **6.** *Obsolete.* Appearance or aspect. —**idioms. as regards.** Concerning. **in** (or **with**) **regard to.** With respect to. [Middle English *regarden,* from Old French *regarder : re-,* re- + *guarder,* to guard (of Germanic origin; see GUARD).]

Usage label

Idioms

SYNONYMS: *regard, esteem, admiration, respect.* These nouns refer to a feeling based on perception of and a measure of approval for the worth of a person or thing. *Regard* is the least forceful and most general: *Please give your parents my warmest regards.* "I once thought you had a kind of regard for her" (George Borrow). *Esteem* connotes considered appraisal and positive regard: "*The near-unanimity of esteem he enjoyed during his lifetime has by no means been sustained since*" (Will Crutchfield). *Admiration* is a feeling of keen approbation: "*Greatness is a spiritual condition worthy to excite love, interest, and admiration*" (Matthew Arnold). *Respect* implies appreciative, often deferential regard resulting from careful assessment: "*I have a great respect for any man who makes his own way in life*" (Winston Churchill). See also Synonyms at **consider.**

Synonyms

USAGE NOTE: *Regard* is traditionally used in the singular in the phrase *in regard* (not *in regards*) *to. Regarding* and *as regards* are also standard in the sense "with reference to." In the same sense *with respect to* is acceptable, but *respecting* is not. • *Respects* is sometimes considered preferable to *regards* in the sense of "particulars": *In some respects* (not *regards*) *the books are alike.*

Usage note

Word origin (etymology)

entry, are words having a meaning opposite from that of the main entry.

Usage

Usage labels indicate when, where, or under what conditions a particular meaning for a word is appropriately used. Common labels are *informal* (or *colloquial*), *slang, nonstandard, dialect, obsolete, archaic, poetic,* and *British.* In the sample entry, two meanings of *regard* are labeled *obsolete* because they are no longer in use.

Dictionaries sometimes include usage notes as well. In the sample entry, the dictionary offers advice on several uses of *regard* not specifically covered by the meanings. Such advice is based on the opinions of many experts and on actual usage in current magazines, newspapers, and books.

43b Discriminate between words that sound alike but have different meanings.

Words that sound alike or nearly alike but have different meanings and spellings are called homophones. The following sets of words are so commonly confused that a good proofreader will double-check their every use.

affect (verb: "to exert an influence")
effect (verb: "to accomplish"; noun: "result")

its (possessive pronoun: "of or belonging to it")
it's (contraction for "it is")

loose (adjective: "free, not securely attached")
lose (verb: "to fail to keep, to be deprived of")

principal (adjective: "most important"; noun: "head of a school")
principle (noun: "a general or fundamental truth")

their (possessive pronoun: "belonging to them")
they're (contraction for "they are")
there (adverb: "that place or position")

who's (contraction for "who is")
whose (possessive form of "who")

your (possessive form of "you")
you're (contraction of "you are")

To check for correct use of these and other commonly confused words, consult the Glossary of Usage, which begins on page 414.

43c Become familiar with the major spelling rules.

1. Use *i* before *e* except after *c* or when sounded like the letter *a*, as in *neighbor* and *weigh*.

i BEFORE *e*	relieve, believe, sieve, frieze
e BEFORE *i*	receive, deceive, sleigh, freight, eight
EXCEPTIONS	seize, either, weird, height, foreign, leisure

2. Generally, drop a final silent -*e* when adding a suffix that begins with a vowel. Keep the final -*e* if the suffix begins with a consonant.

desire, desiring; remove, removable

achieve, achievement; care, careful

Words such as *argument, truly,* and *changeable* are exceptions.

3. When adding -*s* or -*d* to words ending in -*y*, ordinarily change the -*y* to -*ie* when the -*y* is preceded by a consonant but not when it is preceded by a vowel.

comedy, comedies; dry, dried

monkey, monkeys; play, played

With proper names ending in -*y*, however, do not change the -*y* to -*i* even if it is preceded by a consonant: *Dougherty, the Doughertys.*

4. If a final consonant is preceded by a single vowel *and* the consonant ends a one-syllable word or a stressed syllable, double the consonant when adding a suffix beginning with a vowel.

bet, betting; commit, committed; occur, occurrence

5. Add -*s* to form the plural of most nouns; add -*es* to singular nouns ending in -*s, -sh, -ch,* and -*x.*

table, tables; paper, papers

church, churches; dish, dishes

Ordinarily add -*s* to nouns ending in -*o* when the -*o* is preceded by a vowel. Add -*es* when it is preceded by a consonant.

radio, radios; video, videos

hero, heroes; tomato, tomatoes

To form the plural of a hyphenated compound word, add the -*s* to the chief word even if it does not appear at the end.

mother-in-law, mothers-in-law

NOTE: English words derived from other languages such as Latin or French sometimes form the plural as they would in their original language.

medium, media; criterion, criteria; beau, beaux

ESL

Spelling may vary slightly among English-speaking countries. This can prove particularly confusing for ESL students, who may have learned British or Canadian English. Following is a list of some common words spelled differently in American and British English. Consult a dictionary for others.

AMERICAN	BRITISH
canceled, traveled	cancelled, travelled
color, humor	colour, humour
judgment	judgement
check	cheque
realize, apologize	realise, apologise
defense	defence
anemia, anesthetic	anaemia, anaesthetic
theater, center	theatre, centre
fetus	foetus
mold, smolder	mould, smoulder
civilization	civilisation
connection, inflection	connexion, inflexion
licorice	liquorice

43d   Be alert to commonly misspelled words.

absence	benefited	eligible	incredible	phenomenon	sergeant
academic	bureau	embarrass	indispensable	physically	siege
accidentally	business	emphasize	inevitable	picnicking	similar
accommodate	calendar	entirely	intelligence	playwright	sincerely
achievement	candidate	environment	irrelevant	practically	sophomore
acknowledge	cemetery	especially	irresistible	precede	strictly
acquaintance	changeable	exaggerated	knowledge	preference	subtly
acquire	column	exercise	license	preferred	succeed
address	commitment	exhaust	lightning	prejudice	surprise
all right	committed	existence	loneliness	prevalent	thorough
amateur	committee	extraordinary	maintenance	privilege	tragedy
analyze	competitive	extremely	maneuver	proceed	transferred
answer	conceivable	familiar	marriage	professor	tries
apparently	conferred	fascinate	mathematics	pronunciation	truly
appearance	conqueror	February	mischievous	quiet	unnecessarily
arctic	conscience	foreign	necessary	quite	usually
argument	conscientious	forty	noticeable	quizzes	vacuum
arithmetic	conscious	fourth	occasion	receive	vengeance
arrangement	criticism	friend	occurred	referred	villain
ascend	criticize	government	occurrence	restaurant	weird
athlete	decision	grammar	pamphlet	rhythm	whether
athletics	definitely	guard	parallel	roommate	writing
attendance	descendant	harass	particularly	sandwich	
basically	dictionary	height	pastime	schedule	
beginning	disastrous	humorous	permissible	seize	
believe	eighth	incidentally	perseverance	separate	

44   The hyphen

GRAMMAR CHECKERS can flag some, but not all, missing or misused hyphens. For example, the programs can tell you that a hyphen is needed in fractions and compound numbers, such as *two-thirds* and *sixty-four*. They can also tell you how to spell certain compound words, such as *breakup* (not *break-up*).

44a   Consult the dictionary to determine how to treat a compound word.

The dictionary will tell you whether to treat a compound word as a hyphenated compound (*water-repellent*), one word (*waterproof*), or two words (*water table*). If the compound word is not in the dictionary, treat it as two words.

▶ The prosecutor chose not to cross ‿ examine any

witnesses.

▶ Grandma kept a small note book in her apron

pocket.

▶ Alice walked through the looking/glass into a

backward world.

44b   Use a hyphen to connect two or more words functioning together as an adjective before a noun.

▶ Mrs. Douglas gave Toshiko a seashell and some

newspaper ‿ wrapped fish to take home to her

mother.

▶ Priscilla Hood is not yet a well ‿ known candidate.

Newspaper-wrapped and *well-known* are adjectives used before the nouns *fish* and *candidate*.

Generally, do not use a hyphen when such compounds follow the noun.

▶ After our television campaign, Priscilla Hood will

be well/known.

Do not use a hyphen to connect *-ly* adverbs to the words they modify.

▶ A slowly/moving truck tied up traffic.

NOTE: In a series, hyphens are suspended.

Do you prefer first-, second-, or third-class tickets?

44c Hyphenate the written form of fractions and of compound numbers from twenty-one to ninety-nine.

▶ One – fourth of my income goes to pay off the

national debt.

44d Use a hyphen with the prefixes *all-*, *ex-* (meaning "former"), and *self-* and with the suffix *-elect.*

▶ The charity is funneling more money into

self – help projects.

▶ Anne King is our club's president – elect.

44e A hyphen is used in some words to avoid ambiguity or to separate awkward double or triple letters.

Without the hyphen there would be no way to distinguish between words such as *re-creation* and *recreation.*

Bicycling in the country is my favorite recreation.

The film was praised for its astonishing re-creation of nineteenth-century London.

Hyphens are sometimes used to separate awkward double or triple letters in compound words (*anti-intellectual, cross-stitch*). Always check a dictionary for the standard form of the word.

44f If a word must be divided at the end of a line, divide it correctly.

1. Divide words between syllables.

▶ When I returned from overseas, I didn't ~~reco-~~ recog-
~~nize~~
~~gnize~~ nize one face on the magazine covers.

2. Never divide one-syllable words.

▶ He didn't have the courage or the ~~stren-~~ strength
~~gth~~ to open the door.

3. Never divide a word so that a single letter stands alone at the end of a line or fewer than three letters begin a line.

▶ She'll bring her brother with her when she comes ~~a-~~ again.
~~gain.~~

▶ As audience to *The Mousetrap*, Hamlet is a ~~watch-~~ watcher
~~er~~ watching watchers.

4. When dividing a compound word at the end of a line, either make the break between the words that form the compound or put the whole word on the next line.

▶ My niece is determined to become a long-~~dis-~~ distance
~~tance~~ runner when she grows up.

5. To divide long e-mail and Internet addresses, do not use a hyphen. Break the address before a punctuation mark, like this:

Libweb can be reached at http://sunsite .berkeley.edu.Libweb.

Notice that the second line begins with the punctuation mark.

45   Capital letters

In addition to the rules in this section, you can use a good dictionary to tell you when to use capital letters.

> **GRAMMAR CHECKERS** remind you that sentences should begin with capital letters and that some words, such as *Cherokee*, are proper nouns. Many words, however, should be capitalized only in certain contexts, and you must determine when to do so. The program, for example, will not know that *north pole* should be capitalized.

45a   Capitalize proper nouns and words derived from them; do not capitalize common nouns.

Proper nouns are the names of specific persons, places, and things. All other nouns are common nouns. The following types of words are usually capitalized: names for the deity, religions, religious followers, sacred books; words of family relationship used as names; particular places; nationalities and their languages, races, tribes; educational institutions, departments, degrees, particular courses; government departments, organizations, political parties; historical movements, periods, events, documents; specific electronic sources; and trade names.

PROPER NOUNS	COMMON NOUNS
God (used as a name)	a god
Book of Jeremiah	a book
Uncle Pedro	my uncle
Father (used as a name)	my father
Lake Superior	a picturesque lake
the Capital Center	a center for advanced studies
the South	a southern state
Japan, a Japanese garden	an ornamental garden
University of Wisconsin	a good university
Geology 101	geology
Environmental Protection Agency	a federal agency
Phi Kappa Psi	a fraternity
a Democrat	an independent
the Enlightenment	the eighteenth century
the Declaration of Independence	a treaty

the World Wide Web, the Web	a home page
the Internet, the Net	a computer network
Internet Public Library	an online reference site
Kleenex	a tissue

Months, holidays, and days of the week are treated as proper nouns; the seasons and numbers of the days of the month are not.

> Our academic year begins on a Tuesday in early September, right after Labor Day.

> My mother's birthday is in early summer, on the second of June.

Names of school subjects are capitalized only if they are names of languages. Names of particular courses are capitalized.

> This semester Austin is taking math, geography, geology, French, and English.

> Professor Anderson offers Modern American Fiction 501 to graduate students.

Words derived from proper nouns, such as *European* and *Spanish*, are capitalized.

CAUTION: Do not capitalize common nouns to make them seem important: *Our company is currently hiring computer programmers* (not *Company, Computer Programmers*).

45b   Capitalize titles of persons when used as part of a proper name but usually not when used alone.

> Professor Margaret Barnes; Dr. Harold Stevens; John Scott Williams, Jr.; Anne Tilton, LL.D.

> District Attorney Marshall was reprimanded for badgering the witness.

> The district attorney was elected for a two-year term.

Usage varies when the title of an important public figure is used alone: *The president* [or *President*] *vetoed the bill.*

45c Capitalize the first, last, and all major words in titles and subtitles of works such as books, articles, songs, and online documents.

In both titles and subtitles, major words such as nouns, pronouns, verbs, adjectives, and adverbs should be capitalized. Minor words such as articles, prepositions, and coordinating conjunctions are not capitalized unless they are the first or last word of a title or subtitle. Capitalize the second part of a hyphenated term in a title if it is a major word but not if it is a minor word.

To see why some of the following titles are italicized and some are put in quotation marks, see 42a and 37d.

> *The Impossible Theater: A Manifesto*
> *The F-Plan Diet*
> "Fire and Ice"
> "I Want to Hold Your Hand"
> The Canadian Green Page

Capitalize chapter titles and the titles of other major divisions of a work following the same guidelines used for titles of complete works.

> "Work and Play" in Santayana's *The Nature of Beauty*

45d Capitalize the first word of a sentence.

Obviously the first word of a sentence should be capitalized.

> When lightning struck the house, the chimney collapsed.

When a sentence appears within parentheses, capitalize its first word unless the parentheses appear within another sentence.

> Early detection of breast cancer significantly increases survival rates. (See table 2.)

> Early detection of breast cancer significantly increases survival rates (see table 2).

45e Capitalize the first word of a quoted sentence but not a quoted phrase.

> In *Time* magazine Robert Hughes writes, "There are only about sixty Watteau paintings on whose authenticity all experts agree."

> Russell Baker has written that in our country sports are "the opiate of the masses."

If a quoted sentence is interrupted by explanatory words, do not capitalize the first word after the interruption. (See 37f.)

> "If you wanted to go out," he said sharply, "you should have told me."

When quoting poetry, copy the poet's capitalization exactly. Many poets capitalize the first word of every line of poetry; a few contemporary poets dismiss capitalization altogether.

> When I consider everything that grows
> Holds in perfection but a little moment
> —Shakespeare

45f Do not capitalize the first word after a colon unless it begins an independent clause, in which case capitalization is optional.

> Most of the bar's patrons can be divided into two groups: the occasional after-work socializers and the nothing-to-go-home-to regulars.

> This we are forced to conclude: The [*or* the] federal government is needed to protect the rights of minorities.

45g Capitalize abbreviations for departments and agencies of government, other organizations, and corporations; capitalize the call letters of radio and television stations.

> EPA, FBI, OPEC, IBM, WCRB, KNBC-TV

EXERCISE 43/44/45–1 Spelling, the hyphen, and capital letters: Guided practice

Edit the following paragraphs to correct misspellings and errors in the use of the hyphen and capital letters. Rule numbers in the margin refer to appropriate rules in sections 43, 44, and 45. The first revision has been done for you, and a revision of these paragraphs appears in the back of the book.

Columbus's return to Spain from his first exploration was difficult. The *Niña*
and the *Pinta* were ~~seperated,~~ *separated,* the *Niña* almost sank, and the governor on the island   **43d**
of Santa María put Columbus's whole crew in jail. It seemed a miracle that both
boats arrived in the harbor at Palos on the same day.

As difficult as that return was, the reception at court quite made up for it.
Columbus certainly made an all out effort to impress the court, the city, and the en-   **44d**
tire country. Lavishly attired, he recieved a grand welcome as he led his entourage   **43c**
into Barcelona, the spanish capital. It must have been a sight to behold: A proces-   **45a, 45f**
sion like none Barcelona had ever seen before. Leading the parade was a gaudily bedecked horse carrying Columbus, followed by six captive "indians" and all the crew.   **45a**
Everyone but Columbus was carrying boxes, baskets, and cages full of interesting
and exotic items.

When the group reached the throne room, King Ferdinand and Queen Isabella stood up to greet Columbus formally and to admire his apron covered cap-   **44b**
tives. Columbus asked the royal couple to except gifts of plants, shells, darts, thread,   **43b**
and gold. As intrigued as they were with the other gifts, King Ferdinand and Queen
Isabella basicly wanted gold. Luckily, Columbus had collected enough samples of it   **43d**
to satisfy them.

By the end of the first week home, Columbus had such prestige that everyone wanted to accomodate the wishes of the Italian sailor at the court of Spain.   **43d**
Columbus had no doubt that he would receive a Commission for a second voyage of   **45a**
exploration or even colonization.

EXERCISE 43/44/45 – 2 Spelling

Edit the following sentences to correct spelling errors. (Hint: There are ten errors.) Example:

> *incredibly*   *believed*
> Others may have considered him ~~incredibally~~ lucky, but Columbus ~~beleived~~ he had been
> called by God to be the one to find a new way to the Indies.

1. To begin with, he was born in Genoa, Italy, the best place concievable for someone who wanted to be in the sailing busness, since Genoa was a major seaport.

2. Other people said his being born there was all "just chance"; Columbus prefered to think that it was part of God's arrangment for him.

3. He was not suprised to be the sole survivor of a shipwreck that occured when he was twenty-five.

4. Weather others excepted the idea or not, Columbus knew he survived such a disasterous event because God had plans for him.

5. He thought that even his name emphasized his calling: *Christopher* means "Christ-bearing," and he would take Christ's name to the "heatherns" in India.

EXERCISE 43/44/45 – 3 The hyphen

The writer of the following sentences got hyphen-happy. Remove seven of the twelve hyphens. If a sentence needs no hyphens removed, mark it "OK." Example:

> Columbus's all-consuming goal made him think that God/himself had worked/out the fortu-itous marriage Columbus made in 1478.

1. Marrying into a noble-family when he was thirty-three gave Columbus direct-access to the king of Portugal.

2. When the king firmly-declined Columbus's request to finance an exploratory-voyage, this well-known sailor decided he was supposed to go to Spain.

3. Queen Isabella was anxious to make everyone into a practicing-Christian; because Columbus was religious, she did not consider the voyage a half-witted proposal.

4. After his discovery of "India," Columbus received confirmation of his self-given title, Admiral of the Ocean Seas and Viceroy of the Indies.

5. When the *Santa María* was wrecked, Columbus saw the incident as his God-given opportunity to go back post-haste to Spain, get more men, and return to this newly-found land.

EXERCISE 43/44/45–4 Capital letters

Edit the following paragraphs to correct errors in capitalization. The first sentence has been edited for you. You should find ten more errors.

If Columbus had made his return trip first, he might not have been so eager to set out for the ~~indies~~ *Indies*. The voyage turned out all right, but it had its bad times.

To begin with, the *Niña* and the *Pinta* were separated on the way back to Spain. The weather was very bad, especially when the two ships ran into a storm west of the Azores. The *Niña* almost sank. Columbus was so sure it was going down that he put a record of his Discoveries in a small barrel, sealed it completely, and threw it overboard. That way, if the ship went down, there was still a chance that someone would learn of his discoveries. Actually, the ship made it to Santa María, a portuguese island. The authorities there thought Columbus was lying about his adventures and arrested the crew. The crew was released only because Columbus threatened to shoot up the town.

The *Niña* was thrown off course again, but then Columbus's luck turned. The boat came into Lisbon, and Columbus was a guest of king John II for a brief time before he took off for Spain again. Finally, the *Niña* made it home. On March 15, 1493, it sailed into the Harbor at Palos. The *Pinta* arrived shortly afterward on the same day. Such a coincidence certainly seemed to be a sign of divine approval and delighted Columbus. When queen Isabella saw what Columbus had brought back, she was impressed. She thought that god had surely had a hand in the matter. Certainly many influences had played a part in his success that Spring. Even Marco Polo's book *Description of the world* had played a role: Getting Columbus started on the journey. Columbus was convinced that his life was just one miracle after another. "i've been chosen," he might have said. "God has chosen me."

EXERCISE 43/44/45–5 Spelling, the hyphen, and capital letters: Guided review

Correct any errors in spelling, the hyphen, and capital letters in the following paragraphs. Rule numbers in the margin refer to appropriate rules in sections 43, 44, and 45. The first revision has been done for you, and a suggested revision of these paragraphs appears in the back of the book.

After being feted, feasted, and honored on his return from his first voyage

across the ocean, Columbus must have told and ~~re told~~ *retold* the story of his trip. He   **44a**

would have told listeners how, after the ships had sailed for twenty one days, his   **44c**

men threatened to turn back because they had never sailed so far west before.

Columbus, sure of his special calling as an explorer, promised them that they would

sight land within three days. On the evening of the third day, at ten o'clock, he

thought he saw a light and alerted a nearby servant. Both of them lost sight of it al-

most at once. But at two o'clock the next morning, a cannon shot sounded from the

Pinta. "Land! Land!" cried the sailors. Columbus had kept his promise. No wonder

he began to sign his name with a secret code to show that he was more special then

other people.   **43b**

Retelling the story of his voyage, Columbus would have described the beau-

tiful Island that the ships first landed on. He named it San Salvador. He would have   **45a**

told how, at every island he and his men visited, natives had flocked to the boats to

see the strangers. One day, more than a thousand people had come in just one hour.

Columbus had spent three months exploring and setting up a fort before leaving for

the return trip to Spain. And on their return, eight months later, he and his crew

had recieved a royal welcome.   **43c**

Yes, he had had a few problems on the trip out, and the return trip had been

very hard, but one set of memories was indelibly imprinted on Columbus's brain:

The memories of that remarkably successful first voyage.   **45f**

Unit review (40–45): Mechanics

This essay has ten errors in spelling and mechanics. Rule numbers in the margin refer to appropriate rules in sections 40–45. The first revision has been done for you.

Columbus made an all-out effort to find the Indies—India, China, the East   *44d*

Indies, and Japan. Instead, he found Cuba, Venezuela, the Bahamas, and the coasts

of South and Central America. Unable to find gold, he captured 5 hundred natives   *41a*

and had them shipped back to Spain to be sold as slaves. He punished the natives

so severely when they did not bring him gold that in two years one third of them ran   *44c*

away or were killed or sold. Things went from bad to worse; e.g., many settlers died   *40d*

of illness, and some went back to Spain with bad reports of his governance. Con-

vinced that God was unhappy with him for some transgression, Columbus returned

to Spain wearing a monk's course garb and walking humbly. People gave him a new   *43b*

title, Columbus, admiral of the Mosquitoes.   *45b*

Ferdinand and Isabella gave him another opportunity, though, and on May

thirtieth, 1498, Columbus set out again. The voyage was a disaster, with Columbus   *41b*

ending up back in Spain, this time in chains. Columbus got one more chance, but

hurricanes and storms plagued him. He wrote, "other tempests have I seen, but none

so long or so grim as this." He must by now have realized that Dr. Toscanelli did not   *45e*

no his geography very well. Yet "Sail on!" was still his answer to *every* setback.   *43b*

When Columbus got back to Spain, sick and exhausted, queen Isabella died   *45b, 42e*

before he could see her. Columbus died still insisting he had found the Indies. He

had not, of course. He had done far more: He had discovered a new world.

Grammar Basics

46   Introduction to grammar basics

So far, this book has dealt mainly with grammar rules and offered practical advice about correctness. For example, here are some rules of grammar taken from Sections 19–31 of this book:

> Repair sentence fragments.
>
> Make subjects and verbs agree.
>
> Distinguish between pronouns such as *I* and *me.*
>
> Choose adjectives and adverbs with care.
>
> Use the correct form of irregular verbs.
>
> Do not repeat an object or adverb in an adjective clause.

Sections 46–50 describe the building blocks of the English language:

> —parts of speech, such as pronouns and adverbs
>
> —parts of sentences, such as subjects, verbs, and objects
>
> —word groups such as prepositional phrases and subordinate clauses

When you can identify the basic building blocks of a sentence, you are in a good position to understand and apply the rules of grammar, many of which include terms such as *pronoun, adverb, subject, verb, object, phrase,* and *clause.*

47   Parts of speech

Traditional grammar recognizes eight parts of speech: noun, pronoun, verb, adjective, adverb, preposition, conjunction, and interjection. Many words can function as more than one part of speech. For example, depending on its use in a sentence, the word *paint* can be a noun (*The paint is wet*) or a verb (*Please paint the ceiling next*).

A quick-reference chart of the parts of speech appears on page 375.

47a Nouns

As most schoolchildren can attest, a noun is the name of a person, place, or thing.

> The *cat* in *gloves* catches no *mice.*

In addition to the traditional definition of a noun, grammarians describe a noun as follows:

— the kind of word that is often marked with an article (a *spoon*, an *apple*, the *newspaper*)

— the kind of word that can usually be made plural (one *cat*, two *cats*) or possessive (the *cat's* paw)

— the kind of word that when derived from another word typically takes one of these endings: play*er*, just*ice*, happi*ness*, divi*sion*, guid*ance*, refer*ence*, pave*ment*, child*hood*, king*dom*, agen*cy*, tour*ist*, sincer*ity*, censor*ship*

— the kind of word that can fill one of these positions in a sentence: subject, direct object, indirect object, subject complement, object complement, object of the preposition (See 48a and 48b.)

Nouns, in other words, may be identified as much by their form and function as by their meaning.

Nouns sometimes function as adjectives modifying other nouns. Because of their dual function, nouns used in this manner may be called *noun/adjectives.*

> You can't make a *silk* purse out of a *sow's* ear.

Nouns are classified for a variety of purposes. When capitalization is the issue, we speak of *proper* versus *common nouns* (see 45a). If the problem is one of word choice, we may speak of *concrete* versus *abstract nouns* (see 18b). The distinction between *count nouns* and *noncount nouns* is useful primarily for non-native speakers of English (see 30a and 30b). The term *collective noun* refers to a set of nouns that may cause problems with subject-verb or pronoun-antecedent agreement (see 21f and 22b).

47b Pronouns

There are thousands of nouns, and new ones come into the language every year. This is not true of pronouns, which number about one hundred and are extremely resistant to change. Most of the pronouns in English are listed in this section.

A pronoun is a word used in place of a noun. Usually the pronoun substitutes for a specific noun, known as its *antecedent.*

> When the *wheel* squeaks, *it* is greased.

Although most pronouns function as substitutes for nouns, some can function as adjectives modifying nouns.

> *This* hanging will surely be a lesson to me.

Because they have the form of a pronoun and the function of an adjective, such pronouns may be called *pronoun/adjectives.*

Pronouns are classified as personal, possessive, intensive and reflexive, relative, interrogative, demonstrative, indefinite, and reciprocal.

PERSONAL PRONOUNS Personal pronouns refer to specific persons or things. They always function as noun equivalents.

> *Singular:* I, me, you, she, her, he, him, it
>
> *Plural:* we, us, you, they, them

POSSESSIVE PRONOUNS Possessive pronouns indicate ownership.

> *Singular:* my, mine, your, yours, her, hers, his, its
>
> *Plural:* our, ours, your, yours, their, theirs

Some of these possessive pronouns function as adjectives modifying nouns: *my, your, his, her, its, our, their.*

INTENSIVE AND REFLEXIVE PRONOUNS Intensive pronouns emphasize a noun or another pronoun (The senator *herself* met us at the door). Reflexive pronouns, which have the same form as intensive pronouns, name a receiver of an action identical with the doer of the action (Paula cut *herself*).

Singular: myself, yourself, himself, herself, itself

Plural: ourselves, yourselves, themselves

RELATIVE PRONOUNS Relative pronouns introduce subordinate clauses functioning as adjectives (The man *who robbed us* was never caught). In addition to introducing the clause, the relative pronoun, in this case *who*, points back to a noun or pronoun that the clause modifies (*man*). (See 49b.)

who, whom, whose, which, that

Some grammarians also treat *whichever, whoever, whomever, what,* and *whatever* as relative pronouns. These words introduce noun clauses; they do not point back to a noun or pronoun. (See 49b.)

INTERROGATIVE PRONOUNS Interrogative pronouns introduce questions (*Who* is expected to win the election?).

who, whom, whose, which, what

DEMONSTRATIVE PRONOUNS Demonstrative pronouns identify or point to nouns. Frequently they function as adjectives (*This* chair is my favorite), but they may also function as noun equivalents (*This* is my favorite chair).

this, that, these, those

INDEFINITE PRONOUNS Indefinite pronouns refer to nonspecific persons or things. Most are always singular (*everyone, each*); some are always plural (*both, many*); a few may be singular or plural (see 21e). Most indefinite pronouns function as noun equivalents (*Something* is burning), but some can also function as adjectives (*All* campers must check in at the lodge).

all	each	many	one
another	either	neither	several
any	everybody	nobody	some
anybody	everyone	none	somebody
anyone	everything	no one	someone
anything	few	nothing	something
both			

RECIPROCAL PRONOUNS Reciprocal pronouns refer to individual parts of a plural antecedent (By turns, we helped *each other* through college).

each other, one another

NOTE: Pronouns cause a variety of problems for writers. See pronoun-antecedent agreement (22), pronoun reference (23), distinguishing between pronouns such as *I* and *me* (24), and distinguishing between *who* and *whom* (25).

47c Verbs

The verb of a sentence usually expresses action (*jump, think*) or being (*is, become*). It is composed of a main verb possibly preceded by one or more helping verbs:

               MV
The best fish *swim* near the bottom.

           HV   **MV**
A marriage *is* not *built* in a day.

          HV **HV**   **MV**
Even God *has been defended* with nonsense.

Notice that words can intervene between the helping and the main verb (*is* not *built*).

Helping verbs

There are twenty-three helping verbs in English: forms of *have, do,* and *be,* which may also function as main verbs; and nine modals, which function only as helping verbs. The forms of *have, do,* and *be* change form to indicate tense; the nine modals do not.

FORMS OF *HAVE, DO,* AND *BE*
have, has, had

do, does, did

be, am, is, are, was, were, being, been

MODALS

can, could, may, might, must, shall, should, will, would

The phrase *ought to* is often classified as a modal as well.

Main verbs

The main verb of a sentence is always the kind of word that would change form if put into these test sentences:

BASE FORM	Usually I (*walk, ride*).
PAST TENSE	Yesterday I (*walked, rode*).
PAST PARTICIPLE	I have (*walked, ridden*) many times before.
PRESENT PARTICIPLE	I am (*walking, riding*) right now.
-S FORM	Usually he/she/it (*walks, rides*).

If a word doesn't change form when slipped into these test sentences, you can be certain that it is not a main verb. For example, the noun *revolution,* though it may seem to suggest an action, can never function as a main verb. Just try to make it behave like one (*Today I revolution . . . Yesterday I revolutioned . . .*) and you'll see why.

When both the past-tense and the past-participle forms of a verb end in *-ed,* the verb is regular (*walked, walked*). Otherwise, the verb is irregular (*rode, ridden*). (See 27a.)

The verb *be* is highly irregular, having eight forms instead of the usual five: the base form *be;* the present-tense forms *am, is,* and *are;* the past-tense forms *was* and *were;* the present participle *being;* and the past participle *been.*

Helping verbs combine with the various forms of main verbs to create tenses. For a survey of tenses, see 28a.

NOTE: Some verbs are followed by words that look like prepositions but are so closely associated with the verb that they are a part of its meaning. These words are known as *particles.* Common verb-particle combinations include *bring up, call off, drop off, give in, look up, run into,* and *take off.*

A lot of parents *pack up* their troubles and *send* them *off* to camp.

—Raymond Duncan

NOTE: Verbs cause many problems for writers. See subject-verb agreement (21), standard English verb forms (27), verb tense, mood, and voice (28), and ESL problems with verbs (29).

47d   Adjectives

An adjective is a word used to modify, or describe, a noun or pronoun. An adjective usually answers one of these questions: Which one? What kind of? How many?

> the *lame* elephant [Which elephant?]
>
> *valuable old* stamps [What kind of stamps?]
>
> *sixteen* candles [How many candles?]

Grammarians also define adjectives according to their form and their typical position in a sentence, as follows:

— the kind of word that usually comes before a noun in a noun phrase (a *frisky* puppy, an *amiable young* man)

— the kind of word that can follow a linking verb and describe the subject (The ship was *unsinkable;* Talk is *cheap*) (See 48b.)

— the kind of word that when derived from another part of speech typically takes one of these endings: wonder*ful,* courte*ous,* luck*y,* fool*ish,* pleasur*able,* colon*ial,* help*less,* defens*ible,* urg*ent,* disgust*ing,* friend*ly,* spectacul*ar,* secre*tive*

The definite article *the* and the indefinite articles *a* and *an* are also classified as adjectives.

Some possessive, demonstrative, and indefinite pronouns can function as adjectives: *their, its, this* (see 47b).

NOTE: Writers sometimes misuse adjectives (see 26b). Speakers of English as a second language often encounter problems with the articles *a, an,* and *the* and occasionally have trouble placing adjectives correctly (see 30 and 31d).

47e Adverbs

An adverb is a word used to modify, or qualify, a verb (or verbal), an adjective, or another adverb. It usually answers one of these questions: When? Where? How? Why? Under what conditions? To what degree?

> Pull *gently* at a weak rope. [Pull how?]

> Read the best books *first*. [Read when?]

Adverbs that modify a verb are also defined according to their form and their typical position in a sentence, as follows:

—the kind of word that can appear nearly anywhere in a sentence and is often movable (he *sometimes* jogged after work; *sometimes* he jogged after work)

—the kind of word that when derived from an adjective typically takes an *-ly* ending (nice, nice*ly;* profound, profound*ly*)

Adverbs modifying adjectives or other adverbs usually intensify or limit the intensity of the word they modify.

> Be *extremely* good, and you will be *very* lonesome.

Adverbs modifying adjectives and other adverbs are not movable. We can't say "Be good *extremely*" or "*Extremely* be good."

The negators *not* and *never* are classified as adverbs. A word such as *cannot* contains the helping verb *can* and the adverb *not*. A contraction such as *can't* contains the helping verb *can* and a contracted form of the adverb *not*.

Adverbs can modify prepositions (Helen left *just* before midnight), prepositional phrases (The budget is *barely* on target), subordinate clauses (We will try to attend, *especially* if you will be there), or whole sentences (*Certainly* Joe did not intend to insult you).

NOTE: Writers sometimes misuse adverbs (see 26a). Speakers of English as a second language may have trouble placing adverbs correctly (see 31d).

47f Prepositions

A preposition is a word placed before a noun or pronoun to form a phrase modifying another word in the sentence. The prepositional phrase nearly always functions as an adjective or as an adverb. (See 49a.)

> The road *to hell* is usually paved *with good intentions.*

To hell functions as an adjective, modifying the noun *road; with good intentions* functions as an adverb, modifying the verb *is paved.*

There are a limited number of prepositions in English. The most common ones are included in the following list.

about	beyond	next	through
above	but	of	throughout
across	by	off	till
after	concerning	on	to
against	considering	onto	toward
along	despite	opposite	under
among	down	out	underneath
around	during	outside	unlike
as	except	over	until
at	for	past	unto
before	from	plus	up
behind	in	regarding	upon
below	inside	respecting	with
beside	into	round	within
besides	like	since	without
between	near	than	

Some prepositions are more than one word long. *Along with, as well as, in addition to,* and *next to* are common examples.

NOTE: Except for certain idiomatic uses (see 18d), prepositions cause few problems for native speakers of English. For second language speakers, however, prepositions can cause considerable difficulty (see 29d and 31f).

47g Conjunctions

Conjunctions join words, phrases, or clauses, and they indicate the relation between the elements joined.

COORDINATING CONJUNCTIONS A coordinating conjunction is used to connect grammatically equal elements. The coordinating conjunctions are *and, but, or, nor, for, so,* and *yet.*

> Poverty is the parent of revolution *and* crime.

> Admire a little ship, *but* put your cargo in a big one.

In the first sentence, *and* connects two nouns; in the second, *but* connects two independent clauses.

CORRELATIVE CONJUNCTIONS   Correlative conjunctions come in pairs: *either . . . or; neither . . . nor; not only . . . but also; whether . . . or; both . . . and.* Like coordinating conjunctions, they connect grammatically equal elements.

> *Either* Jack Sprat *or* his wife could eat no fat.

SUBORDINATING CONJUNCTIONS   A subordinating conjunction introduces a subordinate clause and indicates its relation to the rest of the sentence. (See 49b.) The most common subordinating conjunctions are *after, although, as, as if, because, before, even though, how, if, in order that, once, rather than, since, so that, than, that, though, unless, until, when, where, whether, while,* and *why.*

> *If* you want service, serve yourself.

CONJUNCTIVE ADVERBS   A conjunctive adverb may be used with a semicolon to connect independent clauses; it usually serves as a transition between the clauses. The most common conjunctive adverbs are *consequently, finally, furthermore, however, moreover, nevertheless, similarly, then, therefore,* and *thus.* (See the chart on p. 375 for a more complete list.)

> When we want to murder a tiger, we call it sport; *however,* when the tiger wants to murder us, we call it ferocity.

NOTE: The ability to distinguish between conjunctive adverbs and coordinating conjunctions will help you avoid run-on sentences and make punctuation decisions (see 20, 32a, and 32b). The ability to recognize subordinating conjunctions will help you avoid sentence fragments (see 19).

47h   Interjections

An interjection is a word used to express surprise or emotion (*Oh! Hey! Wow!*).

Parts of speech

A **NOUN** names a person, place, thing, or idea.

    N   N   N
Repetition does not transform a *lie* into *truth.*

A **PRONOUN** substitutes for a noun.

                                   PN PN   PN
When the gods wish to punish *us, they* heed *our* prayers.

Personal pronouns: I, me, you, he, him, she, her, it, we, us, they, them

Possessive pronouns: my, mine, your, yours, her, hers, his, its, our, ours, their, theirs

Intensive and reflexive pronouns: myself, yourself, himself, herself, itself, ourselves, yourselves, themselves

Relative pronouns: that, which, who, whom, whose

Interrogative pronouns: who, whom, whose, which, what

Demonstrative pronouns: this, that, these, those

Indefinite pronouns: all, another, any, anybody, anyone, anything, both, each, either, everybody, everyone, everything, few, many, neither, nobody, none, no one, nothing, one, several, some, somebody, someone, something

Reciprocal pronouns: each other, one another

A **HELPING VERB** comes before a main verb.

Modals: can, could, may, might, must, shall, should, will, would (*also* ought to)

Forms of be: be, am, is, are, was, were, being, been

Forms of have: have, has, had

Forms of do: do, does, did

(The forms of *be, have,* and *do* may also function as main verbs.)

A **MAIN VERB** asserts action, being, or state of being.

    MV   HV   MV
Charity *begins* at home but *should* not *end* there.

A main verb will always change form when put into these positions in sentences:

Usually I _____ .	(*walk, ride*)
Yesterday I _____ .	(*walked, rode*)
I have _____ many times before.	(*walked, ridden*)
I am _____ right now.	(*walking, riding*)
Usually he _____ .	(*walks, rides*)

There are eight forms of the highly irregular verb *be: be, am, is, are, was, were, being, been.*

An **ADJECTIVE** modifies a noun or pronoun, usually answering one of these questions: Which one? What kind of? How many? The articles *a, an,* and *the* are also adjectives.

    ADJ   ADJ
Useless laws weaken *necessary* ones.

An **ADVERB** modifies a verb, adjective, or adverb, usually answering one of these questions: When? Where? Why? How? Under what conditions? To what degree?

                 ADV ADV
People think *too historically.*

A **PREPOSITION** indicates the relationship between the noun or pronoun that follows it and another word in the sentence.

                P   P
A journey *of* a thousand miles begins *with* a single step.

Common prepositions: about, above, across, after, against, along, among, around, as, at, before, behind, below, beside, besides, between, beyond, but, by, concerning, considering, despite, down, during, except, for, from, in, inside, into, like, near, next, of, off, on, onto, opposite, out, outside, over, past, plus, regarding, respecting, round, since, than, through, throughout, till, to, toward, under, underneath, unlike, until, unto, up, upon, with, within, without

A **CONJUNCTION** connects words or word groups.

Coordinating conjunctions: and, but, or, nor, for, so, yet

Subordinating conjunctions: after, although, as, as if, because, before, even though, how, if, in order that, once, rather than, since, so that, than, that, though, unless, until, when, where, whether, while, why

Correlative conjunctions: either . . . or, neither . . . nor, not only . . . but also, both . . . and, whether . . . or

Conjunctive adverbs: accordingly, also, anyway, besides, certainly, consequently, conversely, finally, furthermore, hence, however, incidentally, indeed, instead, likewise, meanwhile, moreover, nevertheless, next, nonetheless, otherwise, similarly, specifically, still, subsequently, then, therefore, thus

An **INTERJECTION** expresses surprise or emotion. (*Oh! Wow! Hey! Hooray!*)

EXERCISE 47–1 Parts of speech: Preview

In the following paragraph, label the part of speech of each italicized word. Use these codes: noun (N), pronoun (PN), verb (V), adjective (ADJ), adverb (ADV), preposition (P), conjunction (C). The first four words have been marked for you, and answers to this exercise appear in the back of the book.

                         ADV   ADJ   P
           The *somewhat formal* words *of* our Declaration of Independence contain a declaration
       N
and a *promise.* The *final* lines of that declaration *ring* out *like* the Liberty Bell *itself:*

> We, *therefore,* the representatives of the United States of America . . . *do, in* the
>
> name *and* by the authority of the good people of these *colonies,* solemnly *pub-*
>
> *lish* and declare that these United Colonies *are* . . . *free* and independent states.
>
> . . . And for the support *of* this declaration, *with* a *firm reliance* on Divine Prov-
>
> idence, we *mutually* pledge to each other our *lives,* our fortunes, and our
>
> sacred *honor.*

EXERCISE 47–2 Nouns and noun/adjectives

A. Each of the following word groups contains only one noun. Circle the noun. Example:

national   nationwide   (nation)

1. defendable   defend   defenses

2. speaking   speaker   speak

3. just   justice   justly

4. normal   normally   normality

5. repetition   repeating   repeated

B. Each of the following sentences has three nouns or noun/adjectives and a blank for you to put in a fourth. Underline each noun (including noun/adjectives). Then put a noun or a noun/adjective in the blank. Example:

> When they apply for American, *citizenship*, refugee immigrants must study some famous American documents.

6. Schoolchildren and new citizens have similar _____ assignments.

7. They both must learn the _____ of allegiance to the country's flag.

8. Many of these people also memorize the opening words of the _____ of Independence.

9. The Preamble to the Constitution is often assigned, as well as some famous speeches and the national _____.

10. If students pass their _____ on all this, they are promoted; if immigrants pass theirs, they are welcomed into American citizenship.

EXERCISE 47–3 Nouns and noun/adjectives

All of the following paired sentences contain some form of the word *exhibit*. In each pair, circle the letter of the sentence that uses the word *exhibit* as a noun or noun/adjective and be prepared to explain how you know it is a noun. (Hint: There is only one noun/adjective.) Example:

    (a.) The Declaration of Independence is on exhibit at the National Archives in Washington, D.C.

    b. The Archives exhibit the Declaration of Independence for many tourist groups.

1a.   Many people do not realize that the exhibits in the national museums change frequently.

  b.   Each museum exhibits a wide variety of materials.

2a.   Museums can exhibit something of interest to almost any visitor.

  b.   It is impossible to predict which exhibit any one visitor will enjoy.

3a.   Most children prefer an interactive exhibit over any other kind.

  b.   The children can exhibit their own skill in operating the interactive devices.

4a.   Most of the exhibit halls have excellent signs and explanations about what the visitor can see.

  b.   Curators can exhibit rare items safely in specially constructed cases.

5a.   When the museums are exhibiting items borrowed from another place, visitors have a limited time to visit the displays.

  b.   When exhibits contain items from other collections, however, many more people can see and enjoy those items.

EXERCISE 47–4 Pronouns and pronoun/adjectives

A. Circle the five pronouns in each group of words. Example:

	(his)	(they)	under	(whoever)	(no one)	(themselves)
1.	I	she	of	he	ours	everyone
2.	her	me	it	to	whose	many
3.	for	him	you	us	this	someone
4.	they	my	that	we	from	some
5.	in	them	mine	your	these	nothing
6.	at	yours	her	his	all	none
7.	hers	our	its	nobody	another	over
8.	under	myself	their	yours	each	several
9.	from	theirs	who	which	either	something
10.	whom	those	any	both	few	through

B. Underline the pronouns (including pronoun/adjectives) in the following sentences. Except in the example, there are two in each sentence. Example:

> Our Declaration of Independence includes these famous words: "We hold these truths to be self-evident."

11.   Whoever reads the Declaration of Independence finds a message for everyone.

12.   It says that all people are created equal.

13.   Furthermore, the Declaration declares, "They are endowed by their Creator with certain unalienable rights."

14.   "Among these are life, liberty, and the pursuit of happiness" may be its most famous line.

15.   Refugees who apply for citizenship are claiming those rights.

EXERCISE 47–5 Verbs

All of the following paired sentences contain some form of the word *promise*. In each pair, circle the letter of the sentence that uses a form of the word *promise* as a verb. (Hint: The words *promised* and *promising* can sometimes function as adjectives.)

a. The founders of this country made certain promises to each other.

(b.) Each document of this country promises special things to the people who live here.

1a. In a way, the Constitution is a set of promises.

b. The government promises to do certain things for citizens.

2a. In turn, the citizens must promise to obey certain laws.

b. The citizens' promise is just as important as the government's.

3a. Some early citizens thought the Constitution had not promised them enough rights.

b. They thought that the promised rights were not specific enough.

4a. By adding a Bill of Rights to the Constitution, citizens demanded a promise about freedom of religion.

b. The Bill of Rights does indeed promise freedom of religion.

5a. One of the most promising signs of political health in the colonies was their insistence on gaining certain rights.

b. Whenever citizens repeat their oath of allegiance, they are promising anew to honor the Constitution.

EXERCISE 47–6 Adjectives and adverbs

A. Label each of the following words as an adjective (ADJ) or an adverb (ADV). You should find twelve adjectives and eight adverbs. Example:

clean *ADJ*

1. inexpensive _____	8. beautiful _____	15. rich _____
2. very _____	9. sometimes _____	16. lonely _____
3. rude _____	10. political _____	17. oily _____
4. not _____	11. ten _____	18. slowly _____
5. crazy _____	12. never _____	19. always _____
6. lovely _____	13. tired _____	20. common _____
7. extremely _____	14. aloud _____	

B. Label the adjectives (ADJ) and adverbs (ADV) in the following sentences. Ignore the articles *a*, *an*, and *the*. You should find ten adjectives and five adverbs. Example:

                                               ADJ   *ADV*   *ADJ*
The Constitution and the Bill of Rights are separate, but they go together as a single document.

21. The Bill of Rights is the ten amendments that immediately follow the Constitution.

22. The First Amendment is the most familiar of the famous rights.

23. It guarantees religious freedom and freedom of speech for American citizens.

24. It also guarantees freedom of the press, an extremely important freedom in a democratic country.

25. Because representatives to the original Congress valued the right to discuss legislation publicly, the Bill of Rights assures citizens of the right to hold meetings and to petition the federal government.

EXERCISE 47–7 Prepositions and conjunctions

In the following sentences, label all prepositions (P), coordinating conjunctions (CC), and subordinating conjunctions (SUB). The numbers in the brackets after each sentence indicate how many of each you should find. Example:

SUB   P   P   CC
When the Bill of Rights was adopted, it gave to American citizens rights and guarantees none
P   CC
of the colonists or their predecessors had enjoyed. [3P, 2CC, 1SUB]

1. When the founders of the United States wrote the Bill of Rights, they were recalling their past troubles with England. [3P, 1SUB]

2. They were also hoping that this new country and its laws would be different. [1CC, 1SUB]

3. Before the American Revolution, English officers and their men had been quartered in colonists' homes. [2P, 1CC]

4. The colonists often objected, but they could do nothing about the situation. [1P, 1CC]

5. Although they petitioned and appealed, nothing changed. [1CC, 1SUB]

6. Because the colonists objected to this practice, they put a special amendment about it in the Bill of Rights. [4P, 1SUB]

7. That amendment says that the government cannot make people give free room and board to soldiers unless the country is at war. [2P, 1CC, 2SUB]

8. Another problem was that, although the colonists objected, under English rule they and their homes could be searched by any magistrate or his appointees. [2P, 2CC, 2SUB]

9. Another amendment to the Bill of Rights would protect citizens from unreasonable searches; searching a citizen's home would require a warrant. [3P]

10. Because the Bill of Rights was added to the Constitution, Americans are still protected from these and several other intrusions by the government. [4P, 1CC, 1SUB]

EXERCISE 47–8 Parts of speech: Review

In the following paragraph, label the parts of speech of the italicized words. Use these codes: noun (N), pronoun (PN), verb (V), adjective (ADJ), adverb (ADV), preposition (P), conjunction (C). The first four words have been marked for you.

           N   V   P

The *framers* of the Declaration of Independence *did* not always agree *with* each other

ADV

politically, but *they* did *agree* on the hopes *and* fears they had for this *new* nation. Political

affiliation *is* not *important* when citizens realize the promise *of* that original declaration:

> We, therefore, the *representatives* of the United States of America . . . do, in
>
> the name, and *by* the authority of the *good* people of these colonies, *solemnly*
>
> publish and *declare*, that these united colonies are . . . free *and independent*
>
> states. . . . And, *for* the support of this declaration, with a firm reliance on . . .
>
> Divine *Providence*, *we* mutually *pledge* to each other our lives, our *fortunes*, and
>
> our *sacred* honor.

48 Sentence patterns

Most English sentences flow from subject to verb to any objects or complements. The vast majority of sentences conform to one of these five patterns:

subject / verb / subject complement

subject / verb / direct object

subject / verb / indirect object / direct object

subject / verb / direct object / object complement

subject / verb

Adverbial modifiers (single words, phrases, or clauses) may be added to any of these patterns, and they may appear nearly anywhere — at the beginning, the middle, or the end.

Predicate is the grammatical term given to the verb plus its objects, complements, and adverbial modifiers.

For a quick-reference chart of sentence patterns, see page 388.

48a Subjects

The subject of a sentence names who or what the sentence is about. The *complete subject* is usually composed of a *simple subject*, always a noun or pronoun, plus any words or word groups modifying the simple subject. To find the complete subject, ask Who? or What?, insert the verb, and finish the question. The answer is the complete subject.

┌─ COMPLETE SUBJECT ─┐
The purity of a revolution usually lasts about two weeks.

Who or what lasts about two weeks? *The purity of a revolution.*

┌──── COMPLETE SUBJECT ────┐
Historical books that contain no lies are extremely tedious.

Who or what are extremely tedious? *Historical books that contain no lies.*

COMPLETE SUBJECT
In every country the sun rises in the morning.

Who or what rises in the morning? *The sun.* Notice that *In every country the sun* is not a sensible answer to the question. *In every country* is a prepositional phrase modifying the verb *rises.* Since sentences frequently open with such modifiers, it is not safe to assume that the subject must always appear first in a sentence.

To find the simple subject, strip away all modifiers in the complete subject. This includes single-word modifiers such as *the* and *historical,* phrases such as *of a revolution,* and subordinate clauses such as *that contain no lies.*

┌ SS ┐
The purity of a revolution usually lasts about two weeks.

┌ SS ┐
Historical books that contain no lies are extremely tedious.

┌ SS ┐
In every country *the sun* rises in the morning.

A sentence may have a compound subject containing two or more simple subjects joined with a coordinating conjunction such as *and, but,* or *or.*

┌── SS ──┐   ┌── SS ──┐
Much industry and little conscience make us rich.

In imperative sentences, which give advice or issue commands, the verb's subject is understood but not actually present in the sentence. The subject of an imperative sentence is understood to be *you,* as in the following example.

[*You*] Hitch your wagon to a star.

Although the subject ordinarily comes before the verb, occasionally it does not. When a sentence begins with *There is* or *There are* (or *There was* or *There were*), the subject follows the verb. The word *There* is an expletive in such constructions, an empty word serving merely to get the sentence started.

┌── SS ──┐
There is *no substitute for victory.*

Occasionally a writer will invert a sentence for effect.

┌─ SS ─┐
Happy is *the nation that has no history.*

Happy is an adjective, so it cannot be the subject. Turn this sentence around and its structure becomes obvious: *The nation that has no history is happy.*

In questions, the subject frequently appears in an unusual position, sandwiched between parts of the verb.

┌─ SS ─┐
Do *married men* make the best husbands?

Turn the question into a statement, and the words will appear in their usual order: *Married men do make the best husbands.* (*Do make* is the verb.)

NOTE: The ability to recognize the subject of a sentence will help you edit for a variety of problems such as sentence fragments (19), subject-verb agreement (21), and choice of pronouns such as *I* and *me* (24). If English is not your native language, see also 31a and 31b.

48b Verbs, objects, and complements

Section 47c explains how to find the verb of a sentence, which consists of a main verb possibly preceded by one or more helping verbs. A sentence's verb is classified as linking, transitive, or intransitive, depending on the kinds of objects or complements the verb can (or cannot) take.

Linking verbs and subject complements

Linking verbs link the subject to a subject complement, a word or word group that completes the meaning of the subject by renaming or describing it. If the subject complement renames the subject, it is a noun or noun equivalent (sometimes called a *predicate noun*).

┌──────── S ────────┐ ┌─ V ─┐┌─ SC ─┐
The handwriting on the wall may be a forgery.

If the subject complement describes the subject, it is an adjective or adjective equivalent (sometimes called a *predicate adjective*).

S V SC
Love is blind.

Whenever they appear as main verbs (rather than helping verbs), the forms of *be*—*be, am, is, are, was, were, being, been*—usually function as linking verbs. In the preceding examples, for instance, the main verbs are *be* and *is.*

Verbs such as *appear, become, feel, grow, look, make, seem, smell, sound,* and *taste* are sometimes linking, depending on the sense of the sentence.

┌─ S ─┐┌─ V ─┐┌─ SC ─┐
At the touch of love, everyone becomes a poet.

┌─── S ───┐   ┌─ V ─┐┌SC┐
At first sight, original art often looks ugly.

When you suspect that a verb such as *becomes* or *looks* is linking, check to see if the word or words following it rename or describe the subject. In the sample sentences, *a poet* renames *everyone,* and *ugly* describes *art.*

Transitive verbs and direct objects

A transitive verb takes a direct object, a word or word group that names a receiver of the action.

┌──── S ────┐┌─ V ─┐┌──── DO ────┐
The little snake studies the ways of the big
serpent.

In such sentences, the subject and verb alone will seem incomplete. Once we have read *The little snake studies,* for example, we want to know the rest: *The little snake studies what?* The answer to the question What? (or Whom?) is the complete direct object: *the ways of the big serpent.* The simple direct object is always a noun or pronoun, in this case *ways.* To find it, simply strip away all modifiers.

Transitive verbs usually appear in the active voice, with the subject doing the action and a direct object receiving the action. Active-voice sentences can be transformed into the passive voice, with the subject receiving the action instead. (See 48c.)

Transitive verbs, indirect objects, and direct objects

The direct object of a transitive verb is sometimes preceded by an indirect object, a noun or pronoun telling to whom or for whom the action of the sentence is done.

```
 S     V   IO ┌ DO ┐      S ┌─ V ─┐ IO ┌
```
You show me a hero, and I will write you a
```
 ┌ DO ┐
```
tragedy.

The simple indirect object is always a noun or pronoun. To test for an indirect object, insert the word *to* or *for* before the word or word group in question. If the sentence makes sense, the word or word group is an indirect object.

You show [to] me a hero, and I will write [for] you a tragedy.

An indirect object may be turned into a prepositional phrase using *to* or *for*: *You show a hero to me, and I will write a tragedy for you.*

Only certain transitive verbs take indirect objects. Common examples are *give, ask, bring, find, get, hand, lend, offer, pay, pour, promise, read, send, show, teach, tell, throw,* and *write.*

Transitive verbs, direct objects, and object complements

The direct object of a transitive verb is sometimes followed by an object complement, a word or word group that completes the direct object's meaning by renaming or describing it.

```
 ┌ S ┐      ┌ V ┐┌ DO ┐┌────── OC ──────────┐
```
People now call a spade an agricultural implement.

```
 ┌ S ┐ ┌ V ┐ ┌────── DO ──────┐ ┌ OC ┐
```
Love makes all hard hearts gentle.

When the object complement renames the direct object, it is a noun or pronoun (such as *implement*). When it describes the direct object, it is an adjective (such as *gentle*).

Intransitive verbs

Intransitive verbs take no objects or complements. Their pattern is always subject/verb.

```
     S     V
```
Money talks.

```
 ┌──── S ────┐   ┌ V ┐
```
Revolutions never go backward.

Nothing receives the actions of talking and going in these sentences, so the verbs are in-

transitive. Notice that such verbs may or may not be followed by adverbial modifiers. In the second sentence, *backward* is an adverb modifying *go.*

NOTE: The dictionary will tell you whether a verb is transitive or intransitive. Some verbs have both transitive and intransitive functions.

TRANSITIVE
Sandra flew her Cessna over the canyon.

INTRANSITIVE
A bald eagle flew overhead.

In the first example, *flew* has a direct object that receives the action: *her Cessna.* In the second example, the verb is followed by an adverb (*overhead*), not by a direct object.

48c   Pattern variations

Although most sentences follow one of the five patterns in the chart on page 388, variations of these patterns commonly occur in questions, commands, sentences with delayed subjects, and passive transformations.

Questions and commands

Questions are sometimes patterned in normal word order, with the subject preceding the verb.

```
     S   ┌ V ┐
```
Who will take the first step?

Just as frequently, however, the pattern of a question is inverted, with the subject appearing between the helping and main verbs or after the verb.

```
 HV   S   MV
```
Will you take the first step?

```
     V ┌──── S ────┐
```
Why is the first step so difficult?

In commands, the subject of the sentence is an understood *you.*

[You] Keep your mouth shut and your eyes open.

Sentences with delayed subjects

Writers sometimes choose to delay the subject of a sentence to achieve a special effect such as suspense or humor.

Sentence patterns

Subject / linking verb / subject complement

    S   V   SC
Advertising is legalized lying. [*Legalized lying* renames *Advertising*.]

    S   V   SC
Great intellects are skeptical. [*Skeptical* describes *Great intellects*.]

Subject / transitive verb / direct object

    S   V   DO
A stumble may prevent a fall.

Subject / transitive verb / indirect object / direct object

    S   V   IO   DO
Fate gives us our relatives.

Subject / transitive verb / direct object / object complement

    S   V   DO   OC
Our fears do make us traitors. [*Traitors* renames *us*.]

    S   V   DO   OC
The pot calls the kettle black. [*Black* describes *the kettle*.]

Subject / intransitive verb

    S   V
Time flies.

               V
Behind the phony tinsel of Hollywood lies the
   S
real tinsel.

The subject of the sentence is also delayed in sentences opening with the expletive *There* or *It*. When used as expletives, the words *There* and *It* have no strict grammatical function; they serve merely to get the sentence started.

    V   S
There are many paths to the top of the mountain.

    V   S
It is not good to wake a sleeping lion.

The subject in the second example is an infinitive phrase. (See 49c.)

Passive transformations

Transitive verbs, those that can take direct objects, usually appear in the active voice. In the active voice, the subject does the action and a direct object receives the action.

ACTIVE
    S   V   DO
The early bird sometimes catches the early worm.

Sentences in the active voice may be transformed into the passive voice, with the subject receiving the action instead.

PASSIVE
    S   HV   MV
The early worm is sometimes caught by the early bird.

What was once the direct object (*the early worm*) has become the subject in the passive-voice transformation, and the original subject appears in a prepositional phrase beginning with *by*. The *by* phrase is frequently omitted in passive-voice constructions.

PASSIVE
The early worm is sometimes caught.

Verbs in the passive voice can be identified by their form alone. The main verb is always a past participle, such as *caught* (see 47c), preceded by a form of *be* (*be, am, is, are, was, were, being, been*): *is caught*. Sometimes adverbs intervene (*is sometimes caught*).

NOTE: Writers sometimes use the passive voice when the active voice would be more appropriate (see 14a). For a review of the uses of the active and the passive voice, see 28c.

EXERCISE 48–1 Sentence patterns: Preview

Label the function of each italicized word or word group in the following paragraphs. Use these abbreviations: subject (S), verb (V), subject complement (SC), direct object (DO), indirect object (IO), and object complement (OC). The first sentence has been done for you, and answers to this exercise appear in the back of the book.

                        S   *V*   *DO*

New art *forms* often *lead* the *public* to a new way of looking at things. Frequently, however, viewers are not yet ready to understand the new forms.

    A *group* of French artists *had* this *problem* in the 1800s. These artists completely changed their way of painting. Instead of painting in the subdued, dark tones of a formal studio, *they* often *went* outdoors. One of their new techniques was the use of color. *They* nearly always *gave* their *paintings* great *bursts* of color like sunlight on a field. Art *lovers* in France *were surprised* by such bright colors on the artists' canvases. People often called such paintings "open-air paintings." These *artists* usually *made* even their indoor *scenes* very *bright* with light and colors. Through an open window onto a bouquet of flowers or a bright-haired child *would pour* bright *sunshine*. *Were* Pierre-Auguste Renoir's *paintings* always *bright* and *cheerful*? Yes, and those of Claude Monet, Camille Pissarro, and Paul Cézanne were equally pleasant. These *painters*, now called "impressionists," *are admired* all over the world today, but in their own time the artists had to educate their viewers.

    Twentieth-century artists had the same problem. Two new art *forms* from that period *are* good *examples*, "op art" and "pop art." *Both* of these *showed* their *viewers* everyday *objects* in quite different ways. Both eventually attracted a following. But like many artists before them, the op-art and pop-art painters had to educate their viewers.

EXERCISE 48–2 Subjects

A. Each of the following sentences has three words or word groups italicized. One of these words or word groups is the subject. Find it and label it "S." Example:

> S
> Many *artists* have *preferred* certain colors for their *work*.

1. During one *part* of his life, *Picasso* preferred the color *blue*.

2. *There* are many famous *paintings* from *this* period.

3. "*Blue*" refers not only to the predominant *color* of these paintings but also to their *mood*.

4. In these paintings *you* will find *outcasts* or victims of *society* as the main characters.

5. Do the *derelicts and beggars* in these pictures reflect *Picasso's* own sense of *isolation*?

B. In the following paragraph, complete subjects have been italicized. Label the simple subject (or subjects) "SS." The first sentence has been done for you.

> SS   SS
> *Pierre-August Renoir and his young friends* founded a new movement called "impressionism." Instead of trying to reproduce a scene exactly, *impressionist painters like Renoir and his friends* blended small brush strokes of different colors to give a general impression of a scene. Up close, *a careful observer of a restaurant scene* sees no solid edges on a table or a lady's hat, just small dabs of paint. At a distance, however, *that same careful observer* will see clearly the picture in the artist's mind. At first *the art world* laughed at and rejected the new movement. However, there is now *no serious argument about the importance of the impressionist movement.*

EXERCISE 48–3 Direct objects and subject complements

A. Subjects and verbs have been labeled in the following sentences. Label each italicized word as a simple direct object (DO) or a simple subject complement (SC). Example:

> s　　v　　SC
> Pierre-Auguste Renoir's parents were *supportive* of their son's ambitions.

1. Renoir's love of art was *clear* to his parents.
2. When he was a *boy* of thirteen, they apprenticed *him* to a porcelain artist.
3. Renoir first learned the potter's *trade*.
4. Soon he was quite *skillful* at making and firing vases.
5. He enjoyed the *task* of decorating the vases even more.

B. Using the pattern of each sentence as a model, write a short sentence of your own on any subject. Example:

> S/V/SC: Renoir was an artist.
>
> _____*Casey was a ballplayer.*_____

6. S/V: Renoir studied.

_____

7. S/V: Renoir studied hard.

_____

8. S/V/SC: He became an excellent painter.

_____

9. S/V/SC: His paintings are cheerful.

_____

10. S/V/DO: Café owners liked his murals.

_____

EXERCISE 48–4 Indirect objects and object complements

A. Subjects, verbs, and direct objects are labeled in the following sentences. Label each italicized word as a simple indirect object (IO) or a simple object complement (OC). Example:

         s   v *IO*   DO
Renoir's parents gave *him* a good start in his chosen profession.

                                s   v   DO

1. Besides his parents, other people considered the young Renoir a fine *painter*.
        s v   DO
2. He had shown local *businessmen* some of his work.
         s   v   DO
3. Owners of some Paris cafés gave *him* painting jobs.
      s   v   DO
4. He made the walls of their cafés *beautiful*.
           s   v   ⌐——— DO ———⌐
5. The lovely scenes made both customers and owners *happy*.

B. Using the pattern of each sentence as a model, write a short sentence of your own on any subject. Example:

     S/V/DO/OC: Renoir called his style of painting "impressionist."

          Casey called his style of batting "the best."

6. S/V/IO/DO: Paris café owners offered Renoir much work.

7. S/V/IO/DO: They gave him twenty orders for murals.

8. S/V/DO/OC: They considered his work exceptional.

9. S/V/DO/OC: People called him "the happy painter."

10. S/V: His popularity increased.

EXERCISE 48–5 Direct objects, indirect objects, object complements

Underline the verb of each sentence. Then label the complete direct object (DO) and any complete indirect objects (IO) or object complements (OC). Example:

```
          ┌ DO ┐                    ┌─────── DO ───────┐┌────── OC ──────┐
Many people enjoy pop art. They find this new kind of art a refreshing change.
```

1. During World War II, American mass media flooded London.

2. The effect of that flood fascinated many London artists.

3. Using the American material, British artists gave the world a new art form.

4. To produce their art, the artists used images from popular culture.

5. Someone named the new art "pop art."

6. Most Americans find pop art very appealing.

7. To some, it reflects the optimism of the 1960s.

8. Items like flags, signs, and comic strips gave pop artists their subject matter.

9. Artists like Jasper Johns and Roy Lichtenstein preceded the more famous Andy Warhol.

10. Of all these artists, Andy Warhol best understood the media's power to affect people's thinking.

EXERCISE 48–6 Pattern variations: Delayed subjects and understood subjects

Underline the simple subjects in the following sentences. (Hint: These are tricky. The subjects are not always where you expect them, and you may even have to supply an understood *you*.) Examples:

Have you ever heard of "color-field painting"?

You   **Read this exercise to find out something about it.**

1. Making its appearance in the 1940s was a new kind of painting.

2. Was there any difficulty in explaining this new style?

3. No—look at paintings by Mark Rothko or Morris Louis for examples of this new color-field painting.

4. On their canvases are layers of color "washes."

5. What kinds of washes are they?

6. Among them are oil paints, inks, and acrylic.

7. Can colors all by themselves, with no "picture" of anything, make a painting?

8. Careful study of *Blue Veil* by Louis will reveal layer upon layer of different colors of acrylic, but no images.

9. There are many examples of color-field painting in art galleries today.

10. Visit a gallery to discover your own reaction to this kind of painting.

EXERCISE 48–7 Pattern variations: Passive verbs

In the following sentences, underline the verb twice and label it "VP" if it is passive. You should find six passive verbs. Example:

            VP

Jasper Johns <u>has</u> often <u>been called</u> a pioneer of pop art.

1. Andy Warhol, a former commercial artist, was fascinated by everyday objects.

2. In his view, the beauty of everyday objects like soup cans was too often overlooked by people.

3. He was obsessed with America's casual attitude toward criminal executions and horrible accidents.

4. To make people aware of such things, he painted instead of writing or talking.

5. His silk-screened pictures of electric chairs speak for themselves.

6. His works have frequently been labeled "ironic" by art critics.

7. In his *Gold Marilyn Monroe*, Marilyn Monroe has been painted against a gold background, like an ancient religious icon.

8. Because of Warhol's clever use of pop-art technique, however, her image has been cheapened.

9. In the painting, Marilyn Monroe looks like a sleazy Virgin Mary.

10. By exercising his skill, Warhol succeeded in sending a message about American values.

EXERCISE 48–8 Sentence patterns: Review

Label the function of each italicized word or word group in the following paragraph. Use these codes: subject (S), verb (V), subject complement (SC), direct object (DO), indirect object (IO), and object complement (OC). The first sentence has been done for you.

         S   V   DO

Renoir definitely *had* firm *ideas* about work and about getting along with people. As for work, he believed that *people* everywhere *should use* their *hands* every day. He certainly did, and because he did, *friends* often *called* this hardworking *man* a *workman-painter*. Being called a workman-painter pleased Renoir. Work seemed to be more important to him than the finished product. "The only *reward* for work *is* the *work* itself," he said. He got along with people very well; even his enemies seemed to like him. When his opponents attacked his views, *he* frequently *responded* by suggesting a compromise. *He* freely *offered* other *people* his own successful *techniques* for getting along with his opponents. According to Renoir, *you* certainly *should give* your *enemies* a *chance*. You should also avoid a fight whenever possible. Why? If you avoid fights, your *enemies* often *will become* your *friends*. The *joy* in Renoir's paintings *might be explained* by these approaches to life.

49 Subordinate word groups

Subordinate word groups include prepositional phrases, subordinate clauses, verbal phrases, appositives, and absolutes. Not all of these word groups are subordinate in quite the same way. Some are subordinate because they are modifiers; others function as noun equivalents, not as modifiers.

49a Prepositional phrases

A prepositional phrase begins with a preposition such as *at*, *by*, *for*, *from*, *in*, *of*, *on*, *to*, or *with* (see 47f) and usually ends with a noun or noun equivalent: *on the table*, *for him*, *with great fanfare*. The noun or noun equivalent is known as the *object of the preposition*.

Prepositional phrases function either as adjectives modifying a noun or pronoun or as adverbs modifying a verb, an adjective, or another adverb. When functioning as an adjective, a prepositional phrase nearly always appears immediately following the noun or pronoun it modifies.

Variety is the spice *of life.*

Adjective phrases usually answer one or both of the questions Which one? and What kind of? If we ask Which spice? or What kind of spice? we get a sensible answer: *the spice of life.*

Adverbial prepositional phrases that modify the verb can appear nearly anywhere in a sentence.

Do not judge a tree *by its bark.*

Tyranny will *in time* lead to revolution.

To the ant, a few drops of rain are a flood.

Adverbial word groups usually answer one of these questions: When? Where? How? Why? Under what conditions? To what degree?

Do not judge a tree *how? By its bark.*

Tyranny will lead to revolution *when? In time.*

A few drops of rain are a flood *under what conditions? To the ant.*

If a prepositional phrase is movable, you can be certain that it is adverbial; adjectival prepositional phrases are wedded to the words they modify. At least some of the time, adverbial modifiers can be moved to other positions in the sentence.

By their fruits you shall know them.

You shall know them *by their fruits.*

In questions and subordinate clauses, a preposition may appear after its object.

What are you afraid *of?*

We avoided the clerk *whom* John had warned us *about.*

NOTE: The ability to recognize the object of a preposition will help you distinguish between pronouns such as *I* and *me* (see 24b).

49b Subordinate clauses

Subordinate clauses are patterned like sentences, having subjects and verbs and sometimes objects or complements. But they function within sentences as adjectives, adverbs, or nouns. They cannot stand alone as complete sentences.

A subordinate clause usually begins with a subordinating conjunction or a relative pronoun.

SUBORDINATING CONJUNCTIONS

after	even though	so that	when
although	how	than	where
as	if	that	whether
as if	in order that	though	while
because	rather than	unless	why
before	since	until	

RELATIVE PRONOUNS

that	who	whom	whose	which

The chart on page 399 classifies these words according to the kinds of clauses (adjective, adverb, or noun) they introduce.

Adjective clauses

Like other word groups functioning as adjectives, adjective clauses modify nouns or pronouns. An adjective clause nearly always appears immediately following the noun or pronoun it modifies.

The arrow *that has left the bow* never returns.

Relatives are persons *who live too near and visit too often.*

To test whether a subordinate clause functions as an adjective, ask the adjective questions: Which one? What kind of? The answer should make sense. Which arrow? *The arrow that has left the bow.* What kind of persons? *Persons who live too near and visit too often.*

Most adjective clauses begin with a relative pronoun (*who, whom, whose, which,* or *that*), which marks them as grammatically subordinate. In addition to introducing the clause, the relative pronoun points back to the noun that the clause modifies.

The fur *that warms a monarch* once warmed a bear.

Relative pronouns are sometimes "understood."

The things [*that*] *we know best* are the things [*that*] *we haven't been taught.*

Occasionally an adjective clause is introduced by a relative adverb, usually *when, where,* or *why.*

Home is the place *where you slip in the tub and break your neck.*

The parts of an adjective clause are often arranged as in sentences (subject/verb/object or complement).

                              S   V   DO
We often forgive the people *who bore us.*

Frequently, however, the object or complement appears first, violating the normal order of subject/verb/object.

                           DO   S   V
We rarely forgive those *whom we bore.*

To determine the subject of a clause, ask Who? or What? and insert the verb. Don't be surprised if the answer is an echo, as in the first adjective clause above: Who bore us? *Who.* To find any objects or complements, read the subject and the verb and then ask Who? Whom? or What? Again, be prepared for a possible echo, as in the second adjective clause: We bore whom? *Whom.*

NOTE: For punctuation of adjective clauses, see 32e and 33e. If English is not your native language, see 31c for a common problem with adjective clauses.

Adverb clauses

Adverb clauses usually modify verbs, in which case they may appear nearly anywhere in a sentence — at the beginning, at the end, or in the middle. Like other adverbial word groups, they tell when, where, why, under what conditions, or to what degree an action occurred or a situation existed.

When the well is dry, we know the worth of water.

Venice would be a fine city *if it were only drained.*

When do we know the worth of water? *When the well is dry.* Under what conditions would Venice be a fine city? *If it were only drained.*

Unlike adjective clauses, adverb clauses are frequently movable. In the preceding example sentences, for instance, the adverb clauses can be moved without affecting the meaning of the sentences.

We know the worth of water *when the well is dry.*

If it were only drained, Venice would be a fine city.

When an adverb clause modifies an adjective or an adverb, it is not movable; it must appear next to the word it modifies. In the

Words that introduce subordinate clauses

WORDS INTRODUCING ADVERB CLAUSES

Subordinating conjunctions: after, although, as, as if, because, before, even though, if, in order that, rather than, since, so that, than, that, though, unless, until, when, where, whether, while

WORDS INTRODUCING ADJECTIVE CLAUSES

Relative pronouns: that, which, who, whom, whose

Relative adverbs: when, where, why

WORDS INTRODUCING NOUN CLAUSES

Relative pronouns: that, which, who, whom, whose

Other pronouns: whoever, whomever, what, whatever, whichever

Subordinating conjunctions: how, if, when, whenever, where, wherever, whether, why

following examples the *because* clause modifies the adjective *angry,* and the *than* clause modifies the adverb *faster.*

> Angry *because the mayor had not kept his promises,* we worked for his defeat.

> Joan can run faster *than I can bicycle.*

Adverb clauses always begin with a subordinating conjunction (see the chart at the top of this page for a list). Subordinating conjunctions introduce clauses and express their relation to the rest of the sentence.

Adverb clauses are sometimes elliptical, with some of their words being "understood."

> When [*it is*] *painted,* the room will look larger.

Noun clauses

Because they do not function as modifiers, noun clauses are not subordinate in the same sense as are adjective and adverb clauses. They are called subordinate only because they cannot stand alone: They must function within a sentence, always as nouns.

A noun clause functions just like a single-word noun, usually as a subject, subject complement, direct object, or object of a preposition.

> ┌──── **s** ────┐
> *Whoever gossips to you* will gossip of you.

> ┌──── **DO** ────┐
> We never forget *that we buried the hatchet.*

A noun clause begins with a word that marks it as subordinate (see the top of this page for a list). The subordinating word may or may not play a significant role in the clause. In the preceding example sentences, *whoever* is the subject of its clause, but *that* does not perform a function in its clause.

As with adjective clauses, the parts of a noun clause may appear out of their normal order (subject/verb/object).

>   **DO**   **S**   **V**
> Talent is *what you possess.*

The parts of a noun clause may also appear in their normal order.

>   **S**   **V**   **DO**
> Genius is *what possesses you.*

49c Verbal phrases

A verbal is a verb form that does not function as the verb of a clause. Verbals include infinitives (the word *to* plus the base form of the verb), present participles (the *-ing* form of the verb), and past participles (the verb form usually ending in *-d, -ed, -n, -en,* or *-t*). (See 27a and 47c.)

INFINITIVE	PRESENT PARTICIPLE	PAST PARTICIPLE
to dream	dreaming	dreamed
to choose	choosing	chosen
to build	building	built
to grow	growing	grown

Instead of functioning as the verb of a clause, a verbal or a verbal phrase functions as an adjective, a noun, or an adverb.

ADJECTIVE
Stolen grapes are especially sweet.

NOUN
Continual *dripping* wears away a stone.

ADVERB
Were we born *to suffer?*

Verbals can take objects, complements, and modifiers to form verbal phrases; the phrases usually lack subjects.

Living well is the best revenge.

Governments exist *to protect the rights of minorities.*

The verbal *Living* is modified by the adverb *well;* the verbal *to protect* is followed by a direct object, *the rights of minorities.*

Like single-word verbals, verbal phrases function as adjectives, nouns, or adverbs. In the sentences just given, for example, *living well* functions as a noun used as the subject of the sentence, and *to protect the rights of minorities* functions as an adverb, answering the question Why?

Verbal phrases are ordinarily classified as participles, gerunds, and infinitives. This classification is based partly on form (whether the verbal is a present participle, a past participle, or an infinitive) and partly on function (whether the whole phrase functions as an adjective, a noun, or an adverb).

NOTE: For advice on editing dangling verbal phrases, see 12e.

Participial phrases

Participial phrases always function as adjectives. Their verbals are either present participles, always ending in *-ing,* or past participles, frequently ending in *-d, -ed, -n, -en,* or *-t* (see 27a).

Participial phrases frequently appear immediately following the noun or pronoun they modify.

Congress shall make no law *abridging the freedom of speech or of the press.*

Truth *kept in the dark* will never save the world.

Unlike other adjectival word groups, however, which must always follow the noun or pronoun they modify, participial phrases are often movable. They can precede the word they modify.

Being weak, foxes are distinguished by superior tact.

They may also appear at some distance from the word they modify.

History is something that never happened, *written by someone who wasn't there.*

Gerund phrases

Gerund phrases are built around present participles (verb forms ending in *-ing*), and they always function as nouns: usually as subjects, subject complements, direct objects, or objects of a preposition.

——— s ———
Justifying a fault doubles it.

——— sc ———
The secret of education is *respecting the pupil.*

——— do ———
Kleptomaniacs can't help *helping themselves.*

— obj of prep —
The hen is an egg's way of *producing another egg.*

Infinitive phrases

Infinitive phrases, usually constructed around *to* plus the base form of the verb (*to call, to drink*), can function as nouns, as adjectives, or as adverbs.

When functioning as a noun, an infinitive phrase may appear in almost any noun slot in a sentence, usually as a subject, subject complement, or direct object.

┌────── **S** ──────┐
To side with truth is noble.

┌────────── **DO** ──────────┐
Never try *to leap a chasm in two jumps.*

Infinitive phrases functioning as adjectives usually appear immediately following the noun or pronoun they modify.

We do not have the right *to abandon the poor.*

The infinitive phrase modifies the noun *right.* Which right? *The right to abandon the poor.*
  Adverbial infinitive phrases usually qualify the meaning of the verb, telling when, where, how, why, under what conditions, or to what degree an action occurred.

He cut off his nose *to spite his face.*

Why did he cut off his nose? *To spite his face.*

NOTE: In some constructions, the infinitive is unmarked; in other words, the *to* does not appear: *No one can make you [to] feel inferior without your consent.* (See 29c.)

49d Appositive phrases

Though strictly speaking they are not subordinate word groups, appositive phrases function somewhat as adjectives do, to describe nouns or pronouns. Instead of modifying nouns or pronouns, however, appositive phrases rename them. In form they are nouns or noun equivalents.
  Appositives are said to be "in apposition" to the nouns or pronouns they rename.

Politicians, *acrobats at heart,* can sit on a fence and yet keep both ears to the ground.

Acrobats at heart is in apposition to the noun *politicians.*

49e Absolute phrases

An absolute phrase modifies a whole clause or sentence, not just one word, and it may appear nearly anywhere in the sentence. It consists of a noun or noun equivalent usually followed by a participial phrase.

His words dipped in honey, the senator mesmerized the crowd.

The senator mesmerized the crowd, *his words dipped in honey.*

EXERCISE 49–1 Subordinate word groups: Preview

In the following paragraphs, underline prepositional and verbal phrases once; underline subordinate clauses twice. The first sentence has been done for you; you should find fifteen phrases and five subordinate clauses. Answers to this exercise appear in the back of the book.

Louise Nevelson, who was once called "the finest living American artist," did not earn that title easily.

From her earliest years, she was artistically inclined. Drawing colorful pictures was a favorite childhood pastime. To decorate her room, she collected boxes of pretty rocks, shells, and fabric pieces. Encouraging her artistic interest, her family provided the independence that she needed.

Her husband, Charles Nevelson, who was a wealthy New York businessman, provided her with financial independence, but Louise Nevelson needed personal independence too. The marriage lasted for only eleven years. Then she and her son, Mike, went to her family home. Mike stayed there while his mother studied abroad. Studying, working, and making new friends, Louise developed the self-confidence to follow her own vision.

At times she must have wondered whether or not she had done the right thing. During Louise Nevelson's busiest and most exciting years, her paintings and sculptures were not popular with either the critics or the public. Later, however, her work won critical acclaim, and she was recognized throughout the art world. Rewarded and acclaimed, Louise Nevelson knew that she had made the right decision.

EXERCISE 49–2 Prepositional phrases

Underline the twenty prepositional phrases in the following sentences. Example:

Children learn many things <u>from their parents.</u>

1. From her builder-father, Louise Nevelson learned an important tradition that had been handed down for generations.

2. Like many other Jewish traditions, it is recorded in the Talmud.

3. The Talmud is a book about Jewish history and laws; it is studied by Jewish scholars.

4. According to the Talmud, Jews should always leave some part of a new house unfinished or unpainted.

5. The unfinished part is there for a reason: It makes people remember the destruction of Jerusalem's Second Temple.

6. As an adult, Louise moved into a dozen or more "new homes."

7. Sometimes she abided by the tradition, but sometimes she forgot about it.

8. Finally, she began at last to understand this tradition that had been handed down for all those years.

9. She saw that over the years she had often left some work unfinished in her studio.

10. Both her work and her life were like her house: Only with an unfinished corner could they grow and change.

EXERCISE 49–3 Subordinate clauses

A. Underline the subordinate clauses in the following sentences. Example:

> **When Louise was part of a struggling young artists' group in New York,** she met Diego
> Rivera.

1. Diego Rivera, who was a Mexican mural painter, introduced Louise Nevelson to other
   artists and their friends.

2. One of the people whom she met, Marjorie Eaton, became her roommate.

3. Louise also met Ben Shahn while she was working with Rivera.

4. When Louise began working with Ben, she felt at ease with her art for the first time.

5. She knew that she had found her niche.

B. Identify each of the following word groups as a prepositional phrase or a subordinate
clause. Example:

a. After work	_prepositional phrase_
b. After she had worked	_subordinate clause_

6a. Before she went to class _____

 b. Before her painting class _____

7a. Since her happy childhood days _____

 b. Since she had a happy childhood _____

8a. Till the closing bell _____

 b. Till the bell rang _____

9a. After the mural was done _____

 b. After the next sculpture show _____

10a. Until she mastered the skill _____

 b. Until her first exhibition _____

EXERCISE 49–4 Prepositional and verbal phrases

Some of the phrases in the following paragraphs are italicized. Label these phrases prepositional (Prep), gerund (Ger), infinitive (Inf), or participial (Part). The first one has been done for you.

Louise Nevelson's first one-woman show came about because she was determined
Inf
to have her work recognized. Her first choice of a showplace was the Nierendorf Gallery. *Exhibiting there* would put her in the same place where Picasso, Matisse, and Paul Klee had been exhibited. *Showing New York City's best modern art* had helped build a strong reputation for this gallery.

Nevelson went alone to the gallery. First she found Mr. Nierendorf, the gallery's manager. Then, *introducing herself quickly,* she stated quite simply that she wanted an exhibition in his gallery. He was surprised at her forthrightness, but he was also impressed. When he protested that he did not know her work, Nevelson simply invited him *to come and see it.*

He did — the next day — and he offered her a show in twenty-one days. *During the next weeks,* Nevelson got her pieces ready. When the show opened, it was Nierendorf's first exhibition *of an American artist.*

With a few exceptions, art critics liked the show. *Excited by her work,* one critic said that he would have "hailed these sculptural expressions as by surely a great figure among moderns" — if he had not found out the artist was a woman. That left-handed compliment did more harm to the critic than to the artist. Other critics compared her work favorably to Mayan work, *seeing similar forms and rhythms.* Still others commented on the work's "wit" and "zest" and "interest in movement."

Accepted very well, the exhibition was extended past its closing time and gave Nevelson opportunities *to meet some important people* — but not a single piece of art was sold.

EXERCISE 49–5 Verbal phrases

The verbal phrase in each sentence has been italicized. Study it; then compose your own sentence on any subject, using a verbal phrase the same way. Example:

Working with other artists made Louise Nevelson very happy.

Playing against other teams made Carmella nervous.

1. *Enjoying each other's company,* the members of Ben Shahn's artist group often ate together.

   _____

2. Frequently, they would paint a picture right then and there *to celebrate their joy.*

   _____

3. *Needing the white tablecloth for their canvas,* the artists would push aside the dishes and food.

   _____

4. *Totally involved in their project,* they would look for "paint."

   _____

5. *Finding something to use for paint* was not usually a problem.

   _____

6. *Making paint from wine drops or pepper or anything else handy* gave them pleasure.

   _____

7. Each artist had a chance to *add to the picture.*

   _____

8. They enjoyed *adding details to each other's parts of the picture.*

   _____

9. *Relaxed and refreshed,* they would leave the restaurant content.

   _____

10. No one knows why the restaurant owner allowed them *to do this repeatedly to his tablecloths!*

   _____

EXERCISE 49–6 Subordinate word groups: Review

In the following paragraphs, underline prepositional and verbal phrases once; underline subordinate clauses twice. The first sentence has been done for you; you should find twenty more subordinate word groups.

Perhaps becoming a queen is one of every little girl's fantasies. During one experimental stage, Louise Nevelson gave herself that title. She called herself "Queen of the Black Black." While she was experimenting, she used only black materials in her artwork. She decided to make all her surroundings black also. Painting her walls black was the first step. Then she attacked the floors. She did not want to paint them; instead, she used stain to get the desired effect. Stained very dark, the floors did not reflect much light. Her work used no other color, and she insisted that black was "the total color."

At fifty-eight, Louise Nevelson was finally recognized. She became an artist who could expect regular exhibits, sales, and commissions. Museums and collectors bought her work eagerly, paying her well. She was awarded honorary degrees from various universities and accepted invitations to attend White House dinners. She enjoyed receiving these honors, but her greatest pleasure came later.

When Louise Nevelson celebrated her eightieth birthday, her hometown gave her what she had always wanted: The local museum exhibited her work, and the town bestowed a title upon her— "Queen of the City."

50   Sentence types

Sentences are classified in two ways: according to their structure (simple, compound, complex, and compound-complex) and according to their purpose (declarative, imperative, interrogative, and exclamatory).

50a   Sentence structures

Depending on the number and types of clauses they contain, sentences are classified as simple, compound, complex, or compound-complex.

Clauses come in two varieties: independent and subordinate. An independent clause is a full sentence pattern that does not function within another sentence pattern: It contains a subject and verb plus any objects, complements, and modifiers of that verb, and it either stands alone or could stand alone. A subordinate clause is a full sentence pattern that functions within a sentence as an adjective, an adverb, or a noun but that cannot stand alone as a complete sentence. (See 49b.)

Simple sentences

A simple sentence is one independent clause with no subordinate clauses.

> ┌────── **INDEPENDENT CLAUSE** ──────┐
> Without music, life would be a mistake.

This sentence contains a subject (*life*), a verb (*would be*), a complement (*a mistake*), and an adverbial modifier (*Without music*).

A simple sentence may contain compound elements—a compound subject, verb, or object, for example—but it does not contain more than one full sentence pattern. The following sentence is simple because its two verbs (*enters* and *spreads*) share a subject (*Evil*).

> ┌────── **INDEPENDENT CLAUSE** ──────┐
> Evil enters like a needle and spreads like an oak.

Compound sentences

A compound sentence is composed of two or more independent clauses with no subordinate clauses. The independent clauses are usually joined with a comma and a coordinating con-

junction (*and, but, or, nor, for, so, yet*) or with a semicolon. (See 8.)

> ┌── **INDEPENDENT CLAUSE** ──┐   ┌─ **INDEPENDENT** ─
> One arrow is easily broken, but you can't break
> ─ **CLAUSE** ──┐
> a bundle of ten.

> ┌────── **INDEPENDENT CLAUSE** ──────┐ ┌─
> We are born brave, trusting, and greedy; most
> ─ **INDEPENDENT CLAUSE** ──┐
> of us have remained greedy.

Complex sentences

A complex sentence is composed of one independent clause with one or more subordinate clauses. (See 49b.)

> **ADJECTIVE**
>   **SUBORDINATE**
>   ┌─── **CLAUSE** ───┐
> They that sow in tears shall reap in joy.

> **ADVERB**
>   **SUBORDINATE**
>   ┌─── **CLAUSE** ───┐
> If you scatter thorns, don't go barefoot.

> **NOUN**
> ┌────── **SUBORDINATE CLAUSE** ──────┐
> What the scientists have in their briefcases is terrifying.

Compound-complex sentences

A compound-complex sentence contains at least two independent clauses and at least one subordinate clause. The following sentence contains two full sentence patterns that can stand alone.

> ┌ **INDEPENDENT CLAUSE** ┐   ┌─ **INDEPENDENT** ─
> Tell me what you eat, and I will tell you what
> ─ **CLAUSE** ┐
> you are.

And each independent clause contains a subordinate clause, making the sentence both compound and complex.

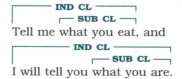

> ┌──── **IND CL** ────┐
>   ┌─ **SUB CL** ─┐
> Tell me what you eat, and
> ┌──── **IND CL** ────┐
>   ┌─ **SUB CL** ─┐
> I will tell you what you are.

50b Sentence purposes

Writers use declarative sentences to make statements, imperative sentences to issue requests or commands, interrogative sentences to ask questions, and exclamatory sentences to make exclamations.

DECLARATIVE	The echo always has the last word.
IMPERATIVE	Love your neighbor.
INTERROGATIVE	Are second thoughts always wisest?
EXCLAMATORY	I want to wash the flag, not burn it!

EXERCISE 50–1 Sentence types: Preview

Indicate on the blank after each sentence in the following paragraphs whether the sentence is simple (S), compound (C), complex (CX), or compound-complex (CC). The first blank has been filled for you, and answers to this exercise appear in the back of the book.

Both were famous for breaking with tradition and starting a new way of thinking about art, but Pierre-Auguste Renoir and Louise Nevelson were different in many ways. __C__

A nineteenth-century man born in France, Renoir traveled to Italy to study the Renaissance artists' work; Nevelson, a twentieth-century woman born in America, traveled to Europe to study all kinds of art. ____ Although he devoted several years to drawing, most of Renoir's work was in painting. ____ Nevelson, on the other hand, explored many of the arts besides painting; she worked extensively in music, dance, and sculpture. ____

Renoir loved brightness and bursts of color; she loved darkness and tones of black. ____ He created and finished everything while he was out of doors; she did her work inside a studio. ____ Renoir avoided lines, even blurring outlines to make one part of a painting blend into another. ____ Nevelson was so fond of line that she painted different parts of her sculpture in different colors; she wanted to accentuate the sculpture's form. ____

Unlike Renoir, who liked to paint people and group scenes, Nevelson constructed abstract forms. ____ Using paints and oils, Renoir fashioned homey, identifiable scenes that his viewers could easily recognize. ____ Using discarded milk crates and burned pieces of wood, Nevelson constructed puzzling, enigmatic sculptures different from those of any other artist. ____

EXERCISE 50–2 Sentence types

A. In the following sentences, underline subordinate clauses. Then determine the sentence type and indicate it in the blank: simple, compound, complex, or compound-complex. Example:

> <u>Because Louise Nevelson was always sure of herself</u>, she could not change direction.
> __*complex*_____

1. The techniques that the artists Pierre-Auguste Renoir and Louise Nevelson used to handle their anger were quite different. _____

2. Renoir tried to turn anger aside; because he often deflected it with a compromise, the other person seemed to win the argument. _____

3. Once, angry and disappointed at the lack of sales after a major exhibition, Nevelson burned two hundred canvases and all of the sculptures in the show. _____

4. Nevelson said that she used her anger to provide energy on many occasions.
    _____

5. Of course the two never met, but wouldn't it have been fun to watch them together?
    _____

B. Write five sentences of your own of the kind indicated. Underline your subordinate clauses.

6. Simple: _____

    _____

7. Compound: _____

    _____

8. Complex: _____

    _____

9. Complex: _____

    _____

10. Compound-complex: _____

    _____

EXERCISE 50–3 Sentence types: Review

Indicate on the blank after each sentence in the following paragraphs whether the sentence is simple (S), compound (C), complex (CX), or compound-complex (CC). The first blank has been filled for you.

Was there anything that artists Pierre-Auguste Renoir and Louise Nevelson had in common? _CX_ Yes, both showed an interest in art when they were children, and both traveled to another country to study art after they were grown. ____ In addition, although the colors were different, both had periods when they used only one color in their work. ____ And both had to overcome significant odds. ____ Nevelson's problems were mostly emotional and financial, but Renoir's were physical. ____ Renoir's painful arthritis crippled his hands as he grew older; he could paint only by having his brushes tied to his hands. ____

These artists were alike in ways significant to the art world. ____ Both broke free of long-standing accepted traditions in their field and introduced new techniques. ____ Both connected with their viewers in ways that forced the viewers to respond. ____ Both started new ways of looking at things; whether they painted a flowering tree or a stack of burned wood, these artists made viewers see objects differently. ____ They had to fight for and wait for recognition, but both won fame: Renoir and Nevelson were recognized during their lifetimes as artists of particular importance. ____

Glossary of Usage

This glossary includes words commonly confused (such as *accept* and *except*), words commonly misused (such as *hopefully*), and words that are nonstandard (such as *hisself*). It also lists colloquialisms and jargon. Colloquialisms are expressions that may be appropriate in informal speech but are inappropriate in formal writing. Jargon is needlessly technical or pretentious language that is inappropriate in most contexts. If an item is not listed here, consult the index. For irregular verbs (such as *sing, sang, sung*), see 27a. For idiomatic use of prepositions, see 18d.

a, an   Use *an* before a vowel sound, *a* before a consonant sound: *an apple, a peach.* Problems sometimes arise with words beginning with *h*. If the *h* is silent, the word begins with a vowel sound, so use *an*: *an hour, an heir, an honest senator, an honorable deed.* If the *h* is pronounced, the word begins with a consonant sound, so use *a: a hospital, a hymn, a historian, a hotel.* When an abbreviation or acronym begins with a vowel sound, use *an: an EKG, an MRI, an AIDS* patient.

accept, except   *Accept* is a verb meaning "to receive." *Except* is usually a preposition meaning "excluding." *I will accept all the packages except that one. Except* is also a verb meaning "to exclude." *Please except that item from the list.*

adapt, adopt   *Adapt* means "to adjust or become accustomed"; it is usually followed by *to. Adopt* means "to take as one's own." *Our family adopted a Vietnamese orphan, who quickly adapted to his new surroundings.*

adverse, averse   *Adverse* means "unfavorable." *Averse* means "opposed" or "reluctant"; it is usually followed by *to. I am averse to your proposal because it could have an adverse impact on the economy.*

advice, advise   *Advice* is a noun, *advise* a verb. *We advise you to follow John's advice.*

affect, effect   *Affect* is usually a verb meaning "to influence." *Effect* is usually a noun meaning "result." *The drug did not affect the disease, and it had adverse side effects. Effect* can also be a verb meaning "to bring about." *Only the president can effect such a change.*

aggravate   *Aggravate* means "to make worse or more troublesome." *Overgrazing aggravated the soil erosion.* In formal writing, avoid the colloquial use of *aggravate* meaning "to annoy or irritate." *Her babbling annoyed* (not *aggravated*) *me.*

agree to, agree with   *Agree to* means "to give consent." *Agree with* means "to be in accord" or "to come to an understanding." *He agrees with me about the need for change, but he won't agree to my plan.*

ain't   *Ain't* is nonstandard. Use *am not, are not* (*aren't*), or *is not* (*isn't*). *I am not* (not *ain't*) *going home for spring break.*

all ready, already   *All ready* means "completely prepared." *Already* means "previously." *Susan was all ready for the concert, but her friends had already left.*

all right   *All right* is written as two words. *Alright* is nonstandard.

all together, altogether   *All together* means "everyone gathered." *Altogether* means "entirely." *We were not altogether certain that we could bring the family all together for the reunion.*

allude   To *allude* to something is to make an indirect reference to it. Do not use *allude* to mean "to refer directly." *In his lecture the professor referred* (not *alluded*) *to several pre-Socratic philosophers.*

allusion, illusion   An *allusion* is an indirect reference. An *illusion* is a misconception or false impression. *Did you catch my allusion to Shakespeare? Mirrors give the room an illusion of depth.*

a lot   *A lot* is two words. Do not write *alot. We have had a lot of rain this spring.* See also *lots, lots of.*

among, between   See *between, among.*

amongst   In American English, *among* is preferred.

amoral, immoral   *Amoral* means "neither moral nor immoral"; it also means "not caring about moral judgments." *Immoral* means "morally wrong." *Until recently, most business courses were taught from an amoral perspective. Murder is immoral.*

amount, number   Use *amount* with quantities that cannot be counted; use *number* with those that can. *This recipe calls for a large amount of sugar. We have a large number of toads in our garden.*

an   See *a, an.*

and etc.   *Et cetera* (*etc.*) means "and so forth"; therefore, *and etc.* is redundant. See also *etc.*

and/or   Avoid the awkward construction *and/or* except in technical or legal documents.

angry at, angry with   To write that one is *angry at* another person is nonstandard. Use *angry with* instead.

ante-, anti-   The prefix *ante-* means "earlier" or "in front of"; the prefix *anti-* means "against" or "opposed to." *William Lloyd Garrison was one of the leaders of the antislavery movement during the antebellum period. Anti-* should be used with a hyphen when it is followed by a capital letter or a word beginning with *i.*

anxious   *Anxious* means "worried" or "apprehensive." In formal writing, avoid using *anxious* to mean "eager." *We are eager* (not *anxious*) *to see your new house.*

anybody, anyone   *Anybody* and *anyone* are singular. (See 21e and 22a.)

anymore   Reserve the adverb *anymore* for negative contexts, where it means "any longer." *Moviegoers are rarely shocked anymore by profanity.* Do not use *anymore* in positive contexts. Use *now* or *nowadays* instead. *Interest rates are so low nowadays* (not *anymore*) *that more people can afford to buy homes.*

anyone   See *anybody, anyone.*

anyone, any one   *Anyone*, an indefinite pronoun, means "any person at all." *Any one*, the pronoun *one* preceded by the adjective *any*, refers to a particular person or thing in a group. *Anyone from Chicago may choose any one of the games on display.*

anyplace   *Anyplace* is informal for *anywhere.* Avoid *anyplace* in formal writing.

anyways, anywheres   *Anyways* and *anywheres* are nonstandard. Use *anyway* and *anywhere.*

as   *As* is sometimes used to mean "because." But do not use it if there is any chance of ambiguity. *We canceled the picnic because* (not *as*) *it began raining. As* here could mean "because" or "when."

as, like   See *like, as.*

as to   *As to* is jargon for *about. He inquired about* (not *as to*) *the job.*

averse   See *adverse, averse.*

awful   The adjective *awful* means "awe-inspiring." Colloquially it is used to mean "terrible" or "bad." The adverb *awfully* is sometimes used in conversation as an intensifier meaning "very." In formal writing, avoid these colloquial uses. *I was very* (not *awfully*) *upset last night. Susan had a terrible* (not *an awful*) *time calming her nerves.*

awhile, a while   *Awhile* is an adverb; it can modify a verb, but it cannot be the object of a preposition such as *for.* The two-word form *a while* is a noun preceded by an article and therefore can be the object of a preposition. *Stay awhile. Stay for a while.*

back up, backup   *Back up* is a verb phrase. *Back up the car carefully. Be sure to back up your hard drive.* A *backup* is a duplicate of electronically stored data. *Keep your backup in a safe place. Backup* can also be used as an adjective. *I regularly create backup disks.*

bad, badly   *Bad* is an adjective, *badly* an adverb. (See 26a and 26b.) *They felt bad about being early and ruining the surprise. Her arm hurt badly after she slid headfirst into second base.*

being as, being that   *Being as* and *being that* are nonstandard expressions. Write *because* or *since* instead. *Because* (not *Being as*) *I slept late, I had to skip breakfast.*

beside, besides   *Beside* is a preposition meaning "at the side of" or "next to." *Annie Oakley slept with her gun beside her bed. Besides* is a preposition meaning "except" or "in addition to." *No one besides Terrie can have that ice cream. Besides* is also an adverb meaning "in addition." *I'm not hungry; besides, I don't like ice cream.*

between, among   Ordinarily, use *among* with three or more entities, *between* with two. *The prize was divided among several contestants. You have a choice between carrots and beans.*

bring, take   Use *bring* when an object is being transported toward you, *take* when it is being moved away. *Please bring me a glass of water. Please take these flowers to Mr. Scott.*

burst, bursted; bust, busted   *Burst* is an irregular verb meaning "to come open or fly apart suddenly or violently." Its principal parts are *burst, burst, burst.* The past-tense form *bursted* is nonstandard. *Bust* and *busted* are slang for *burst* and, along with *bursted,* should not be used in formal writing.

can, may   The distinction between *can* and *may* is fading, but many careful writers still observe it in formal writing. *Can* is traditionally reserved for ability, *may* for permission. *Can you ski down the advanced slope without falling? May I help you?*

capital, capitol   *Capital* refers to a city, *capitol* to a building where lawmakers meet. *Capital* also refers to wealth or resources. *The capitol has undergone extensive renovations. The residents of the state capital protested the development plans.*

censor, censure   *Censor* means "to remove or suppress material considered objectionable." *Censure* means "to criticize severely." *The library's new policy of censoring controversial books has been censured by the media.*

cite, site   *Cite* means "to quote as an authority or example." *Site* is usually a noun meaning "a particular place." *He cited the zoning law in his argument against the proposed site of the gas station.* Locations on the Internet are usually referred to as *sites. The library's Web site improves every week.*

climactic, climatic   *Climactic* is derived from *climax,* the point of greatest intensity in a series or progression of events. *Climatic* is derived from *climate* and refers to meteorological conditions. *The climactic period in the dinosaurs' reign was reached just before severe climatic conditions brought on an ice age.*

coarse, course   *Coarse* means "crude" or "rough in texture." *The coarse weave of the wall hanging gave it a three-dimensional quality. Course* usually refers to a path, a playing field, or a unit of study; the expression *of course* means "certainly." *I plan to take a course in car repair this summer. Of course, you are welcome to join me.*

compare to, compare with   *Compare to* means "to represent as similar." *She compared him to a wild stallion. Compare with* means "to examine the ways in which two things are similar." *The study compared the language ability of apes with that of dolphins.*

complement, compliment   *Complement* is a verb meaning "to go with or complete" or a noun meaning "something that completes." *Compliment* as a verb means "to flatter"; as a noun it means "flattering remark." *Her skill at rushing the net complements his skill at volleying. Mother's flower arrangements receive many compliments.*

conscience, conscious   *Conscience* is a noun meaning "moral principles." *Conscious* is an adjective meaning "aware or alert." *Let your conscience be your guide. Were you conscious of his love for you?*

continual, continuous   *Continual* means "repeated regularly and frequently." *She grew weary of the continual telephone calls. Continuous* means "extended or prolonged without interruption." *The broken siren made a continuous wail.*

could care less   *Could care less* is a nonstandard expression. Write *couldn't care less* instead. *He couldn't* (not *could*) *care less about his psychology final.*

could of   *Could of* is nonstandard for *could have. We could have* (not *could of*) *had steak for dinner if we had been hungry.*

council, counsel   A *council* is a deliberative body, and a *councilor* is a member of such a body. *Counsel* usually means "advice" and can also mean "lawyer"; *counselor* is one who gives advice or guidance. *The councilors met to draft the council's position paper. The pastor offered wise counsel to the troubled teenager.*

criteria   *Criteria* is the plural of *criterion,* which means "a standard or rule or test on which a judgment or decision can be based." *The only criterion for the scholarship is ability.*

data   *Data* is a plural noun technically meaning "facts or propositions." But *data* is increasingly being accepted as a singular noun. *The new data suggest* (or *suggests*) *that our theory is correct.* (The singular *datum* is rarely used.)

different from, different than   Ordinarily, write *different from. Your sense of style is different from Jim's.* However, *different than* is acceptable to avoid an awkward construction. *Please let me know if your plans are different than* (to avoid *from what*) *they were six weeks ago.*

differ from, differ with   *Differ from* means "to be unlike"; *differ with* means "to disagree." *She differed with me about the wording of the agreement. My approach to the problem differed from hers.*

disinterested, uninterested   *Disinterested* means "impartial, objective"; *uninterested* means "not interested." *We sought the advice of a disinterested counselor to help us solve our problem. He was uninterested in anyone's opinion but his own.*

don't   *Don't* is the contraction for *do not. I don't want any. Don't* should not be used as the contraction for *does not,* which is *doesn't. He doesn't* (not *don't*) *want any.* (See 27c.)

double negative   Standard English allows two negatives only if a positive meaning is intended. *The runners were not unhappy with their performance.* Double negatives used to emphasize negation are nonstandard. *Jack doesn't have to answer to anybody* (not *nobody*).

due to   *Due to* is an adjective phrase and should not be used as a preposition meaning "because of." *The trip was canceled because of* (not *due to*) *lack of interest. Due to* is acceptable as a subject complement and usually follows a form of the verb *be. His success was due to hard work.*

each   *Each* is singular. (See 21e and 22a.)

effect   See *affect, effect.*

e.g.   In formal writing, replace the Latin abbreviation *e.g.* with its English equivalent: *for example* or *for instance.*

either *Either* is singular. (See 21e and 22a.) (For *either . . . or* constructions, see 21d and 22d.)

elicit, illicit *Elicit* is a verb meaning "to bring out" or "to evoke." *Illicit* is an adjective meaning "unlawful." *The reporter was unable to elicit any information from the police about illicit drug traffic.*

emigrate from, immigrate to *Emigrate* means "to leave one country or region to settle in another." *In 1900, my grandfather emigrated from Russia to escape the religious pogroms. Immigrate* means "to enter another country and reside there." *Many Mexicans immigrate to the United States to find work.*

eminent, imminent *Eminent* means "outstanding" or "distinguished." *We met an eminent professor of Greek history. Imminent* means "about to happen." *The announcement is imminent.*

enthused Many people object to the use of *enthused* as an adjective. Use *enthusiastic* instead. *The children were enthusiastic* (not *enthused*) *about going to the circus.*

-ess Many people find the *-ess* suffix demeaning. Write *poet,* not *poetess; Jew,* not *Jewess; author,* not *authoress.*

etc. Avoid ending a list with *etc.* It is more emphatic to end with an example, and in most contexts readers will understand that the list is not exhaustive. When you don't wish to end with an example, *and so on* is more graceful than *etc.* See also *and etc.*

eventually, ultimately Often used interchangeably, *eventually* is the better choice to mean "at an unspecified time in the future" and *ultimately* is better to mean "the furthest possible extent or greatest extreme." *He knew that eventually he would complete his degree. The existentialist considered suicide the ultimately rational act.*

everybody, everyone *Everybody* and *everyone* are singular. (See 21e and 22a.)

everyone, every one *Everyone* is an indefinite pronoun. *Every one,* the pronoun *one* preceded by the adjective *every,* means "each individual or thing in a particular group." *Every one* is usually followed by *of. Everyone wanted to go. Every one of the missing books was found.*

except See *accept, except.*

expect Avoid the colloquial use of *expect* meaning "to believe, think, or suppose." *I think* (not *expect*) *it will rain tonight.*

explicit, implicit *Explicit* means "expressed directly" or "clearly defined"; *implicit* means "implied, unstated." *I gave him explicit instructions not to go swimming. My mother's silence indicated her implicit approval.*

farther, further *Farther* usually describes distances. *Further* usually suggests quantity or degree. *Chicago is farther from Miami than I thought. You extended the curfew further than you should have.*

female, male The terms *female* and *male* are jargon when used to refer to specific people. *Two women* (not *females*) *and one man* (not *male*) *applied for the position.*

fewer, less *Fewer* refers to items that can be counted; *less* refers to general amounts. *Fewer people are living in the city. Please put less sugar in my tea.*

finalize *Finalize* is jargon meaning "to make final or complete." Use ordinary English instead. *The architect prepared final drawings* (not *finalized the drawings*).

firstly *Firstly* sounds pretentious, and it leads to the ungainly series *firstly, secondly, thirdly, fourthly,* and so on. Write *first, second, third* instead.

further See *farther, further.*

get *Get* has many colloquial uses. In writing, avoid using *get* to mean the following: "to evoke an emotional response" (*That music always gets to me*); "to annoy" (*After a while his sulking got to me*); "to take revenge on" (*I got back at him by leaving the room*); "to become" (*He got sick*); "to start or

begin" (*Let's get going*). Avoid using *have got to* in place of *must. I must* (not *have got to*) *finish this paper tonight.*

good, well *Good* is an adjective, *well* an adverb. (See 26.) *He hasn't felt good about his game since he sprained his wrist last season. She performed well on the uneven parallel bars.*

hanged, hung *Hanged* is the past-tense and past-participle form of the verb *hang* meaning "to execute." *The prisoner was hanged at dawn. Hung* is the past-tense and past-participle form of the verb *hang* meaning "to fasten or suspend." *The stockings were hung by the chimney with care.*

hardly Avoid expressions such as *can't hardly* and *not hardly,* which are considered double negatives. *I can* (not *can't*) *hardly describe my elation at getting the job.*

has got, have got *Got* is unnecessary and awkward in such constructions. It should be dropped. *We have* (not *have got*) *three days to prepare for the opening.*

he At one time *he* was commonly used to mean "he or she." Today such usage is inappropriate. (See 17f and 22a.)

he/she, his/her In formal writing, use *he or she* or *his or her.* For alternatives to these wordy constructions, see 17f and 22a.

hisself *Hisself* is nonstandard. Use *himself.*

hopefully *Hopefully* means "in a hopeful manner." *We looked hopefully to the future.* Do not use *hopefully* in constructions such as the following: *Hopefully, your daughter will recover soon.* Indicate who is doing the hoping: *I hope that your daughter will recover soon.*

hung See *hanged, hung.*

i.e. In formal writing, replace the Latin abbreviation *i.e.* with its English equivalent: *that is.*

if, whether Use *if* to express a condition and *whether* to express alternatives. *If you go on a trip, whether it be to Nebraska or New Jersey, remember to bring traveler's checks.*

illusion See *allusion, illusion.*

immigrate, emigrate See *emigrate from, immigrate to.*

imminent See *eminent, imminent.*

immoral See *amoral, immoral.*

implement *Implement* is a pretentious way of saying "do," "carry out," or "accomplish." Use ordinary language instead. *We carried out* (not *implemented*) *the director's orders with some reluctance.*

imply, infer *Imply* means "to suggest or state indirectly"; *infer* means "to draw a conclusion." *John implied that he knew all about computers, but the interviewer inferred that John was inexperienced.*

in, into *In* indicates location or condition; *into* indicates movement or a change in condition. *They found the lost letters in a box after moving into the house.*

individual *Individual* is a pretentious substitute for *person. We invited several persons* (not *individuals*) *from the audience to participate in the experiment.*

ingenious, ingenuous *Ingenious* means "clever." *Sarah's solution to the problem was ingenious. Ingenuous* means "naive" or "frank." *For a successful manager, Ed is surprisingly ingenuous.*

in regards to *In regards to* confuses two different phrases: *in regard to* and *as regards.* Use one or the other. *In regard to* (or *As regards*) *the contract, ignore the first clause.*

irregardless *Irregardless* is nonstandard. Use *regardless.*

is when, is where These mixed constructions are often incorrectly used in definitions. *A run-off election is a second election held to break a tie* (not *is when a second election breaks a tie*). (See 11c.)

it is   *It is* is nonstandard when used to mean "there is." *There is* (not *It is*) *a fly in my soup.*

its, it's   *Its* is a possessive pronoun; *it's* is a contraction for *it is.* (See 36c and 36e.) *The dog licked its wound whenever its owner walked into the room. It's a perfect day to walk the twenty-mile trail.*

kind(s)   *Kind* is singular and should be treated as such. Don't write *These kind of chairs are rare.* Write instead *This kind of chair is rare. Kinds* is plural and should be used only when you mean more than one kind. *These kinds of chairs are rare.*

kind of, sort of   Avoid using *kind of* or *sort of* to mean "somewhat." *The movie was somewhat* (not *kind of*) *boring.* Do not put *a* after either phrase. *That kind of* (not *kind of a*) *salesclerk annoys me.*

lead, led   *Lead* is a noun referring to a metal. *Led* is the past tense of the verb *lead. He led me to the treasure.*

learn, teach   *Learn* means "to gain knowledge"; *teach* means "to impart knowledge." *I must teach* (not *learn*) *my sister to read.*

leave, let   *Leave* means "to exit." Avoid using it with the nonstandard meaning "to permit." *Let* (not *leave*) *me help you with the dishes.*

less   See *fewer, less.*

let, leave   See *leave, let.*

liable   *Liable* means "obligated" or "responsible." Do not use it to mean "likely." *You're likely* (not *liable*) *to trip if you don't tie your shoelaces.*

lie, lay   *Lie* is an intransitive verb meaning "to recline or rest on a surface." Its principal parts are *lie, lay, lain. Lay* is a transitive verb meaning "to put or place." Its principal parts are *lay, laid, laid.* (See 27b.)

like, as   *Like* is a preposition, not a subordinating conjunction. It can be followed only by a noun or a noun phrase. *As* is a subordinating conjunction that introduces a subordinate clause. In casual speech you may say *She looks like she hasn't slept* or *You don't know her like I do.* But in formal writing, use *as. She looks as if she hasn't slept. You don't know her as I do.* (See prepositions and subordinating conjunctions, 47f and 47g.)

loose, lose   *Loose* is an adjective meaning "not securely fastened." *Lose* is a verb meaning "to misplace" or "to not win." *Did you lose your only loose pair of work pants?*

lots, lots of   *Lots* and *lots of* are colloquial substitutes for *many, much,* or *a lot.* Avoid using them in formal writing.

male, female   See *female, male.*

mankind   Avoid *mankind* whenever possible. It offends many readers because it excludes women. Use *humanity, humans, the human race,* or *humankind* instead.

may   See *can, may.*

maybe, may be   *Maybe* is an adverb meaning "possibly." *May be* is a verb phrase. *Maybe the sun will shine tomorrow. Tomorrow may be a brighter day.*

may of, might of   *May of* and *might of* are nonstandard for *may have* and *might have. We may have* (not *may of*) *had too many cookies.*

media, medium   *Media* is the plural of *medium. Of all the media that cover the Olympics, television is the medium that best captures the spectacle of the events.*

most   *Most* is colloquial when used to mean "almost" and should be avoided. *Almost* (not *Most*) *everyone went to the parade.*

must of   See *may of.*

myself   *Myself* is a reflexive or intensive pronoun. Reflexive: *I cut myself.* Intensive: *I will drive you myself.* Do not use *myself* in place of *I* or *me. He gave the flowers to Melinda and me* (not *myself*). (See also 24.)

neither   *Neither* is singular. (See 21e and 22a.) For *neither . . . nor* constructions, see 21d and 22d.

none   *None* is usually singular. (See 21e.)

nowheres   *Nowheres* is nonstandard for *nowhere.*

number   See *amount, number.*

of   Use the verb *have,* not the preposition *of,* after the verbs *could, should, would, may, might,* and *must. They must have* (not *of*) *left early.*

off of   *Off* is sufficient. Omit *of. The ball rolled off* (not *off of*) *the table.*

OK, O.K., okay   All three spellings are acceptable, but in formal speech and writing avoid these colloquial expressions for consent or approval.

parameters   *Parameter* is a mathematical term that has become jargon for "fixed limit," "boundary," or "guideline." Use ordinary English instead. *The task force was asked to work within certain guidelines* (not *parameters*).

passed, past   *Passed* is the past tense of the verb *pass. Mother passed me another slice of cake. Past* usually means "belonging to a former time" or "beyond a time or place." *Our past president spoke until past midnight. The hotel is just past the next intersection.*

percent, per cent, percentage   *Percent* (also spelled *per cent*) is always used with a specific number. *Percentage* is used with a descriptive term such as *large* or *small,* not with a specific number. *The candidate won 80 percent of the primary vote. Only a small percentage of registered voters turned out for the election.*

phenomena   *Phenomena* is the plural of *phenomenon,* which means "an observable occurrence or fact." *Strange phenomena occur at all hours of the night in that house, but last night's phenomenon was the strangest of all.*

plus   *Plus* should not be used to join independent clauses. *This raincoat is dirty; moreover* (not *plus*), *it has a hole in it.*

precede, proceed   *Precede* means "to come before." *Proceed* means "to go forward." *As we proceeded up the mountain path, we noticed fresh tracks in the mud, evidence that a group of hikers had preceded us.*

principal, principle   *Principal* is a noun meaning "the head of a school or organization" or "a sum of money." It is also an adjective meaning "most important." *Principle* is a noun meaning "a basic truth or law." *The principal expelled her for three principal reasons. We believe in the principle of equal justice for all.*

proceed, precede   See *precede, proceed.*

quote, quotation   *Quote* is a verb; *quotation* is a noun. Avoid using *quote* as a shortened form of *quotation.* *Her quotations* (not *quotes*) *from Shakespeare intrigued us.*

raise, rise   *Raise* is a transitive verb meaning "to move or cause to move upward." It takes a direct object. *I raised the shades. Rise* is an intransitive verb meaning "to go up." It does not take a direct object. *Heat rises.*

real, really   *Real* is an adjective; *really* is an adverb. *Real* is sometimes used informally as an adverb, but avoid this use in formal writing. *She was really* (not *real*) *angry.* (See 26a.)

reason is because   Use *that* instead of *because.* *The reason I'm late is that* (not *because*) *my car broke down.* (See 11c.)

reason why   The expression *reason why* is redundant. *The reason* (not *The reason why*) *Jones lost the election is clear.*

relation, relationship   *Relation* describes a connection between things. *Relationship* describes a connection between people. *There is a relation between poverty and infant mortality. Our business relationship has cooled over the years.*

respectfully, respectively   *Respectfully* means "showing or marked by respect." *Respectively* means "each in the order given." *He respectfully submitted his opinion to the judge. John, Tom, and Larry were a butcher, a baker, and a lawyer, respectively.*

sensual, sensuous   *Sensual* means "gratifying the physical senses," especially those associated with sexual pleasure. *Sensuous* means "pleasing to the senses," especially those involved in the experience of art, music, and nature. *The sensuous music and balmy air led the dancers to more sensual movements.*

set, sit   *Set* is a transitive verb meaning "to put" or "to place." Its principal parts are *set, set, set. Sit* is an intransitive verb meaning "to be seated." Its principal parts are *sit, sat, sat. She set the dough in a warm corner of the kitchen. The cat sat in the warmest part of the room.*

shall, will   *Shall* was once used as the helping verb with *I* or *we: I shall, we shall, you will, he/she/it will, they will.* Today, however, *will* is generally accepted even when the subject is *I* or *we.* The word *shall* occurs primarily in polite questions (*Shall I find you a pillow?*) and in legalistic sentences suggesting duty or obligation (*The applicant shall file form 1080 by December 31*).

should of   *Should of* is nonstandard for *should have. They should have* (not *should of*) *been home an hour ago.*

since   Do not use *since* to mean "because" if there is any chance of ambiguity. *Since we won the game, we have been celebrating with a pitcher of beer. Since* here could mean "because" or "from the time that."

sit   See *set, sit.*

site, cite   See *cite, site.*

somebody, someone   *Somebody* and *someone* are singular. (See 21e and 22a.)

something   *Something* is singular. (See 21e.)

sometime, some time, sometimes   *Sometime* is an adverb meaning "at an indefinite or unstated time." *Some time* is the adjective *some* modifying the noun *time* and is spelled as two words to mean "a period of time." *Sometimes* is an adverb meaning "at times, now and then." *I'll see you sometime soon. I haven't lived there for some time. Sometimes I run into him at the library.*

suppose to   Write *supposed to.*

sure and   *Sure and* is nonstandard for *sure to. We were all taught to be sure to* (not *and*) *look both ways before crossing a street.*

take   See *bring, take.*

than, then   *Than* is a conjunction used in comparisons; *then* is an adverb denoting time. *That pizza is more than I can eat. Tom laughed, and then we recognized him.*

that   See *who, which, that.*

that, which   Many writers reserve *that* for restrictive clauses, *which* for nonrestrictive clauses. (See 32e.)

theirselves   *Theirselves* is nonstandard for *themselves. The two people were able to push the Volkswagen out of the way themselves* (not *theirselves*).

them   The use of *them* in place of *those* is nonstandard. *Please send those* (not *them*) *flowers to the patient in room 220.*

there, their, they're   *There* is an adverb specifying place; it is also an expletive. Adverb: *Sylvia is lying there unconscious.* Expletive: *There are two plums left. Their* is a possessive pronoun. *Fred and Jane finally washed their car. They're* is a contraction of *they are. They're later than usual today.*

they   The use of *they* to indicate possession is nonstandard. Use *their* instead. *Cindy and Sam decided to sell their* (not *they*) *1975 Corvette.*

this kind   See *kind(s).*

to, too, two   *To* is a preposition; *too* is an adverb; *two* is a number. *Too many of your shots slice to the left, but the last two were right on the mark.*

toward, towards   *Toward* and *towards* are generally interchangeable, although *toward* is preferred in American English.

try and   *Try and* is nonstandard for *try to. The teacher asked us all to try to* (not *and*) *write an original haiku.*

ultimately, eventually   See *eventually, ultimately.*

unique   Avoid expressions such as *most unique, more straight, less perfect, very round.* Something either is unique or it isn't. It is illogical to suggest degrees of uniqueness. (See 26c.)

usage   The noun *usage* should not be substituted for *use* when the meaning intended is "employment of." The *use* (not *usage*) *of computers dramatically increased the company's profits.*

use to   Write *used to.*

utilize   *Utilize* means "to make use of." It often sounds pretentious; in most cases, *use* is sufficient. *I used* (not *utilized*) *the best workers to get the job done fast.*

wait for, wait on   *Wait for* means "to be in readiness for" or "await." *Wait on* means "to serve." *We're only waiting for* (not *waiting on*) *Ruth to take us to the game.*

ways   *Ways* is colloquial when used to mean "distance." *The city is a long way* (not *ways*) *from here.*

weather, whether   The noun *weather* refers to the state of the atmosphere. *Whether* is a conjunction referring to a choice between alternatives. *We wondered whether the weather would clear up in time for our picnic.*

well, good   See *good, well.*

where   Do not use *where* in place of *that. I heard that* (not *where*) *the crime rate is increasing.*

which   See *that, which* and *who, which, that.*

while   Avoid using *while* to mean "although" or "whereas" if there is any chance of ambiguity. *Although* (not *While*) *Gloria lost money in the slot machine, Tom won it at roulette.* Here *While* could mean either "although" or "at the same time that."

who, which, that   Do not use *which* to refer to persons. Use *who* instead. *That,* though generally used to refer to things, may be used to refer to a group or class of people. *Fans wondered how an old man who* (not *that* or *which*) *walked with a limp could play football. The team that scores the most points in this game will win the tournament.*

who, whom   *Who* is used for subjects and subject complements; *whom* is used for objects. (See 25.)

who's, whose   *Who's* is a contraction of *who is; whose* is a possessive pronoun. *Who's ready for more popcorn? Whose coat is this?* (See 36c and 36e.)

will   See *shall, will.*

would of   *Would of* is nonstandard for *would have. She would have* (not *would of*) *had a chance to play if she had arrived on time.*

you   In formal writing, avoid *you* in an indefinite sense meaning "anyone." (See 23d.) *Any spectator* (not *You*) *could tell by the way John caught the ball that his throw would be too late.*

your, you're   *Your* is a possessive pronoun; *you're* is a contraction of *you are. Is that your new motorcycle? You're on the list of finalists.* (See 36c and 36e.)

Answers to Tutorials, Guided Practice, and Preview Exercises

TUTORIAL 1, page ix

1. A verb has to agree with its subject. (21)
2. Each pronoun should agree with its antecedent. (22)
3. You should avoid sentence fragments. (19)
4. Don't write a run-on sentence; you must connect the clauses with a comma and a coordinating conjunction or with a semicolon. (20)
5. Discriminate carefully between adjectives and adverbs. (26)
6. Proofread to see if you left any words out. (10)
7. Check for *-ed* verb endings that have been dropped. (27d)
8. In most contexts, avoid passive-voice verbs. (14a or 28c)
9. In choosing proper pronoun case, follow the example of us teachers, who are the experts. (24 and 25)
10. Don't use double negatives. (26d)
11. Watch out for dangling modifiers. (12e)
12. It's important to use apostrophes correctly. (36)
13. A writer must be careful not to shift his or her [*not* their] point of view. *Or* Writers must be careful not to shift their point of view. (13a)
14. If your sentence begins with a long introductory word group, use a comma to separate the word group from the rest of the sentence. (32b)
15. Avoid clichés. (18e)

TUTORIAL 2, page ix

1. The index entry "*anybody*" mentions that the word is singular, so you might not need to look further to realize that the plural *their* is incorrect. The second page reference leads you to section 22, which suggests nonsexist strategies for revision, such as *Students taking the school bus to the volleyball game must bring in a permission slip signed by their parents* or *Anybody taking the school bus to the volleyball game must bring in a permission slip signed by his or her parents.*
2. The index entry "*lay, lie*" (or "*laying* versus *lying*") takes you to section 27b and to the Glossary of Usage, where you will learn that *lying* (meaning "reclining or resting on a surface") is correct.
3. Look up "*only*" and you will be directed to section 12a, which explains that limiting modifiers such as *only* should be placed before the words they modify. The sentence should read *We looked at only two houses before buying the house of our dreams.*
4. Looking up "*you*, inappropriate use of" leads you to section 23d and the Glossary of Usage, which explain that *you* should not be used to mean "anyone in general." You can revise the sentence by using *a person* or *one* instead of *you*, or you can restructure the sentence completely: *In Saudi Arbia, accepting a gift is considered ill-mannered.*
5. The index entries "*I* versus *me*" and "*me* versus *I*" take you to section 24, which explains why *me* is correct.

TUTORIAL 3, page ix

1. Section 32c tells you that although usage varies, most experts advise using a comma between all items in a series—to prevent possible misreadings or ambiguities. To find this section, Ray Farley would probably use the menu system.
2. Maria Sanchez and Mike Lee would consult section 30, on articles. This section is easy to locate on either the brief or the detailed menu.
3. Section 24 explains why *Jane and me* is correct. To find section 24, John Pell could use the menu system to locate section 24, "Pronoun case" (*I* or *me*, etc.). Or he could look up "*I* versus *me*" in the index. Pell could also look up "*myself*" in the index or he could consult the Glossary of Usage, where a cross-reference would direct him to section 24.
4. Selena Young's employees could turn to sections 21 and 27c for help. Young could use the menu system to find these sections if she knew to look under "Subject-verb agreement" or "Standard English verb forms." If she wasn't sure about the grammatical terminology, she could look up "*-s*, as verb ending" or "Verbs, *-s* form of" in the index.
5. Section 26b explains why *I felt bad about her death* is correct. To find section 26b, Joe Thompson could use the menu system if he knew that *bad* versus *badly* is a choice between an adjective and an adverb. Otherwise he could look up "*bad, badly*" in the index or the Glossary of Usage.

TUTORIAL 4, page x

1. The *number* of horses a Comanche warrior had in his possession indicated the wealth of his family.
2. Correct
3. That is the most *unusual* floral arrangement I have ever seen.
4. Changing attitudes *toward* alcohol have *affected* the beer industry.
5. Jenny *should have* known better than to attempt that dive.
6. Everyone in our office is *enthusiastic* about this project.
7. George and Pat are selling *their* house because now that *their* children are grown, *they're* planning to move to Arizona.
8. Correct
9. It is *human* nature to think wisely and act foolishly.
10. Dr. Newman and *I* have agreed to arrange the retirement party.

EXERCISE 8–1, page 87

Suggested revision:

No one who knew Albert Einstein as a young child would ever have believed that he might one day be called the smartest man in the world. None of his teachers could have predicted success for him. A shy, slow learner, Albert always got in trouble in class. He consistently failed the subjects he did not like. His family could not have predicted his success either. Albert could not even get to meals on time. Night after night his parents had to postpone dinner until servants, after searching the house and grounds, found the boy. He would be full of apologies but have no explanation to offer for his lateness except that he was "thinking." Once his angry father dangled his big gold watch at Albert and told him to figure out how late he was. Albert, who could not tell time, was fascinated by the tiny magnetic compass hanging from the watch chain. The boy asked so many questions about the compass that he did not eat much dinner anyway. When Albert begged his father to lend him the compass to sleep with, his father let him borrow it. Years later Einstein wondered whether that little compass had been the beginning of his interest in science.

EXERCISE 9–1, page 93

Suggested revision:

In his own time, this sixteenth century man was known only by his given name, "Leonardo." Today his is still known by that one name. But then and now, that name suggests many different roles for its owner: theatrical producer, biologist, botanist, inventor, engineer, strategist, researcher, and artist.

Sixteenth-century fighting men told how Leonardo had given the Venetians advice about conducting surprise underwater attacks against the invading Turkish fleet and flooding the countryside that the Turkish army had to cross. Engineers knew him as the man who laid out new canals for the city of Milan. Scientists admired him for not only his precise anatomical drawings but also for his discovery that hardening of the arteries could cause death. To Milan's royal court, Leonardo was the artist who was painting impressive portraits, sculpting a bronze horse memorial to the house of Sforza, and at the same time working on a mural of the Last Supper.

Leonardo understood things others did not. He saw a three-dimensional S-curve in all of nature—the flow of water, the movements of animals, and the flight of birds. He called this curve "life-force." We recognize the same S-curve today in the spiraling form of DNA. Leonardo invented the wave theory. He saw that grain bending as the wind blew over it and water rippling from a stone cast into it were the same scientific event. It was as easy for him to see this wave in sound and light as to observe it in fields and streams. The math of his day could not explain all his theories; it was the twentieth century before science showed the world that Leonardo knew what he was talking about.

Leonardo was not blind to the negative aspects of his world. He saw very clearly that the powers of nature could be infinitely destructive and that human beings could be savage. At the same time, he felt a unity that held all life's varied parts together, a unity he could express in his art.

"Leonardo"—it's quite a name!

EXERCISE 10–1, page 99

Suggested revision:

Mary Wollstonecraft, an eighteenth-century writer, may have been England's first feminist. Her entire life reflected her belief in equal rights for women in all areas of their lives: personal, intellectual, and professional.

From childhood, she never had accepted and never would accept the idea that men were superior to women. As a young girl, she knew that her drinking and gambling father deserved less respect than her long-suffering mother. As an adult, she demanded that society give her the same freedom it gave to men.

Wollstonecraft also demanded that men pay attention to her ideas. She did not get their attention by arguing directly on a subject. Instead, she would give an example of what she was objecting to and invite her readers to think about it from various points of view. Working this way, she made few enemies among intellectuals. Indeed, she was attracted to and respected by some of the leading intellectuals of her day. Among them she was as well known on one side of the Atlantic as on the other. Tom Paine, the American orator and writer, probably knew her better than Samuel Johnson, the English writer, did.

Professionally, she was a governess, teacher, and writer. When her father's drinking destroyed the family, she and her sisters had to support themselves. After a stint as governess, Mary joined her two sisters in starting a girls' school. Eventually, financial problems forced the school to close, but not before Mary had acquired enough firsthand experience to write *Thoughts on the Education of Daughters* (1786). As competent as or more competent than other writers of the day, she was a more persuasive advocate for women than most of them.

Modern feminists may find it ironic that current encyclopedia entries for "Wollstonecraft" refer researchers to "Godwin," her married name—where they will find an entry for her longer than the one for her famous husband, William Godwin.

EXERCISE 11–1, page 105

Sometimes it's hard to separate fact from fiction, to know what is history and what is folklore. For example, was there really a Casey Jones? Or are the stories about him simply legends? Casey Jones, John Henry, Johnny Appleseed, Uncle Sam, Santa Claus—which of these were real men? We've been told stories about them all of our lives, but are those stories true?

There really was a railroad engineer people called "Casey" Jones; he got that nickname because of his birthplace, Cayce, Kentucky. There really was a "Cannonball" too; it was the Illinois-

Central's fast mail train. And there really was a train wreck: Engine Number 382 rammed into some freight cars. The accident was not Casey's fault, and he died trying to save his passengers. When workers found his body in the wreckage, Casey's hand was still on the air brake lever. (Air brakes had recently been installed on trains to increase their braking power.)

John Henry was an African American railroad worker of great strength. In legend and song, he died after a timed contest against a steam drill. By using a hammer in each hand, he won the contest. John Henry drilled two 7-foot holes; the steam drill bored only one 9-foot hole. The real John Henry died on the job too, crushed by rocks that fell from the ceiling of a railroad tunnel.

John Chapman, better known as Johnny Appleseed, was a wealthy and well-liked nurseryman who kept moving his place of business west as the frontier moved west. His boyhood friend Sam Wilson supplied meat to the United States troops during the War of 1812. A worker told a government inspector that the "U.S." stamped on the meat stood for "Uncle Sam." Although it was a joke, it caught on, and Congress made the "Uncle Sam" identification official in the 1960s.

That leaves Santa Claus. As far as historians know now, Santa was not real. But legends say that there was once a man who . . .

EXERCISE 12–1, page 113

Suggested revision:

Hearing the name Karl Marx, people usually think of Russia. Marx never lived in Russia at all. Actually, he spent almost all of his adult life in England. He was a political exile for the last half of his life.

Marx lived first in Germany. Born of Jewish parents, he completed his university studies with a Ph.D. at the University of Jena. His favorite professor tried to get Marx an appointment to teach at the university. When that professor was fired, Marx gave up hope of teaching at Jena or any other German university. Because he was denied a university position, Marx had to earn his living as a journalist. He worked briefly as a newspaper editor in Germany.

Next came France, Belgium, and a return to Germany. First Marx and his new bride moved to Paris, where Marx worked for a radical journal and became friendly with Friedrich Engels. When the journal ceased publication, Marx moved to Brussels, Belgium, and then back to Cologne, Germany. He did not hold a regular job, so he tried desperately to earn at least enough money to feed his family.

After living in Paris and Brussels, Marx decided he would settle in London. He and his family lived in abject poverty while Marx earned what little income he could by writing for an American newspaper, the *New York Tribune*.

EXERCISE 13–1, page 119

Suggested revision:

Do you know how slavery began in America or how it ended? When the *Mayflower* landed in September 1620, slaves were already in America. A Dutch ship had unloaded and sold twenty Africans in Jamestown, Virginia, the year before.

But slavery in America began long before that. Many early explorers brought slaves with them to the new land, and some historians claim that one of the men in Christopher Columbus's crew was a slave. From the 1500s to the 1800s, slave ships brought ten million African slaves across the ocean.

Most of the slaves stayed in Latin America and the West Indies, but the southern part of the United States received about six percent of them. Few northerners owned slaves, and opposition to slavery was evident by the time of the American Revolution. Rhode Island prohibited the importation of slaves even before the Revolutionary War. After the war, six northern states abolished slavery at once. Others passed laws to phase out slavery, and even Virginia enacted legislation encouraging slave owners to emancipate their slaves.

But it took a war, a tricky political situation, and a very clever former slave to free all slaves. History gives Lincoln the credit for liberating the slaves during the Civil War, and he deserves some credit, but emancipation was not his idea. Originally, no government officials seriously considered emancipation because they were so focused on winning the war to save the Union. But then a very important black man talked to Lincoln and gave him the idea and the reason. This man said that freeing slaves would be good for the war effort and asked if Lincoln would agree to do it. Who was this man? He was Frederick Douglass, fugitive slave and newspaper editor.

EXERCISE 14–1, page 127

Suggested revision:

Frederick Douglass immensely enjoyed his favorite fantasy about slave owners. In Douglass's dream, everyone conspired against the slave owners. Slaves still in bondage gave no hint of an impending escape. People who helped escaping slaves never indicated that they did so. Slaves who escaped successfully never revealed how they got away. Recaptured slaves told their owners nothing at all. Even some white southerners who sympathized with the slaves gave no information to their slave-owning friends. Douglass enjoyed the final part of his fantasy the most. In it, Douglass imagined slave owners as being too afraid to hunt escaping slaves. The owners distrusted their slaves, their enemies, and even their friends.

EXERCISE 15–1, page 133

Suggested revision:

Everyone has heard of Martin Luther King, Jr. After studying for the ministry at Boston University and earning a doctorate in theology, he went home to the South to work as a minister. He started working in civil rights and became the most influential leader of that cause in America. When he died, the victim of an assassin's bullet, his name was almost synonymous with "civil rights." Historians and biographers have recorded his leadership in the fight to gain basic civil rights for all Americans. Many people who know of his civil rights work, however, are not aware of his skill as a writer. In addition to his carefully crafted and emotional speeches, King produced other important writing.

Among King's most famous writings is his "Letter from a Birmingham Jail." Written to answer a statement published by eight Alabama ministers that King's work was "unwise and untimely," the letter shows King to be a man who had great patience with his critics. Eager to get these ministers to accept his point of view, King reminds them that they are ministers. Their goodwill, he says, should help them see that his views hold value. Instead of attacking them personally, he analyzes their arguments and then presents his own views. Does he use many of the emotional appeals for which he is justly famous? No, in this letter King depends on logic and reasoning as the tools to win his argument.

EXERCISE 16–1, page 141

Suggested revision:

Adam Smith, the founder of modern economics, proposed a theory in the eighteenth century that has made him controversial ever since. This economist, born in Scotland and educated in England, wrote the first complete study of political economy. *The Wealth of Nations* was published in the same year that Americans declared their independence from England—1776. Smith's book pointed out the interdependence of freedom and order, economic processes, and free trade laws. Although Smith's thinking did not really affect economic policies significantly during his lifetime, its influence in the next century was considerable. Among economists, "the invisible hand" and "laissez-faire" are synonymous with Smith's name. History has only made Smith's ideas more controversial. Say "Adam Smith" to conservative businesspeople, and they will smile and respond with words like "He was a good man—really understood how business works!" Say "Adam Smith" to liberal reformers, and they will grimace and mutter something like "He was an evil man—really sold the average citizen down the river." Both of these reactions are extreme, but such responses indicate that the controversy aroused by Smith's ideas is still alive.

EXERCISE 17–1, page 151

Suggested revisions:

A. In the 1800s, an English man named Thomas Robert Malthus became involved in economics. He was very interested in predicting how many more people would be in the world eventually and how much food would be available for them. What he figured out was frightening. He said people kept having children faster than

society could produce enough to feed them. There was no way to avoid it. Hard times and wars would kill most people. According to Malthus, famine, plagues, and even wars were necessary to eliminate some excess people so the remainder could have enough food.

B. Robert Malthus proved that population grows faster than food supplies. His thinking led him to oppose any help for poor people. He believed that by relieving the immediate problems of the poor, the government actually made it harder for people to feed their families. Malthus said that if the government subsidized their basic needs, people would only have more children, thus increasing the population even more. Then the inevitable famine or drought would have to eliminate even more people to help a few survive. Everyone from worker to supervisor was caught in the same predicament. It is no wonder that when the English historian Thomas Carlyle finished reading Malthus's theories, he pronounced economics "the dismal science."

EXERCISE 18–1, page 159

Suggested revision:

Economics is not totally dominated by men. Even in the 1800s, when Thomas Malthus and David Ricardo were the experts, one leading writer about economics was a woman, Jane Marcet. Marcet wrote for the popular press. One of her favorite topics to write about was political economy. In her book *Conversations in Political Economy,* Marcet summarized economic doctrines before 1800. Her aim was different from that of either Malthus or Ricardo. Rather than propounding a new theory of her own, she popularized theories of other people. Twentieth-century women have done more than write about theories that men have proposed. Some of them have taken the initiative to develop their own ideas. Sally Herbert Frankel, for example, made the first official calculations of the Union of South Africa's national income. She is only one of the increasing number of women who make careers in economics.

EXERCISE 19–1, page 169

Suggested revision:

Four young Englishmen added a word to the world's vocabulary in the 1960s, a word that became synonymous with the 1960s, especially with the music of that time. That word was, of course, "Beatles." The Beatles became the most famous popular musical group of the twentieth century, and they may still hold that title when the twentieth century is over.

The Beatles were popular in Liverpool, England, and in Hamburg, Germany, before they came to America on tour and became world-famous. Liverpool and Hamburg loved the four young men and their music. The Beatles' favorite club was the Cavern in Liverpool, where they hung out together, played day and night, and attracted many fans. A Liverpool disk jockey first called attention to them, and a Liverpool music critic and record store owner became their first manager. The disk jockey called them "fantastic," saying that they had "resurrected original rock 'n' roll." The music critic who became their manager, Brian Epstein, made them shape up as a group, promoting them, arranging club dates for them, and badgering record companies for them. He intended to win a recording contract for this exciting new group.

In England, the record buying led to the publicity. In America, the publicity led to the record buying. Everyone wanted copies of the original singles: "Love Me Do," "Please, Please Me," and "From Me to You." In America, audiences made so much noise that no one could hear the music. Crowds of screaming teenagers surrounded the Beatles wherever they went, determined to touch one or more of these famous music makers. Reporters observing the conduct of fans at Beatles' concerts found that they had to invent another word to describe the wild, almost insane behavior of the fans. They called it "Beatlemania."

EXERCISE 20–1, page 179

Suggested revision:

Have you ever heard of the Wobblies? Not many people have these days. That's a shame, because they did at least two things for which they should be remembered. They probably saved the labor movement in America, and they definitely gave American folk music some of its most unforgettable songs. No one really knows how they got their nickname, but almost everyone knows a song or two that they inspired.

The Wobblies were the members of the Industrial Workers of the World (IWW), a small but militant coalition of radical labor groups. The Wobblies could not get along with the major union groups of the day; in fact, they alienated most of those groups.

Although the major unions disliked the Wobblies immensely, they learned some valuable lessons from them. The first lesson was to avoid getting involved in politics. If there was one thing the Wobblies hated more than capitalism, it was politics. The Wobblies avoided politics for one good reason: They believed that political affiliation caused the death of unions. What else did the major unions learn? They learned to deal realistically with workers' problems. Major unions also learned new recruiting techniques from the Wobblies. In addition, they copied the Wobblies in devoting their energy to nuts-and-bolts issues affecting the workers.

The major unions never recognized their debt to the Wobblies, but the debt was still there for later historians to see. When historians began to compile the story of American labor unions, they finally recognized the contributions of the Wobblies.

EXERCISE 21–1, page 193

convey, are, are, are, has, is, seem, enjoy, is, is

EXERCISE 22–1, page 201

Suggested revision:

Everyone has heard of Dorothy and Toto and their tornado "flight" from Kansas to Oz. Everyone also knows that the Oz adventure was pure fantasy and that it ended happily. But another girl from Kansas took real flights all around the real world. Whenever she landed safely after setting one of her many records, everyone rejoiced and sent congratulations to her. When she disappeared on her last flight, the whole world mourned. Not every pilot can claim to have that kind of following.

Neighbors knew that Amelia Earhart would not be a typical "lady." A child as curious, daring, and self-confident as Amelia was bound to stand out among peers. When she and her sister Muriel were young, girls were supposed to play with dolls. If girls played baseball or collected worms, they were called "tomboys" and were often punished. Boys and girls even had different kinds of sleds — the girls' sleds were lightweight, impossible-to-steer box sleds.

But the Earhart family lived by its own rules. Amelia's father, whom she depended on for approval, bought her the boys' sled she longed for. Many fast trips down steep hills gave Amelia a foretaste of flying with the wind in her face.

The closest Amelia came to flying was on a homemade roller coaster. She and her friends built it, using an old woodshed for the base of the ride. They started eight feet off the ground and tried to sled down the slope without falling off. No one was successful on a first attempt, but Amelia kept trying until she had a successful ride. Satisfied at last, she declared that the ride had felt "just like flying."

EXERCISE 23–1, page 207

Suggested revision:

George and Mary Jones lived in Memphis during the Civil War. They were sympathetic to the Union, but the city definitely favored the Confederates. Being caught in the middle made the war years especially hard on them. They looked forward to a much better life after the war.

At first, it seemed that they were going to have that better life. George got a job as a labor organizer, and Mary stayed at home to care for their four healthy children. Then came yellow fever. In nine months, Mary went from a happy wife and mother to a despondent widow who had no children. She had to find work. Because a person must have some meaning for living, she needed work that she could care strongly about.

By 1900, Mary had become involved in union activities all over the United States. She found her calling among the coal miners and their wives, a calling she followed for the next thirty years. Making friends with workers and outwitting private detectives, she held secret meetings to help the miners organize and plan strategy. The newspaper often reported her ability to outwit and outlast mine bosses and lawyers as well as to reawaken courage in disconsolate workers.

Mary Jones spent many nights in jail, but often her jailers did not know what to do with this attractive, gray-haired woman whom

the workers called "Mother." The jailers' confusion simply amused Mary, who was far more used to jail than her jailers could imagine.

EXERCISE 24–1, page 215

They, them, We, her, they, them, they, he, president's, she

EXERCISE 25–1, page 221

whom, whom. Who, whoever, whom
[*Note:* The *whom* in the last sentence may be dropped.]

EXERCISE 26–1, page 229

Novelists have often used their storytelling talents to influence people's thinking. Charles Dickens did it in nineteenth-century England. From *David Copperfield* to *Oliver Twist*, book after book depicted the plight of the poor and other really unfortunate members of society. Harriet Beecher Stowe did it in nineteenth-century America, but with hardly as many books. Her *Uncle Tom's Cabin* depicted slavery so well that the book was very influential in causing the Civil War.

Harriet Beecher Stowe considered slavery sinful and wanted her book to help end slavery quickly and peacefully. People first read parts of the novel ten years before the beginning of the war. An abolitionist magazine published it a few chapters at a time, hoping the effect of the story would make readers feel so bad about slavery that they would rally to the abolitionist cause. Many people, reading *Uncle Tom's Cabin* installment by installment, did become convinced that nothing could be worse than living in slavery on a southern plantation.

None of the abolitionists, who devoted their energy to abolishing slavery, expected a perfect world when the book itself was published in 1852. But they certainly hoped that the book would be influential. It was. Of all the novels published that year, it was the best seller on both sides of the Atlantic. Its popularity was good news for the abolitionists. Harriet Beecher Stowe's wish came true.

EXERCISE 27–1, page 239

What Hollywood film director gets credit for some of the scariest movies ever made, for some of the most incredible special effects anyone has ever dreamed of, and for one of the most popular children's movies ever made? If your answer is Steven Spielberg, you're right. *Jaws* and *Jurassic Park* have frightened millions of viewers. *Raiders of the Lost Ark* and *Close Encounters of the Third Kind* continue to intrigue how-to-do-it fans, and *E.T.* has won the hearts of children and adults throughout the world.

What kind of person is the creator of these widely different films? He is a man who has been in love with a movie camera all his life. His family claims that when Spielberg's father tried to take the first home movies of his young son, Spielberg got up and walked directly toward the camera, as if he already knew how an actor should respond to the lens. As a child, he set up two electric trains going full speed toward each other so that he could film the resulting crash. Once he even talked his mother into boiling a cherry dessert in a pressure cooker until it exploded — so he could film the explosion and the sticky red mess that lay on top of all the counters afterward.

Those events were staged for the fun and information they provided the boy. But he found other uses for his camera as well. His moviemaking gave this nonacademic, nonathletic schoolboy something to do with his after-school hours and provided him with a little bit of popularity and even protection: Other children liked to be in his movies, and the bully who had been picking on him ceased his harassment after having a role in one of them.

EXERCISE 28–1, page 249

Almost everyone has heard about Aesop's fables, but most people know very little about Aesop himself. Most of what we know about Aesop is a mixture of hearsay and conjecture. We do know that he was a slave in Greece. One theory is that before he came to Greece he had lived in Ethiopia for most of his life and that "Aesop" is a much-shortened form of "the Ethiopian."

Aesop was not a storyteller then, though he would have loved to speak well enough to tell a good story. He stuttered so badly that he did not even try to talk. In one story we learn, however, that he could communicate. A neighbor brought a gift of figs to Aesop's master. Greatly pleased, the master planned to enjoy the figs after his bath and directed that they be put in a cool place until he was ready. While the master was bathing, the overseer and his friends ate the figs. When the master discovered the loss of his figs, the other slaves placed the blame on Aesop. They knew that if Aesop were able to speak, he could defend himself, but they did not fear this stammering slave.

The master ordered that Aesop be flogged. Aesop got the master to delay the punishment briefly. Aesop drank a glass of warm water, ran his fingers down his throat, and vomited only water. Pointing at the overseer, he made gestures that the overseer and his friends should do as he had done. They drank the water, ran their fingers down their throats—and vomited figs.

Although Aesop's cleverness saved him from a flogging, it also made an enemy of the overseer. Aesop discovered a basic truth about life: Being right doesn't always help one to make friends.

EXERCISE 29–1, page 261

Suggested revision:

Immigrants have come to the United States from all over the world. Initially, new settlers were mostly European, Irish, or English. By the twentieth century, many Asians had taken the frightening boat trip across the Pacific. Usually the men came first. After they had made enough money for passage, their wives and children were brought over. All were in search of the same good life that earlier European immigrants had sought. Unable to live comfortably in their homelands, a large number of Chinese and Japanese gave them up and settled in the western part of the United States.

These new immigrants worked on the railroads and in the mines. American businesses recruited Chinese labor because it was difficult to find American workers who would accept the wages that were paid. Why did workers decide to come to America anyway? Somehow the idea got started that America was a "golden mountain," where people could pick up gold nuggets after an easy climb. Once they got here, most immigrants worked hard because they hoped to make enough money to bring relatives over to America too.

Before and during World War II, many Germans who had been persecuted by Hitler escaped to America. After the war, thousands of "displaced persons" were welcomed by the United States. Later, refugees from Asia, Africa, Latin America, and the Caribbean wanted to be accepted. Franklin D. Roosevelt once said, "All of our people all over the country, except the pure-blooded Indians, are immigrants or descendants of immigrants." If Roosevelt were alive today, he would know that his statement is still true.

EXERCISE 30–1, page 273

Suggested revision:

The United States has always attracted immigrants. Modern scientists think that the first immigrants arrived at least 25,000 years ago, probably traveling over a land bridge just below the Arctic Circle—from Siberia to Alaska. (Of course the land bridge is no longer there. Scientists think that such a bridge formed during the ice age, when much of the water in the ocean froze into tall glaciers. As it froze, it exposed large strips of land. Hunters probably followed animals across this land bridge.)

Descendants of the original immigrants were still here in 1607 when settlers from England arrived in Virginia. These early settlers were followed by many more. In the hundred and forty years that followed, thousands made the trip to America. Crowded onto small wooden boats, they left behind their kinfolk and their history and crossed the Atlantic Ocean. Making such a trip took bravery and faith in the future.

Some of the settlers came for religious reasons; others came to escape poverty or imprisonment. But all of them came hoping for happiness. They were followed by many others with the same goal. Ever since those first immigrants 25,000 years ago, waves of immigrants have been a common occurrence in America.

EXERCISE 31–1, page 281

Suggested revision:

The Cisneros family lived out an American immigrant's dream. José Romulo Munguia y Torres could not see a way to succeed in his home country, Mexico. This young man, like many Mexicans before him, crossed the Rio Grande from Mexico. In Texas, he found a job, worked, saved his money, bought a house, and started a family.

Two generations later, José's first grandson, Henry, was a professor at the University of Texas. This young professor decided to enter politics. There were many Mexican Americans in San Antonio, where he lived. The Mexican Americans in the part of town where Henry lived were trying to get political power in the city. It was not easy to do so. The powerful white people controlled the city government. The city may have been controlled by the white people, but the Mexican Americans had the most voting power. Not having an elected Mexican American in public office was discouraging to them.

It was very difficult for everyone because neither group really trusted the other at all. Henry Cisneros was the Mexican Americans' first choice to run for city council. This man, whom they had hoped to persuade, was willing to run for election. Henry's friends campaigned for him as the man everyone could trust, and the people elected Henry Cisneros to office. At twenty-eight, Cisneros became a dedicated young city council member, the youngest that San Antonio had ever had. Clearly, Mexican Americans were not the only people in San Antonio who wanted to put Henry Cisneros in office.

EXERCISE 32/33–1, page 297

If a boy wanted to join the football team at Carlisle Indian School, he had to go through a difficult test. Any boy who wanted to be on the team had to stand at one of the goal lines; all the first-string players stood around the field. When the ball was punted to the new boy, he had to catch it and try to get all the way to the other end zone with it. The team members tried to stop him before he could get very far. Only a few players had ever gotten as far as the fifty-yard line, so "Pop" Warner, coach at the Carlisle Indian School, considered it a good test.

One day a quiet Indian boy surprised Pop. The boy caught the ball, started running, wheeled away from the first players who tried to stop him, shook off the others, and ran the ball all the way to the opposite goal line. Convinced that the player's success was an accident, the coach ordered him to run the play again. Brusquely, the coach spoke to the players and reminded them that this workout was supposed to be tackling practice. Jim, the nineteen-year-old six-footer, simply said, "Nobody tackles Jim." Then he ran the ball to the goal line a second time.

Well, almost no one tackled Jim Thorpe successfully for many years. Life itself got him down and made him fumble more often than his football opponents did, but he was usually able to recover and go on. The first blow was the death of his twin brother while the two boys were still in grade school. This tragedy was followed by others; by the time Jim was twenty-five, he had lost his brother, his mother, and his father too. They left him a Native American heritage: His father was half Irish and half Native American, and his mother was the granddaughter of a famous Indian warrior named Chief Black Hawk.

Fortunately or unfortunately, along with his Native American heritage came great pride and stoicism. That pride kept him silent when the greatest blow of all came: He was forced to return the Olympic medals he had won in 1912 because he was declared to be not an amateur. He dealt stoically with his personal tragedies. When infantile paralysis struck his son, Jim Thorpe disappeared for a few days to deal with the tragedy alone. His stoicism also saw him through a demotion to the minor leagues and sad years of unemployment and poverty before his death.

Even death's tackle may not have been totally successful: After Jim Thorpe's death, his Olympic medals were returned, and a town was named after him.

EXERCISE 34–1, page 307

When Cheryl Toussaint came in second in a race she had never planned to run, she started on a road that led to the Olympics and a world record.

Cheryl began running almost by accident one day when she went to watch a city-sponsored track meet in Brooklyn, New York. During the preliminaries, the officials announced an "open" race; it was a race that anyone could enter. Cheryl wanted to enter, but she was dressed in a skirt and sandals. Four things made her run: One friend traded shoes with her, another let her borrow jeans, several called her "chicken" if she didn't run, and one girl dared her to run. Coming in second in that race led this teenager to many places, including Munich, Germany; Toronto, Canada; and Montreal, Canada.

There were, however, many races to run and lessons to learn. Cheryl joined the all-female Atoms Track Club, and she began training under Coach Fred Thompson. Like most coaches, Fred had his own way of testing newcomers. He watched a new runner carefully; however, he gave her no special attention. Instead, he just gave her orders one after another. He would tell Cheryl to run laps, go through exercises, and do practice starts, but he would never comment on how she performed. If the newcomer endured the hard, time-consuming workouts without encouragement or praise, Thompson was sure she was ready for real coaching.

Cheryl quit after two months; for six more months she stayed out. During that time she thought about her attitude toward work, her poor record at school, her pleasure in running, and her lack of goals. When she returned, Thompson welcomed her back; he knew how special Cheryl was. Before he was through with Cheryl Toussaint, Coach Thompson not only convinced her she was college material, but he pushed her to achieve the highest goal of the amateur athlete — the Olympics.

EXERCISE 35-1, page 313

In 1951, Althea Gibson broke the color barrier in women's tennis and became admired all over the world. No one who knew her as a teenager would have predicted her success. By the time Althea Gibson reached her teens, her record showed three indications of trouble: running away from home, dropping out of school, and losing the one job she had been able to find. To survive in her neighborhood, Althea depended on a small welfare allowance, occasional handouts, and plain old luck. She listed her skills as the following: good bowler, great two-on-two basketball player, and fast paddleball player. Even after she began playing tennis and moving in upper-class Harlem society, she resented the efforts of the society ladies to improve her. They busied themselves with tasks such as correcting her manners and restricting her behavior. Looking back, she later summed up her attitude: She [*or* she] said she wasn't ready to study about "how to be a fine lady." At eighteen, she finally got a waitress job, a congenial roommate, and a good friend.

EXERCISE 36-1, page 319

During the 1990 troubles in Panama, American television and newspaper reporters had an exciting piece of news. They reported that for the first time American female soldiers had been engaged in actual combat. Acting as her soldiers' leader, Captain Linda Bray led her troops into combat. Names of two additional women who were involved in combat, Staff Sergeant April Hanley and PFC Christina Proctor, were reported in the newspapers. Theirs were the only names reported, although other women also took part.

It wasn't the first time an American woman had fought in an American battle, but it's not likely that many people are aware of that fact. The Civil War had its female fighters too. Loreta Janeta Velazquez fought for the Confederates in the Civil War after her husband's death. Like many other women whose husbands were killed in the war, she must have asked herself, "Who's going to take his place in battle?" The decision to fight was hers alone. Someone is sure to ask how that was possible, even in those days. Military I.D.'s were not very sophisticated in the 1860s. Someone's willingness to fight was that person's major qualification, and each fighting unit needed to replace its losses as fast as possible. Velazquez simply disguised herself in men's clothing, found a troop needing replacements, and joined the fight. Loreta Janeta Velazquez was Linda Bray's Civil War predecessor.

EXERCISE 37-1, page 327

1. The doctor answered, "You can do nothing but pray."
2. When the bandages were removed and the shades were opened to let in the bright sunlight, the doctor asked, "What do you see?"
3. "Nothing," said the boy. "I see nothing."
4. The village priest said, "I have recently seen a remarkable school." He had just returned from a trip to Paris.
5. "In this school," he added, "blind students are taught to read."
6. "You didn't say 'read,' did you?" asked the boy's father.
7. The boy responded to the priest's words as if they were a trick of some kind: "Now you are joking with me. How can such a thing be possible?"

8. The boy, Louis, thought it would be great fun to visit that school someday.
9. His father promised, "We will go soon, Louis."
10. And so it happened that ten-year-old Louis Braille entered the National Institute for Blind Youths and began the long effort to erase the fear people had of even the word "blind" [*or* blind].

EXERCISE 38-1, page 333

After Louis Braille invented his new system that would allow blind people to read and write, he tested it thoroughly. Students and faculty of the National Institute for Blind Youths were excited at how easily they could master it and encouraged Louis to demonstrate the system to the French educational authorities, who made the rules for the institute. Louis agreed to do so.

When Louis held the demonstration, all went well. What excitement he and his friends felt! But the authorities would not recommend that the institute adopt Louis's new system. Why didn't the French authorities recognize the advantages of Braille's system? Did they have a vested interest in the old system of teaching the blind? Or a real doubt about the system? Whatever their reasons, they delayed the pleasures of reading for thousands of people. In addition, a new director, Dr. Pignier, even outlawed the use of the system at the institute for four years.

Although unhappy and disheartened, Braille never gave up; he knew his system would enable the blind to read.

EXERCISE 39-1, page 340

Suggested revision:

The most famous woman in America is Miss Liberty — a 450,000-pound, 154-foot resident of New York City. For people all over the world, the Statue of Liberty symbolizes America. Yet the idea of the statue did not come from America, England, or even New York itself — but from France. Three men can claim the credit for construction of Miss Liberty: (1) Frédéric-Auguste Bartholdi, sculptor; (2) Alexandre-Gustave Eiffel, structural engineer; and (3) Richard Morris Hunt, architect. France gave the statue to the United States, and the United States provided the pedestal on which it stands.

Two Americans contributed significantly to the statue. The first was Russian immigrant Joseph Pulitzer, then owner and publisher of the *New York World.* He led several fundraising efforts and urged every American to give what he or she could to help build the pedestal. The second American who contributed significantly was Emma Lazarus. She wrote the famous lines on the bronze plaque inside the statue. Her three-word title "The New Colossus" (huge statue) alludes to a statue built in the harbor of Rhodes in ancient Greece. The most quoted lines from "The New Colossus" are probably these: "Give me your tired, your poor, / Your huddled masses yearning to breathe free."

EXERCISE 40/41/42-1, page 351

Suggested revision:

Everyone has heard of Christopher Columbus, but not many people know much about him. Most people learn that he discovered America in A.D. 1492. Some people know that he had three ships, and they might be able to name them. (The ships were the *Niña,* the *Pinta,* and the *Santa María.*) A few people might even remember that Columbus thought he had found the Indies. And those with great self-confidence might be willing to guess at the number of trips he made to his India. (It was four.) Probably no one would be familiar with his favorite word, *adelante.*

If they were asked what Columbus was trying to prove with his expensive journey, most people would reply that he was trying to prove the world is round. They would be wrong. If they were asked what Columbus meant by "the Indies," they would probably say "India." They would be wrong again. If they were asked what Columbus's rank was, they would most likely say "captain." They would be wrong again. If they were asked what his sailors feared most, a number of them would reply, "They feared that the boats would fall off the edge of the earth." And they would be wrong again.

Isn't it strange that people can be so ignorant about a well-known man like Columbus?

EXERCISE 43/44/45–1, page 363

Columbus's return to Spain from his first exploration was difficult. The *Niña* and the *Pinta* were separated, the *Niña* almost sank, and the governor on the island of Santa María put Columbus's whole crew in jail. It seemed a miracle that both boats arrived in the harbor at Palos on the same day.

As difficult as that return was, the reception at court quite made up for it. Columbus certainly made an all-out effort to impress the court, the city, and the entire country. Lavishly attired, he received a grand welcome as he led his entourage into Barcelona, the Spanish capital. It must have been a sight to behold: a procession like none Barcelona had ever seen before. Leading the parade was a gaudily bedecked horse carrying Columbus, followed by six captive "Indians" and all the crew. Everyone but Columbus was carrying boxes, baskets, and cages full of interesting and exotic items.

When the group reached the throne room, King Ferdinand and Queen Isabella stood up to greet Columbus formally and to admire his apron-covered captives. Columbus asked the royal couple to accept gifts of plants, shells, darts, thread, and gold. As intrigued as they were with the other gifts, King Ferdinand and Queen Isabella basically wanted gold. Luckily, Columbus had collected enough samples of it to satisfy them.

By the end of the first week home, Columbus had such prestige that everyone wanted to accommodate the wishes of the Italian sailor at the court of Spain. Columbus had no doubt that he would receive a commission for a second voyage of exploration or even colonization.

EXERCISE 47–1, page 377

Nouns: colonies, reliance, lives, honor
Pronouns: itself, We
Verbs: ring, do, publish, are
Adjectives: final, free, firm
Adverb: mutually
Prepositions: like, in, of, with
Conjunctions: therefore, and

EXERCISE 48–1, page 389

Subjects: group, they, They, lovers, artists, sunshine, paintings, painters, forms, Both
Verbs: had, went, gave, were surprised, made, would pour, Were, are admired, are, showed
Subject complements: bright, cheerful, examples
Direct objects: problem, bursts, scenes, objects
Indirect objects: paintings, viewers
Object complement: bright

EXERCISE 49–1, page 403

Verbal phrases: Drawing colorful pictures; To decorate her room; Encouraging her artistic interest; Studying, working, and making new friends; to follow her own vision; Rewarded and acclaimed
Prepositional phrases: From her earliest years; of pretty rocks, shells, and fabric pieces; with financial independence; for only eleven years; to her family home; At times; During Louise Nevelson's busiest and most exciting years; with either the critics or the public; throughout the art world
Subordinate clauses: that she needed; who was a wealthy New York businessman; while his mother studied abroad; whether or not she had done the right thing; that she had made the right decision

EXERCISE 50–1, page 411

Compound; Complex: Although he devoted several years to drawing (subordinate clause); Compound; Compound; Compound-complex: while he was out of doors (subordinate clause); Simple; Compound-complex: that she painted different parts of her sculpture in different colors (subordinate clause); Complex: who liked to paint people and group scenes (subordinate clause); Complex: that his viewers could easily recognize (subordinate clause); Simple

Index

A List of Charts

Special Help for ESL Students

Correction Symbols

abbr	faulty abbreviation **40**	*inc*	incomplete construction **10**	*pn agr*	pronoun agreement **22**
ad	misuse of adverb or adjective **26**	*irreg*	error in irregular verb **27a**	*proof*	proofreading problem **3c**
add	add needed word **10**	*ital*	italics (underlining) **42**	*ref*	error in pronoun reference **23**
agr	faulty agreement **21, 22**	*jarg*	jargon **17a**	*run-on*	run-on sentence **20**
appr	inappropriate language **17**	*lc*	lowercase letter **45**	*-s*	error in *-s* ending **21, 27c**
art	article **30**	*mix*	mixed construction **11**	*sexist*	sexist language **17f, 22a**
awk	awkward	*mm*	misplaced modifier **12a–d**	*shift*	distracting shift **13**
cap	capital letter **45**	*mood*	error in mood **28b**	*sl*	slang **17d**
case	error in case **24, 25**	*nonst*	nonstandard usage **17d, 27**	*sp*	misspelled word **43**
cliché	cliché **18e**	*num*	error in use of numbers **41**	*sub*	faulty subordination **8c–d**
coh	coherence **7**	*om*	omitted word **10, 30, 31a**	*sv agr*	subject-verb agreement **21, 27c**
coord	faulty coordination **8b**	*p*	error in punctuation	*t*	error in verb tense **28a**
cs	comma splice **20**	⌢	comma **32**	*trans*	transition needed **7e**
dev	inadequate development **6a**	*no ,*	no comma **33**	*usage*	see Glossary of Usage
dm	dangling modifier **12e**	;	semicolon **34**	*v*	voice **14a, 28c**
-ed	error in *-ed* ending **27d**	:	colon **35**	*var*	lack of variety in sentence structure **8, 15**
emph	emphasis **14**	⌄	apostrophe **36**	*vb*	verb error **27, 28**
ESL	English as a second language **29–31**	" "	quotation marks **37**	*w*	wordy **16**
exact	inexact language **18**	. ? !	period, question mark, exclamation point **38**	*//*	faulty parallelism **9**
frag	sentence fragment **19**	— ( ) [ ] … /	dash, parentheses, brackets, ellipsis mark, slash **39**	^	insert
fs	fused sentence **20**	¶	new paragraph **4f**	x	obvious error
gl/us	see Glossary of Usage	*pass*	ineffective passive **14a, 28c**	#	insert space
hyph	error in use of hyphen **44**			⌒	close up space
idiom	idioms **18d**				

A List of Grammatical Terms

absolute phrase **49e**
active voice **28c, 48c**
adjective **47d**
adjective clause **49b**
adverb **47e**
adverb clause **49b**
agreement **21, 22**
antecedent **22, 23, 47b**
appositive phrase **49d**
article **30**
case **24, 25**
clause **49b, 50**
comparative **26c**
complement **48b**
complete subject **48a**
complex sentence **50a**
compound-complex sentence **50a**
compound sentence **50a**
compound subject **48a**
conjunction **47g**
conjunctive adverb **47g**
coordinating conjunction **47g**
correlative conjunction **47g**
demonstrative pronoun **47b**

dependent clause (*See* subordinate clause.)
determiner **30**
direct object **48b**
expletive **48a, 48c**
future tense **28a**
gerund **49c**
gerund phrase **49c**
helping verb **47c**
indefinite pronoun **47b**
independent clause **50a**
indirect object **48b**
infinitive **49c**
infinitive phrase **49c**
intensive pronoun **47b**
interjection **47h**
interrogative pronoun **47b**
intransitive verb **48b**
inverted sentence pattern **48a**
irregular verb **27a**
linking verb **48b**
main clause (*See* independent clause.)
main verb **47c**
modal **29a, 47c**

mood **28b**
noun **47a**
noun/adjective **47a**
noun clause **49b**
object complement **48b**
object of the preposition **49a**
particle **29d**
participial phrase **49c**
participle, present and past **27a, 47c**
parts of speech **47**
passive voice **28c, 48c**
past tense **28a**
perfect tense **28a**
personal pronoun **47b**
possessive pronoun **47b**
predicate **48**
predicate adjective (*See* subject complement.)
predicate noun (*See* subject complement.)
preposition **47f**
prepositional phrase **47f, 49a**
present tense **28a**
progressive tenses **28a**

pronoun **47b**
pronoun/adjective **47b**
reciprocal pronoun **47b**
reflexive pronoun **47b**
regular verb **27a, 47c**
relative adverb **49b**
relative pronoun **47b, 49b**
-s form of verbs **21, 27c**
sentence patterns **48**
sentence types **50**
simple sentence **50a**
simple subject **48a**
subject **48a**
subject complement **48b**
subordinate clause **49b**
subordinating conjunction **47g, 49b**
subordinate word group **49**
superlative **26c**
tense **28a**
transitive verb **48b**
understood subject **48a**
verb **47c, 48b**
verbal phrase **49c**

Detailed Menu